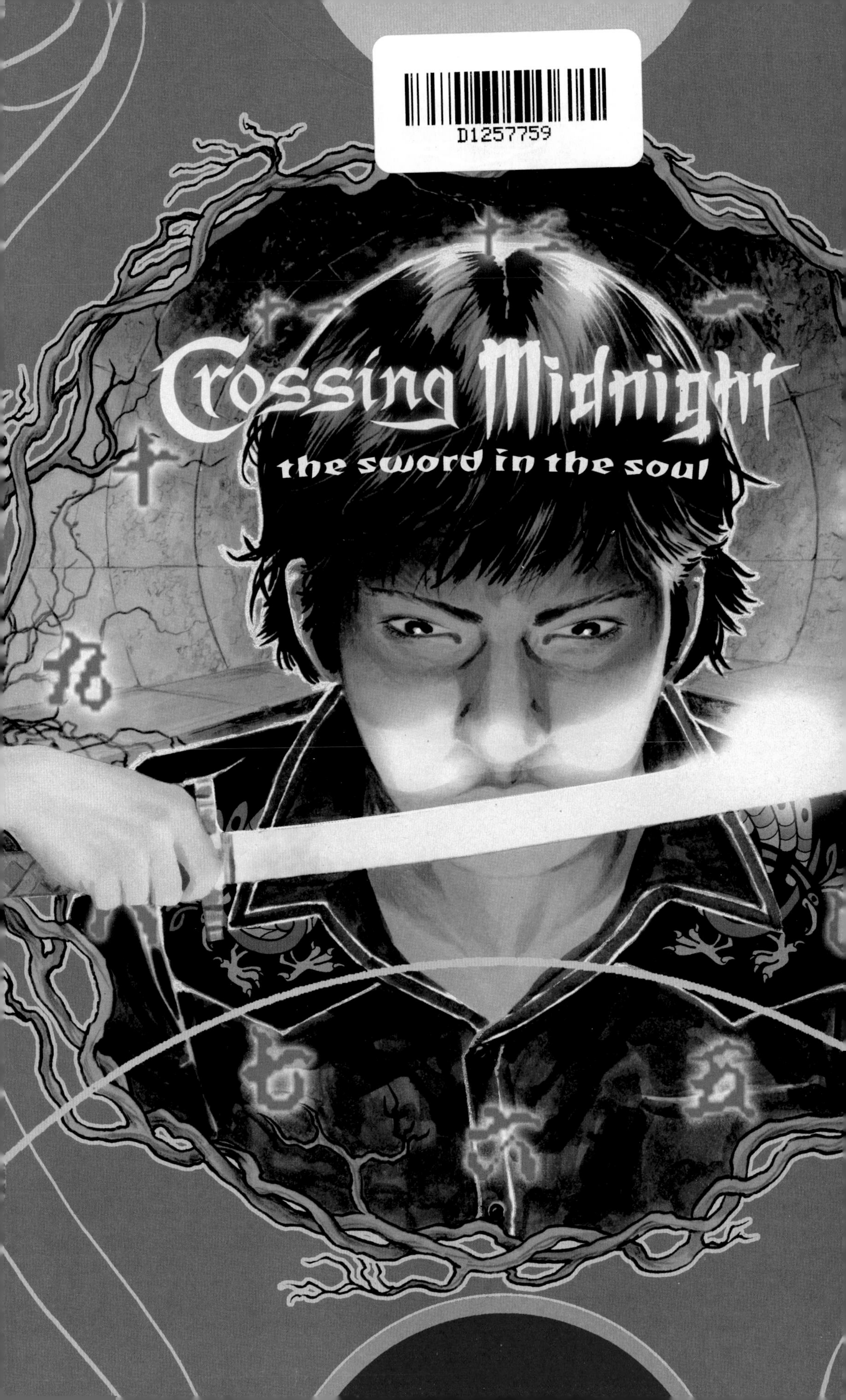
Crossing Midnight
the sword in the soul

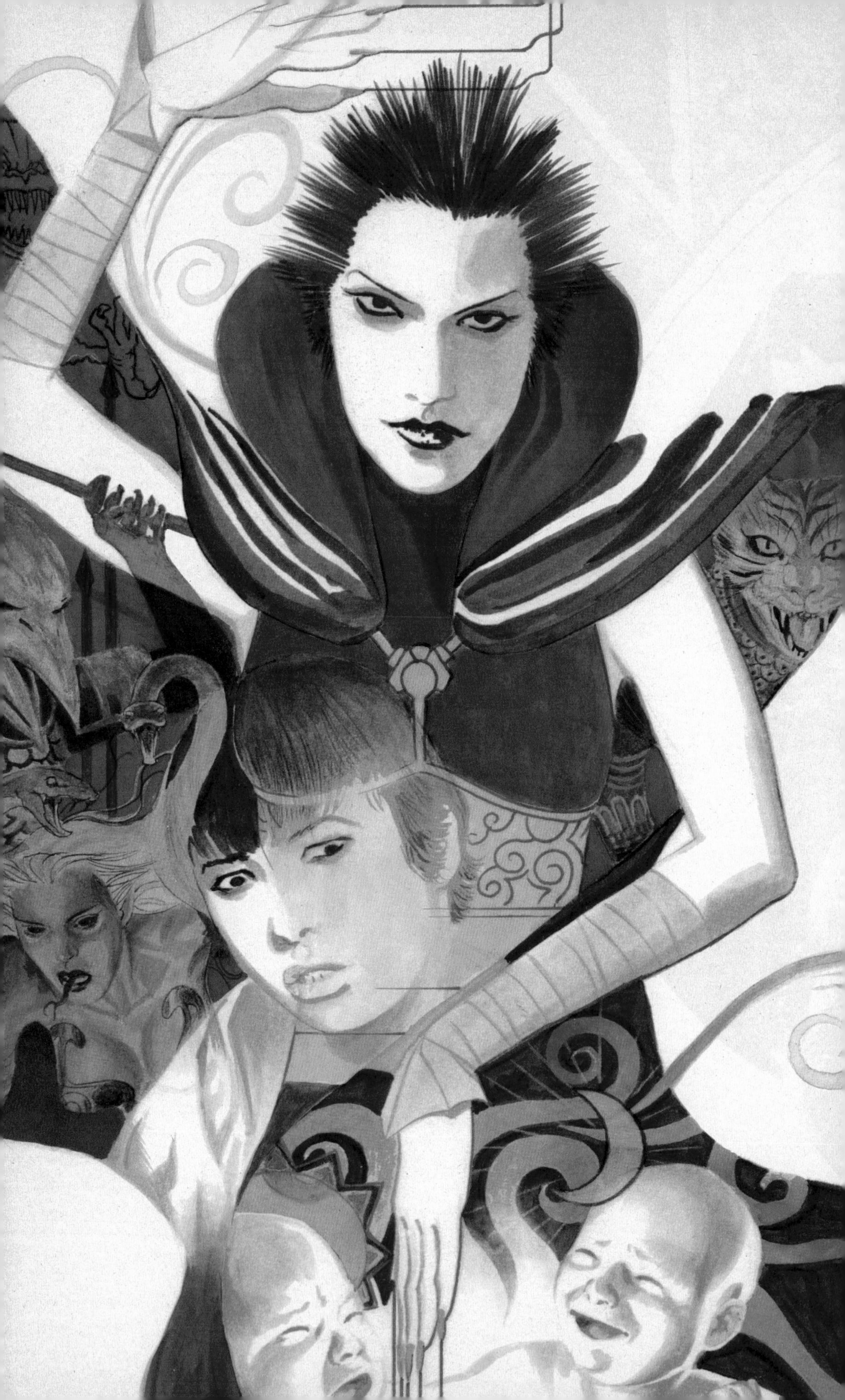

Crossing Midnight

the sword in the soul

Mike Carey
WRITER

Jim Fern
José Villarrubia
Gabriel Hernandez
Mateo Guerrero
J.H. Williams III
ARTISTS

Todd Klein
LETTERER

J.H. Williams III
ORIGINAL SERIES
COVERS

CROSSING MIDNIGHT created by
Mike Carey and **Jim Fern**

Cover illustration by J. H. Williams III
Logo design by Glenn Parsons of Astrolux Design
Publication design by Amelia Grohman

CROSSING MIDNIGHT:
THE SWORD IN THE SOUL

DC Comics, 1700 Broadway, New York, NY 10019
A Warner Bros. Entertainment Company.
Printed in Canada. First Printing.
ISBN: 978-1-4012-1966-6

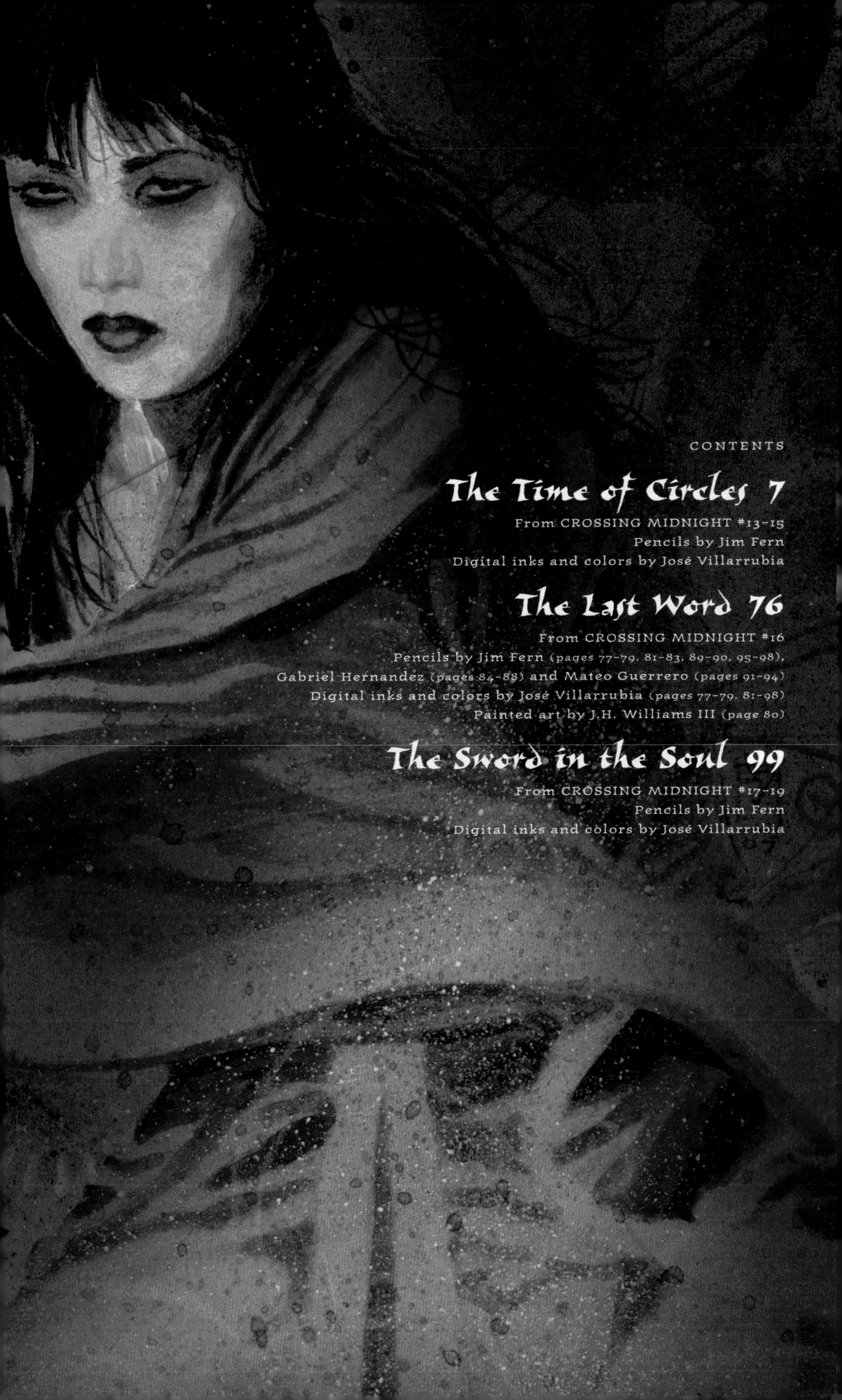

CONTENTS

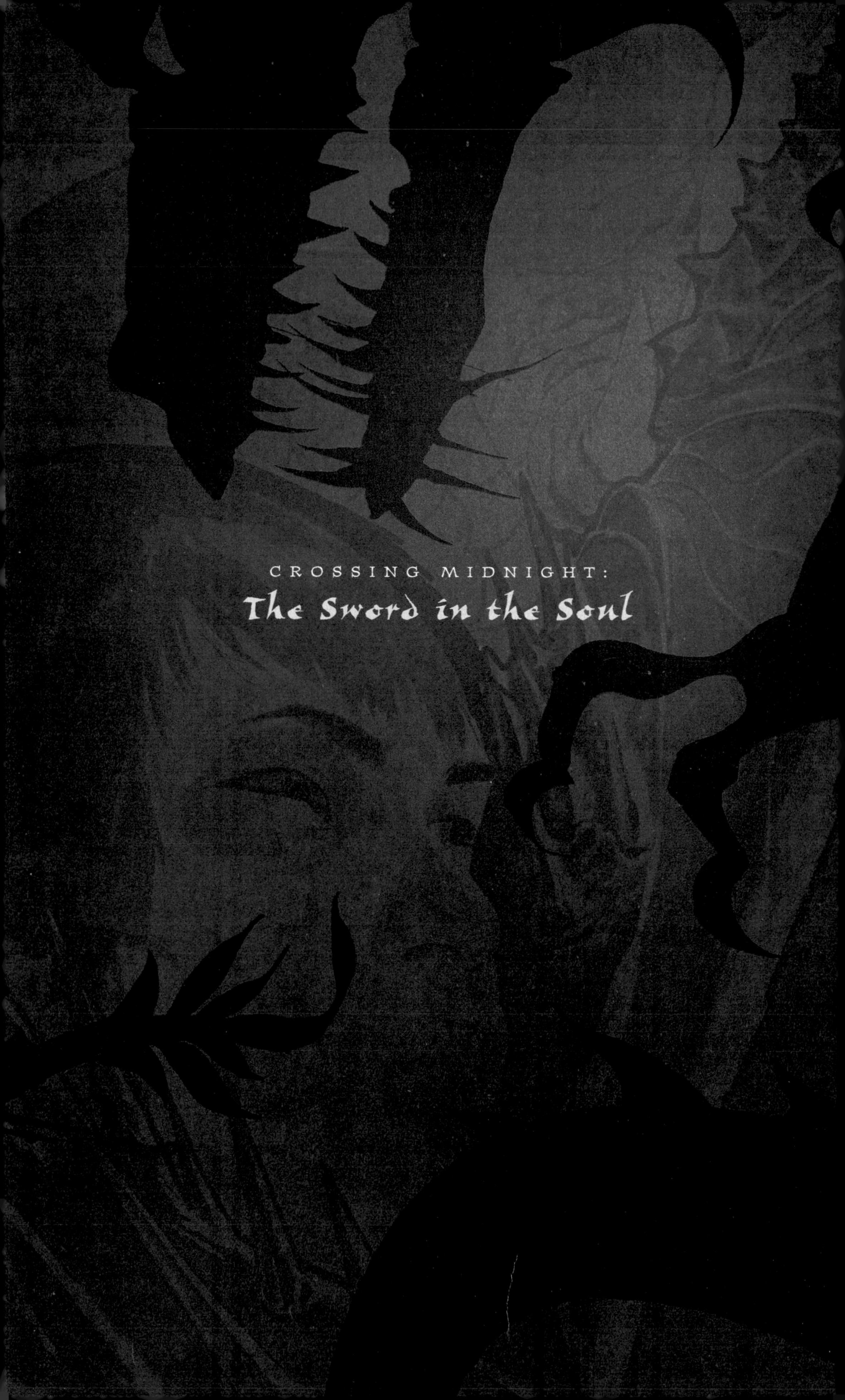

CROSSING MIDNIGHT:

The Sword in the Soul

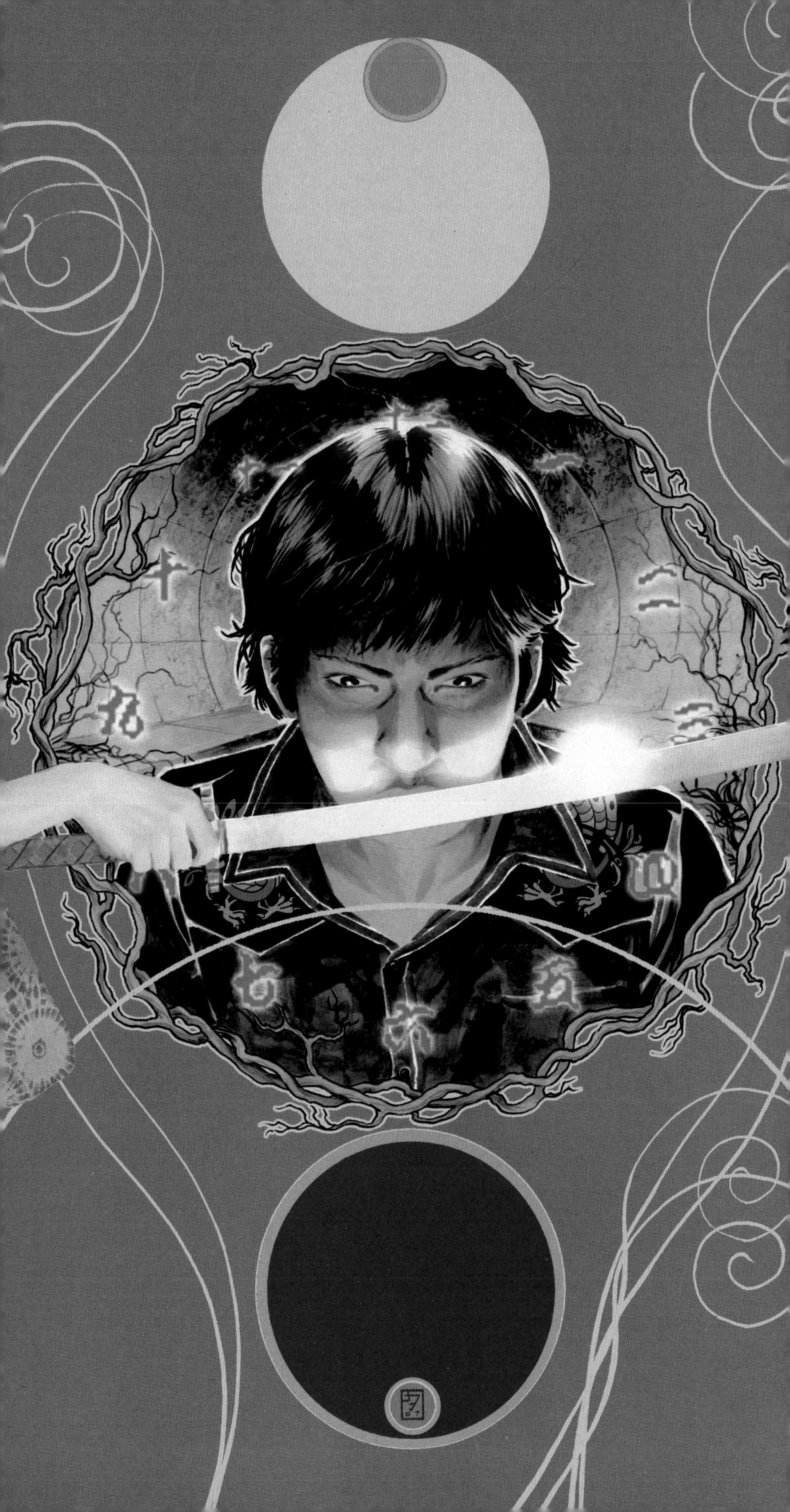

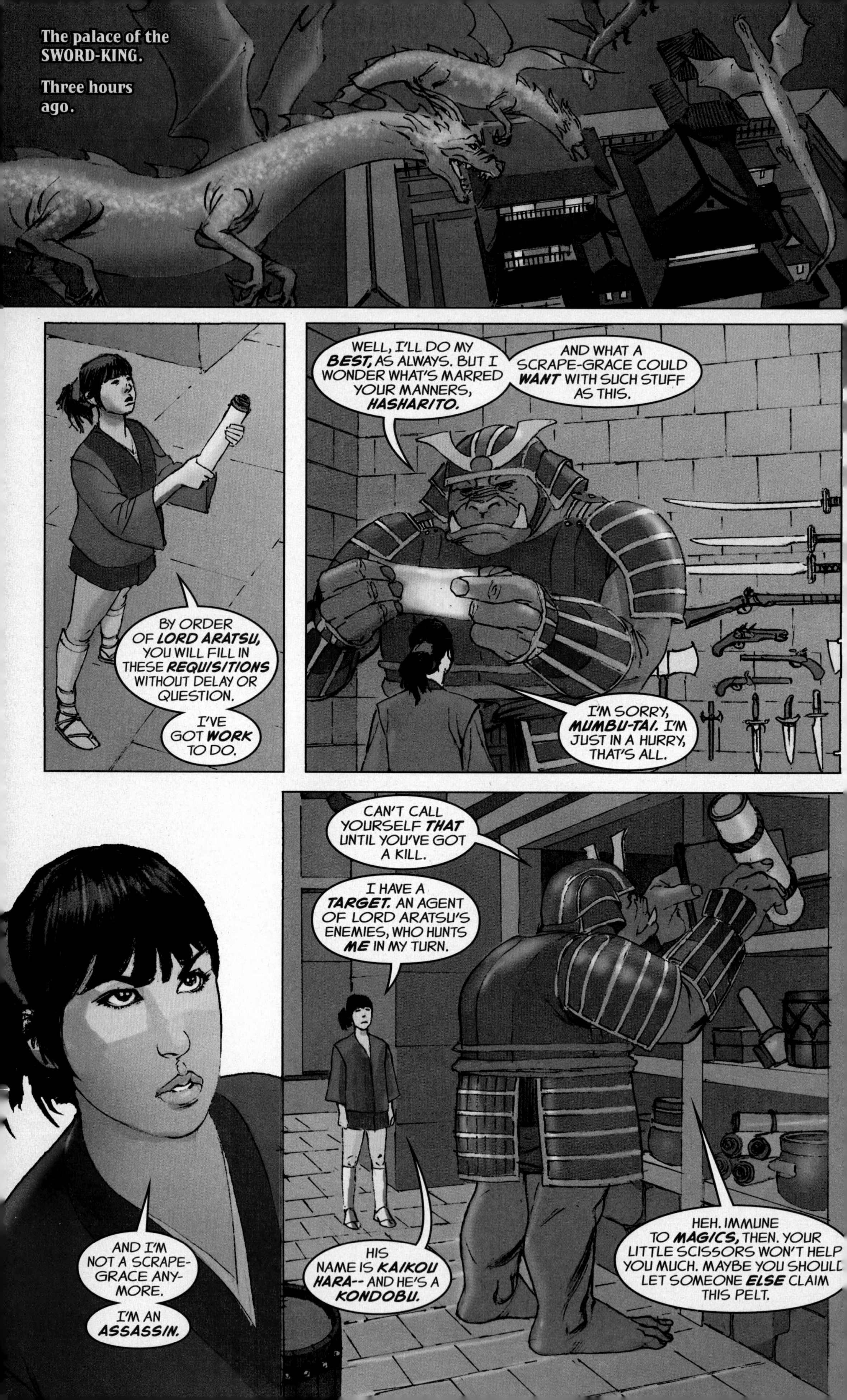
The palace of the SWORD-KING.
Three hours ago.
BY ORDER OF LORD ARATSU, YOU WILL FILL IN THESE REQUISITIONS WITHOUT DELAY OR QUESTION.
I'VE GOT WORK TO DO.
WELL, I'LL DO MY BEST, AS ALWAYS. BUT I WONDER WHAT'S MARRED YOUR MANNERS, HASHARITO.
AND WHAT A SCRAPE-GRACE COULD WANT WITH SUCH STUFF AS THIS.
I'M SORRY, MUMBU-TAI. I'M JUST IN A HURRY, THAT'S ALL.
AND I'M NOT A SCRAPE-GRACE ANY-MORE.
I'M AN ASSASSIN.
CAN'T CALL YOURSELF THAT UNTIL YOU'VE GOT A KILL.
I HAVE A TARGET. AN AGENT OF LORD ARATSU'S ENEMIES, WHO HUNTS ME IN MY TURN.
HIS NAME IS KAIKOU HARA-- AND HE'S A KONDOBU.
HEH. IMMUNE TO MAGICS, THEN. YOUR LITTLE SCISSORS WON'T HELP YOU MUCH. MAYBE YOU SHOULD LET SOMEONE ELSE CLAIM THIS PELT.

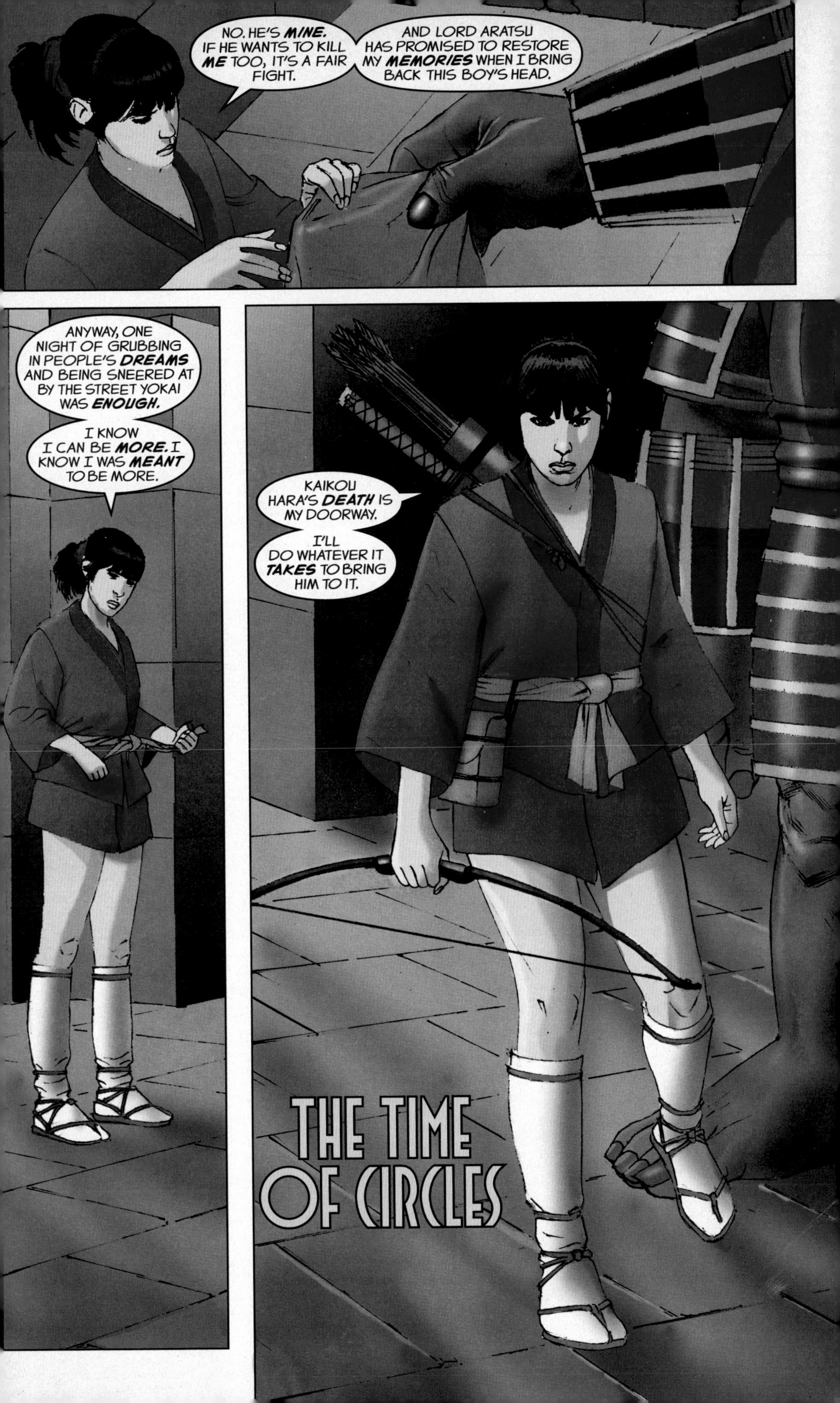

NO. HE'S **MINE.** IF HE WANTS TO KILL **ME** TOO, IT'S A FAIR FIGHT.
AND LORD ARATSU HAS PROMISED TO RESTORE MY **MEMORIES** WHEN I BRING BACK THIS BOY'S HEAD.
ANYWAY, ONE NIGHT OF GRUBBING IN PEOPLE'S **DREAMS** AND BEING SNEERED AT BY THE STREET YOKAI WAS **ENOUGH.**
I KNOW I CAN BE **MORE.** I KNOW I WAS **MEANT** TO BE MORE.
KAIKOU HARA'S **DEATH** IS MY DOORWAY.
I'LL DO WHATEVER IT **TAKES** TO BRING HIM TO IT.
THE TIME OF CIRCLES

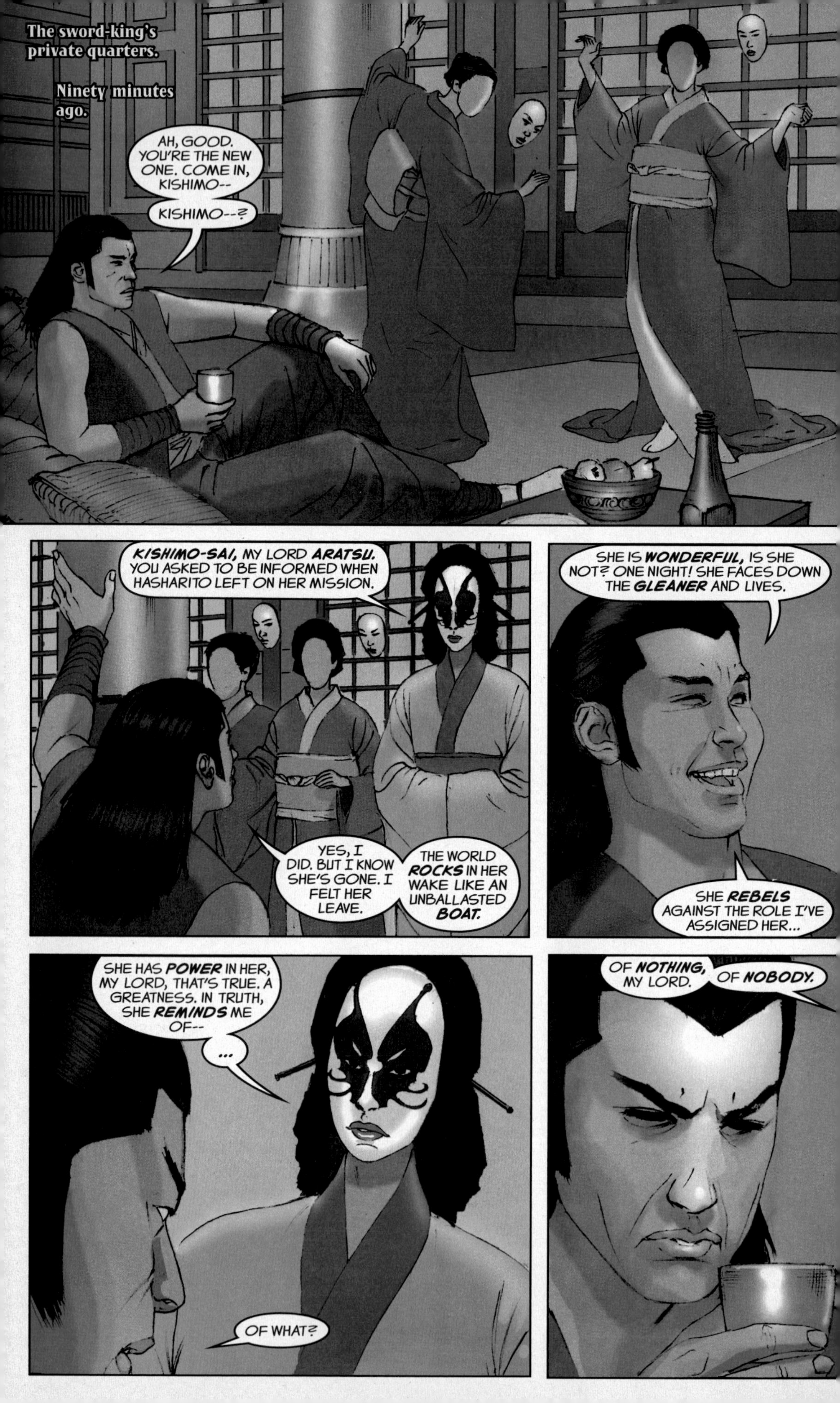

The sword-king's private quarters.
Ninety minutes ago.
AH, GOOD. YOU'RE THE NEW ONE. COME IN, KISHIMO--
KISHIMO--?
KISHIMO-SAI, MY LORD ARATSU. YOU ASKED TO BE INFORMED WHEN HASHARITO LEFT ON HER MISSION.
YES, I DID. BUT I KNOW SHE'S GONE. I FELT HER LEAVE.
THE WORLD ROCKS IN HER WAKE LIKE AN UNBALLASTED BOAT.
SHE IS WONDERFUL, IS SHE NOT? ONE NIGHT! SHE FACES DOWN THE GLEANER AND LIVES.
SHE REBELS AGAINST THE ROLE I'VE ASSIGNED HER...
SHE HAS POWER IN HER, MY LORD, THAT'S TRUE. A GREATNESS. IN TRUTH, SHE REMINDS ME OF--
...
OF WHAT?
OF NOTHING, MY LORD.
OF NOBODY.

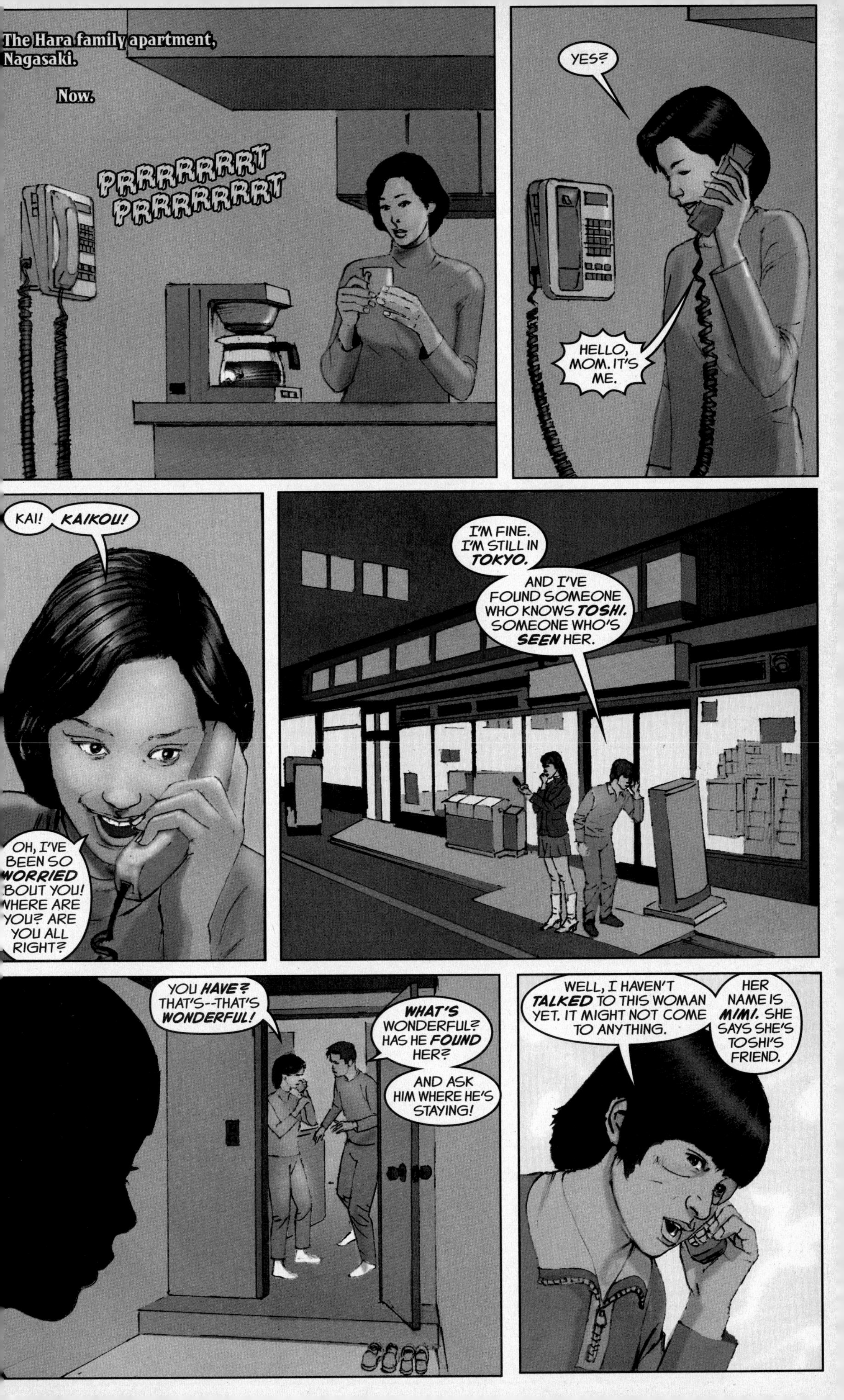
The Hara family apartment, Nagasaki.
Now.
PRRRRRRRT PRRRRRRRT
YES?
HELLO, MOM. IT'S ME.
KAI! KAIKOU!
OH, I'VE BEEN SO WORRIED 'BOUT YOU! WHERE ARE YOU? ARE YOU ALL RIGHT?
I'M FINE. I'M STILL IN TOKYO.
AND I'VE FOUND SOMEONE WHO KNOWS TOSHI. SOMEONE WHO'S SEEN HER.
YOU HAVE? THAT'S--THAT'S WONDERFUL!
WHAT'S WONDERFUL? HAS HE FOUND HER?
AND ASK HIM WHERE HE'S STAYING!
WELL, I HAVEN'T TALKED TO THIS WOMAN YET. IT MIGHT NOT COME TO ANYTHING.
HER NAME IS MIMI. SHE SAYS SHE'S TOSHI'S FRIEND.

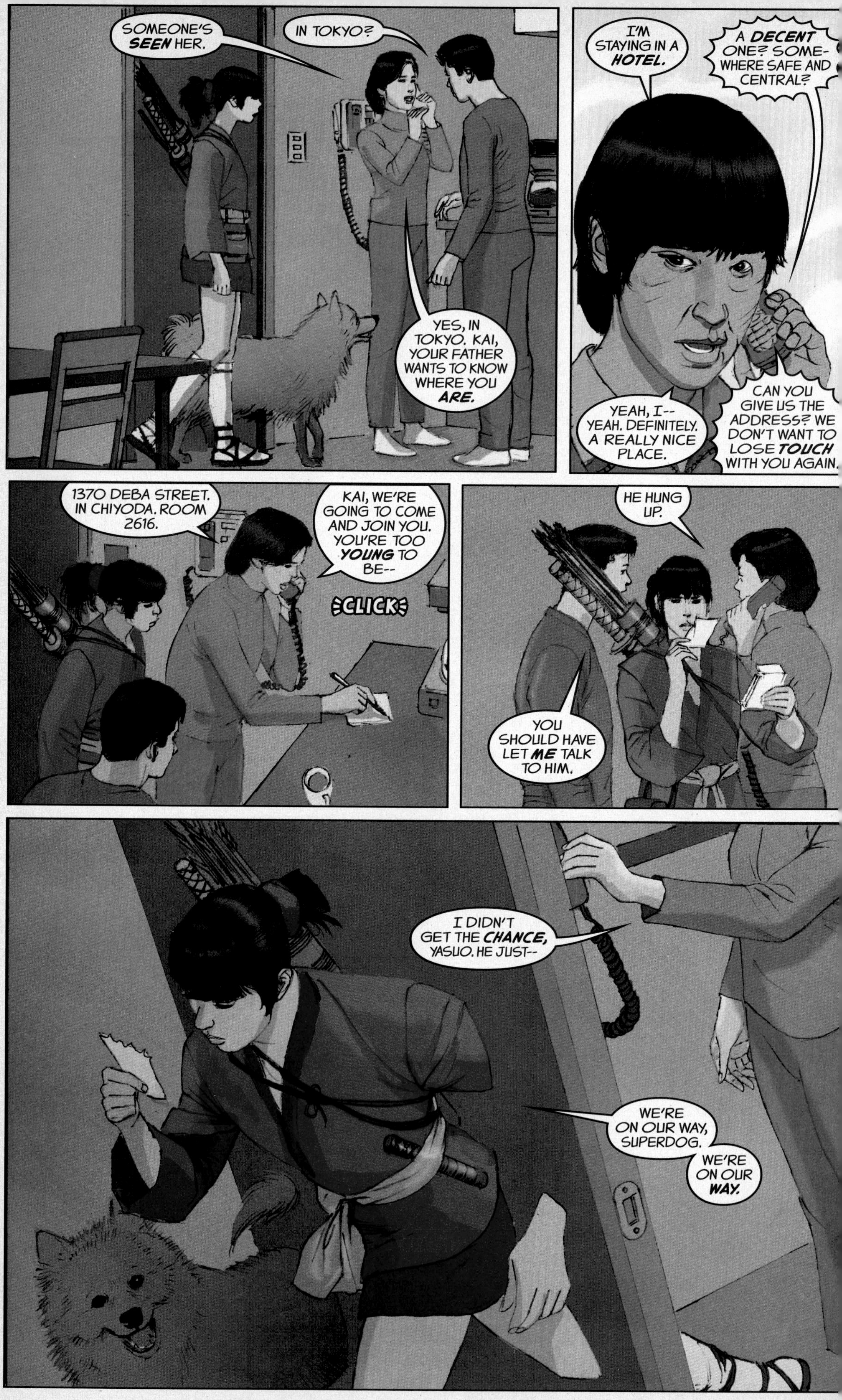
SOMEONE'S SEEN HER.
IN TOKYO?
YES, IN TOKYO. KAI, YOUR FATHER WANTS TO KNOW WHERE YOU ARE.
I'M STAYING IN A HOTEL.
A DECENT ONE? SOMEWHERE SAFE AND CENTRAL?
YEAH, I-- YEAH. DEFINITELY. A REALLY NICE PLACE.
CAN YOU GIVE US THE ADDRESS? WE DON'T WANT TO LOSE TOUCH WITH YOU AGAIN.
1370 DEBA STREET. IN CHIYODA. ROOM 2616.
KAI, WE'RE GOING TO COME AND JOIN YOU. YOU'RE TOO YOUNG TO BE--
CLICK
HE HUNG UP.
YOU SHOULD HAVE LET ME TALK TO HIM.
I DIDN'T GET THE CHANCE, YASUO. HE JUST--
WE'RE ON OUR WAY, SUPERDOG.
WE'RE ON OUR WAY.

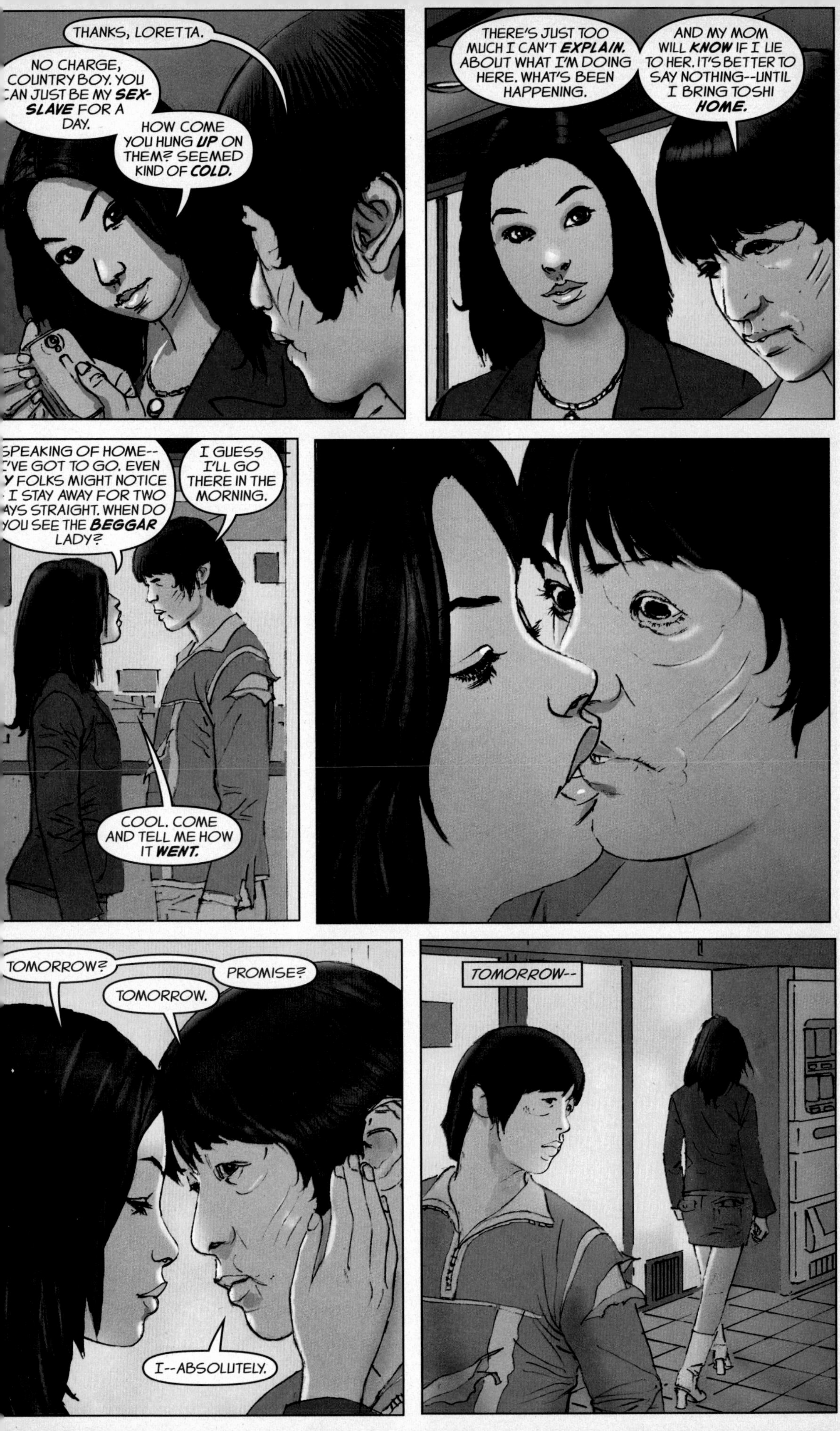
THANKS, LORETTA.
NO CHARGE, COUNTRY BOY. YOU CAN JUST BE MY SEX-SLAVE FOR A DAY.
HOW COME YOU HUNG UP ON THEM? SEEMED KIND OF COLD.
THERE'S JUST TOO MUCH I CAN'T EXPLAIN. ABOUT WHAT I'M DOING HERE. WHAT'S BEEN HAPPENING.
AND MY MOM WILL KNOW IF I LIE TO HER. IT'S BETTER TO SAY NOTHING--UNTIL I BRING TOSHI HOME.
SPEAKING OF HOME--I'VE GOT TO GO. EVEN MY FOLKS MIGHT NOTICE IF I STAY AWAY FOR TWO DAYS STRAIGHT. WHEN DO YOU SEE THE BEGGAR LADY?
I GUESS I'LL GO THERE IN THE MORNING.
COOL. COME AND TELL ME HOW IT WENT.
TOMORROW?
PROMISE?
TOMORROW.
I--ABSOLUTELY.
TOMORROW--

TOMORROW'S ALREADY *HERE*, BECAUSE IT'S TWO IN THE MORNING.

BUT I WANDER THE STREETS OF CHIBA LIKE A *GHOST,* HOUR AFTER HOUR.

AND GHOSTS *WATCH* ME. I'M ON THEIR WAVE-LENGTH NOW. I'M IN THEIR WORLD.

GHOSTS. MONSTERS. LOST SOULS.

BUT THEY DON'T *INTRUDE* BECAUSE THEY CAN SEE WHAT KIND OF A *MOOD* I'M IN.

OR PERHAPS THEY CAN SMELL THAT THE *BLOOD* ON MY HANDS IS THE BLOOD OF THEIR OWN *KIND.*

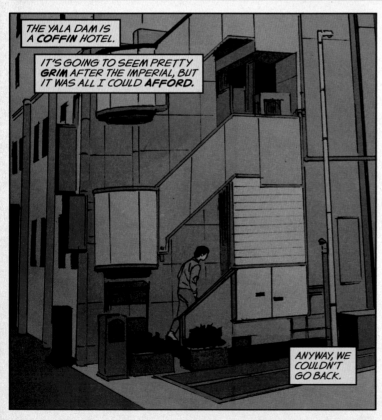

THE YALA DAM IS A *COFFIN* HOTEL.

IT'S GOING TO SEEM PRETTY *GRIM* AFTER THE IMPERIAL, BUT IT WAS ALL I COULD *AFFORD.*

ANYWAY, WE COULDN'T GO BACK.

AND I COULDN'T ASK *LORETTA* FOR MONEY NOW THAT I KNOW SHE HUGS MIDDLE-AGED *SARARIMEN* TO GET IT.

SO IT'S *THIS* PLACE OR NOTHING.

≈CRKKKKKK≈

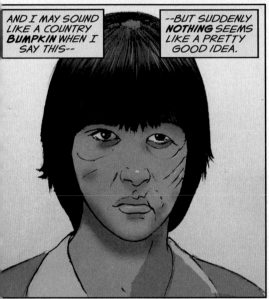

AND I MAY SOUND LIKE A COUNTRY *BUMPKIN* WHEN I SAY THIS--

--BUT SUDDENLY *NOTHING* SEEMS LIKE A PRETTY GOOD IDEA.

SUPPOSE I WENT TO UENO PARK *NOW?* IN THE MIDDLE OF THE NIGHT?

WOULD THIS MIMI-SAMA AGREE TO *SEE* ME?

AND HOW CAN SHE *LIVE* IN A PARK ANYWAY? WHAT DOES THAT *MEAN?*

CUBICLE 2616 HAS THREE *CONDOMS* LYING RIGHT INSIDE THE DOOR.

I GUESS THE LAST RESIDENT WAS TOO *TIRED* AFTER THE THIRD TIME TO CLEAN UP AFTER HIMSELF.

AND I GUESS I'LL SLEEP *LATER.*

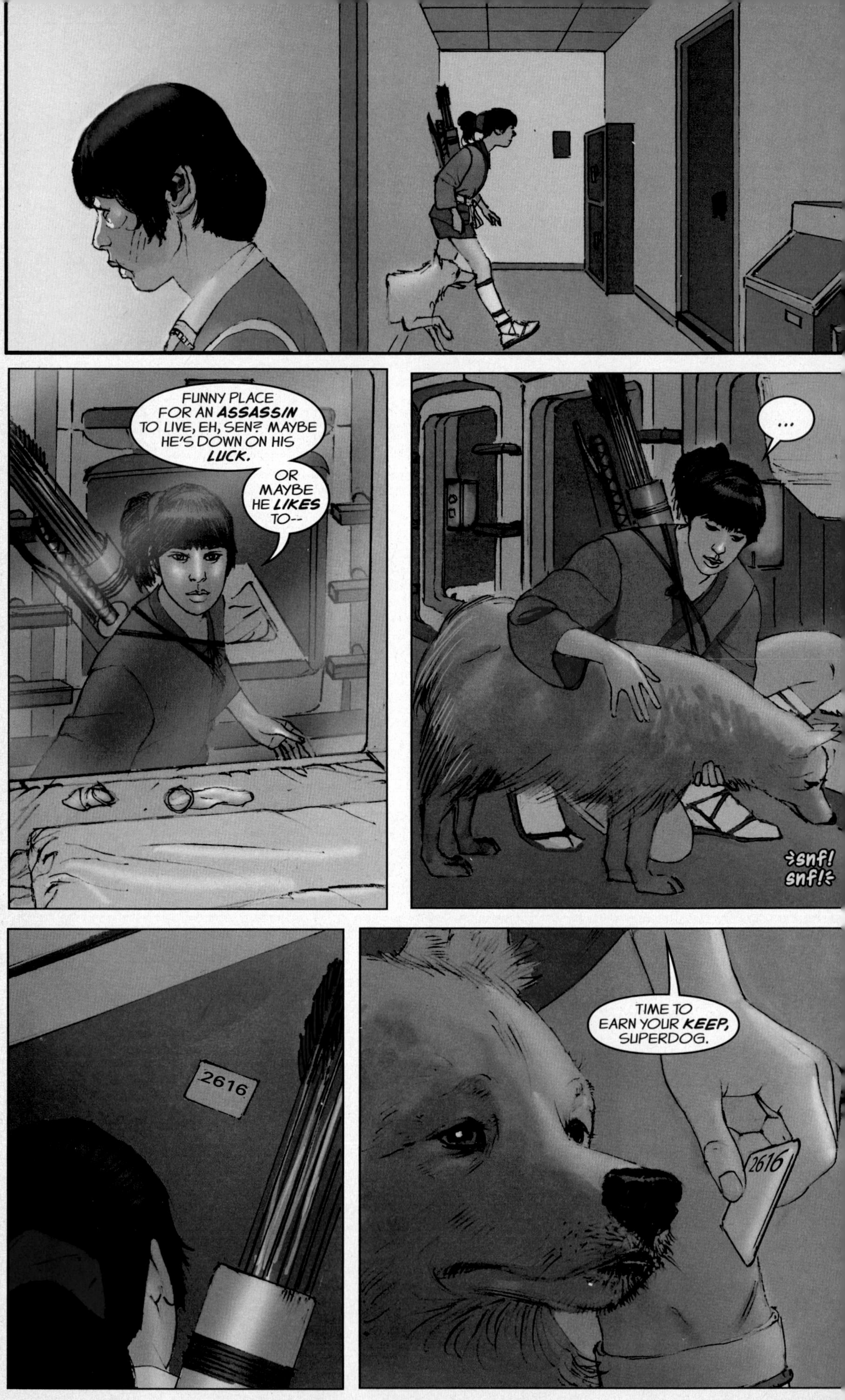
FUNNY PLACE FOR AN ASSASSIN TO LIVE, EH, SEN? MAYBE HE'S DOWN ON HIS LUCK.
OR MAYBE HE LIKES TO--
...
snf! snf!
2616
TIME TO EARN YOUR KEEP, SUPERDOG.
2616

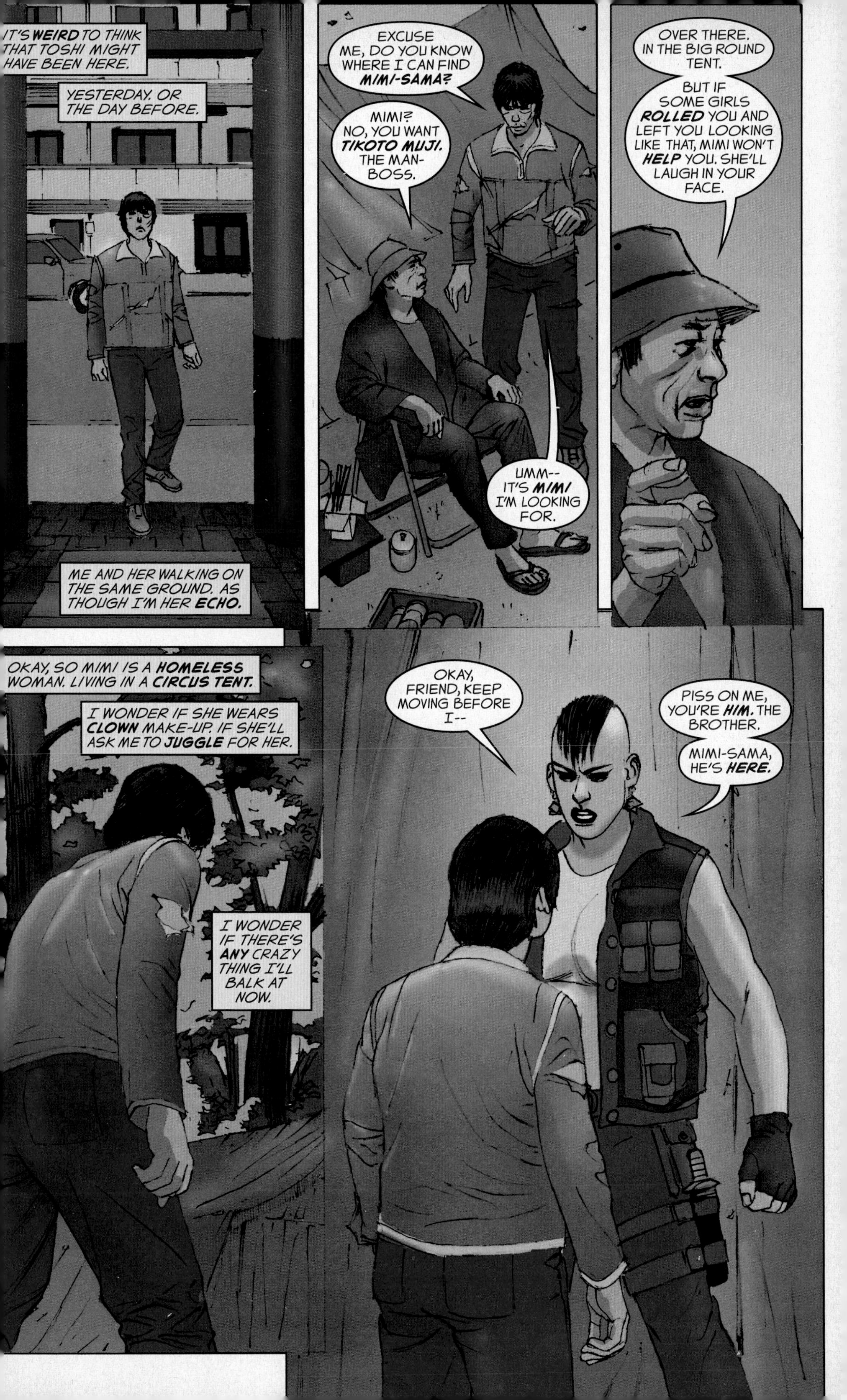

IT'S WEIRD TO THINK THAT TOSHI MIGHT HAVE BEEN HERE.
YESTERDAY. OR THE DAY BEFORE.
ME AND HER WALKING ON THE SAME GROUND. AS THOUGH I'M HER ECHO.
EXCUSE ME, DO YOU KNOW WHERE I CAN FIND MIMI-SAMA?
MIMI? NO, YOU WANT TIKOTO MUJI. THE MAN-BOSS.
UMM-- IT'S MIMI I'M LOOKING FOR.
OVER THERE. IN THE BIG ROUND TENT.
BUT IF SOME GIRLS ROLLED YOU AND LEFT YOU LOOKING LIKE THAT, MIMI WON'T HELP YOU. SHE'LL LAUGH IN YOUR FACE.
OKAY, SO MIMI IS A HOMELESS WOMAN. LIVING IN A CIRCUS TENT.
I WONDER IF SHE WEARS CLOWN MAKE-UP. IF SHE'LL ASK ME TO JUGGLE FOR HER.
I WONDER IF THERE'S ANY CRAZY THING I'LL BALK AT NOW.
OKAY, FRIEND, KEEP MOVING BEFORE I--
PISS ON ME, YOU'RE HIM. THE BROTHER.
MIMI-SAMA, HE'S HERE.

KAIKOU HARA.

I HOPE IT'S NOT TOO **LATE**. STONE-FIST SAID YOU WANTED TO SEE ME, SO I--

EXTREME LOVE!!!

--I THOUGHT-- ...

切恋愛
EXTREME LOVE!!!

STARRING MIMI OGUNO

Y-YOU-- --YOU'RE-- --YOU'RE **MIMI OGUNO**.

YES, I AM. YOU'VE SEEN SOME OF MY **FILMS?**

I--I SAW **INSATIABLE NURSES** AT MY FRIEND'S HOUSE, LOTS OF--LOTS OF TIMES.

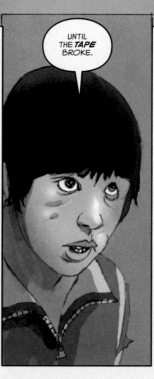

UNTIL THE **TAPE** BROKE.

THEN THERE DOESN'T NEED TO BE ANY CEREMONY OR **STIFFNESS** BETWEEN US, KAIKOU.

WE'RE **INTIMATE** ALREADY.

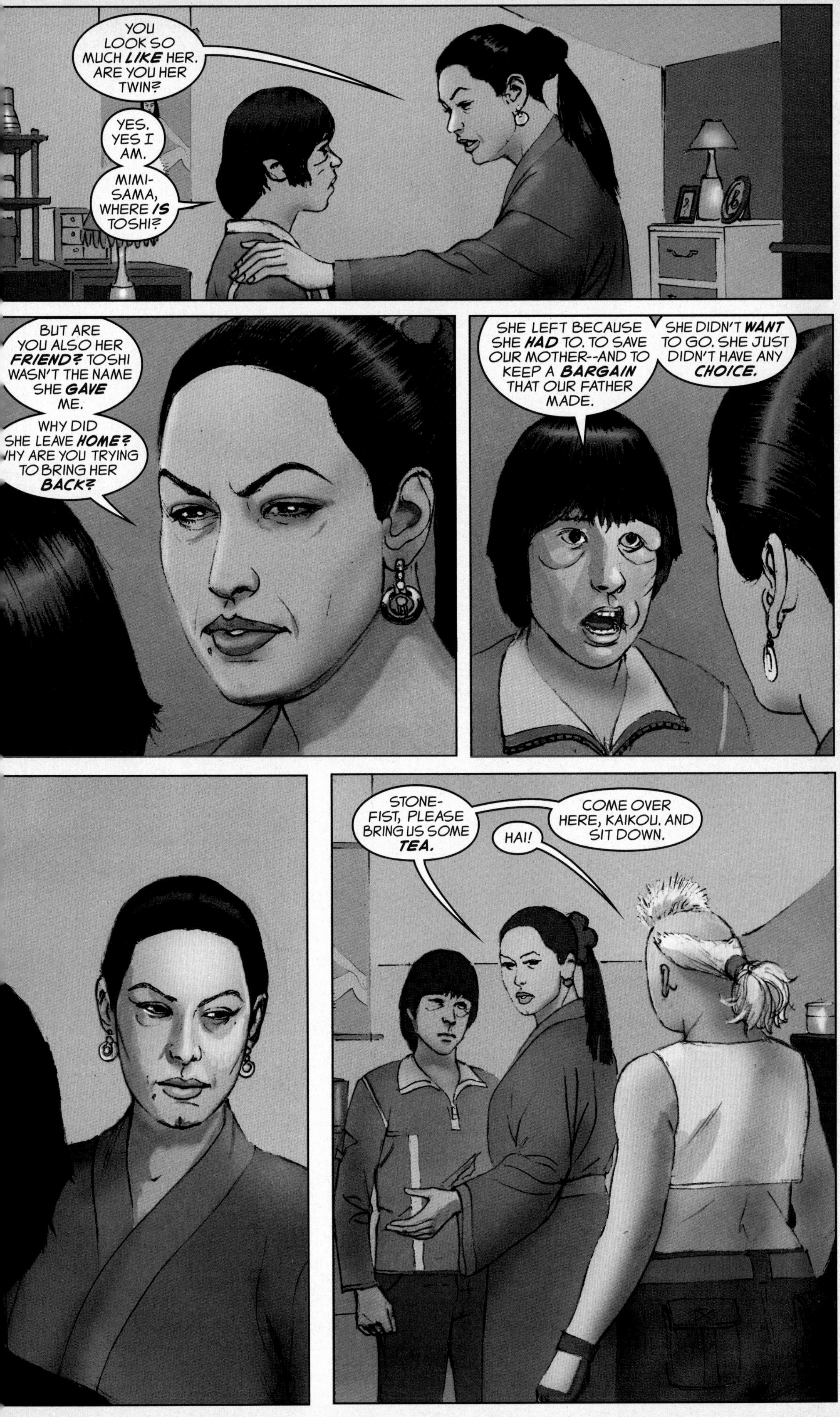

YOU LOOK SO MUCH LIKE HER. ARE YOU HER TWIN?
YES. YES I AM.
MIMI-SAMA, WHERE IS TOSHI?
BUT ARE YOU ALSO HER FRIEND? TOSHI WASN'T THE NAME SHE GAVE ME.
WHY DID SHE LEAVE HOME? WHY ARE YOU TRYING TO BRING HER BACK?
SHE LEFT BECAUSE SHE HAD TO. TO SAVE OUR MOTHER--AND TO KEEP A BARGAIN THAT OUR FATHER MADE.
SHE DIDN'T WANT TO GO. SHE JUST DIDN'T HAVE ANY CHOICE.
STONE-FIST, PLEASE BRING US SOME TEA.
HAI!
COME OVER HERE, KAIKOU. AND SIT DOWN.

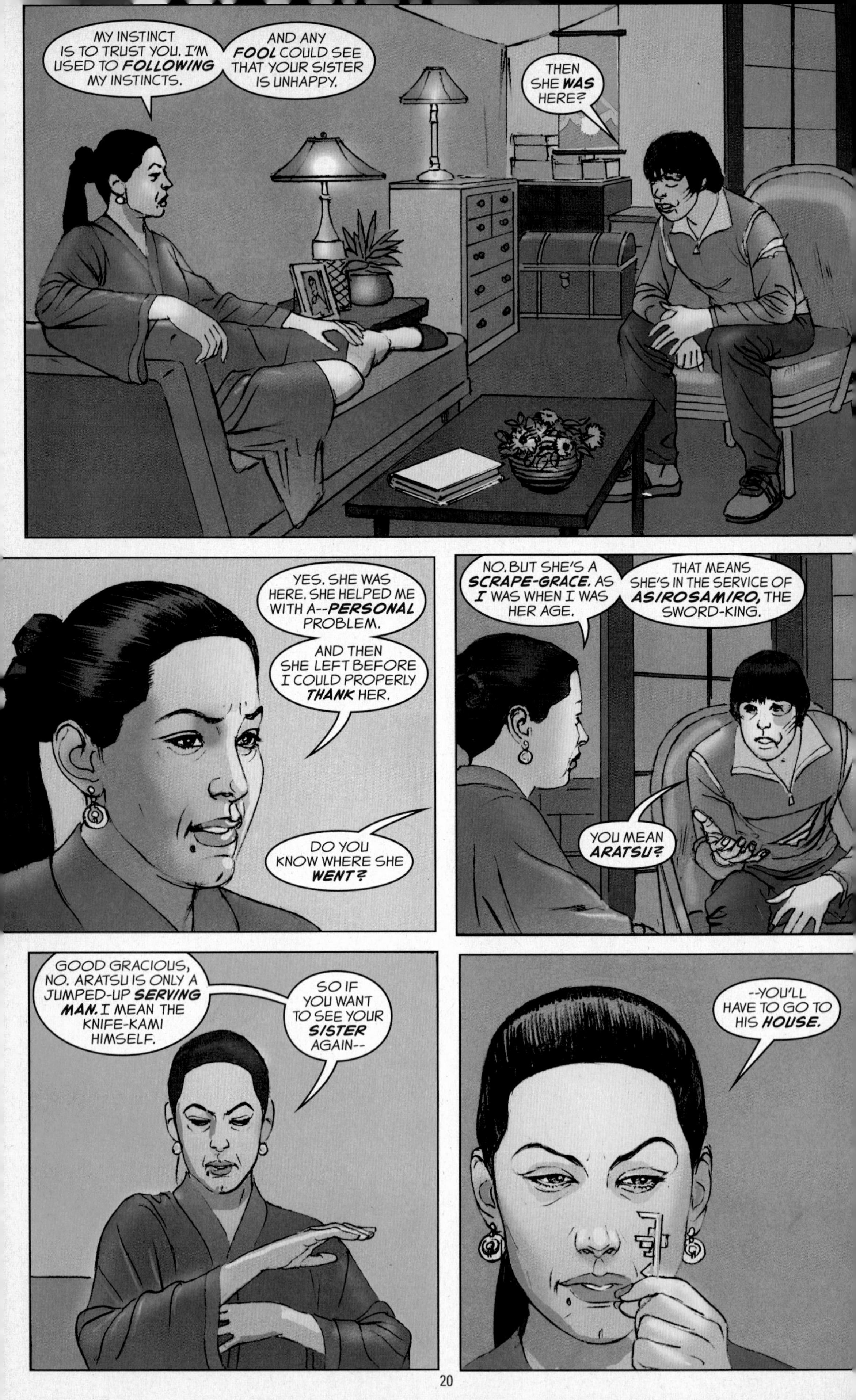
MY INSTINCT IS TO TRUST YOU. I'M USED TO FOLLOWING MY INSTINCTS.
AND ANY FOOL COULD SEE THAT YOUR SISTER IS UNHAPPY.
THEN SHE WAS HERE?
YES. SHE WAS HERE. SHE HELPED ME WITH A--PERSONAL PROBLEM.
AND THEN SHE LEFT BEFORE I COULD PROPERLY THANK HER.
DO YOU KNOW WHERE SHE WENT?
NO. BUT SHE'S A SCRAPE-GRACE. AS I WAS WHEN I WAS HER AGE.
THAT MEANS SHE'S IN THE SERVICE OF ASIROSAMIRO, THE SWORD-KING.
YOU MEAN ARATSU?
GOOD GRACIOUS, NO. ARATSU IS ONLY A JUMPED-UP SERVING MAN. I MEAN THE KNIFE-KAMI HIMSELF.
SO IF YOU WANT TO SEE YOUR SISTER AGAIN--
--YOU'LL HAVE TO GO TO HIS HOUSE.

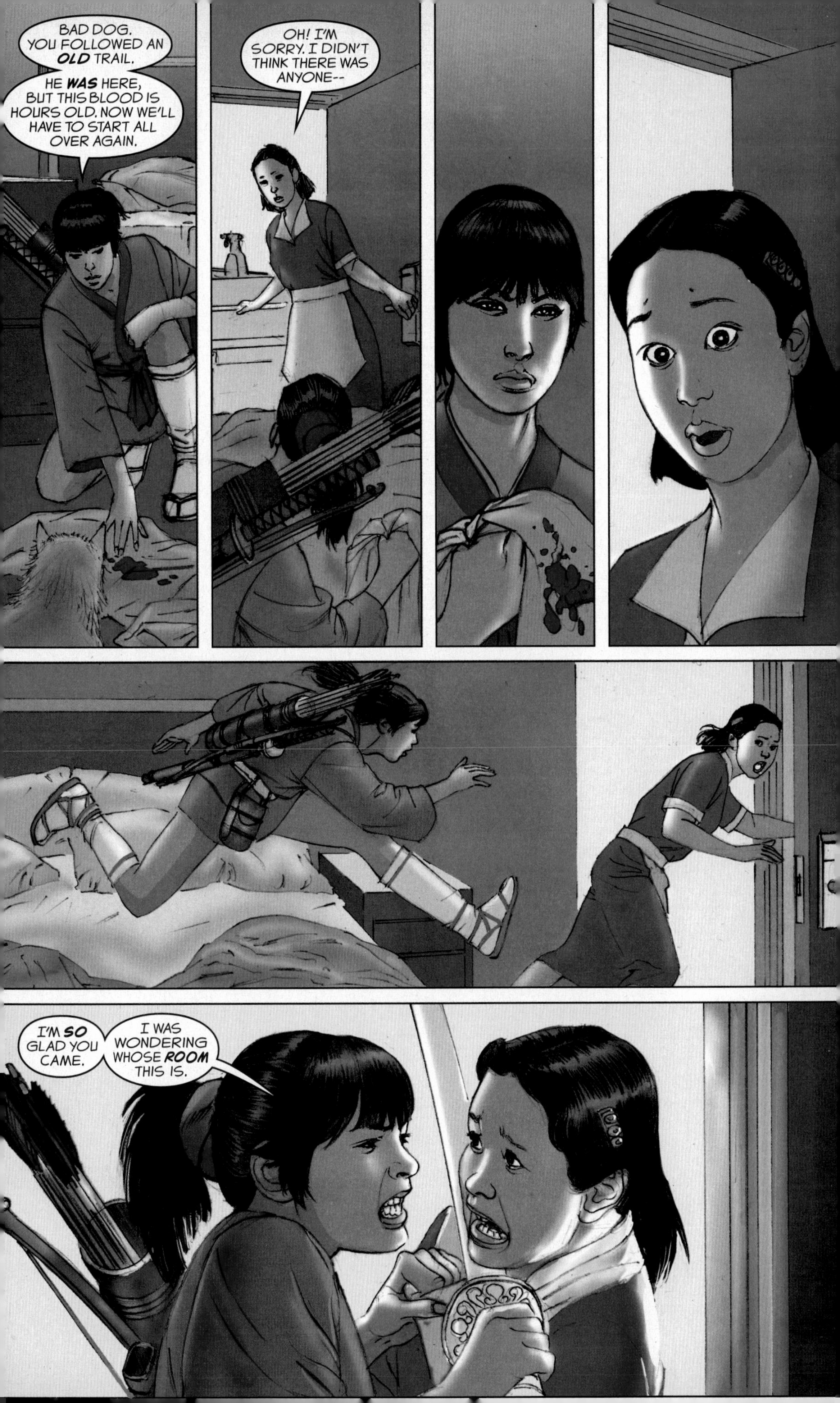
BAD DOG. YOU FOLLOWED AN **OLD** TRAIL.
HE **WAS** HERE, BUT THIS BLOOD IS HOURS OLD. NOW WE'LL HAVE TO START ALL OVER AGAIN.
OH! I'M SORRY. I DIDN'T THINK THERE WAS ANYONE--
I'M **SO** GLAD YOU CAME.
I WAS WONDERING WHOSE **ROOM** THIS IS.

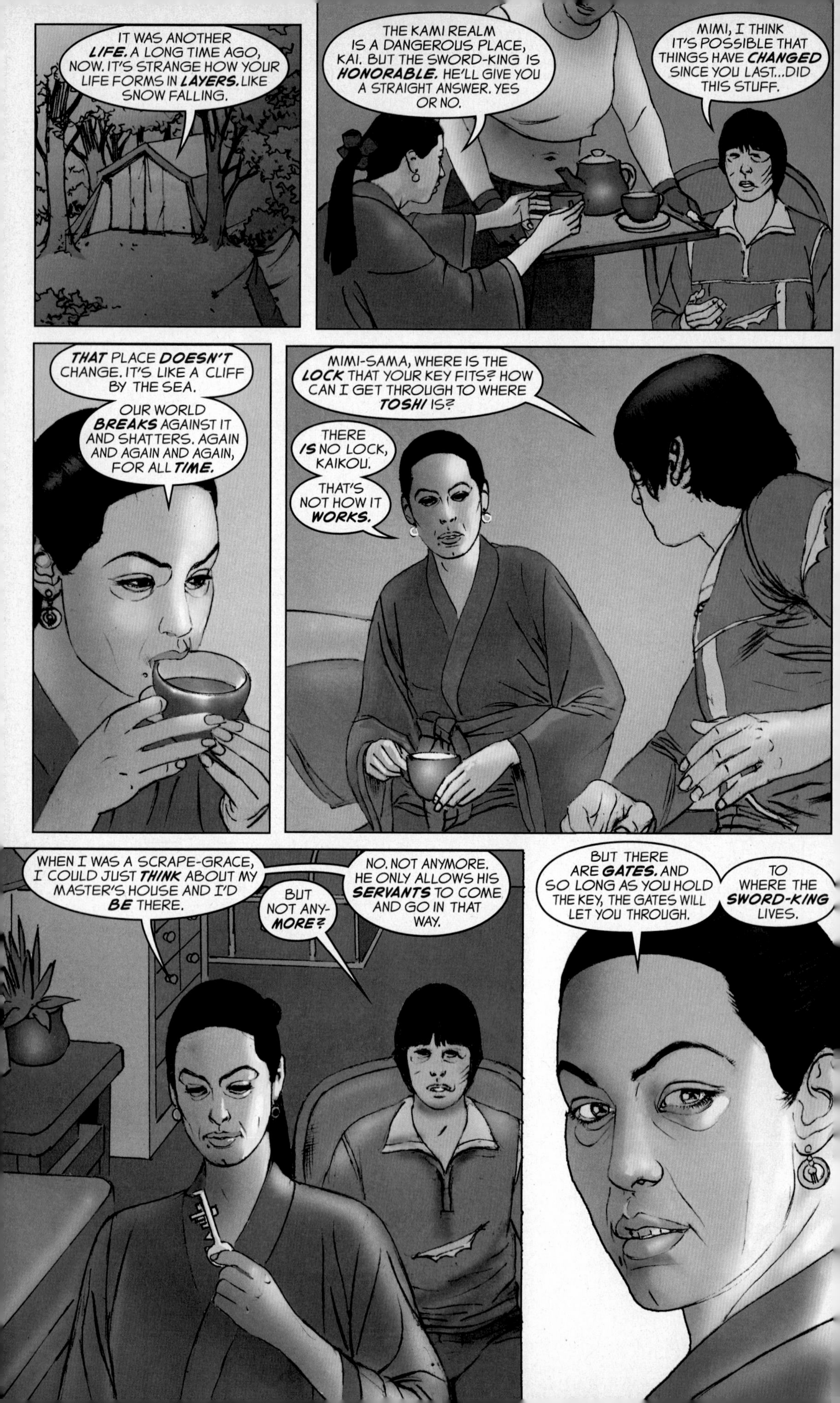
IT WAS ANOTHER LIFE. A LONG TIME AGO, NOW. IT'S STRANGE HOW YOUR LIFE FORMS IN LAYERS. LIKE SNOW FALLING.
THE KAMI REALM IS A DANGEROUS PLACE, KAI. BUT THE SWORD-KING IS HONORABLE. HE'LL GIVE YOU A STRAIGHT ANSWER. YES OR NO.
MIMI, I THINK IT'S POSSIBLE THAT THINGS HAVE CHANGED SINCE YOU LAST...DID THIS STUFF.
THAT PLACE DOESN'T CHANGE. IT'S LIKE A CLIFF BY THE SEA.
OUR WORLD BREAKS AGAINST IT AND SHATTERS. AGAIN AND AGAIN AND AGAIN, FOR ALL TIME.
MIMI-SAMA, WHERE IS THE LOCK THAT YOUR KEY FITS? HOW CAN I GET THROUGH TO WHERE TOSHI IS?
THERE IS NO LOCK, KAIKOU.
THAT'S NOT HOW IT WORKS.
WHEN I WAS A SCRAPE-GRACE, I COULD JUST THINK ABOUT MY MASTER'S HOUSE AND I'D BE THERE.
BUT NOT ANY-MORE?
NO. NOT ANYMORE. HE ONLY ALLOWS HIS SERVANTS TO COME AND GO IN THAT WAY.
BUT THERE ARE GATES. AND SO LONG AS YOU HOLD THE KEY, THE GATES WILL LET YOU THROUGH.
TO WHERE THE SWORD-KING LIVES.

CAN YOU TELL ME WHERE THESE GATES ARE? OR *TAKE* ME TO ONE?

THE NEAREST IS AT THE *NISHIDAI* SUBWAY STATION. THE EASTBOUND TUNNEL ON THE MITA LINE.

STONE-FIST WILL TAKE YOU THERE.

I WAS EXPECTING THE KEY TO BE *COLD* TO THE TOUCH. BUT IT WAS WARM, AND IT *SQUIRMED* IN MY HAND LIKE SOMETHING ALIVE.

EVEN AFTER ALL I'D BEEN THROUGH--IT *SCARED* ME.

STAY WITH HIM. KEEP HIM SAFE.

DON'T WORRY, MIMI-SAMA. ANYONE WHO TRIES TO HURT HIM WILL EAT THEIR OWN *TEETH.*

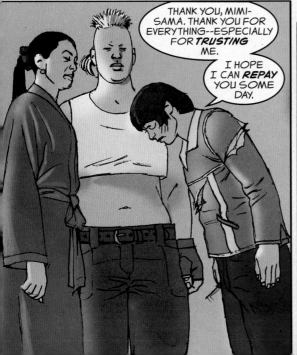

THANK YOU, MIMI-SAMA. THANK YOU FOR EVERYTHING--ESPECIALLY FOR *TRUSTING* ME.

I HOPE I CAN *REPAY* YOU SOME DAY.

COME BACK *ALIVE,* KAIKOU.

AND WATCH *INSATIABLE NURSES II*--IT'S A FAR BETTER MOVIE.

LORETTA!

WHAT ARE YOU *DOING* IN THERE?

I'M BLEACHING MY *EYEBROWS!*

GOD, CAN I GET A *MOMENT'S* PEACE?

YOU'VE BEEN IN THERE FORTY-FIVE *MINUTES!*

WELL, IF THAT'S HOW LONG IT TAKES, THEN THAT'S HOW LONG IT *TAKES.*

I'M NOT RUSHING THE FINAL *RINSE* BECAUSE YOUR BLADDER IS TOO SMALL TO--

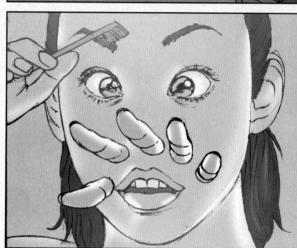

HI. YOU MUST BE *LORETTA.* TELL ME ABOUT *KAIKOU HARA.*

WHILE YOUR *HEAD* IS STILL ATTACHED TO YOUR NECK.

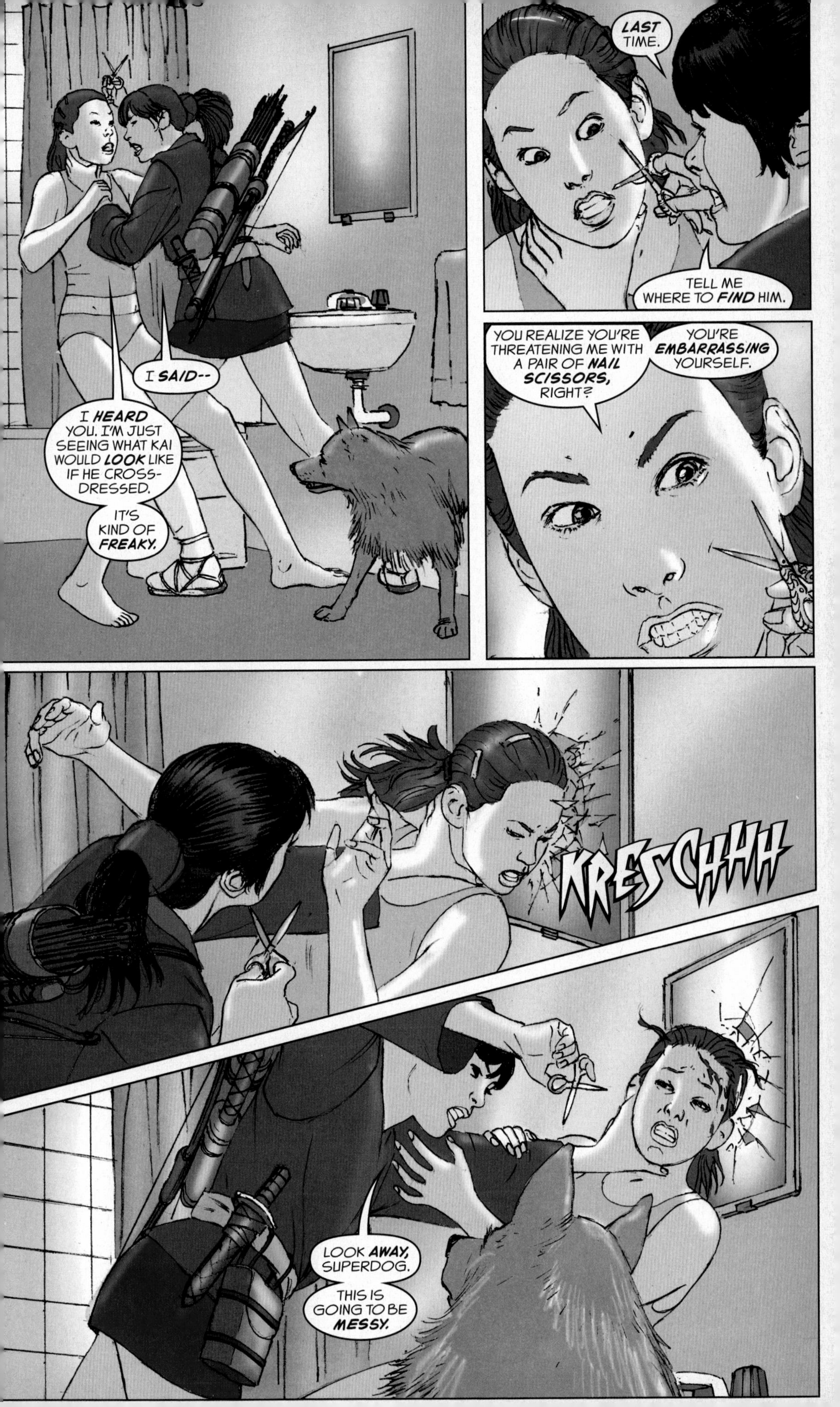
I SAID--
I HEARD YOU. I'M JUST SEEING WHAT KAI WOULD LOOK LIKE IF HE CROSS-DRESSED.
IT'S KIND OF FREAKY.
LAST TIME.
TELL ME WHERE TO FIND HIM.
YOU REALIZE YOU'RE THREATENING ME WITH A PAIR OF NAIL SCISSORS, RIGHT?
YOU'RE EMBARRASSING YOURSELF.
KRESCHHH
LOOK AWAY, SUPERDOG.
THIS IS GOING TO BE MESSY.

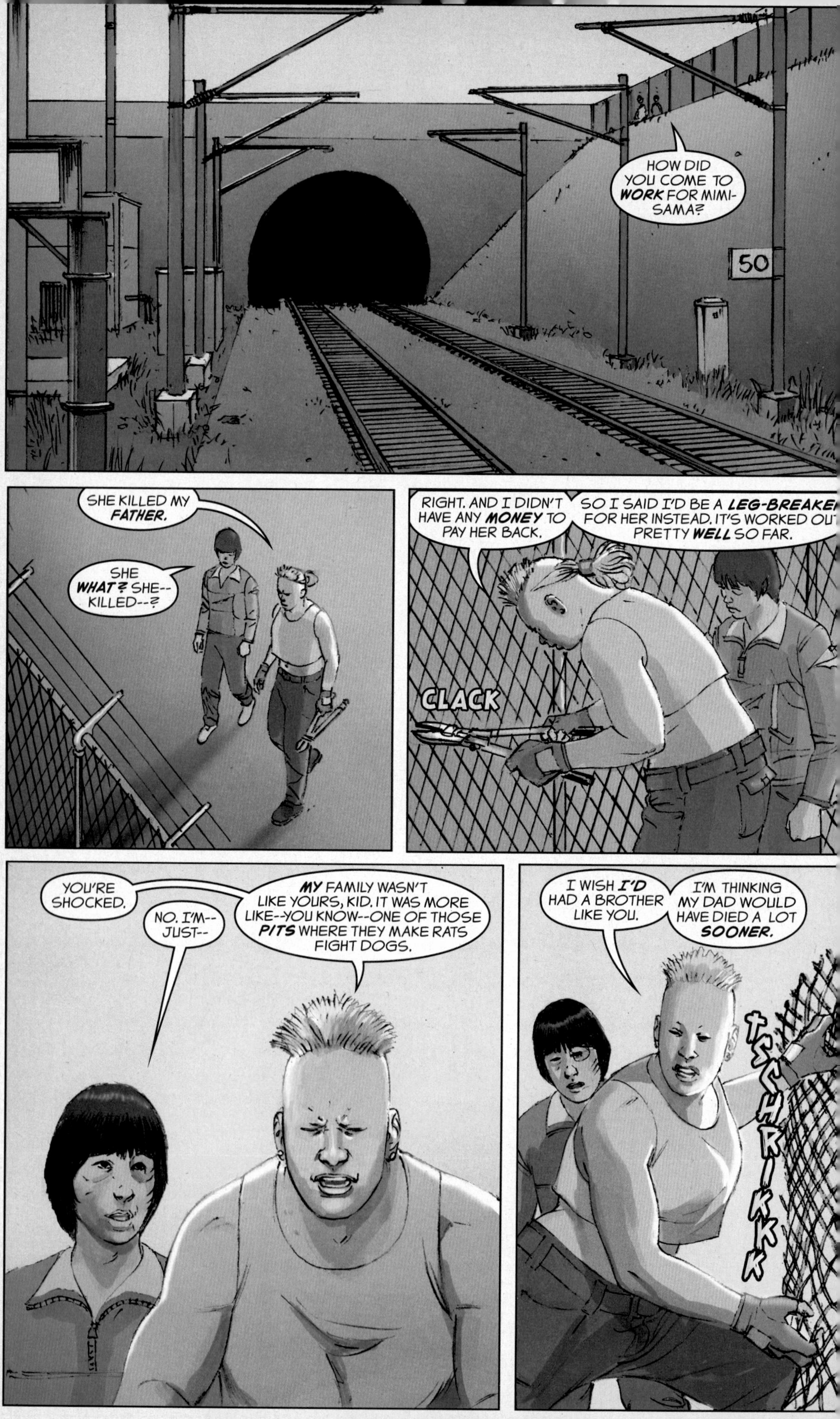
HOW DID YOU COME TO WORK FOR MIMI-SAMA?
50
SHE KILLED MY FATHER.
SHE WHAT? SHE-- KILLED--?
RIGHT. AND I DIDN'T HAVE ANY MONEY TO PAY HER BACK.
SO I SAID I'D BE A LEG-BREAKER FOR HER INSTEAD. IT'S WORKED OUT PRETTY WELL SO FAR.
CLACK
YOU'RE SHOCKED.
NO. I'M-- JUST--
MY FAMILY WASN'T LIKE YOURS, KID. IT WAS MORE LIKE--YOU KNOW--ONE OF THOSE PITS WHERE THEY MAKE RATS FIGHT DOGS.
I WISH I'D HAD A BROTHER LIKE YOU.
I'M THINKING MY DAD WOULD HAVE DIED A LOT SOONER.
TSHRIKKK

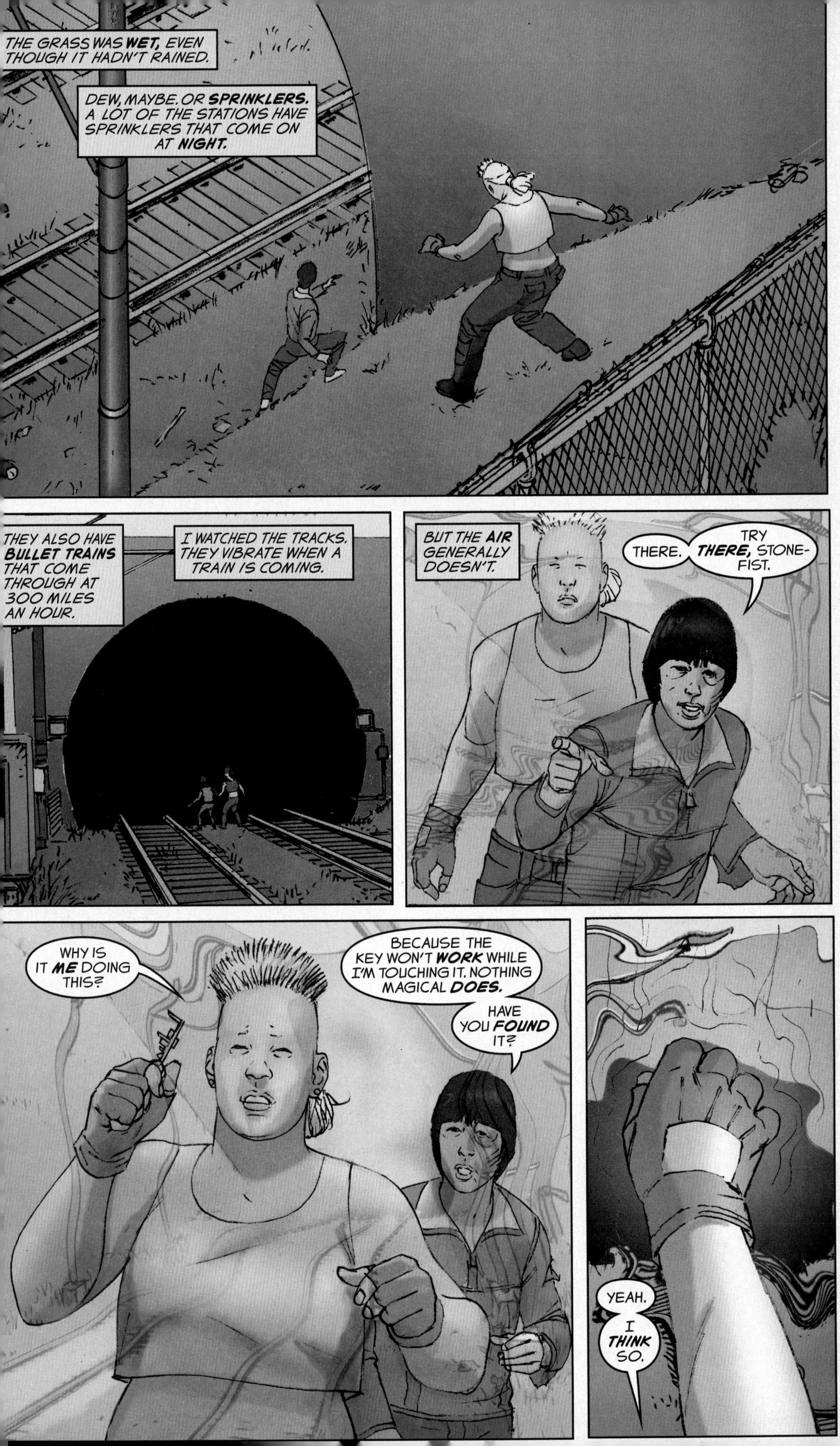
THE GRASS WAS WET, EVEN THOUGH IT HADN'T RAINED.
DEW, MAYBE. OR SPRINKLERS. A LOT OF THE STATIONS HAVE SPRINKLERS THAT COME ON AT NIGHT.
THEY ALSO HAVE BULLET TRAINS THAT COME THROUGH AT 300 MILES AN HOUR.
I WATCHED THE TRACKS. THEY VIBRATE WHEN A TRAIN IS COMING.
BUT THE AIR GENERALLY DOESN'T.
THERE.
TRY THERE, STONE-FIST.
WHY IS IT ME DOING THIS?
BECAUSE THE KEY WON'T WORK WHILE I'M TOUCHING IT. NOTHING MAGICAL DOES.
HAVE YOU FOUND IT?
YEAH.
I THINK SO.

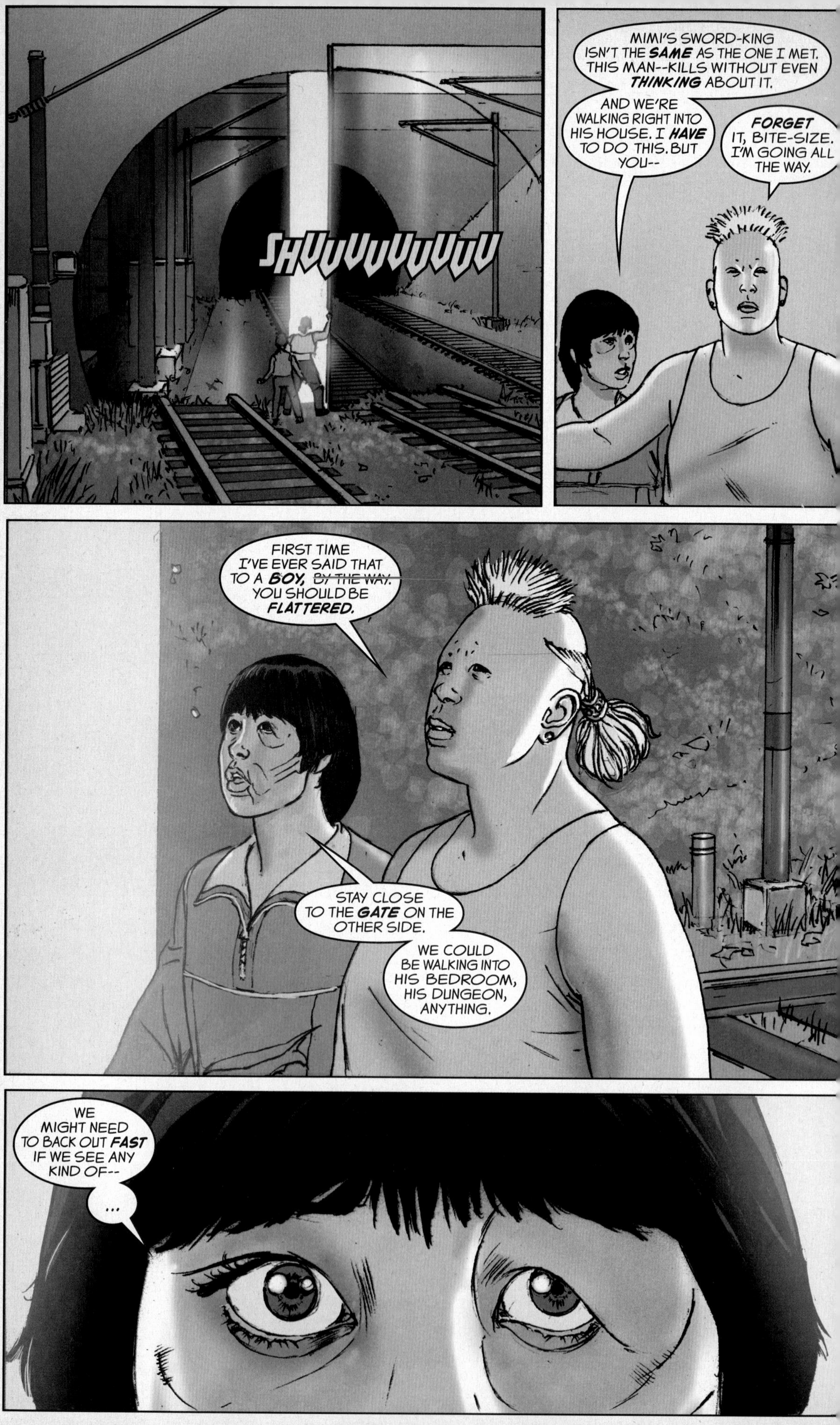
SHVVVVVVVVVV
MIMI'S SWORD-KING ISN'T THE SAME AS THE ONE I MET. THIS MAN--KILLS WITHOUT EVEN THINKING ABOUT IT.
AND WE'RE WALKING RIGHT INTO HIS HOUSE. I HAVE TO DO THIS. BUT YOU--
FORGET IT, BITE-SIZE. I'M GOING ALL THE WAY.
FIRST TIME I'VE EVER SAID THAT TO A BOY, BY THE WAY. YOU SHOULD BE FLATTERED.
STAY CLOSE TO THE GATE ON THE OTHER SIDE.
WE COULD BE WALKING INTO HIS BEDROOM, HIS DUNGEON, ANYTHING.
WE MIGHT NEED TO BACK OUT FAST IF WE SEE ANY KIND OF--
...

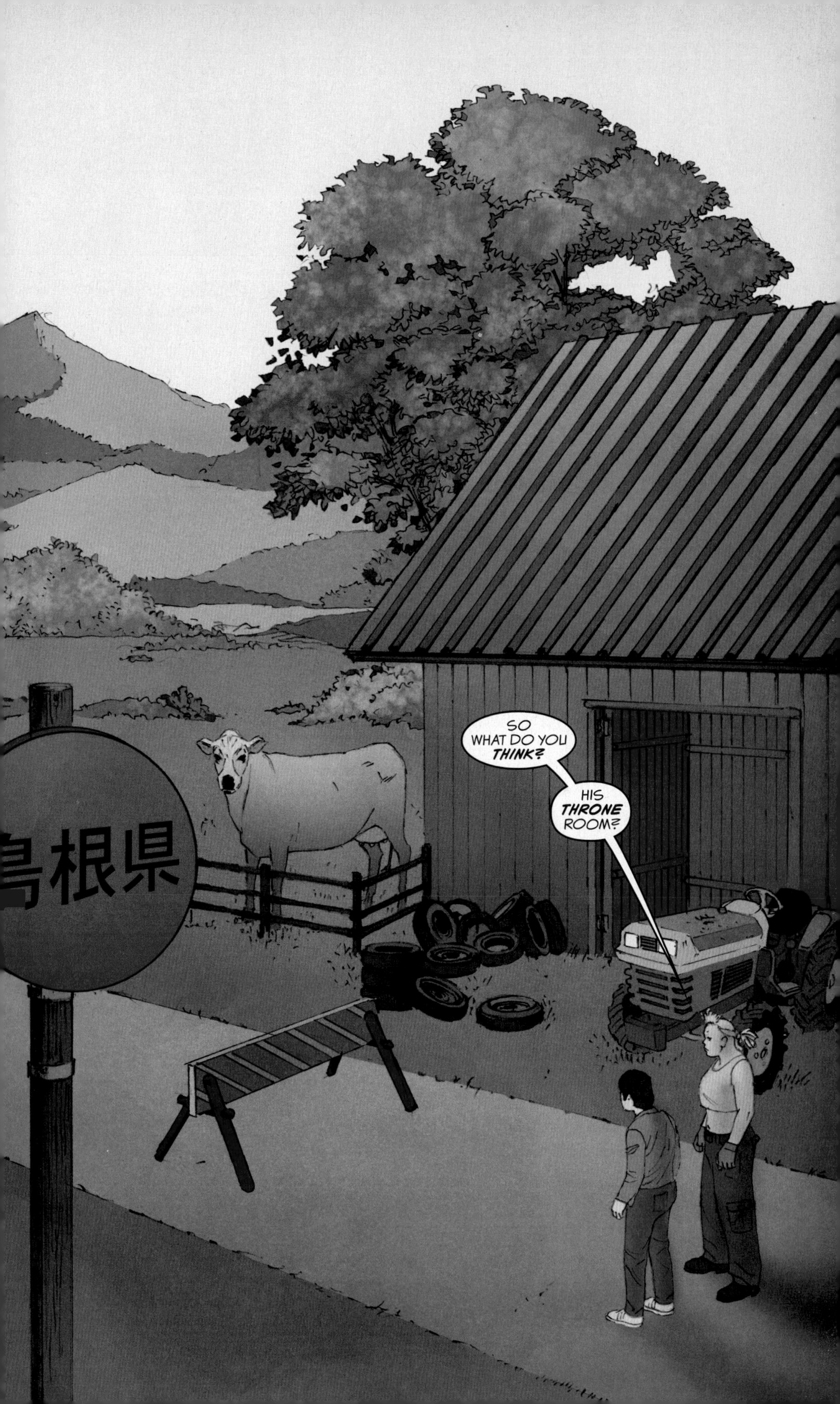
島根県
SO WHAT DO YOU THINK?
HIS THRONE ROOM?

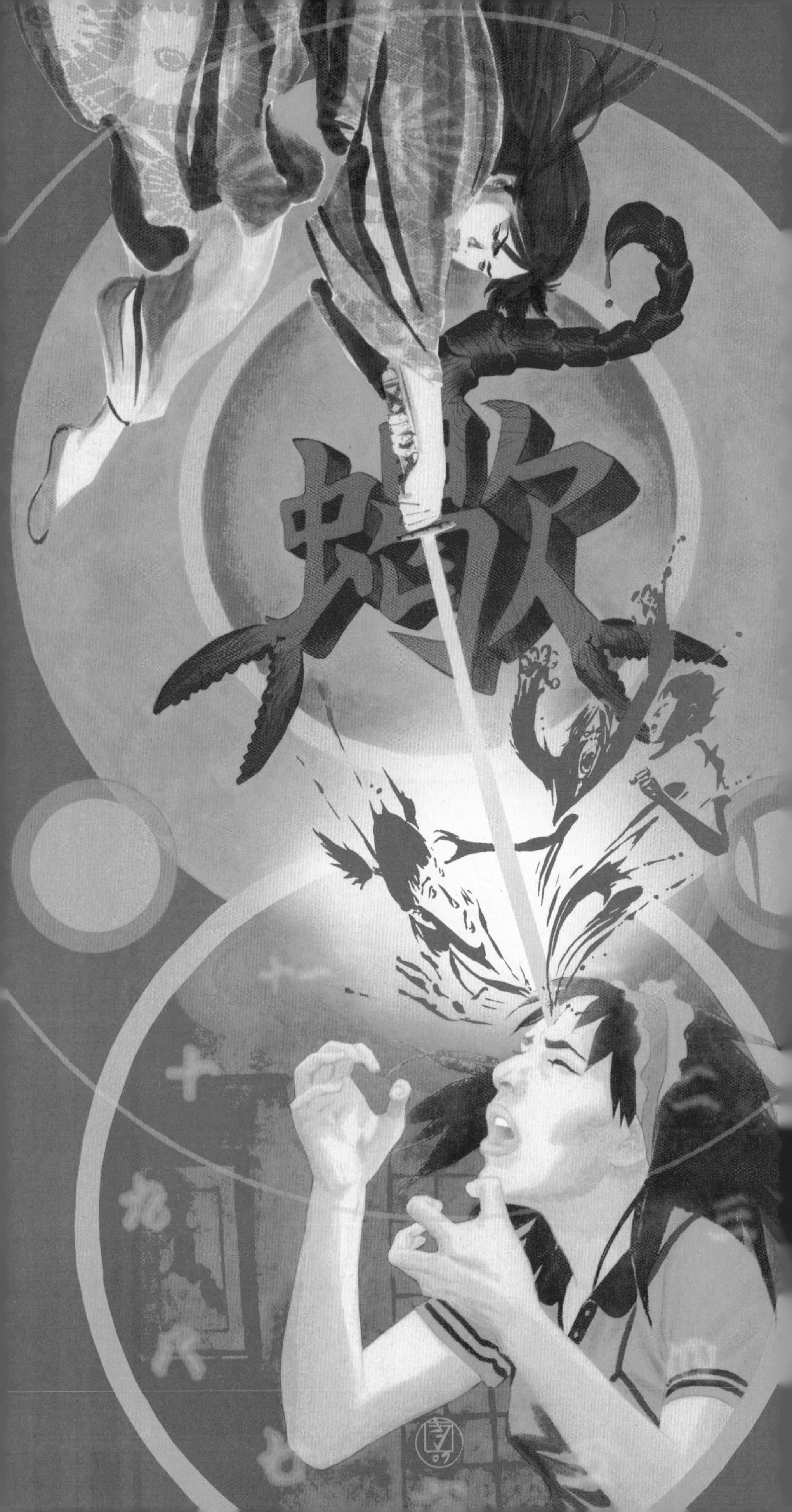
蠍

BEEN HERE LESS THAN TWO HOURS, AND ALREADY I WANT TO **KILL** SOMEONE.

LOCK MY **THIGHS** ON EITHER SIDE OF THEIR HEAD, FLEX AND **TWIST.**

IT'S BECAUSE OF THE **ISLANDS.**

BECAUSE JAPAN IS LIKE A **BREAD ROLL** BROKEN INTO CRUMBS AND SPRINKLED ON THE **SEA.**

IDZUMI TAISHA?

HAI! DZUMI TAISHA, SUTSU **MAIRU.** SOKO.

EVERY MILE YOU TRAVEL AWAY FROM TOKYO IS **TEN** MILES-- AND TEN **YEARS.**

SO BY THE TIME YOU GET TO **SHIMANE** PROVINCE YOU'RE RIGHT AT THE EDGE OF THE **WORLD.**

AND BACK IN THE FUCKING **STONE AGE.**

OR MAYBE IT'S BECAUSE OF THE **KID.**

I MEAN, ONE OF THE **ADVANTAGES** OF THE DYKE LIFESTYLE IS THAT YOU DON'T HAVE TO **DEAL** WITH THAT STUFF.

OU DON'T HAVE TO BE RESPONSIBLE FOR **ANYONE** UNLESS YOU **REALLY WANT** TO BE.

YOU FIGHT YOUR WAY OUT FROM UNDER ALL THE POINTLESS FUCKING PARAPHERNALIA AND-- YOU'RE FREE. YOU'RE **YOURSELF.**

SO WHY AM I **ENJOYING** THIS? PLAYING **MOMMA?**

AND HOW AM I EVER GONNA LOOK *CUTLASS* IN THE *FACE* AGAIN?

WE'RE IN *IDZUMO,* IN SHIMANE PROVINCE. ABOUT FIVE MILES DOWN THE ROAD FROM THE *TAISHA* SHRINE.

BUT THAT'S *CRAZY,* STONE-FIST.

MIMI-SAMA SAID THE KEY WOULD TAKE US TO THE *SWORD-KING'S* HOUSE--IN THE REALM OF THE *KAMI.*

BUT WE'RE STILL IN OUR *OWN* WORLD-- THE NORMAL WORLD. IN THE MIDDLE OF *NOWHERE.*

AND NOW IT'S STOPPED WORKING ALTOGETHER.

THIS *ISN'T* THE MIDDLE OF NOWHERE, KAI. THIS IS NOWHERE'S STINKING, SHIT-CAKED *REAR END.*

THE ONLY *PHONE* HERE IS IN THE MAYOR'S HOUSE, AND THEY WOULDN'T EVEN LET ME IN.

THEY'VE NEVER SEEN ANYTHING *LIKE* ME HERE. BUT AT LEAST I GOT US A ROOM. AND TOMORROW WE CAN HITCH A RIDE AS FAR AS--

HEY, YOU! MAN-BITCH!

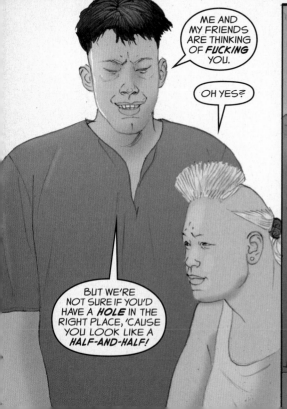

ME AND MY FRIENDS ARE THINKING OF *FUCKING* YOU.

OH YES?

BUT WE'RE NOT SURE IF YOU'D HAVE A *HOLE* IN THE RIGHT PLACE, 'CAUSE YOU LOOK LIKE A *HALF-AND-HALF!*

LIKE A *WHAT?*

YOU KNOW. HALF *MAN,* HALF WOMAN.

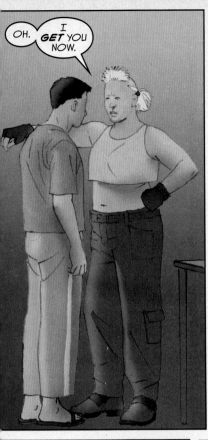

OH. I **GET** YOU NOW.

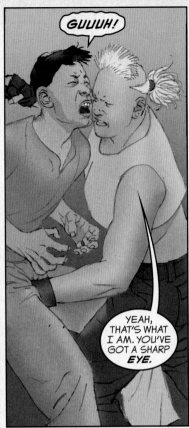

GUUUH!

YEAH, THAT'S WHAT I AM. YOU'VE GOT A SHARP **EYE.**

BUT MAYBE BEING **HALF** A MAN IS ENOUGH.

YOU'LL HAVE TO LET ME **KNOW.**

NN! NN! NNN**NN!**

ANYONE ELSE WANT A CUDDLE?

NO?

HEY, NICE TO MEET YOU BOYS. YOU REALLY KNOW HOW TO TURN A LADY'S **HEAD.**

DID YOU **HAVE** TO HURT HIM?

WHAT, THAT **BOTHERED** YOU? LOOK, A BIT OF VIOLENCE CAN BE LIKE--**OIL** ON THE WHEELS.

MAKE THINGS GO **SMOOTHER.**

THE KID LOOKS AWAY. OKAY, SO MAYBE I'LL HOLD BACK A LITTLE NEXT TIME. IF I KNOW HE'S WATCHING.

SHIT! I WONDER WHAT IT WOULD HAVE BEEN LIKE TO HAVE **HIS** CHILDHOOD.

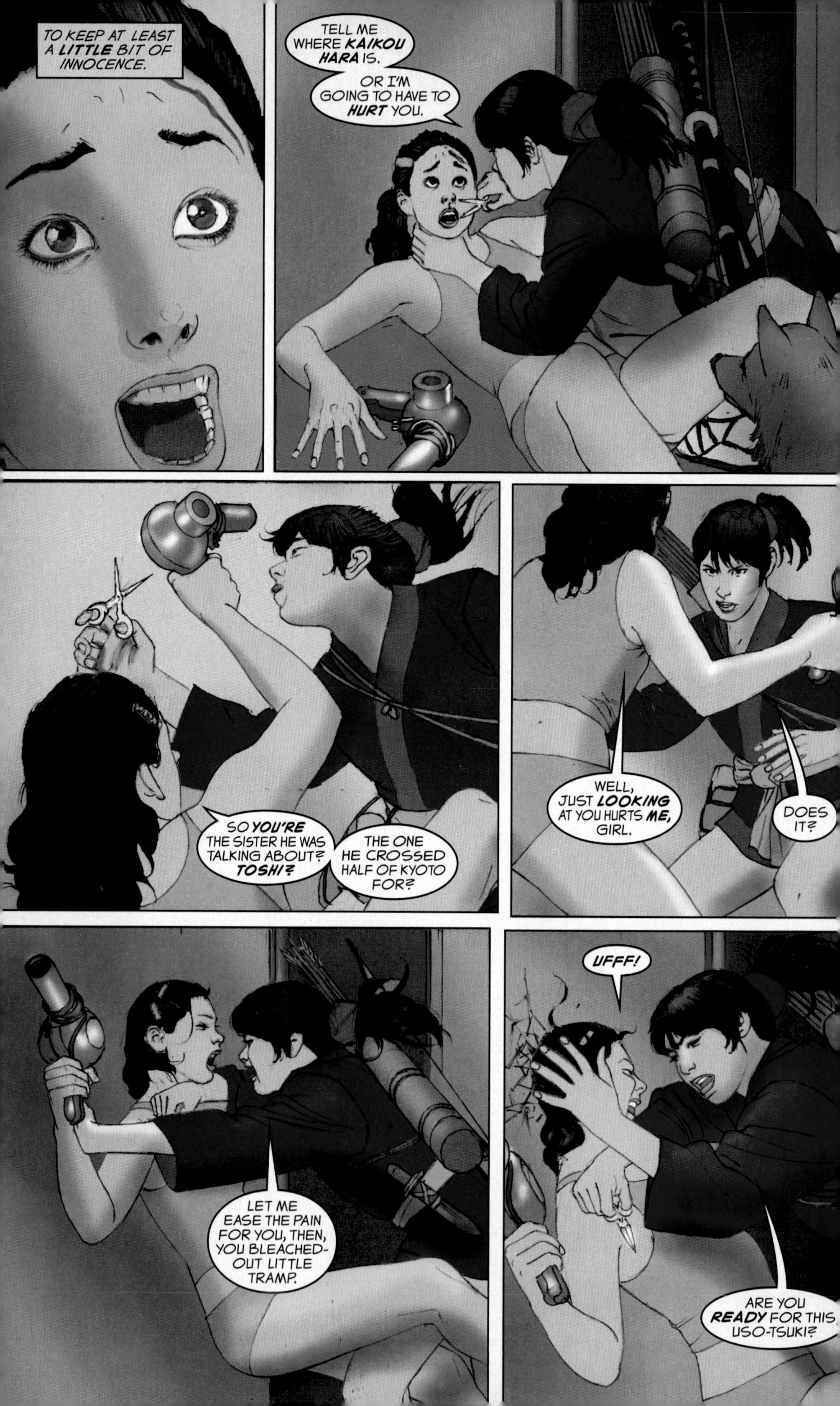
TO KEEP AT LEAST A LITTLE BIT OF INNOCENCE.
TELL ME WHERE KAIKOU HARA IS.
OR I'M GOING TO HAVE TO HURT YOU.
SO YOU'RE THE SISTER HE WAS TALKING ABOUT? TOSHI?
THE ONE HE CROSSED HALF OF KYOTO FOR?
WELL, JUST LOOKING AT YOU HURTS ME, GIRL.
DOES IT?
LET ME EASE THE PAIN FOR YOU, THEN, YOU BLEACHED-OUT LITTLE TRAMP.
UFFF!
ARE YOU READY FOR THIS USO-TSUKI?

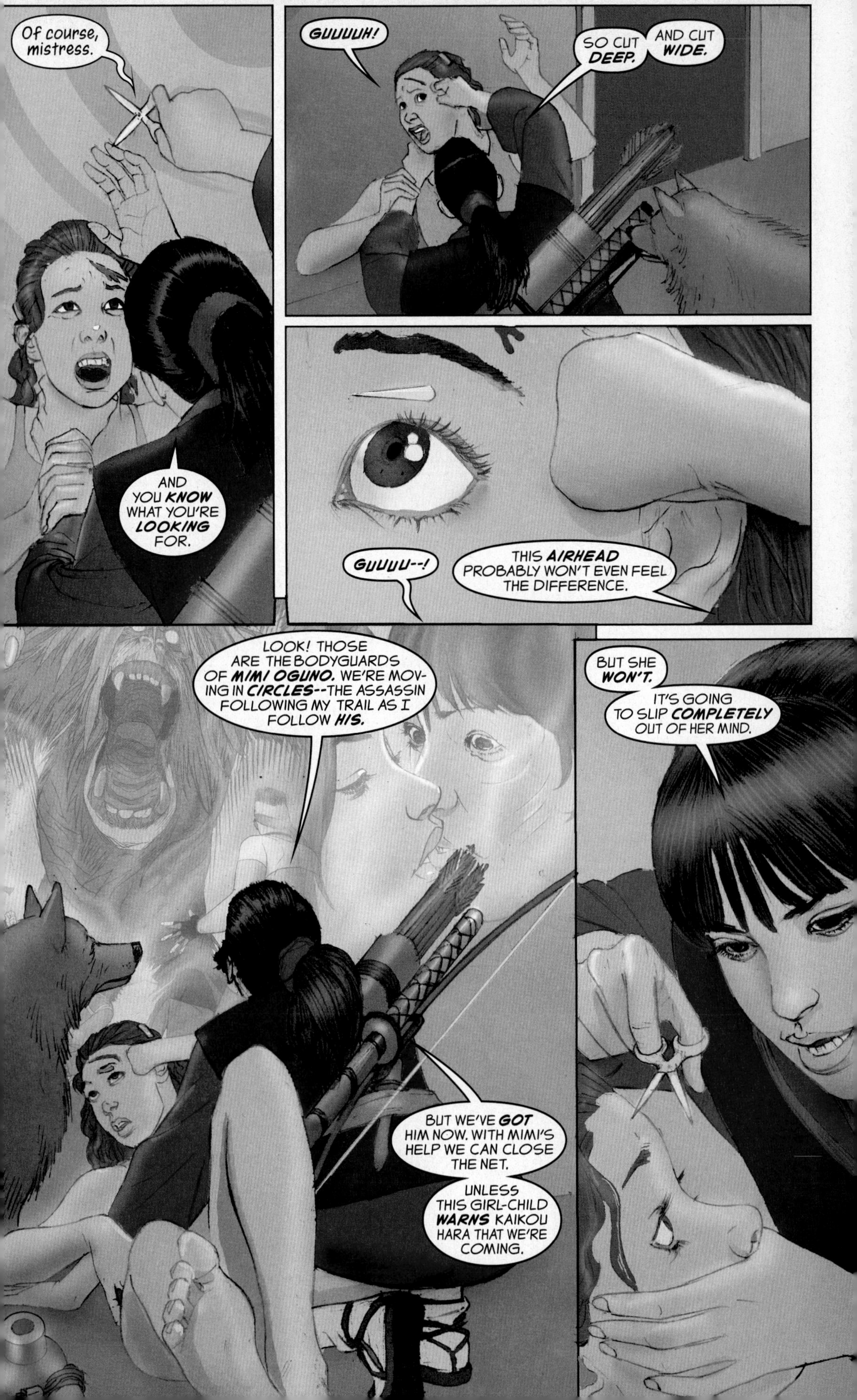

Of course, mistress.
AND YOU KNOW WHAT YOU'RE LOOKING FOR.
GUUUUH!
SO CUT DEEP.
AND CUT WIDE.
GUUUU--!
THIS AIRHEAD PROBABLY WON'T EVEN FEEL THE DIFFERENCE.
LOOK! THOSE ARE THE BODYGUARDS OF MIMI OGUNO. WE'RE MOVING IN CIRCLES--THE ASSASSIN FOLLOWING MY TRAIL AS I FOLLOW HIS.
BUT WE'VE GOT HIM NOW. WITH MIMI'S HELP WE CAN CLOSE THE NET.
UNLESS THIS GIRL-CHILD WARNS KAIKOU HARA THAT WE'RE COMING.
BUT SHE WON'T.
IT'S GOING TO SLIP COMPLETELY OUT OF HER MIND.

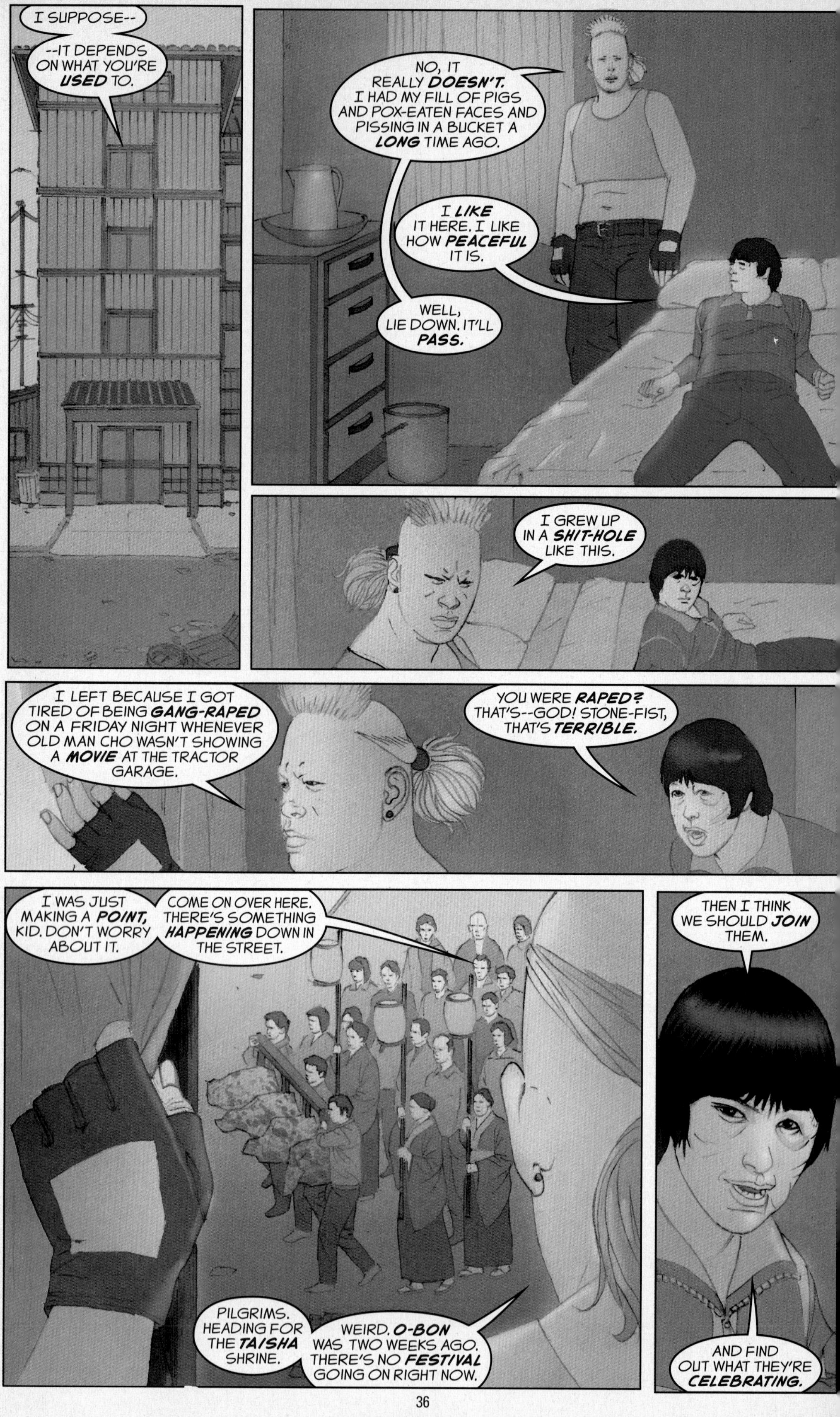
I SUPPOSE--
--IT DEPENDS ON WHAT YOU'RE USED TO.
NO, IT REALLY DOESN'T. I HAD MY FILL OF PIGS AND POX-EATEN FACES AND PISSING IN A BUCKET A LONG TIME AGO.
I LIKE IT HERE. I LIKE HOW PEACEFUL IT IS.
WELL, LIE DOWN. IT'LL PASS.
I GREW UP IN A SHIT-HOLE LIKE THIS.
I LEFT BECAUSE I GOT TIRED OF BEING GANG-RAPED ON A FRIDAY NIGHT WHENEVER OLD MAN CHO WASN'T SHOWING A MOVIE AT THE TRACTOR GARAGE.
YOU WERE RAPED? THAT'S--GOD! STONE-FIST, THAT'S TERRIBLE.
I WAS JUST MAKING A POINT, KID. DON'T WORRY ABOUT IT.
COME ON OVER HERE. THERE'S SOMETHING HAPPENING DOWN IN THE STREET.
PILGRIMS. HEADING FOR THE TAISHA SHRINE.
WEIRD. O-BON WAS TWO WEEKS AGO. THERE'S NO FESTIVAL GOING ON RIGHT NOW.
THEN I THINK WE SHOULD JOIN THEM.
AND FIND OUT WHAT THEY'RE CELEBRATING.

WHY DID I EVEN *MENTION* THAT?

I *HATE* PEOPLE WHO WHINE ABOUT HOW HARD THEY HAD IT. LIKE IT EXPLAINS ANYTHING, OR *EXCUSES* ANYTHING.

BECAUSE IT *DOESN'T.*

NO MATTER WHAT *SHIT* POURS DOWN ON YOU, IT'S YOUR OWN *CHOICE* TO STAND UNDER IT OR MOVE OUT OF THE *WAY.*

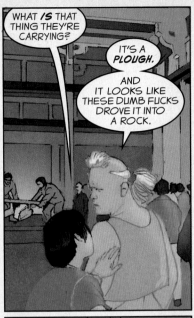

WHAT *IS* THAT THING THEY'RE CARRYING?

IT'S A *PLOUGH.*

AND IT LOOKS LIKE THESE DUMB FUCKS DROVE IT INTO A ROCK.

SPIRITS, YOU SEE THE *FAVOR* THESE YOUR SUPPLICANTS HOPE AND PRAY FOR.

MAKE THIS IMPLEMENT *WHOLE,* I BEG YOU, THAT THEIR LIVELIHOODS SHOULD NOT BE PUT AT *RISK.*

P-PRAISE THEM! PRAISE THEIR HOLY NAMES!

GREAT-SOULED ONES, WE THANK YOU AND HONOR YOU IN OUR HEARTS.

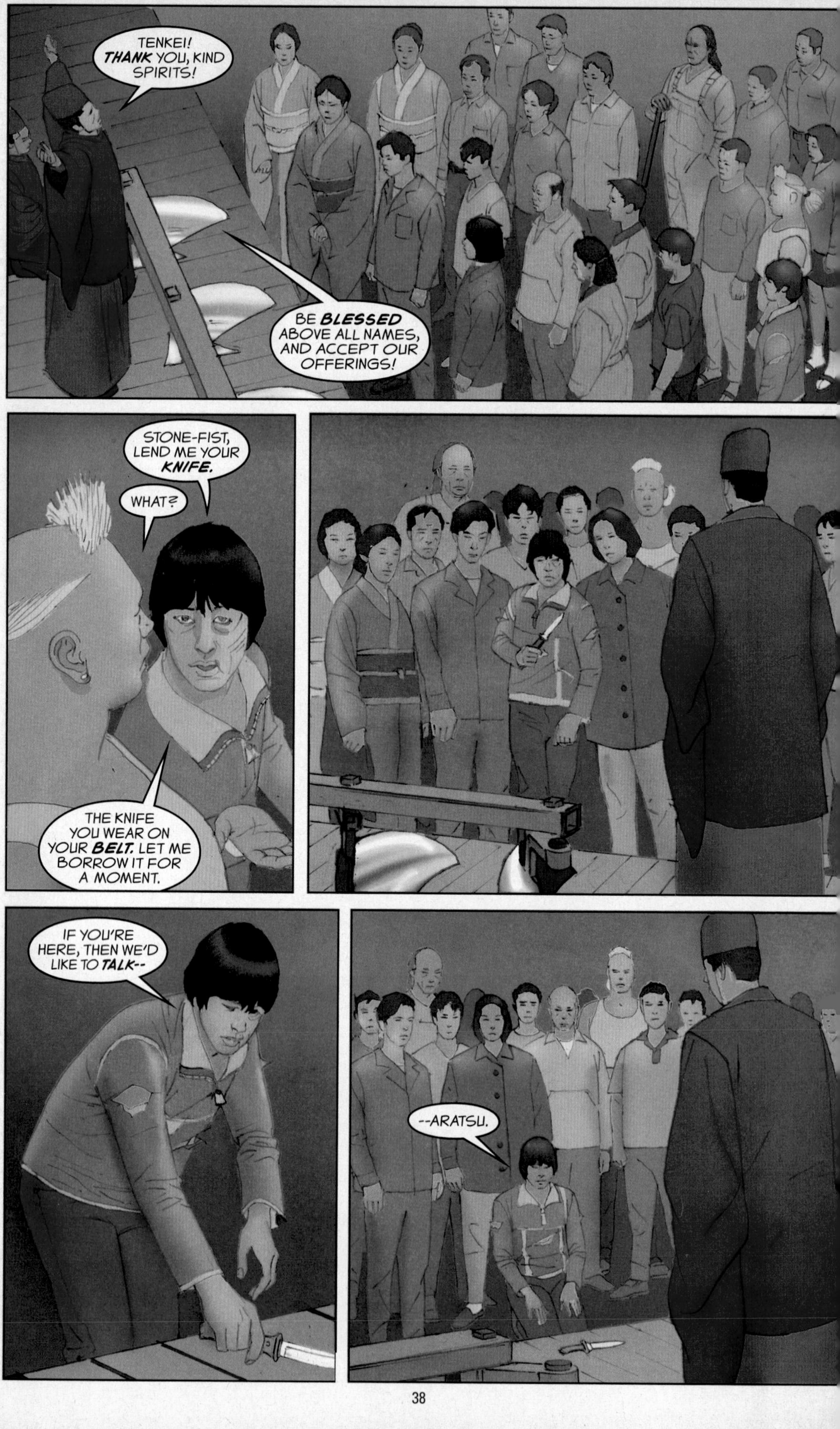
TENKEI! THANK YOU, KIND SPIRITS!
BE BLESSED ABOVE ALL NAMES, AND ACCEPT OUR OFFERINGS!
STONE-FIST, LEND ME YOUR KNIFE.
WHAT?
THE KNIFE YOU WEAR ON YOUR BELT. LET ME BORROW IT FOR A MOMENT.
IF YOU'RE HERE, THEN WE'D LIKE TO TALK--
--ARATSU.

KRA-TISCHH

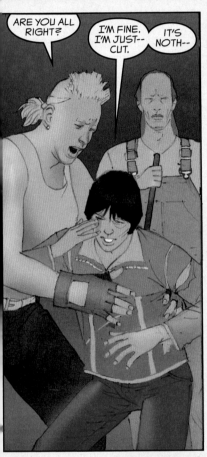

ARE YOU ALL RIGHT?

I'M FINE. I'M JUST-- CUT.

IT'S NOTH--

...

KAI!

WAIT FOR ME! DON'T RUN OFF BY YOUR--

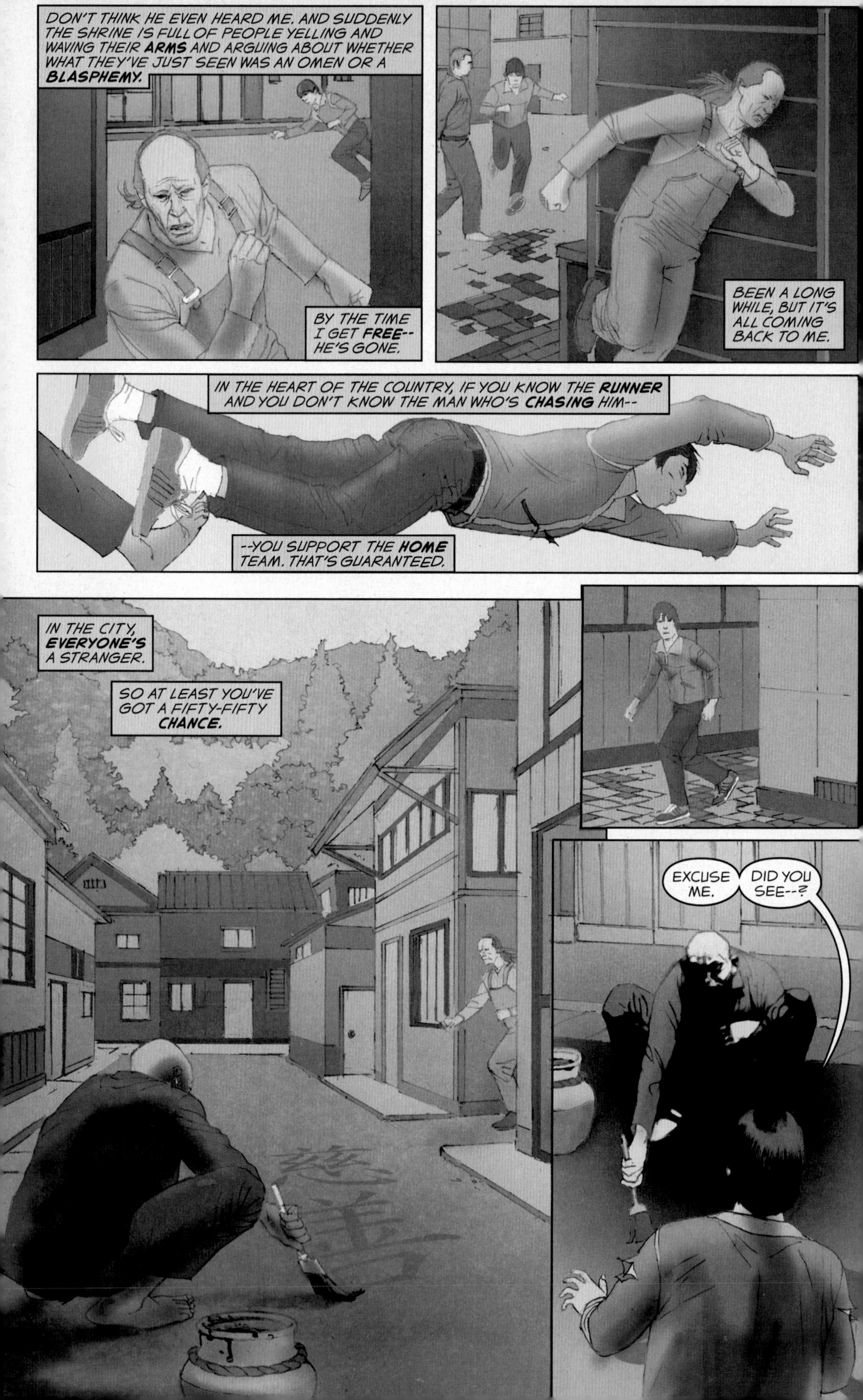
DON'T THINK HE EVEN HEARD ME. AND SUDDENLY THE SHRINE IS FULL OF PEOPLE YELLING AND WAVING THEIR ARMS AND ARGUING ABOUT WHETHER WHAT THEY'VE JUST SEEN WAS AN OMEN OR A BLASPHEMY.
BY THE TIME I GET FREE-- HE'S GONE.
BEEN A LONG WHILE, BUT IT'S ALL COMING BACK TO ME.
IN THE HEART OF THE COUNTRY, IF YOU KNOW THE RUNNER AND YOU DON'T KNOW THE MAN WHO'S CHASING HIM--
--YOU SUPPORT THE HOME TEAM. THAT'S GUARANTEED.
IN THE CITY, EVERYONE'S A STRANGER.
SO AT LEAST YOU'VE GOT A FIFTY-FIFTY CHANCE.
EXCUSE ME.
DID YOU SEE--?

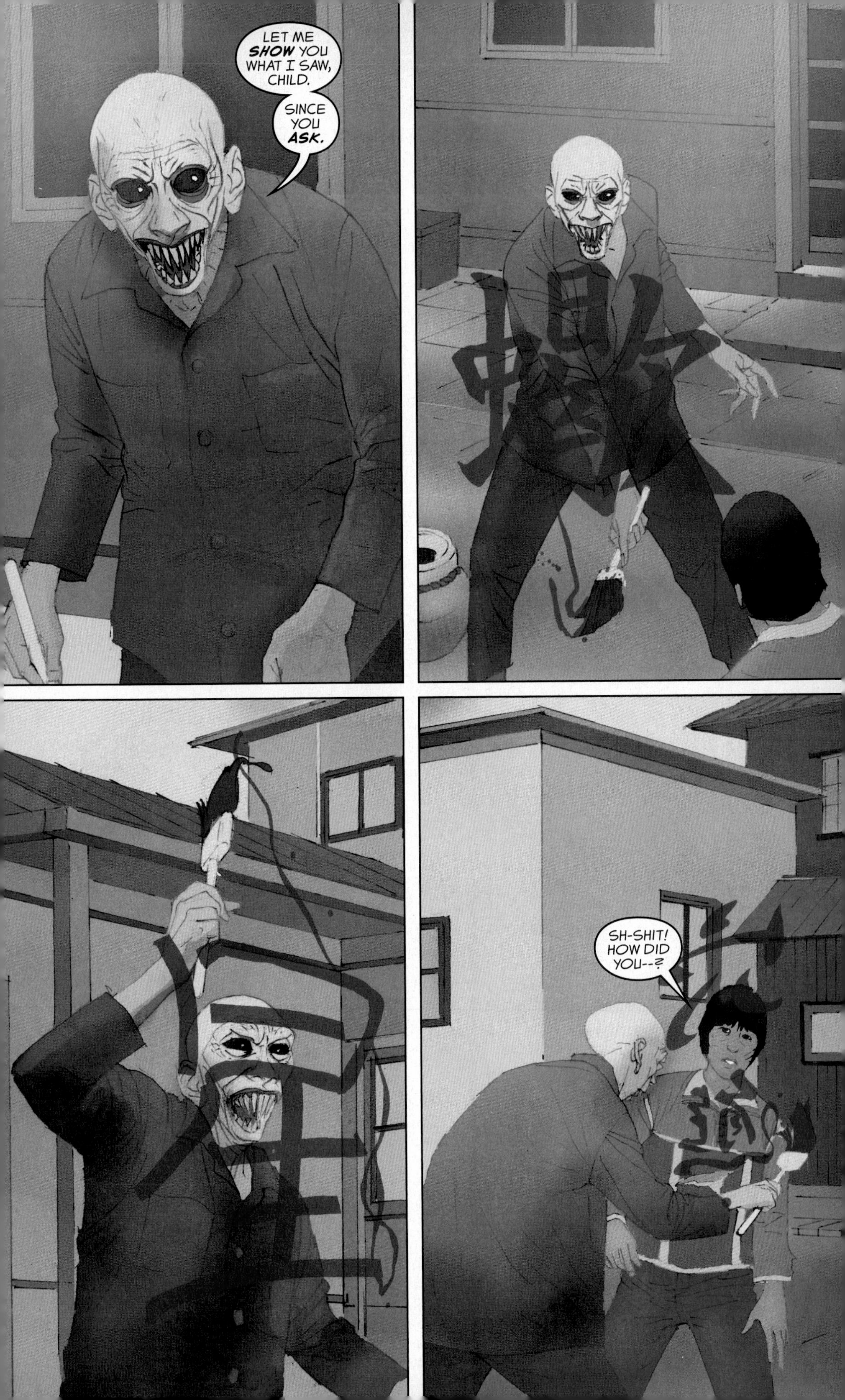
LET ME SHOW YOU WHAT I SAW, CHILD.
SINCE YOU ASK.
SH-SHIT! HOW DID YOU--?

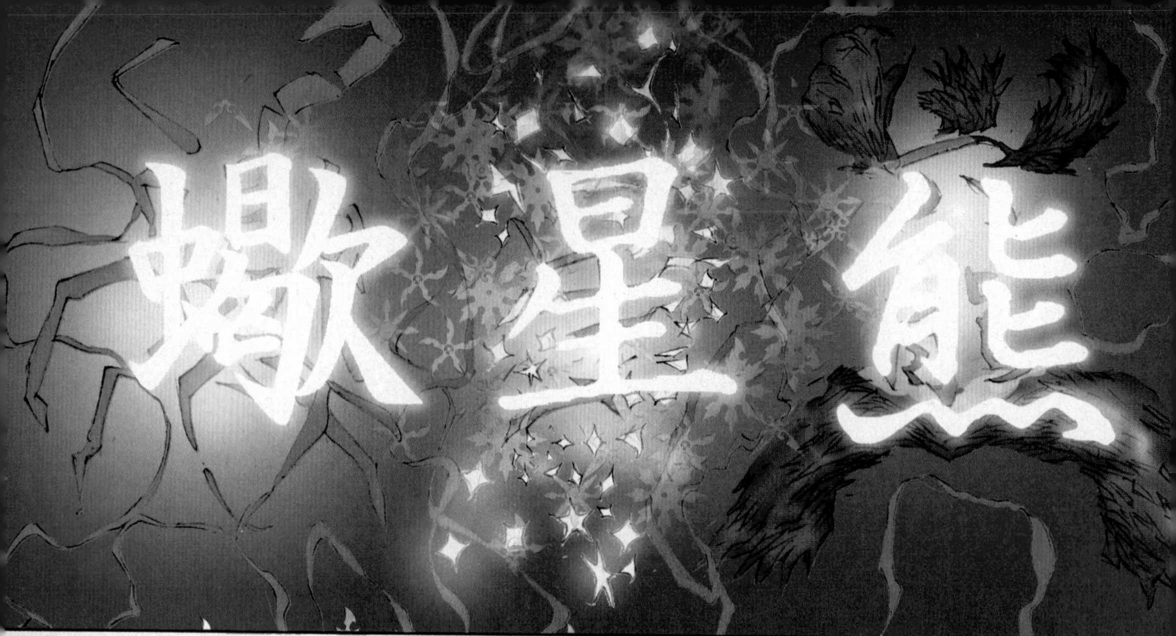
蠍 星 熊

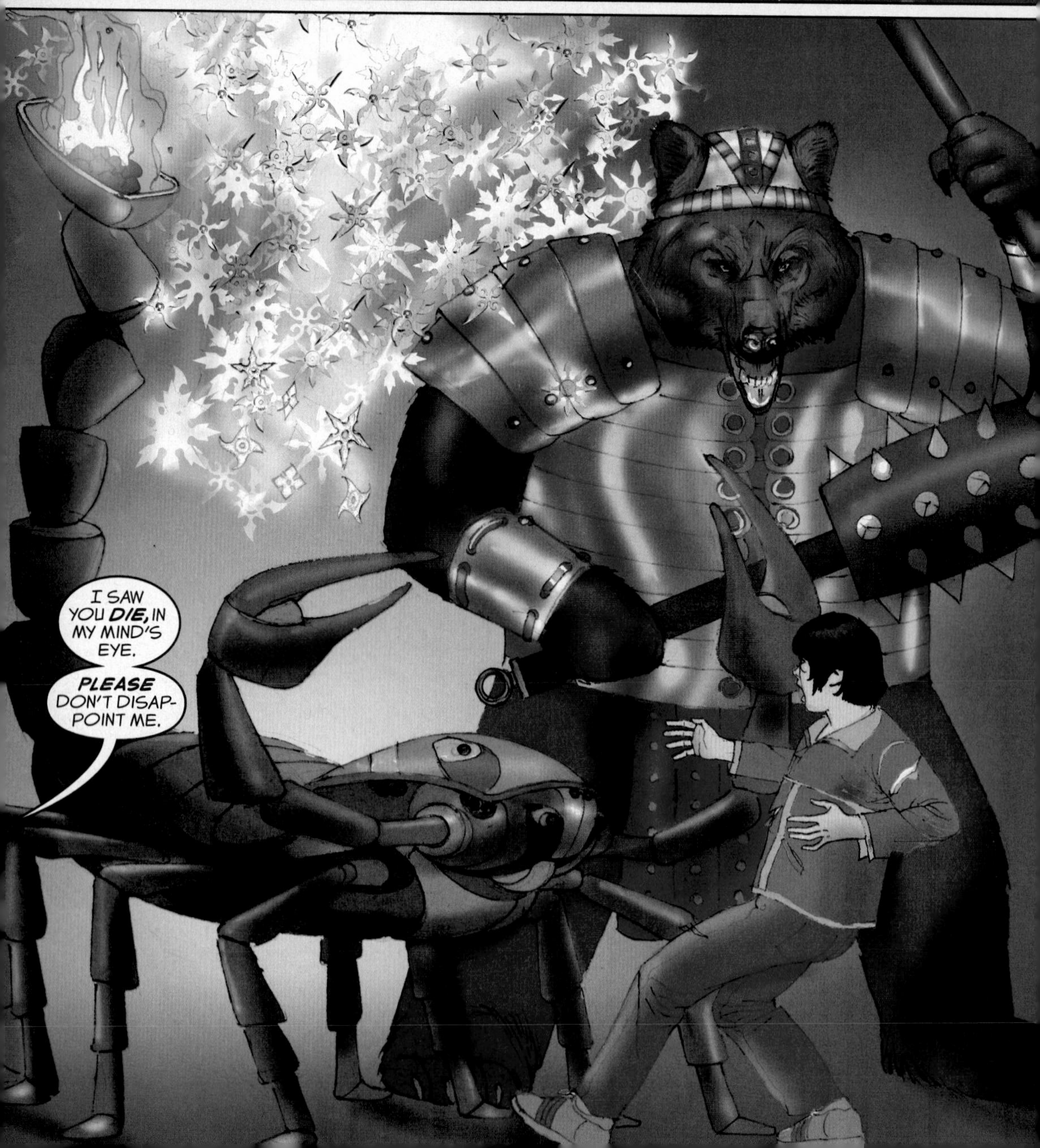
I SAW YOU **DIE,** IN MY MIND'S EYE.
PLEASE DON'T DISAP-POINT ME.

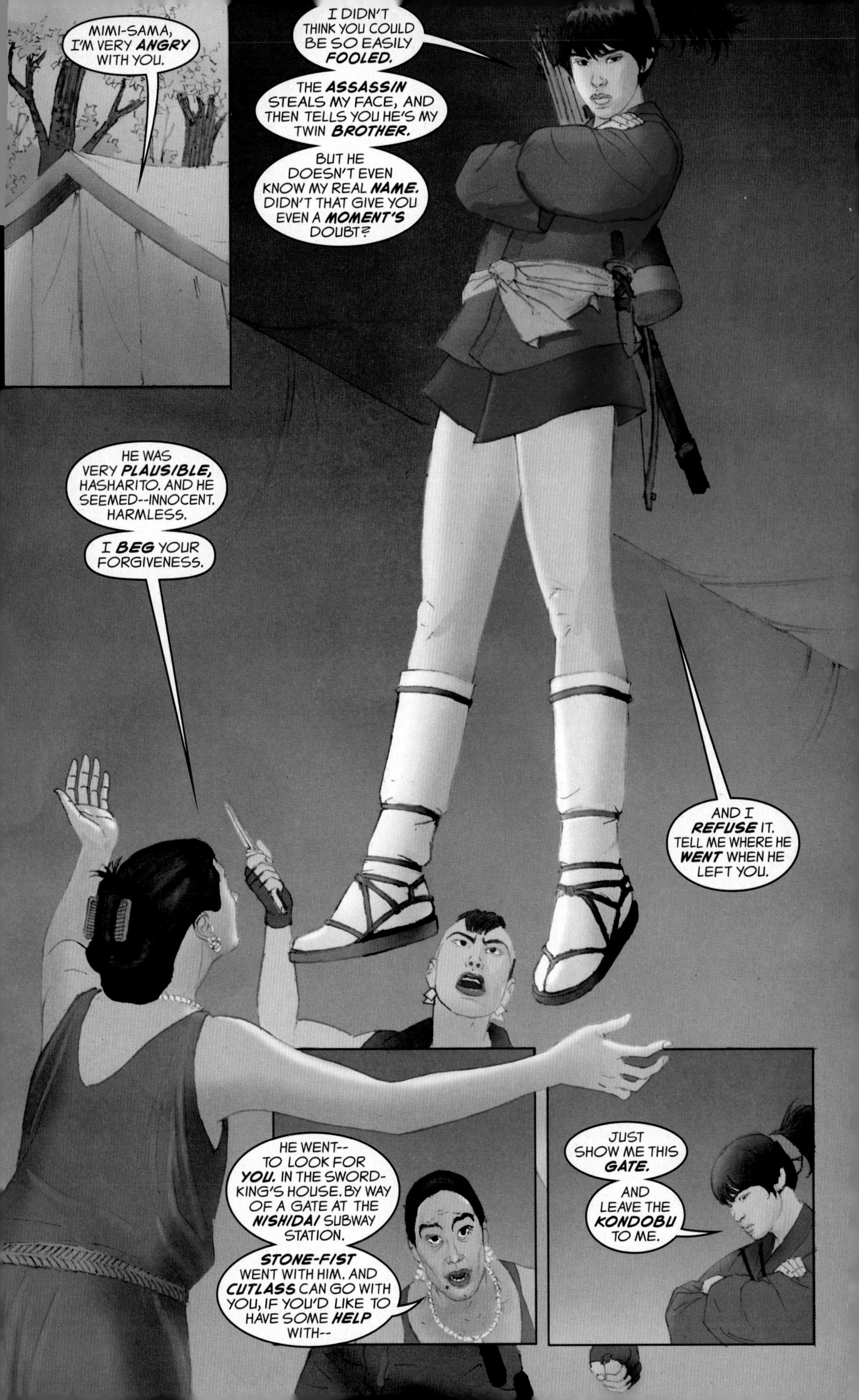
MIMI-SAMA, I'M VERY ANGRY WITH YOU.
I DIDN'T THINK YOU COULD BE SO EASILY FOOLED.
THE ASSASSIN STEALS MY FACE, AND THEN TELLS YOU HE'S MY TWIN BROTHER.
BUT HE DOESN'T EVEN KNOW MY REAL NAME. DIDN'T THAT GIVE YOU EVEN A MOMENT'S DOUBT?
HE WAS VERY PLAUSIBLE, HASHARITO. AND HE SEEMED--INNOCENT. HARMLESS.
I BEG YOUR FORGIVENESS.
AND I REFUSE IT. TELL ME WHERE HE WENT WHEN HE LEFT YOU.
HE WENT-- TO LOOK FOR YOU. IN THE SWORD-KING'S HOUSE. BY WAY OF A GATE AT THE NISHIDAI SUBWAY STATION.
STONE-FIST WENT WITH HIM. AND CUTLASS CAN GO WITH YOU, IF YOU'D LIKE TO HAVE SOME HELP WITH--
JUST SHOW ME THIS GATE.
AND LEAVE THE KONDOBU TO ME.

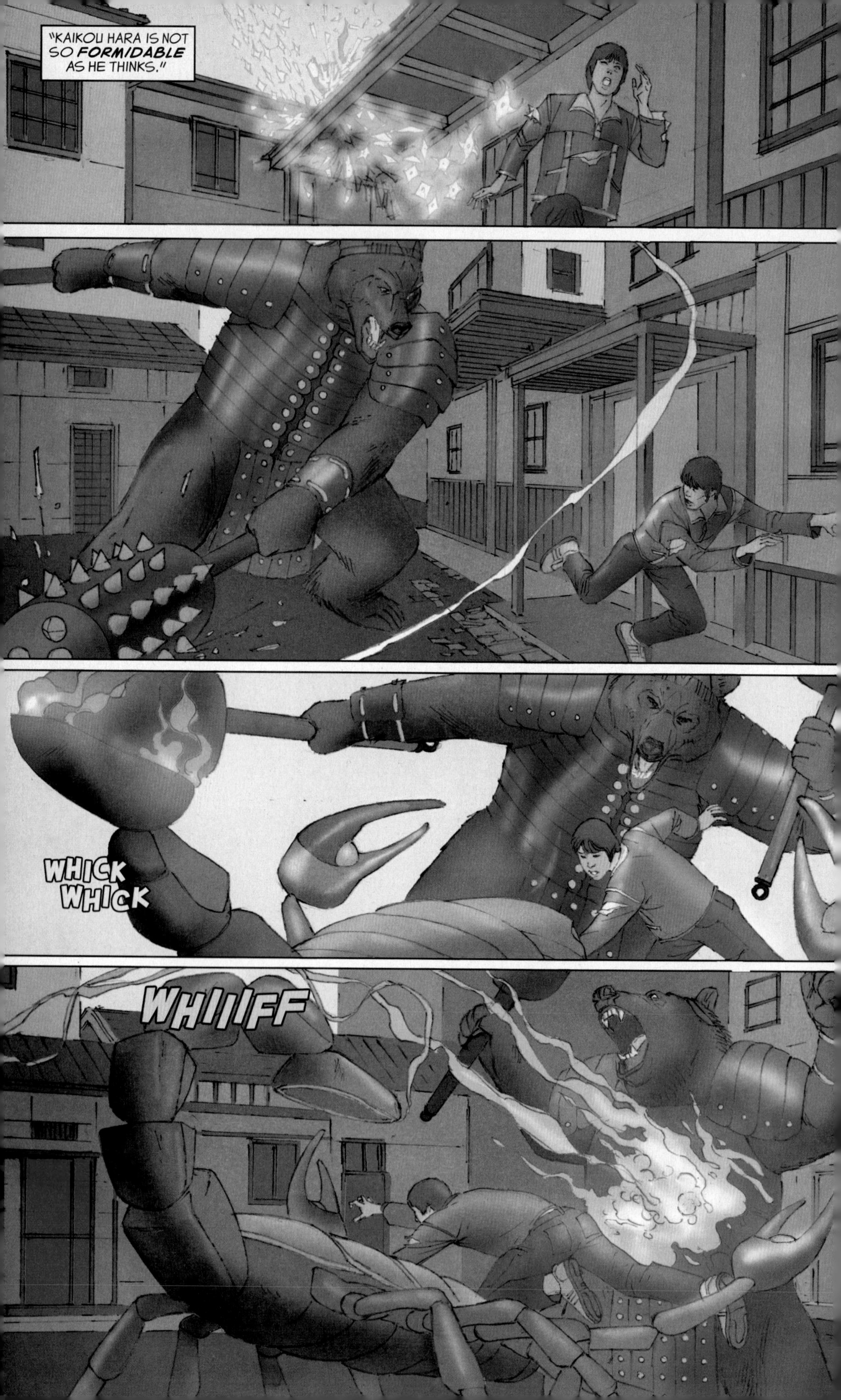
"KAIKOU HARA IS NOT SO **FORMIDABLE** AS HE THINKS."
WHICK WHICK
WHIIIFF

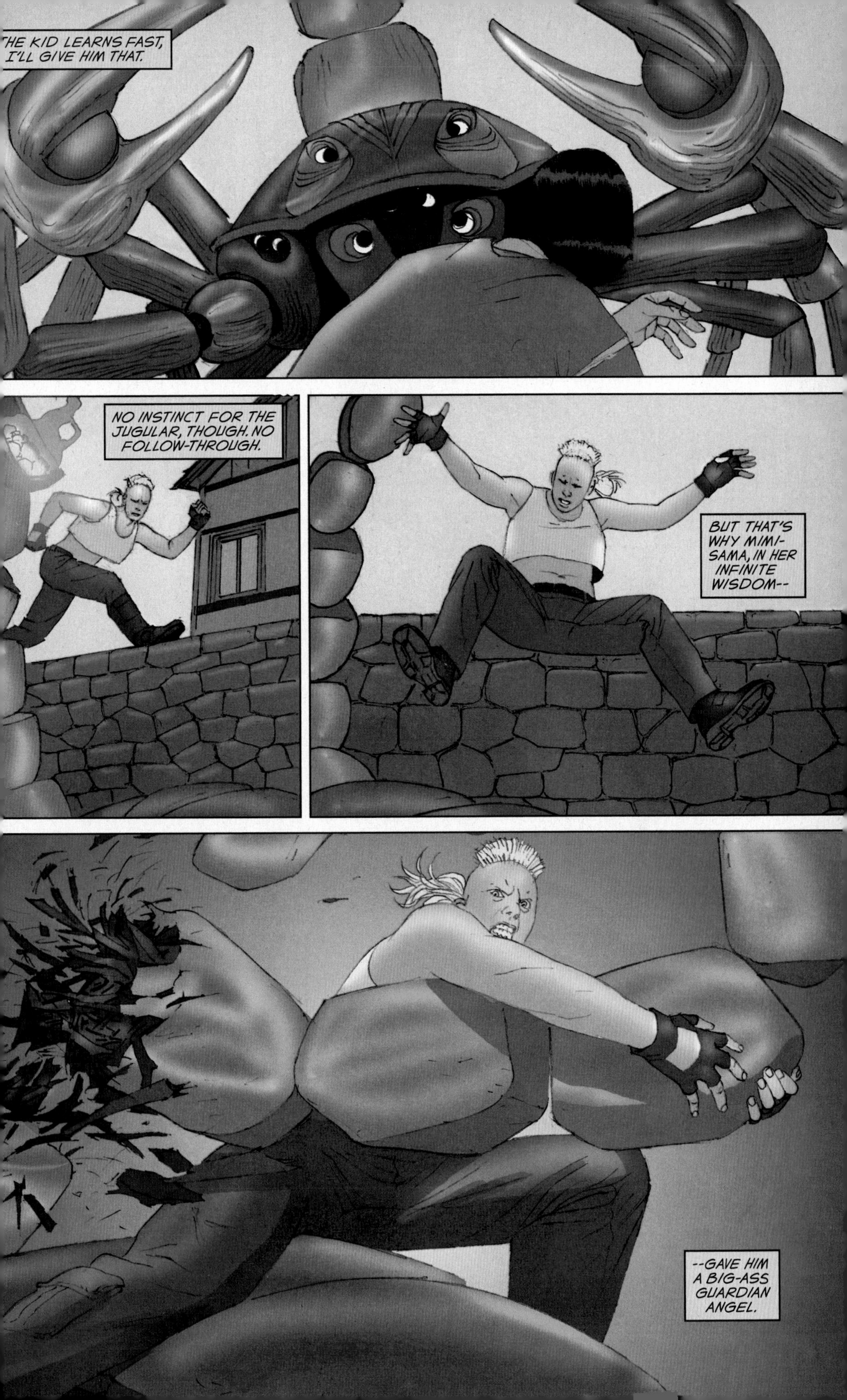
THE KID LEARNS FAST, I'LL GIVE HIM THAT.
NO INSTINCT FOR THE JUGULAR, THOUGH. NO FOLLOW-THROUGH.
BUT THAT'S WHY MIMI-SAMA, IN HER INFINITE WISDOM--
--GAVE HIM A BIG-ASS GUARDIAN ANGEL.

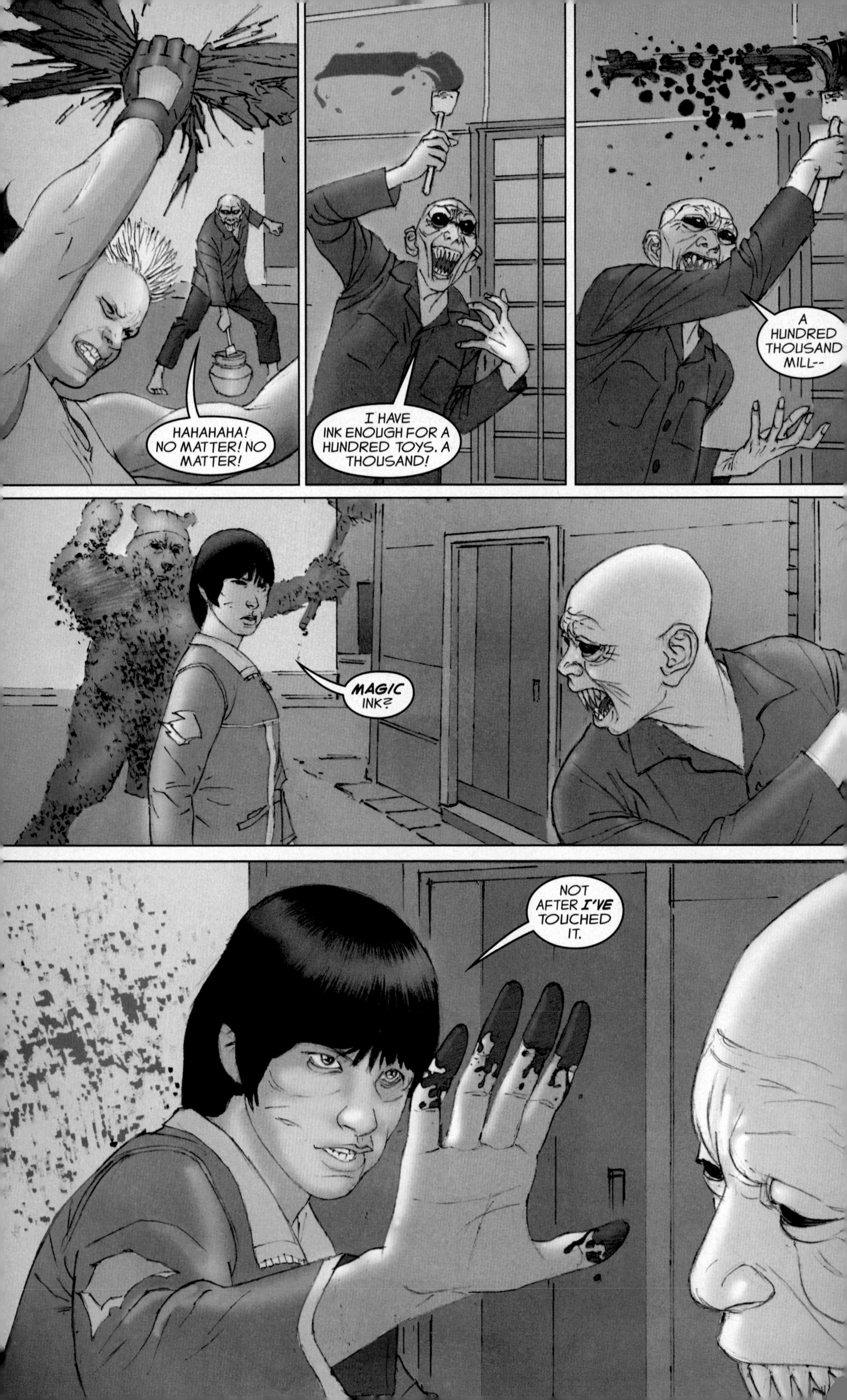
HAHAHAHA! NO MATTER! NO MATTER!
I HAVE INK ENOUGH FOR A HUNDRED TOYS. A THOUSAND!
A HUNDRED THOUSAND MILL--
MAGIC INK?
NOT AFTER I'VE TOUCHED IT.

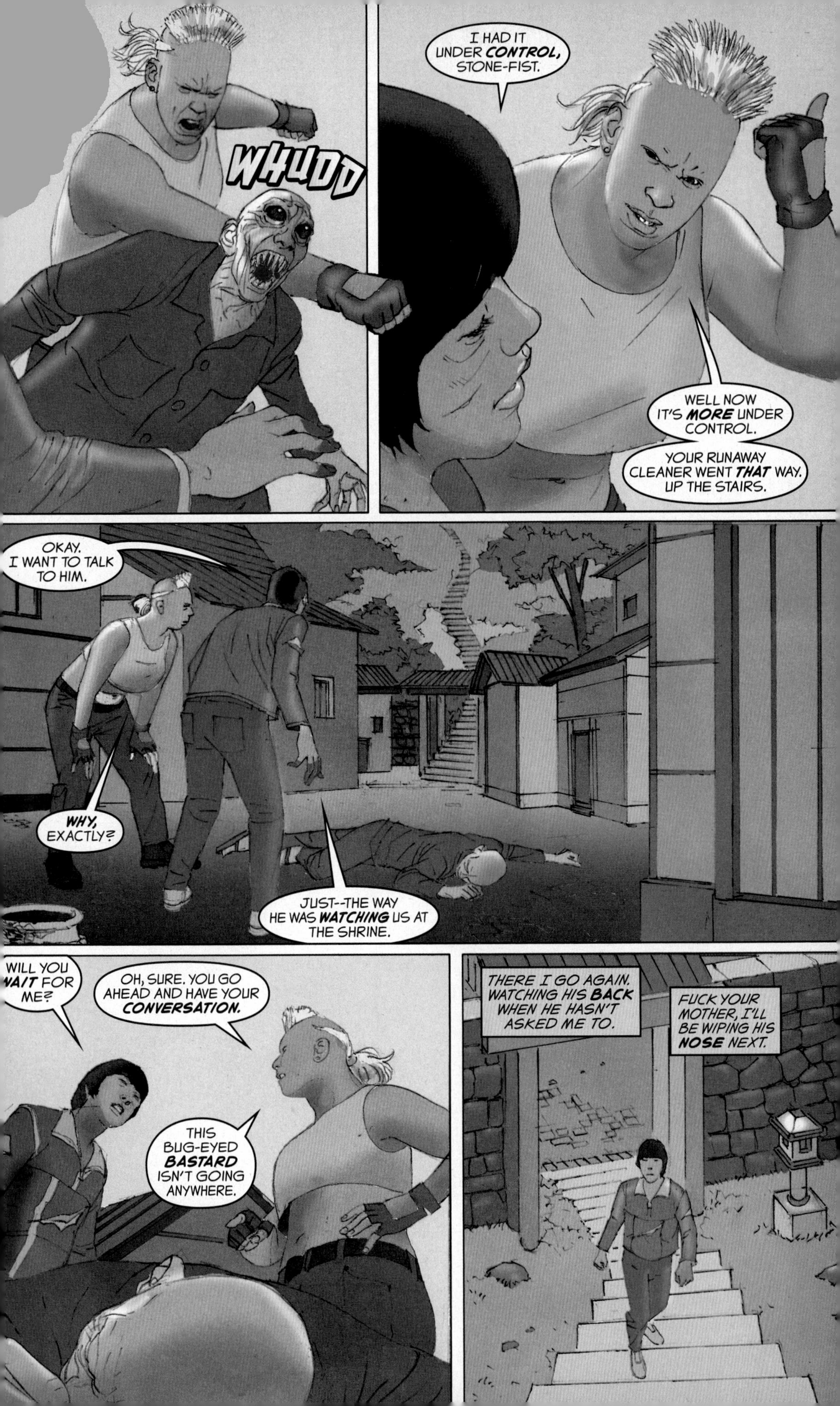
WHUDD
I HAD IT UNDER CONTROL, STONE-FIST.
WELL NOW IT'S MORE UNDER CONTROL.
YOUR RUNAWAY CLEANER WENT THAT WAY. UP THE STAIRS.
OKAY. I WANT TO TALK TO HIM.
WHY, EXACTLY?
JUST--THE WAY HE WAS WATCHING US AT THE SHRINE.
WILL YOU WAIT FOR ME?
OH, SURE. YOU GO AHEAD AND HAVE YOUR CONVERSATION.
THIS BUG-EYED BASTARD ISN'T GOING ANYWHERE.
THERE I GO AGAIN. WATCHING HIS BACK WHEN HE HASN'T ASKED ME TO.
FUCK YOUR MOTHER, I'LL BE WIPING HIS NOSE NEXT.

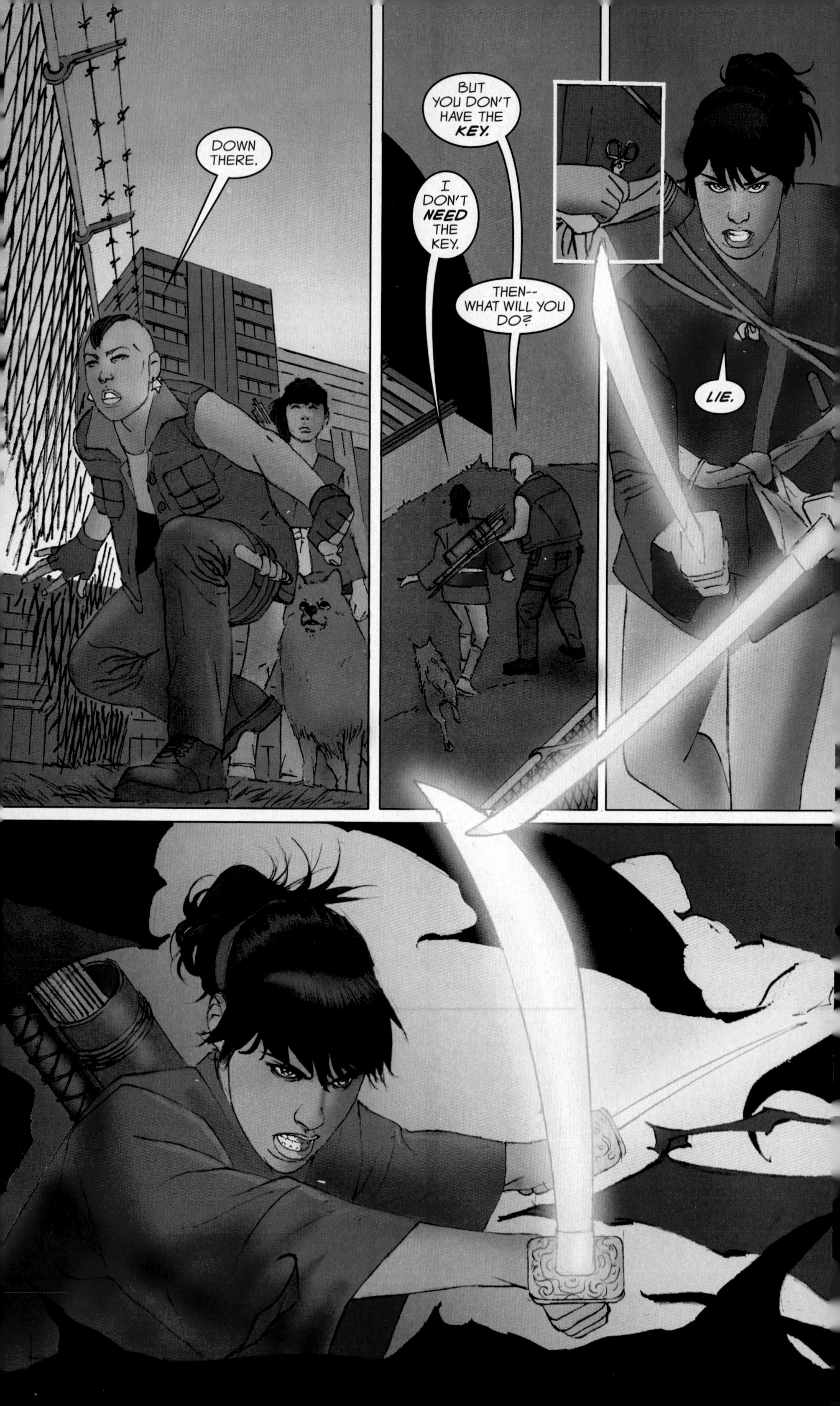
DOWN THERE.
BUT YOU DON'T HAVE THE KEY.
I DON'T NEED THE KEY.
THEN-- WHAT WILL YOU DO?
LIE.

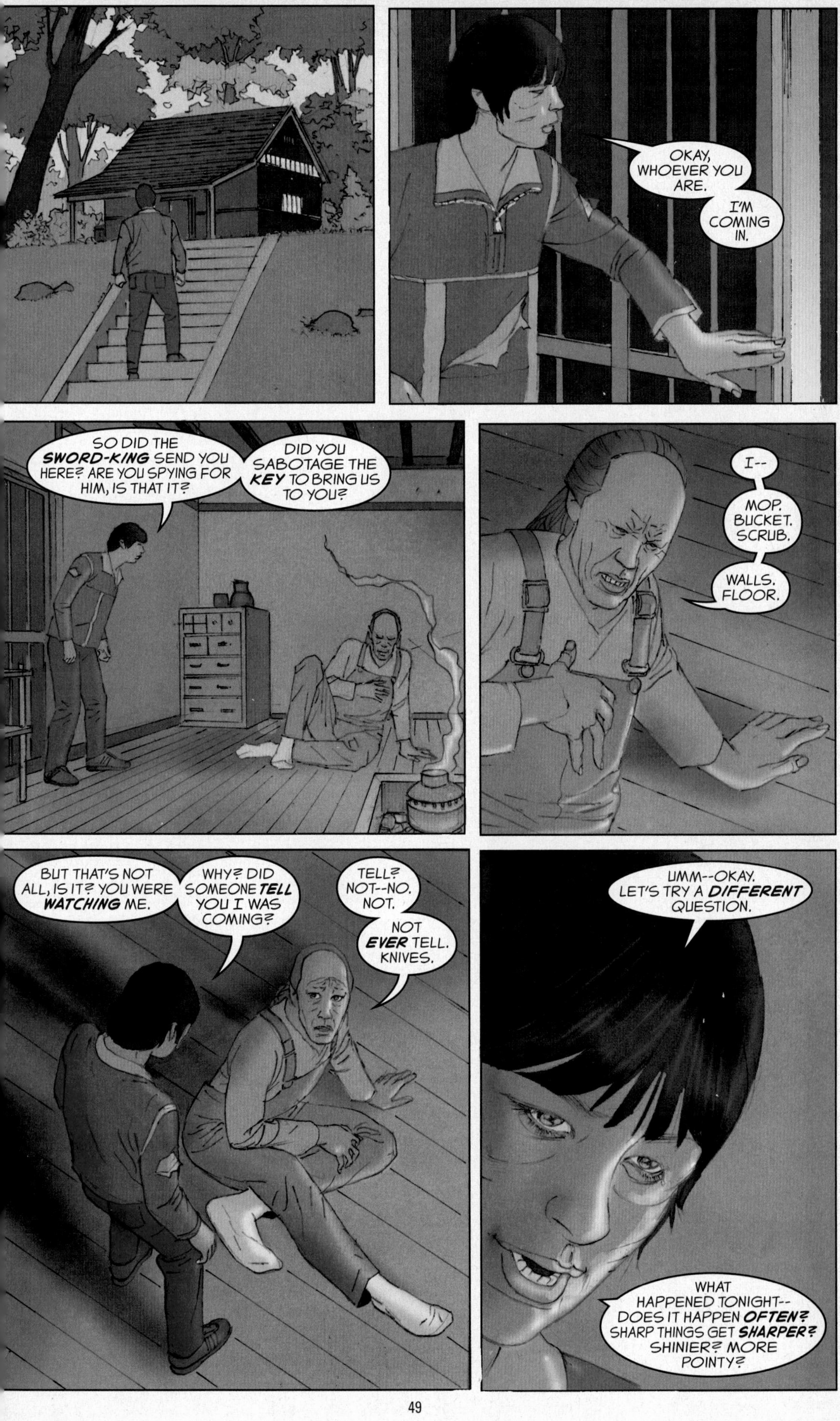
OKAY, WHOEVER YOU ARE.
I'M COMING IN.
SO DID THE SWORD-KING SEND YOU HERE? ARE YOU SPYING FOR HIM, IS THAT IT?
DID YOU SABOTAGE THE KEY TO BRING US TO YOU?
I--
MOP. BUCKET. SCRUB.
WALLS. FLOOR.
BUT THAT'S NOT ALL, IS IT? YOU WERE WATCHING ME.
WHY? DID SOMEONE TELL YOU I WAS COMING?
TELL? NOT--NO. NOT.
NOT EVER TELL. KNIVES.
UMM--OKAY. LET'S TRY A DIFFERENT QUESTION.
WHAT HAPPENED TONIGHT-- DOES IT HAPPEN OFTEN? SHARP THINGS GET SHARPER? SHINIER? MORE POINTY?

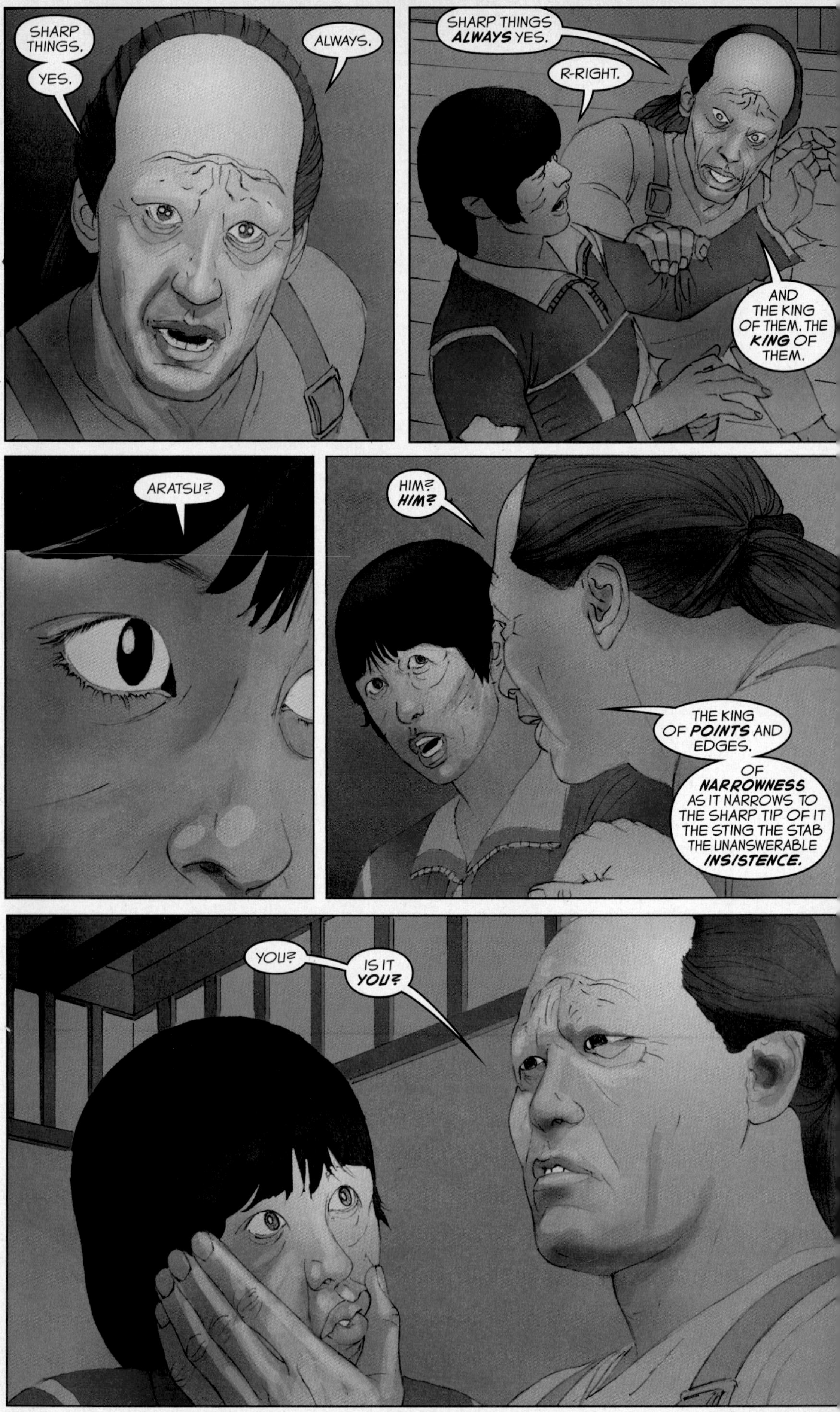
SHARP THINGS.
YES.
ALWAYS.
SHARP THINGS ALWAYS YES.
R-RIGHT.
AND THE KING OF THEM. THE KING OF THEM.
ARATSU?
HIM? HIM?
THE KING OF POINTS AND EDGES.
OF NARROWNESS AS IT NARROWS TO THE SHARP TIP OF IT THE STING THE STAB THE UNANSWERABLE INSISTENCE.
YOU?
IS IT YOU?

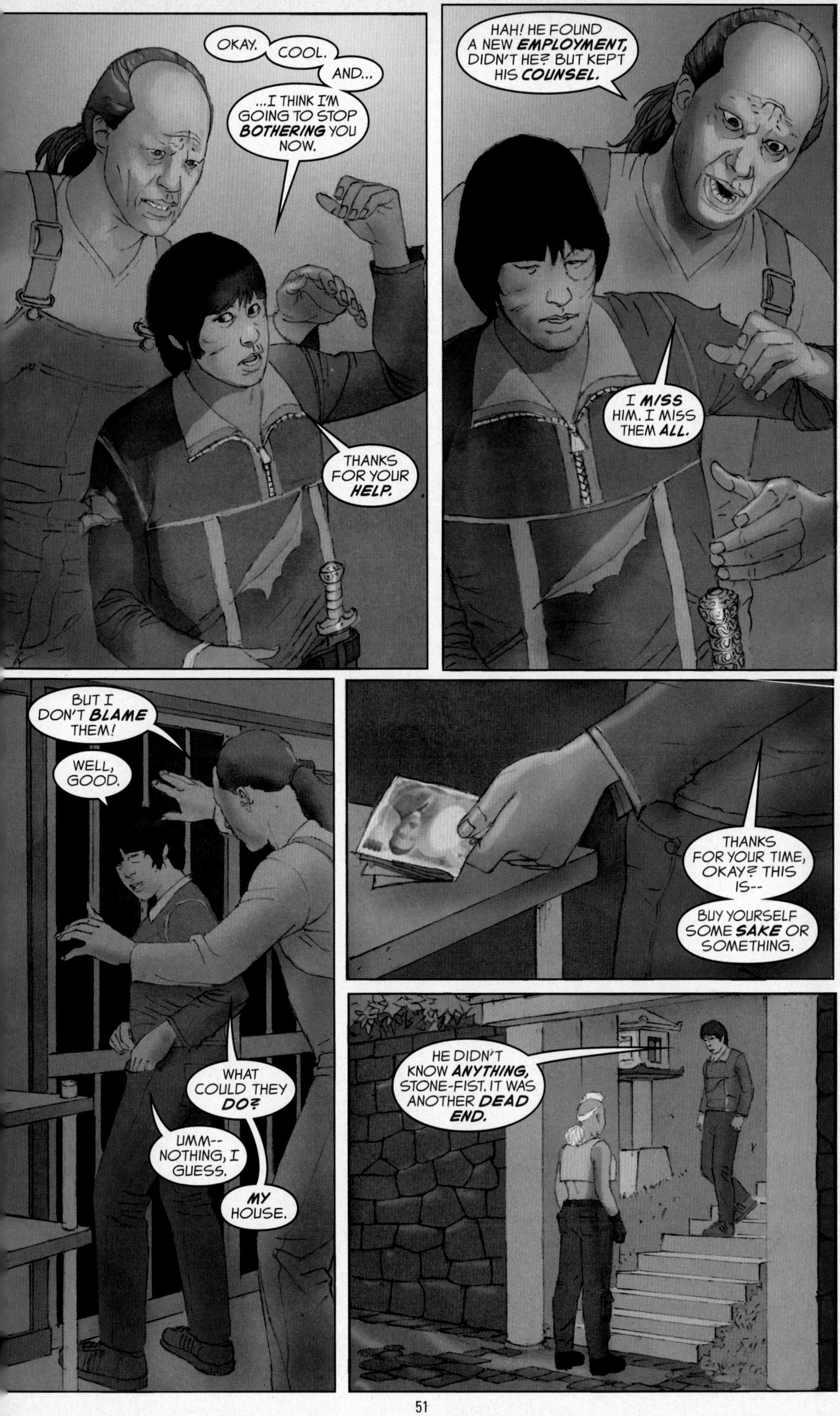
OKAY.
COOL.
AND...
...I THINK I'M GOING TO STOP BOTHERING YOU NOW.
THANKS FOR YOUR HELP.
HAH! HE FOUND A NEW EMPLOYMENT, DIDN'T HE? BUT KEPT HIS COUNSEL.
I MISS HIM. I MISS THEM ALL.
BUT I DON'T BLAME THEM!
WELL, GOOD.
WHAT COULD THEY DO?
UMM-- NOTHING, I GUESS.
MY HOUSE.
THANKS FOR YOUR TIME, OKAY? THIS IS--
BUY YOURSELF SOME SAKE OR SOMETHING.
HE DIDN'T KNOW ANYTHING, STONE-FIST. IT WAS ANOTHER DEAD END.

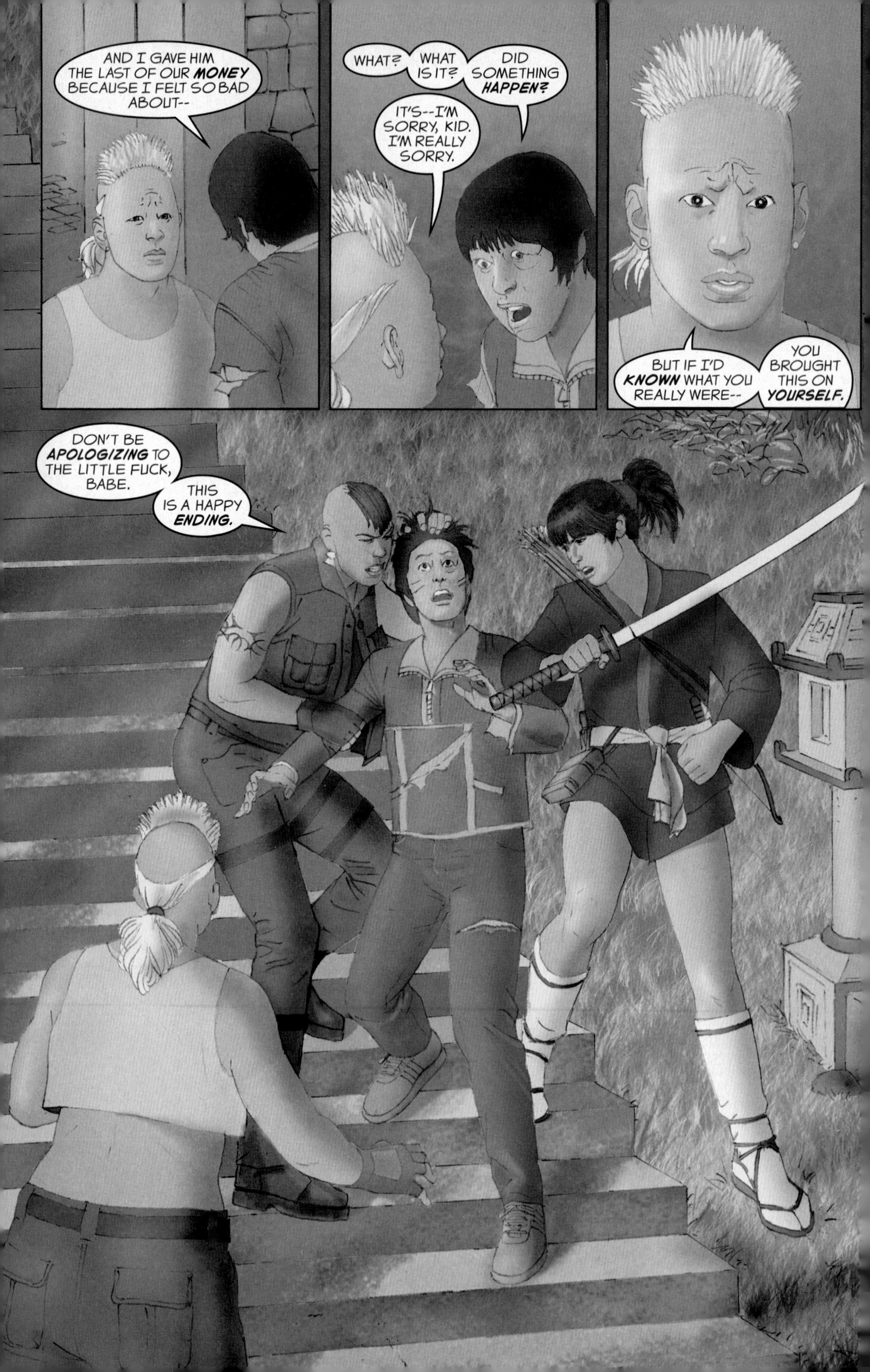
AND I GAVE HIM THE LAST OF OUR MONEY BECAUSE I FELT SO BAD ABOUT--
WHAT?
WHAT IS IT?
DID SOMETHING HAPPEN?
IT'S--I'M SORRY, KID. I'M REALLY SORRY.
BUT IF I'D KNOWN WHAT YOU REALLY WERE--
YOU BROUGHT THIS ON YOURSELF.
DON'T BE APOLOGIZING TO THE LITTLE FUCK, BABE.
THIS IS A HAPPY ENDING.

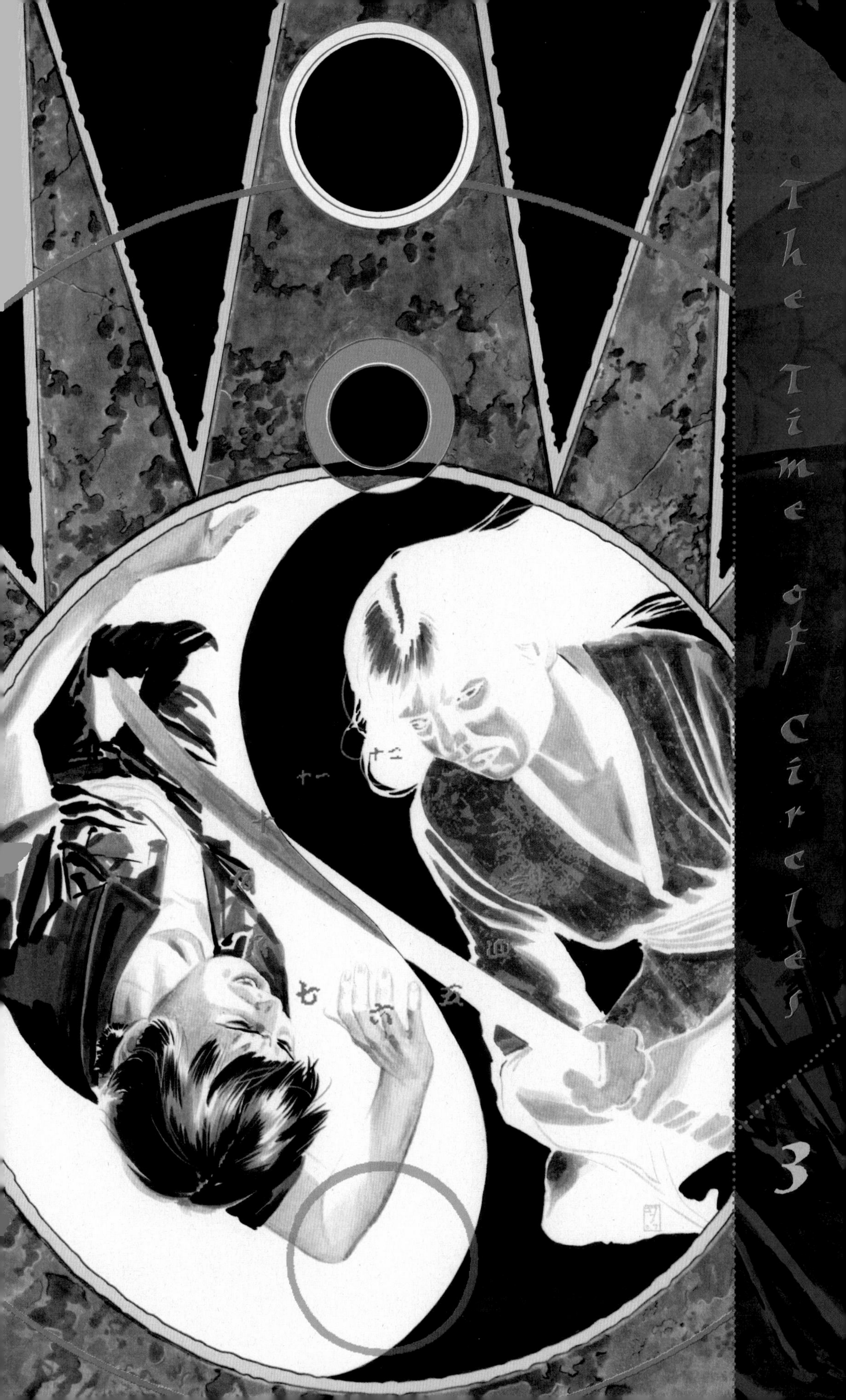
The Time of Circles
3

SO I WENT ON A **QUEST**. THAT'S WHAT IT COMES DOWN TO. AND WHAT I WAS LOOKING FOR WAS **MYSELF**.

HASHARITO, WHOEVER **SHE** IS.

I KNOW HOW **TIRED** THAT SOUNDS. I KNOW **EVERYBODY** SAYS IT.

MOSTLY WHEN THEY GET PAST **FORTY**. WHEN THE RHYTHMS OF THEIR **LIFE** START TO SEEM TOO FAMILIAR.

AND THEY WANT TO BELIEVE THERE'S **MORE** TO THEM THAN WHAT THEY DO FOR A LIVING.

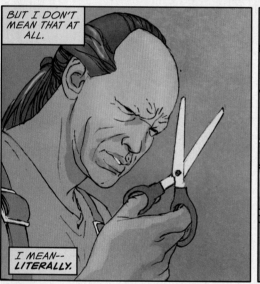

BUT I DON'T MEAN THAT AT ALL.

I MEAN-- **LITERALLY**.

MY PAST IS A **HOLE**. NEATLY DUG, AND SQUARED OFF, LIKE A **GRAVE**.

AN EMPTY **SPACE** I THOUGHT I COULD FILL.

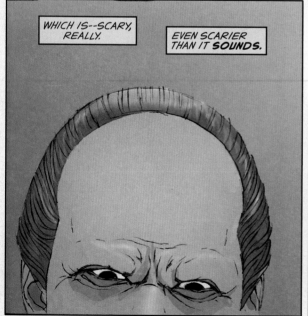

WHICH IS--SCARY, REALLY.

EVEN SCARIER THAN IT **SOUNDS**.

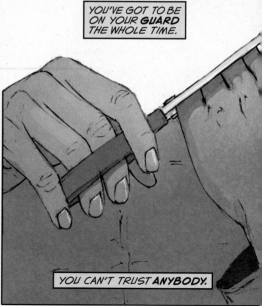

YOU'VE GOT TO BE ON YOUR **GUARD** THE WHOLE TIME.

YOU CAN'T TRUST **ANYBODY**.

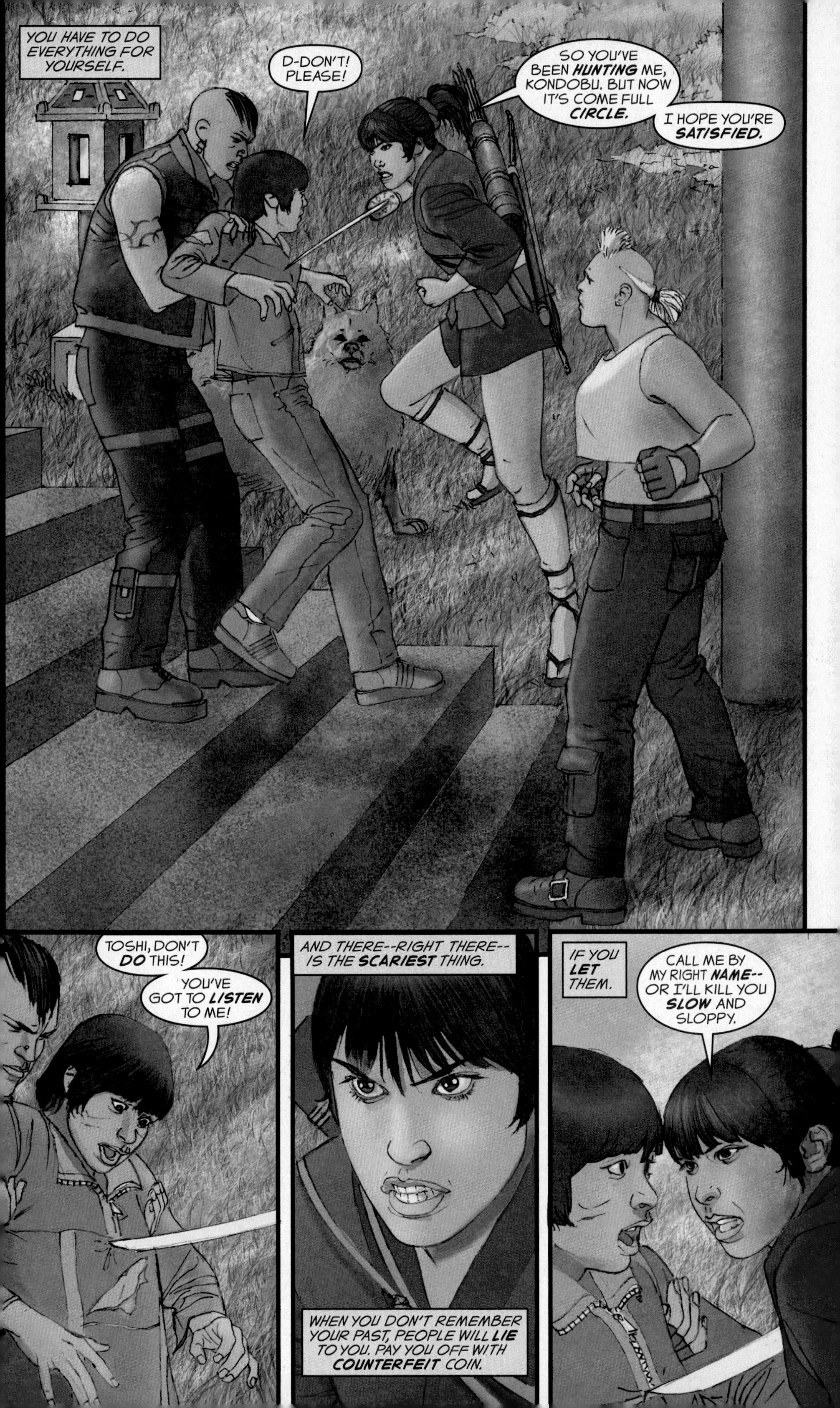
YOU HAVE TO DO EVERYTHING FOR YOURSELF.
D-DON'T! PLEASE!
SO YOU'VE BEEN HUNTING ME, KONDOBU. BUT NOW IT'S COME FULL CIRCLE.
I HOPE YOU'RE SATISFIED.
TOSHI, DON'T DO THIS!
YOU'VE GOT TO LISTEN TO ME!
AND THERE--RIGHT THERE--IS THE SCARIEST THING.
WHEN YOU DON'T REMEMBER YOUR PAST, PEOPLE WILL LIE TO YOU. PAY YOU OFF WITH COUNTERFEIT COIN.
IF YOU LET THEM.
CALL ME BY MY RIGHT NAME--OR I'LL KILL YOU SLOW AND SLOPPY.

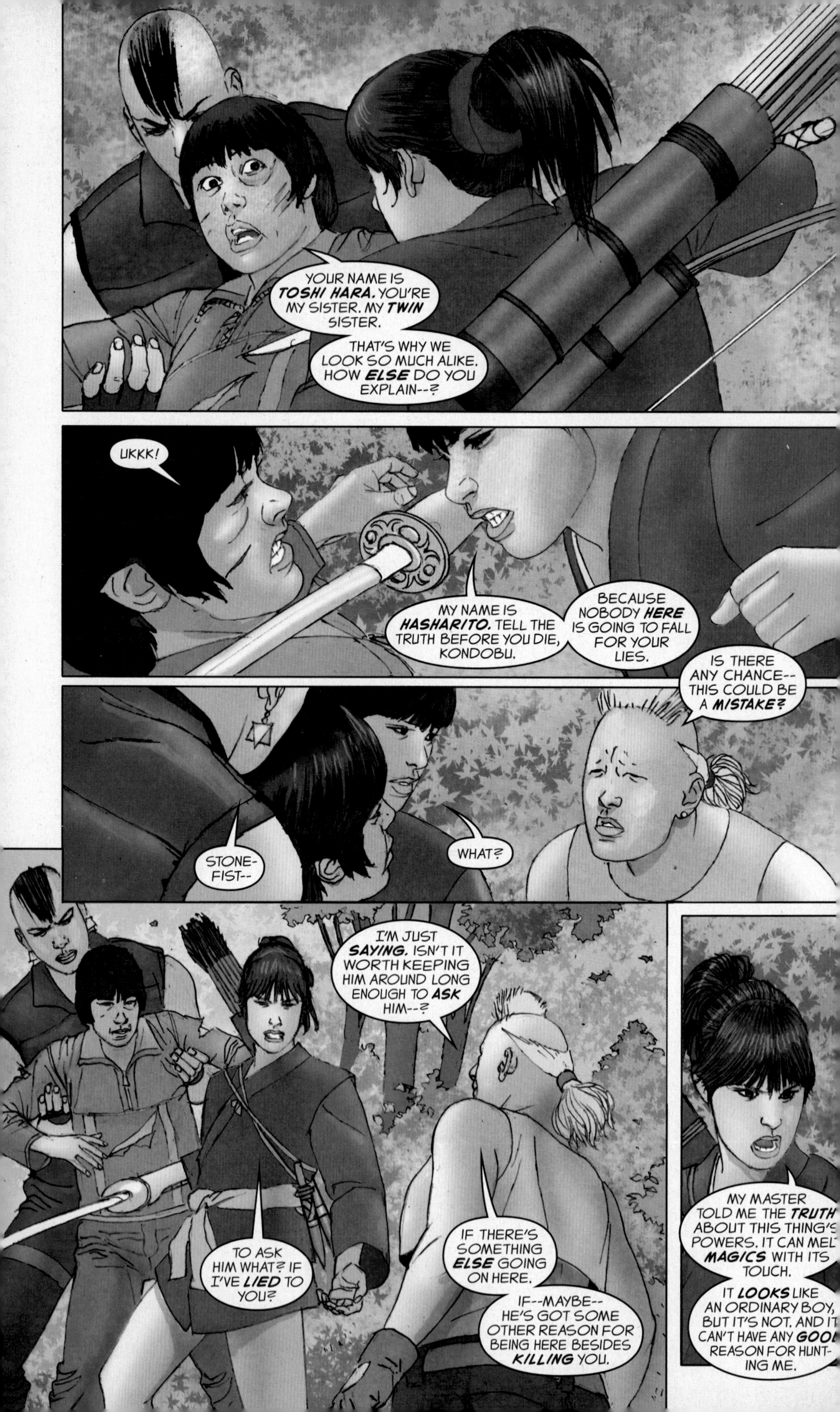
YOUR NAME IS TOSHI HARA. YOU'RE MY SISTER. MY TWIN SISTER.
THAT'S WHY WE LOOK SO MUCH ALIKE. HOW ELSE DO YOU EXPLAIN--?
UKKK!
MY NAME IS HASHARITO. TELL THE TRUTH BEFORE YOU DIE, KONDOBU.
BECAUSE NOBODY HERE IS GOING TO FALL FOR YOUR LIES.
IS THERE ANY CHANCE-- THIS COULD BE A MISTAKE?
STONE-FIST--
WHAT?
I'M JUST SAYING. ISN'T IT WORTH KEEPING HIM AROUND LONG ENOUGH TO ASK HIM--?
TO ASK HIM WHAT? IF I'VE LIED TO YOU?
IF THERE'S SOMETHING ELSE GOING ON HERE.
IF--MAYBE-- HE'S GOT SOME OTHER REASON FOR BEING HERE BESIDES KILLING YOU.
MY MASTER TOLD ME THE TRUTH ABOUT THIS THING'S POWERS. IT CAN MELT MAGICS WITH ITS TOUCH.
IT LOOKS LIKE AN ORDINARY BOY, BUT IT'S NOT. AND IT CAN'T HAVE ANY GOOD REASON FOR HUNTING ME.

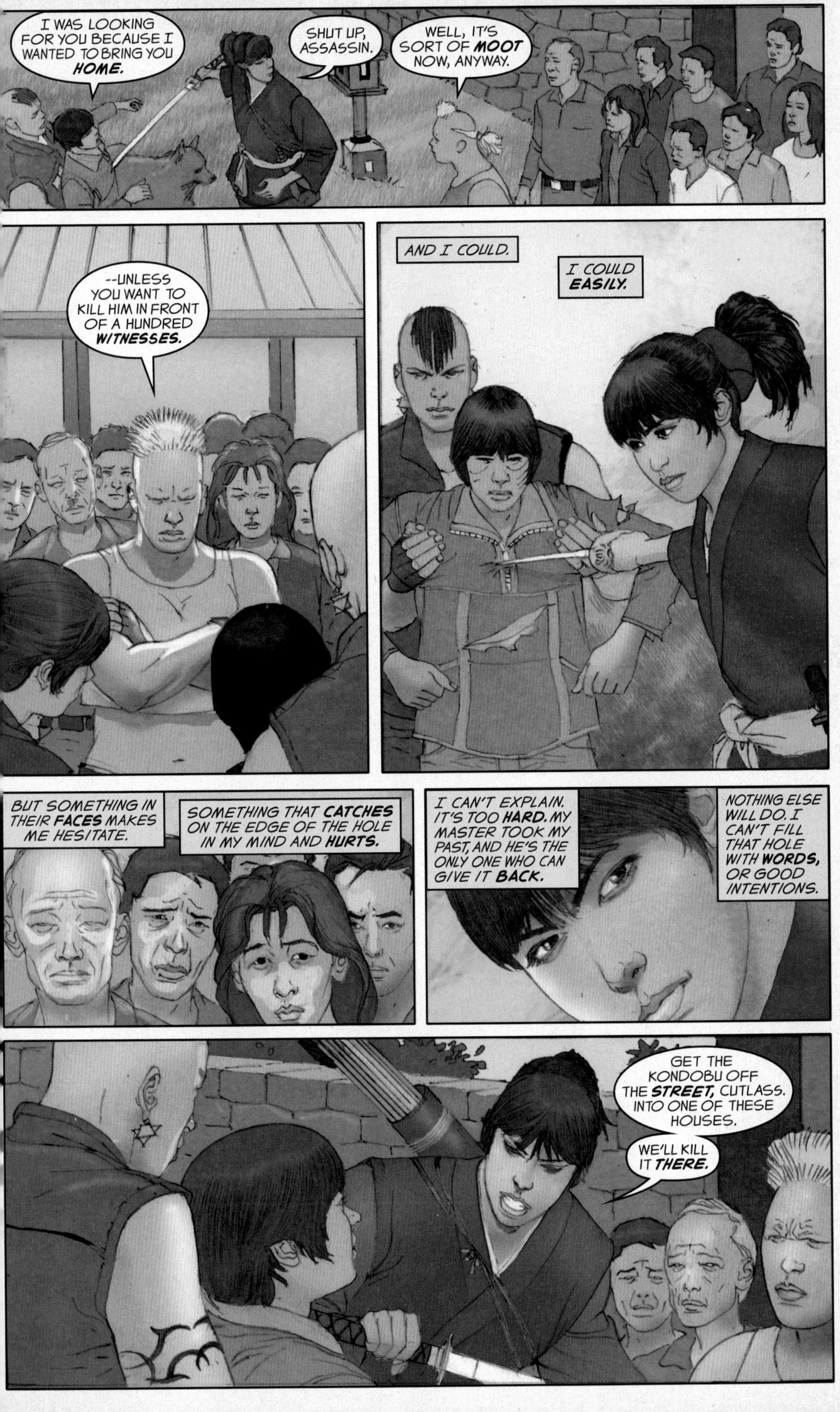
I WAS LOOKING FOR YOU BECAUSE I WANTED TO BRING YOU **HOME.**
SHUT UP, ASSASSIN.
WELL, IT'S SORT OF **MOOT** NOW, ANYWAY.
--UNLESS YOU WANT TO KILL HIM IN FRONT OF A HUNDRED **WITNESSES.**
AND I COULD.
I COULD **EASILY.**
BUT SOMETHING IN THEIR **FACES** MAKES ME HESITATE.
SOMETHING THAT **CATCHES** ON THE EDGE OF THE HOLE IN MY MIND AND **HURTS.**
I CAN'T EXPLAIN. IT'S TOO **HARD.** MY MASTER TOOK MY PAST, AND HE'S THE ONLY ONE WHO CAN GIVE IT **BACK.**
NOTHING ELSE WILL DO. I CAN'T FILL THAT HOLE WITH **WORDS,** OR GOOD INTENTIONS.
GET THE KONDOBU OFF THE **STREET,** CUTLASS. INTO ONE OF THESE HOUSES.
WE'LL KILL IT **THERE.**

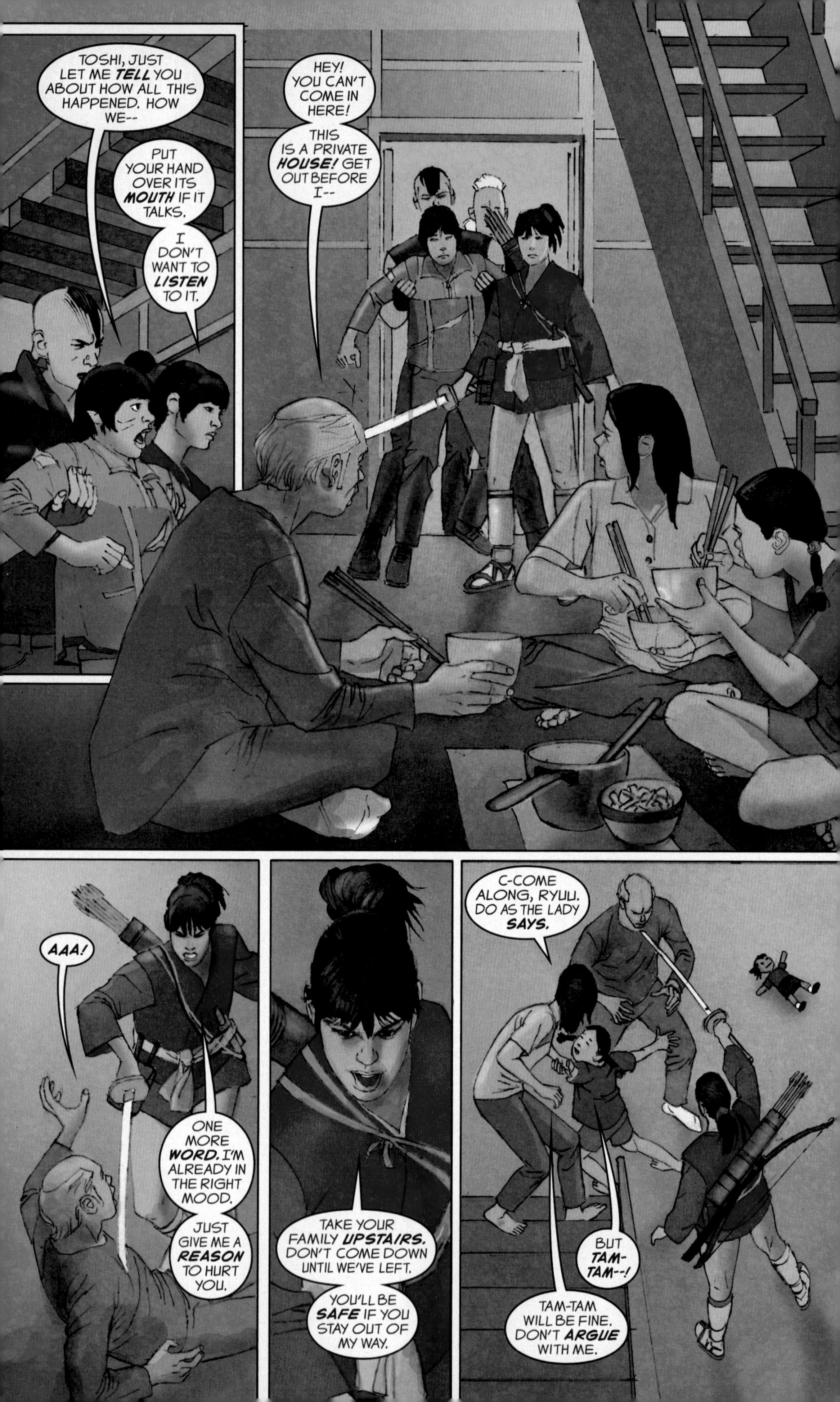

TOSHI, JUST LET ME TELL YOU ABOUT HOW ALL THIS HAPPENED. HOW WE--
PUT YOUR HAND OVER ITS MOUTH IF IT TALKS.
I DON'T WANT TO LISTEN TO IT.
HEY! YOU CAN'T COME IN HERE!
THIS IS A PRIVATE HOUSE! GET OUT BEFORE I--
AAA!
ONE MORE WORD. I'M ALREADY IN THE RIGHT MOOD.
JUST GIVE ME A REASON TO HURT YOU.
TAKE YOUR FAMILY UPSTAIRS. DON'T COME DOWN UNTIL WE'VE LEFT.
YOU'LL BE SAFE IF YOU STAY OUT OF MY WAY.
C-COME ALONG, RYUU. DO AS THE LADY SAYS.
BUT TAM-TAM--!
TAM-TAM WILL BE FINE. DON'T ARGUE WITH ME.

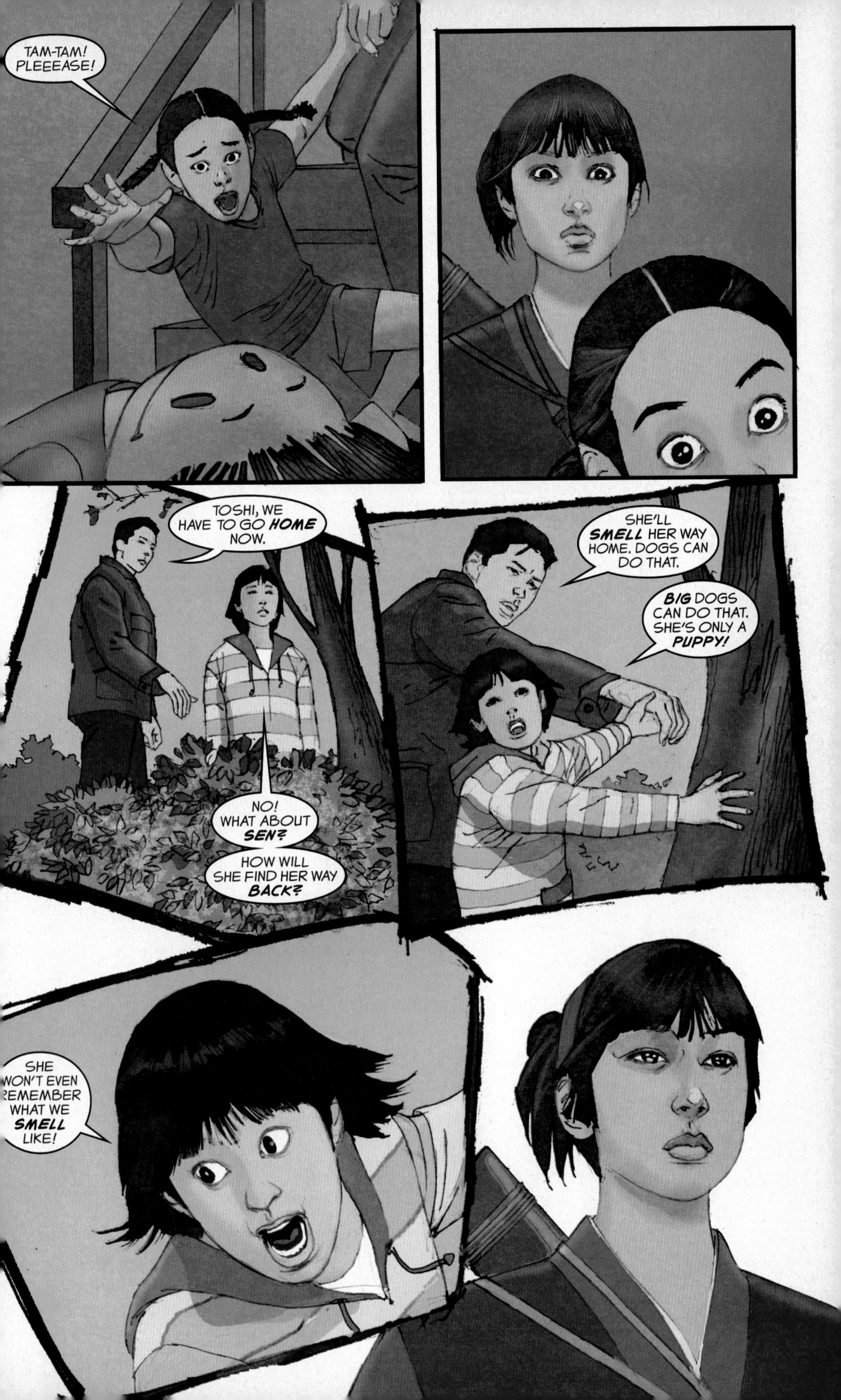
TAM-TAM! PLEEEASE!
TOSHI, WE HAVE TO GO HOME NOW.
NO! WHAT ABOUT SEN?
HOW WILL SHE FIND HER WAY BACK?
SHE'LL SMELL HER WAY HOME. DOGS CAN DO THAT.
BIG DOGS CAN DO THAT. SHE'S ONLY A PUPPY!
SHE WON'T EVEN REMEMBER WHAT WE SMELL LIKE!

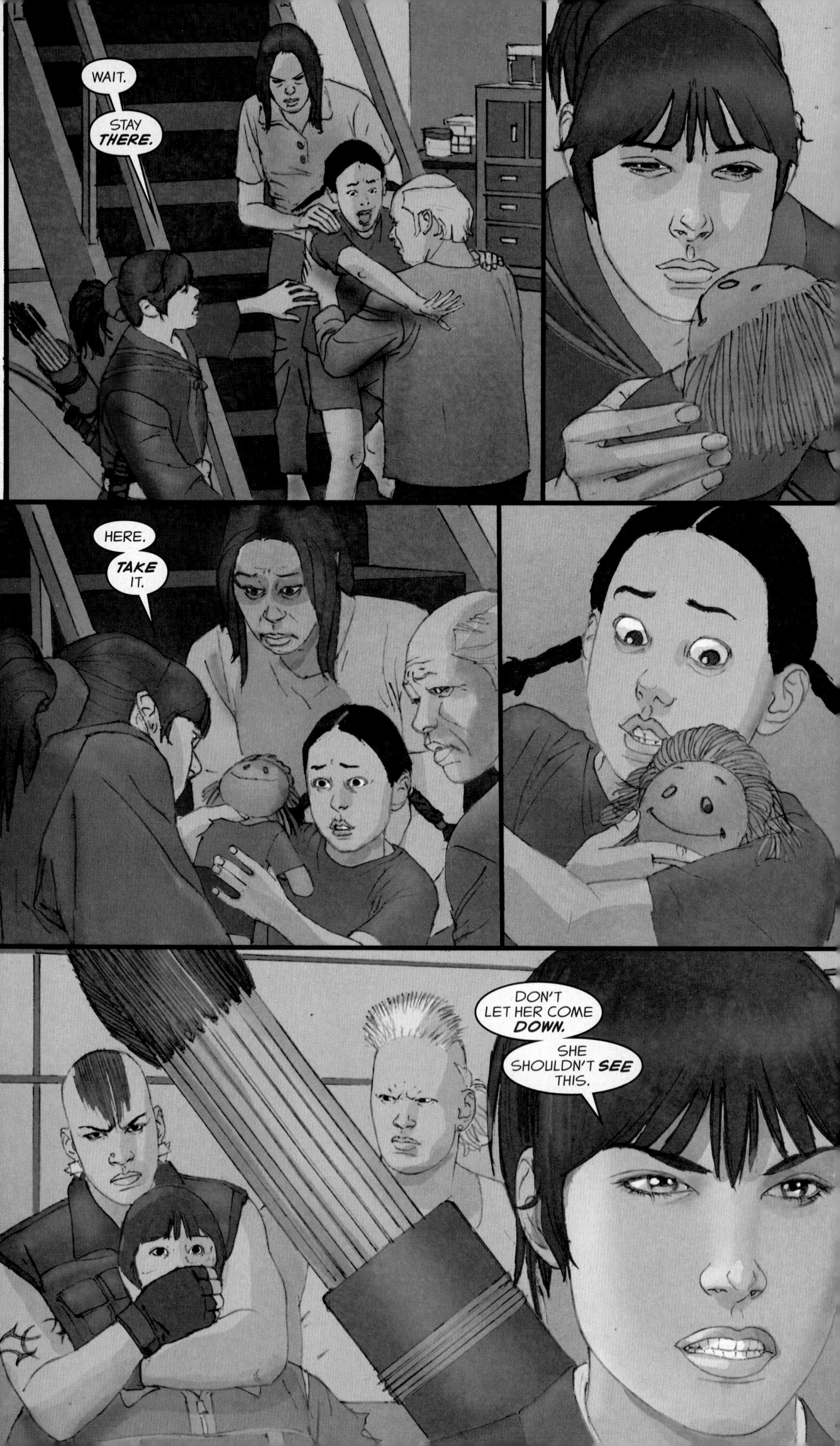
WAIT.
STAY THERE.
HERE. TAKE IT.
DON'T LET HER COME DOWN.
SHE SHOULDN'T SEE THIS.

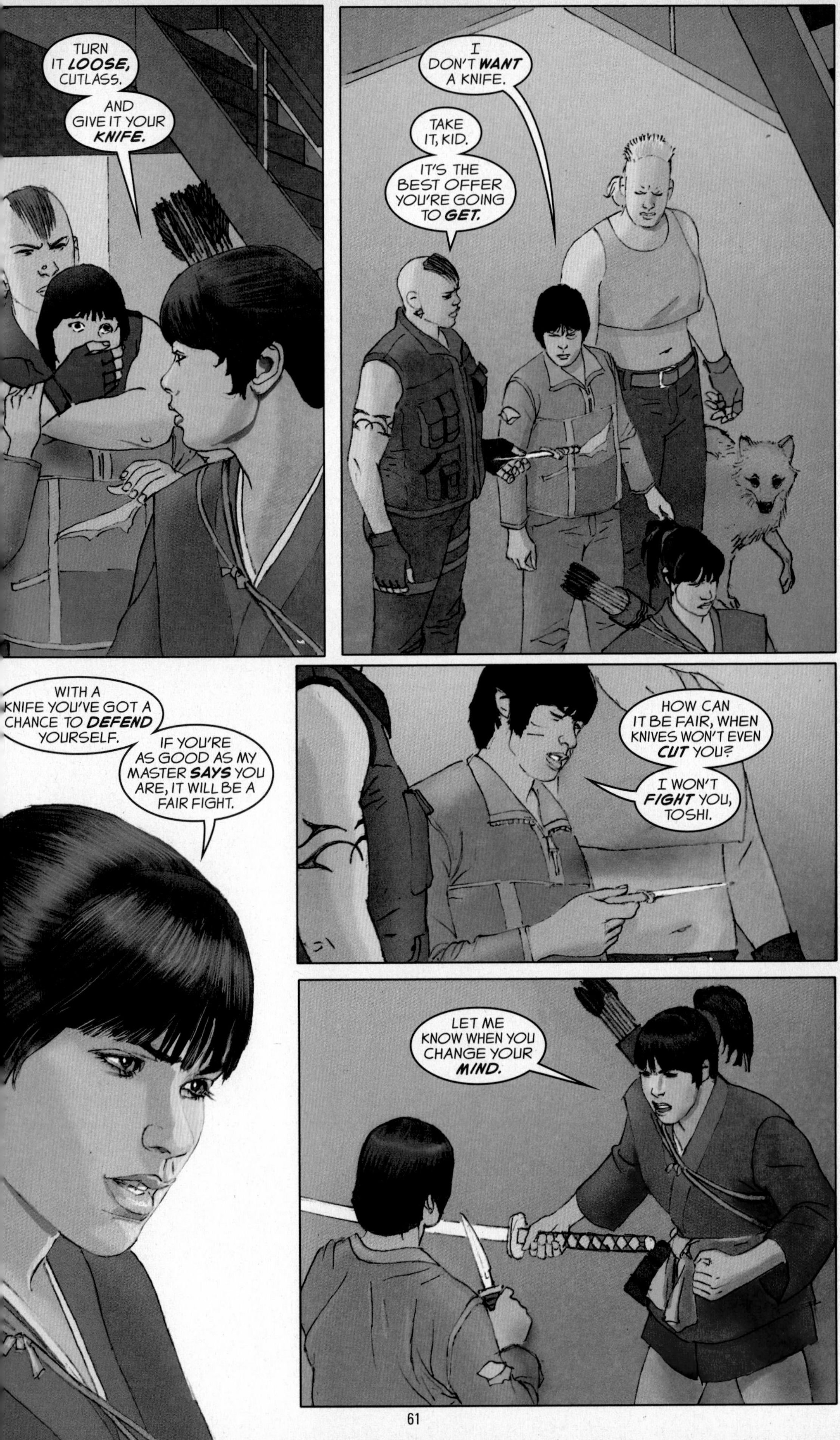
TURN IT LOOSE, CUTLASS.
AND GIVE IT YOUR KNIFE.
I DON'T WANT A KNIFE.
TAKE IT, KID.
IT'S THE BEST OFFER YOU'RE GOING TO GET.
WITH A KNIFE YOU'VE GOT A CHANCE TO DEFEND YOURSELF.
IF YOU'RE AS GOOD AS MY MASTER SAYS YOU ARE, IT WILL BE A FAIR FIGHT.
HOW CAN IT BE FAIR, WHEN KNIVES WON'T EVEN CUT YOU?
I WON'T FIGHT YOU, TOSHI.
LET ME KNOW WHEN YOU CHANGE YOUR MIND.

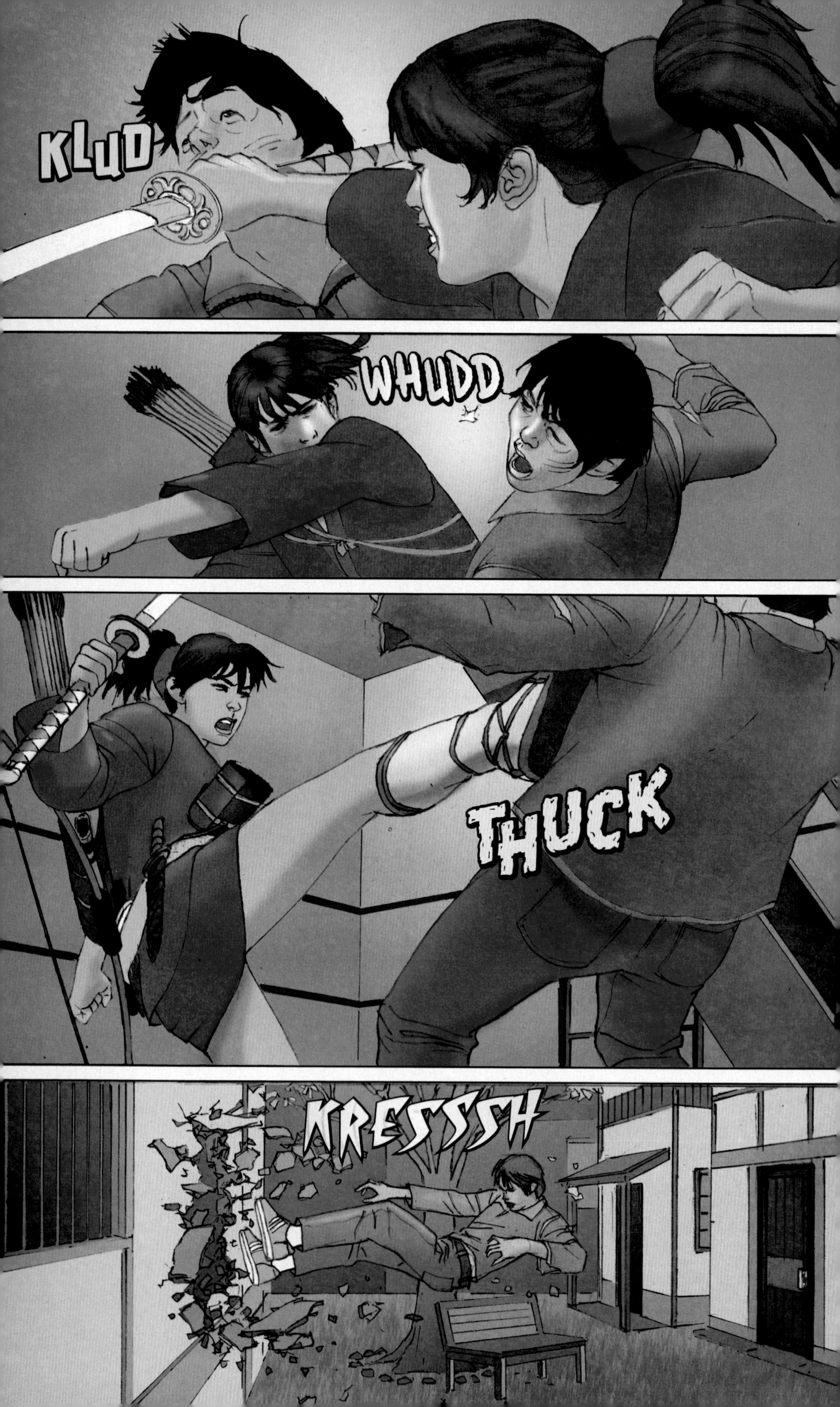
KLUD
WHUDD
THUCK
KRESSSH

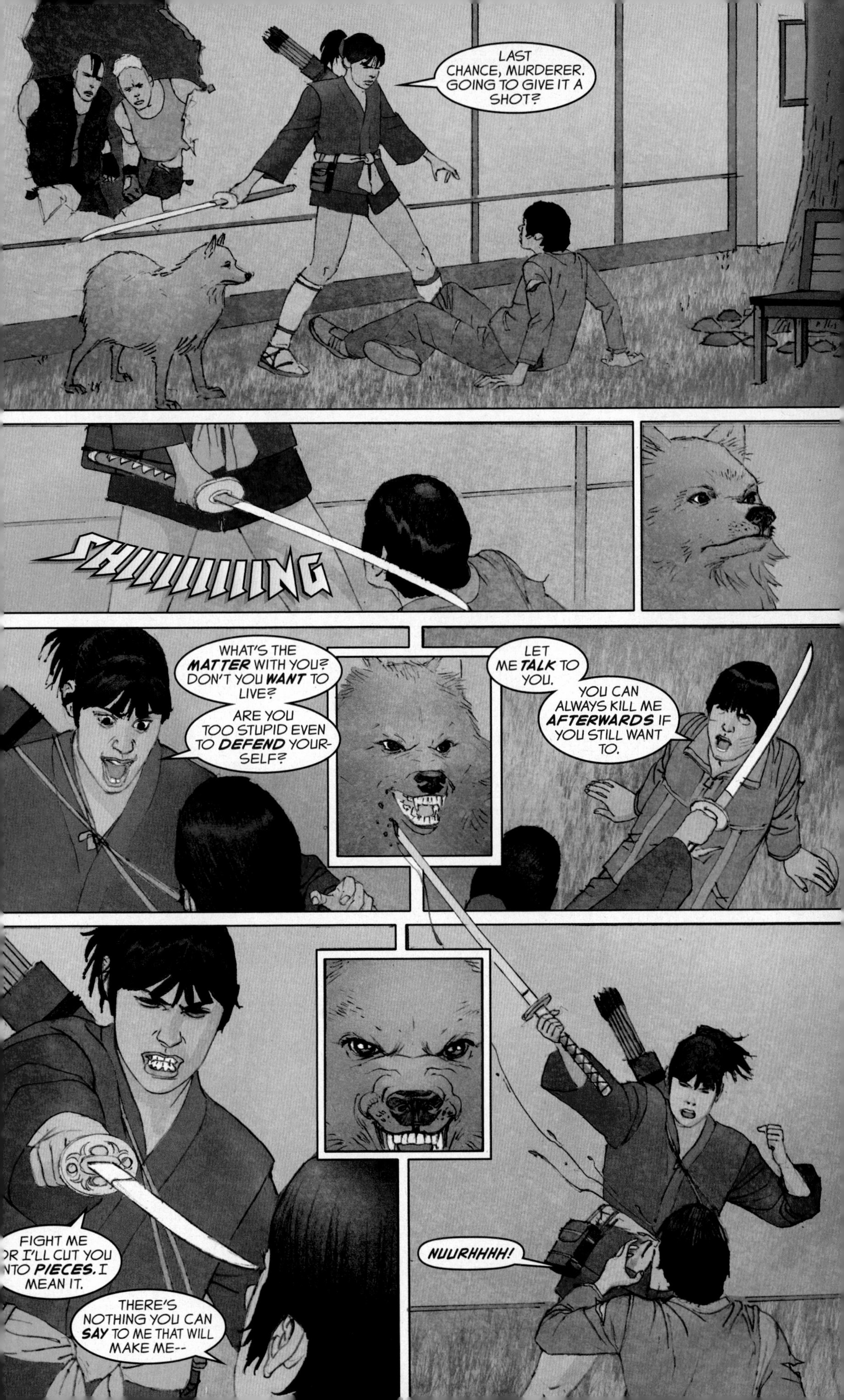
LAST CHANCE, MURDERER. GOING TO GIVE IT A SHOT?
SHIIIIIIIING
WHAT'S THE MATTER WITH YOU? DON'T YOU WANT TO LIVE?
ARE YOU TOO STUPID EVEN TO DEFEND YOURSELF?
LET ME TALK TO YOU.
YOU CAN ALWAYS KILL ME AFTERWARDS IF YOU STILL WANT TO.
FIGHT ME OR I'LL CUT YOU INTO PIECES. I MEAN IT.
THERE'S NOTHING YOU CAN SAY TO ME THAT WILL MAKE ME--
NUURHHHH!

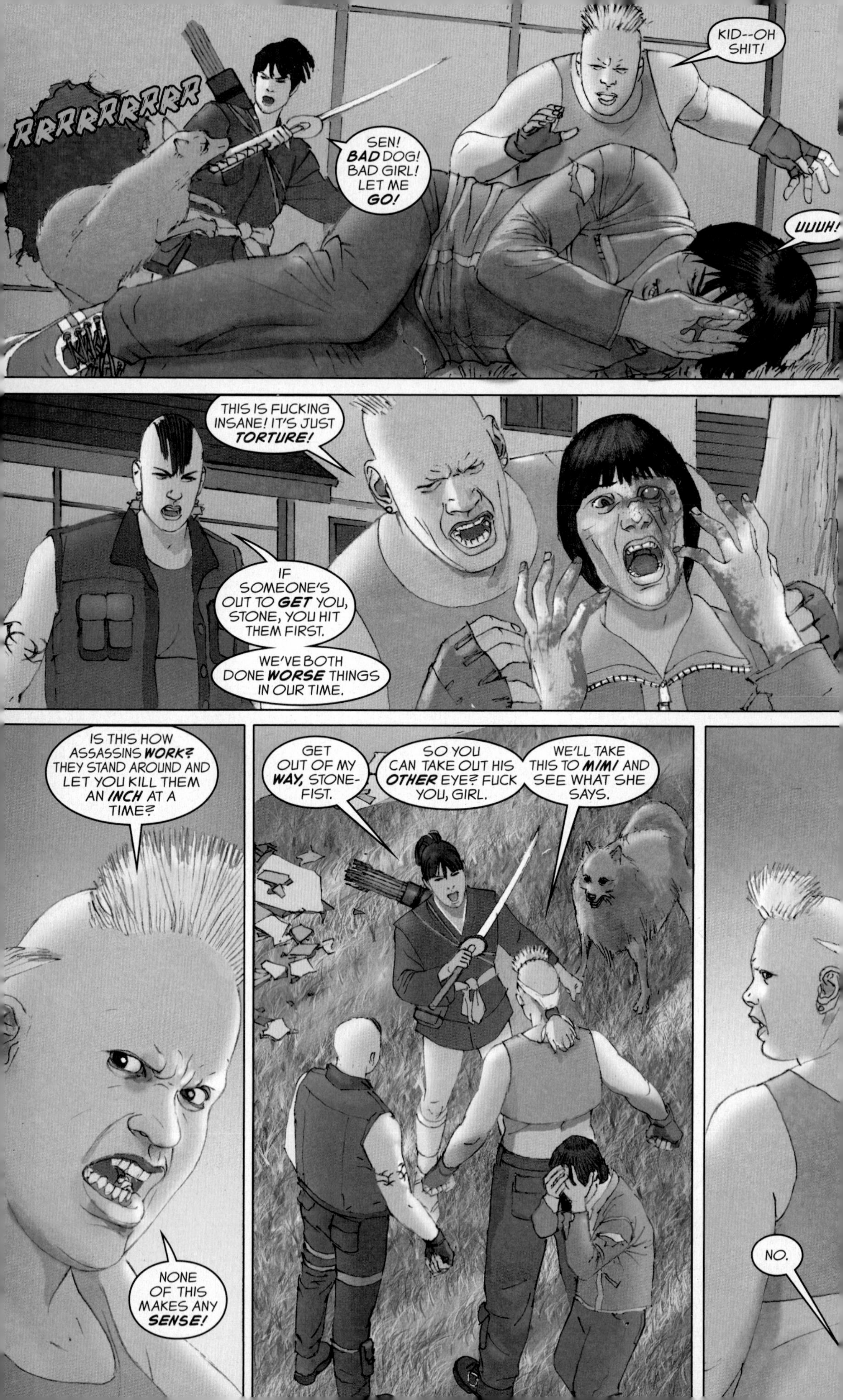
RRRRRRRRRR
SEN! BAD DOG! BAD GIRL! LET ME GO!
KID--OH SHIT!
UUUH!
THIS IS FUCKING INSANE! IT'S JUST TORTURE!
IF SOMEONE'S OUT TO GET YOU, STONE, YOU HIT THEM FIRST.
WE'VE BOTH DONE WORSE THINGS IN OUR TIME.
IS THIS HOW ASSASSINS WORK? THEY STAND AROUND AND LET YOU KILL THEM AN INCH AT A TIME?
NONE OF THIS MAKES ANY SENSE!
GET OUT OF MY WAY, STONE-FIST.
SO YOU CAN TAKE OUT HIS OTHER EYE? FUCK YOU, GIRL.
WE'LL TAKE THIS TO MIMI AND SEE WHAT SHE SAYS.
NO.

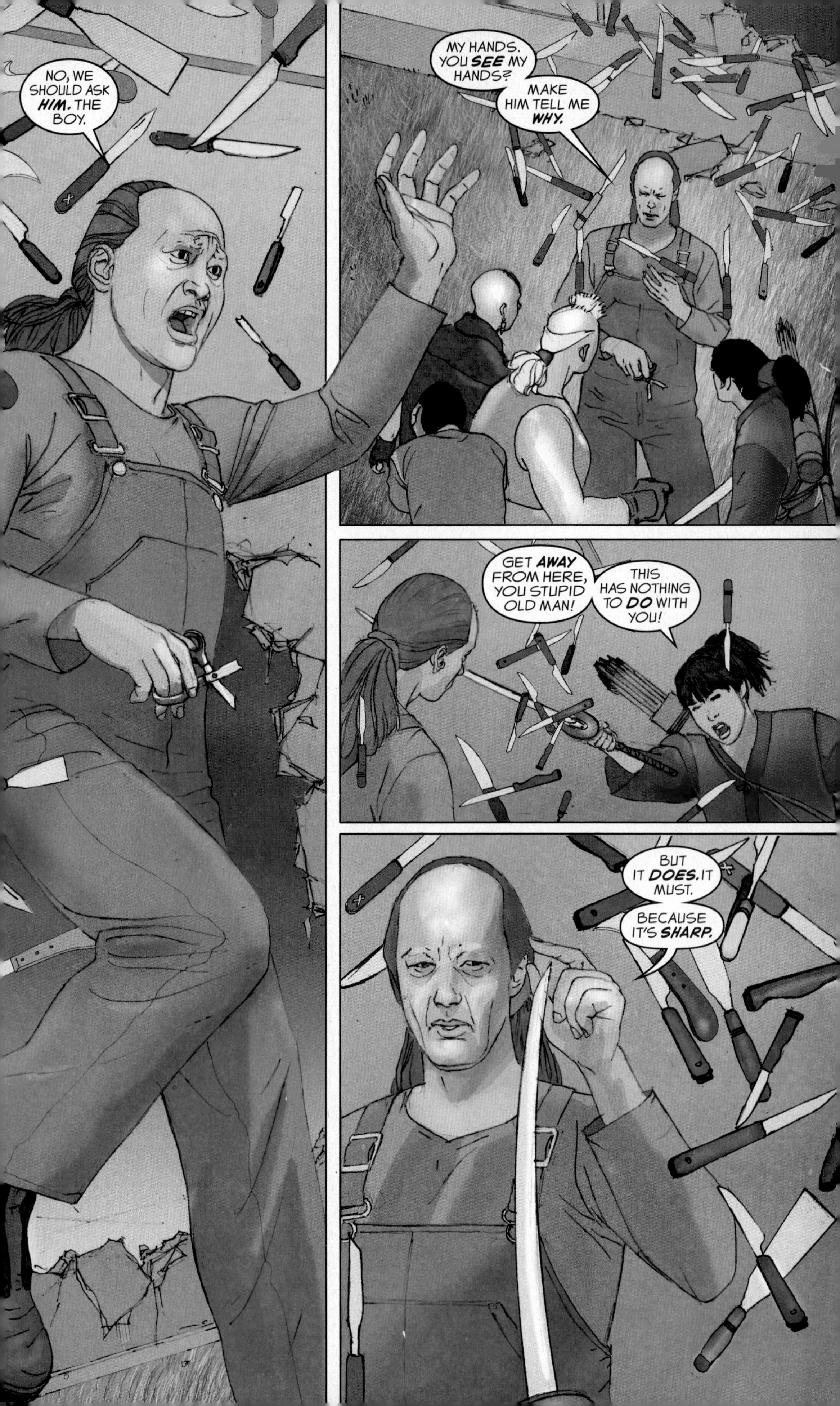
NO, WE SHOULD ASK *HIM.* THE BOY.
MY HANDS. YOU *SEE* MY HANDS?
MAKE HIM TELL ME *WHY.*
GET *AWAY* FROM HERE, YOU STUPID OLD MAN!
THIS HAS NOTHING TO *DO* WITH YOU!
BUT IT *DOES.* IT MUST.
BECAUSE IT'S *SHARP.*

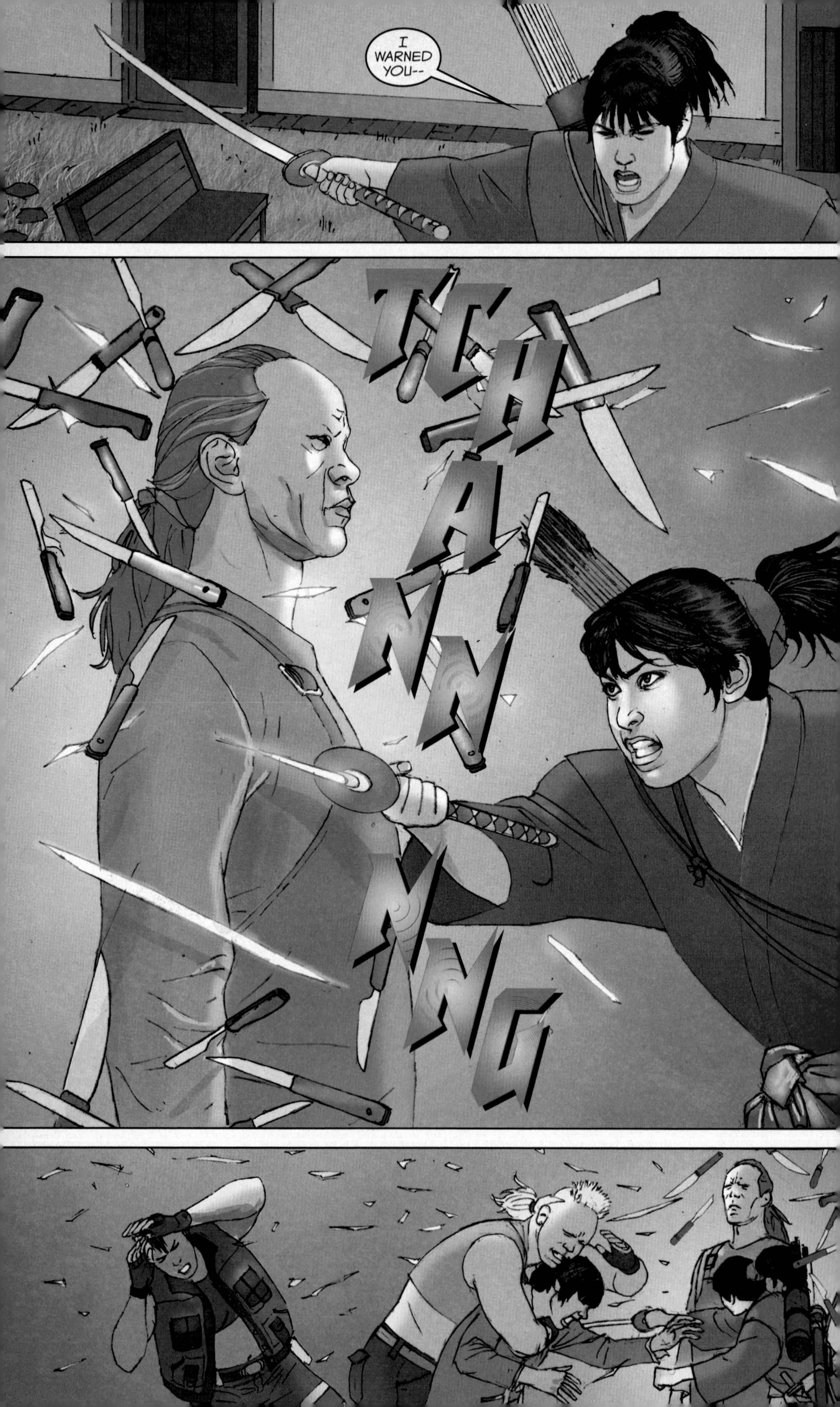
I WARNED YOU--
TCHAANNNNG

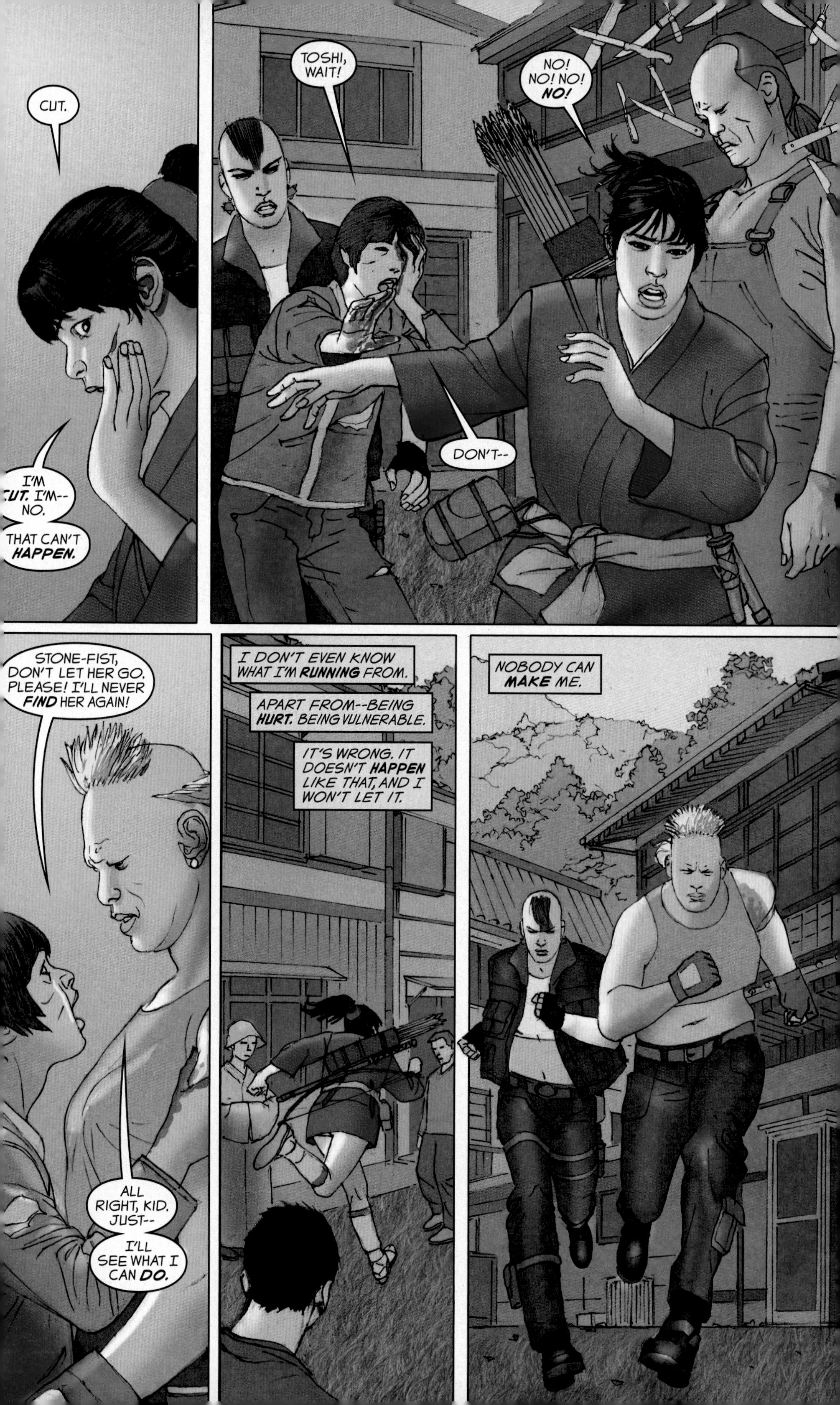
CUT.
I'M CUT. I'M-- NO.
THAT CAN'T HAPPEN.
TOSHI, WAIT!
NO! NO! NO! NO!
DON'T--
STONE-FIST, DON'T LET HER GO. PLEASE! I'LL NEVER FIND HER AGAIN!
ALL RIGHT, KID. JUST--
I'LL SEE WHAT I CAN DO.
I DON'T EVEN KNOW WHAT I'M RUNNING FROM.
APART FROM--BEING HURT. BEING VULNERABLE.
IT'S WRONG. IT DOESN'T HAPPEN LIKE THAT, AND I WON'T LET IT.
NOBODY CAN MAKE ME.

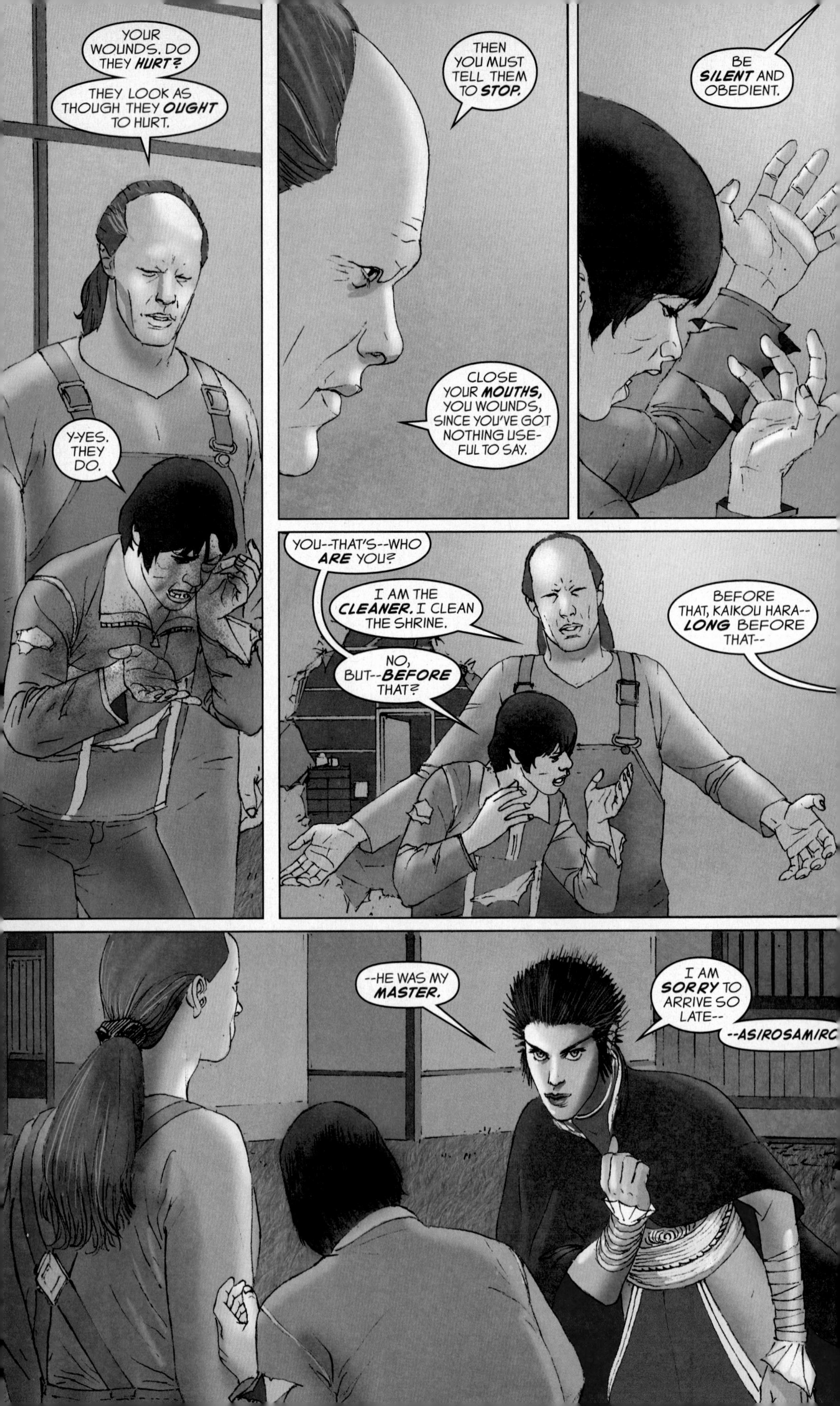
YOUR WOUNDS. DO THEY HURT?
THEY LOOK AS THOUGH THEY OUGHT TO HURT.
THEN YOU MUST TELL THEM TO STOP.
BE SILENT AND OBEDIENT.
Y-YES. THEY DO.
CLOSE YOUR MOUTHS, YOU WOUNDS, SINCE YOU'VE GOT NOTHING USE-FUL TO SAY.
YOU--THAT'S--WHO ARE YOU?
I AM THE CLEANER. I CLEAN THE SHRINE.
NO, BUT--BEFORE THAT?
BEFORE THAT, KAIKOU HARA--LONG BEFORE THAT--
--HE WAS MY MASTER.
I AM SORRY TO ARRIVE SO LATE--
--ASIROSAMIRO

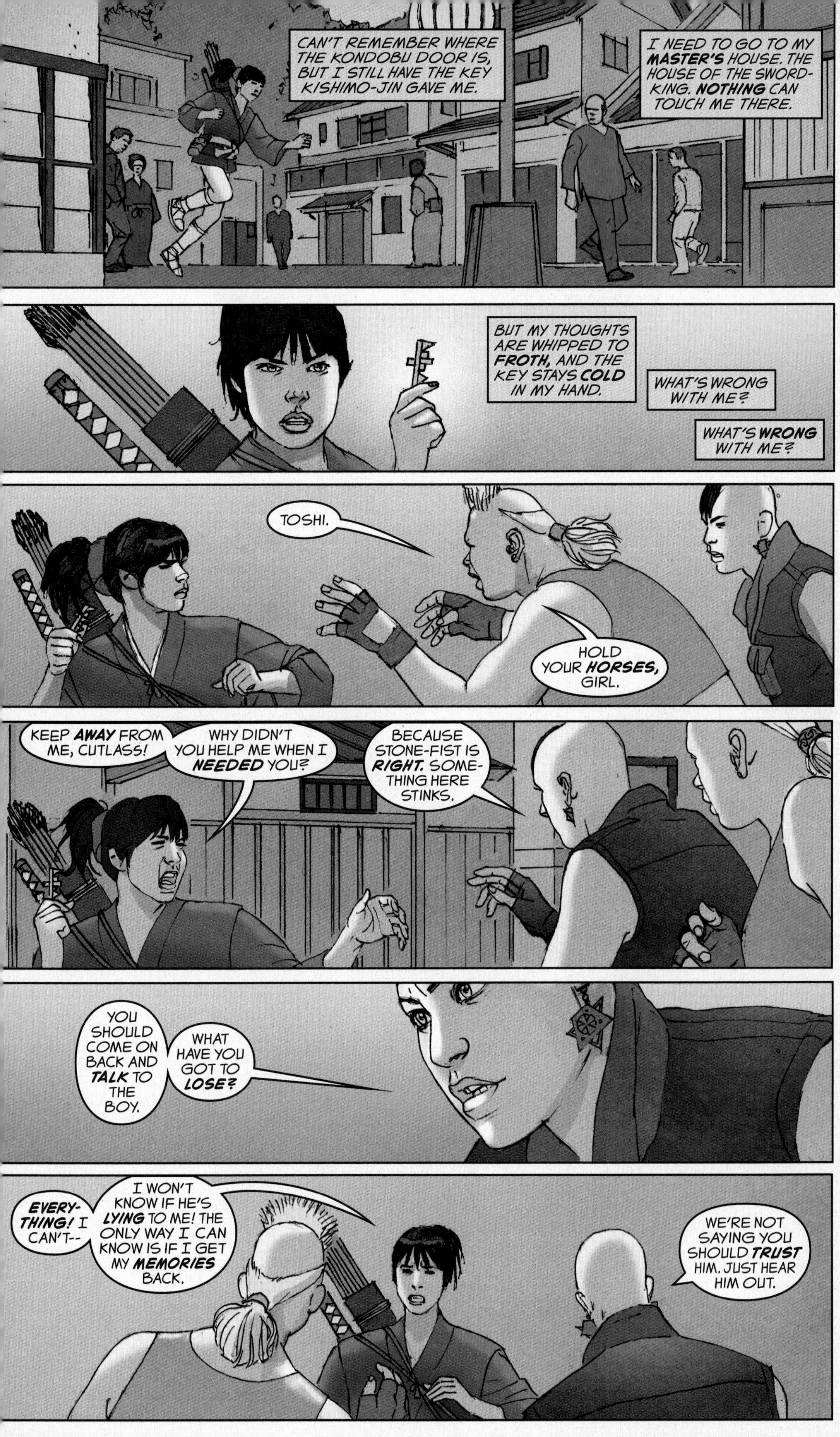
CAN'T REMEMBER WHERE THE KONDOBU DOOR IS, BUT I STILL HAVE THE KEY KISHIMO-JIN GAVE ME.
I NEED TO GO TO MY MASTER'S HOUSE. THE HOUSE OF THE SWORD-KING. NOTHING CAN TOUCH ME THERE.
BUT MY THOUGHTS ARE WHIPPED TO FROTH, AND THE KEY STAYS COLD IN MY HAND.
WHAT'S WRONG WITH ME?
WHAT'S WRONG WITH ME?
TOSHI.
HOLD YOUR HORSES, GIRL.
KEEP AWAY FROM ME, CUTLASS!
WHY DIDN'T YOU HELP ME WHEN I NEEDED YOU?
BECAUSE STONE-FIST IS RIGHT. SOMETHING HERE STINKS.
YOU SHOULD COME ON BACK AND TALK TO THE BOY.
WHAT HAVE YOU GOT TO LOSE?
EVERYTHING! I CAN'T--
I WON'T KNOW IF HE'S LYING TO ME! THE ONLY WAY I CAN KNOW IS IF I GET MY MEMORIES BACK.
WE'RE NOT SAYING YOU SHOULD TRUST HIM. JUST HEAR HIM OUT.

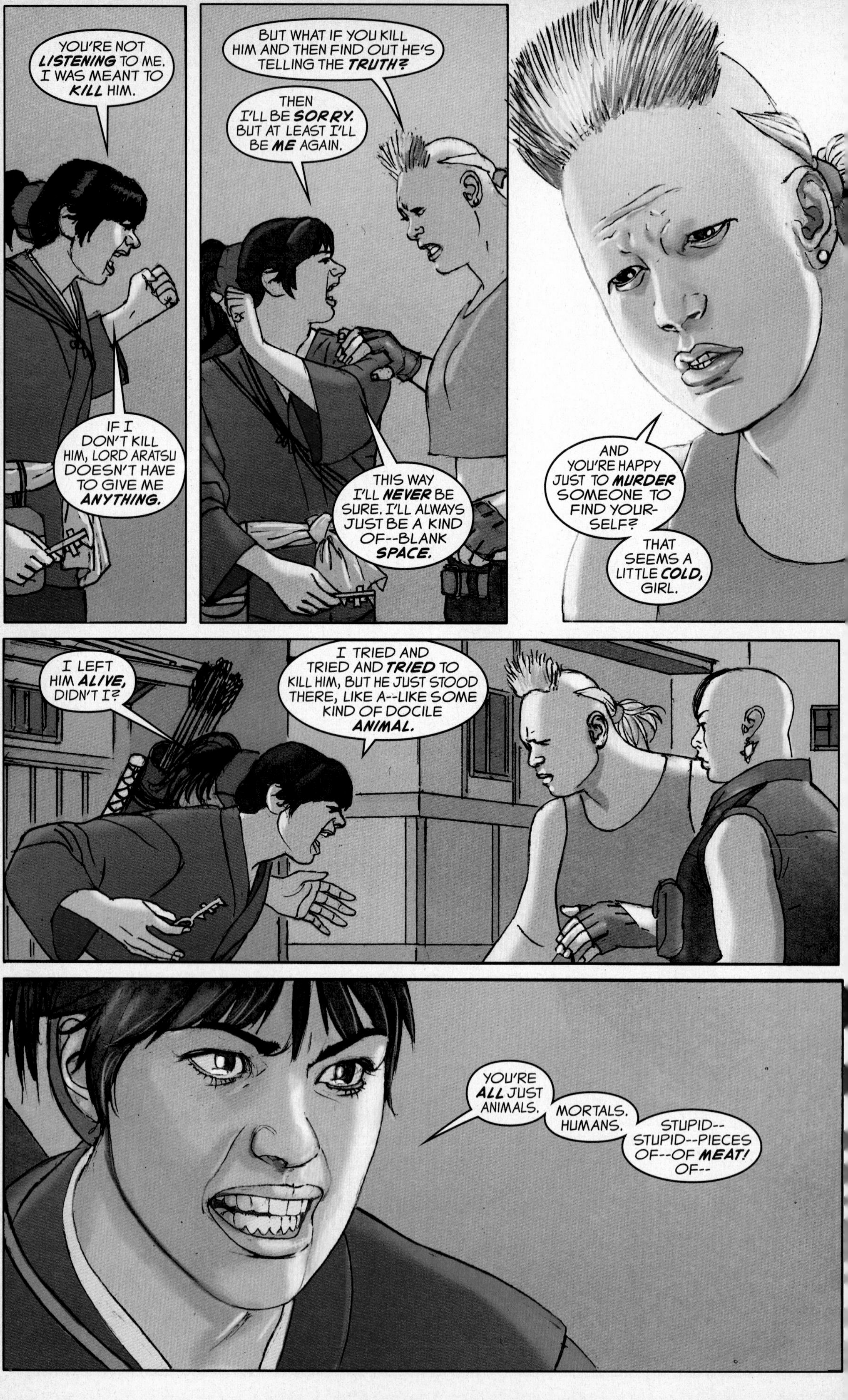
YOU'RE NOT LISTENING TO ME. I WAS MEANT TO KILL HIM.
IF I DON'T KILL HIM, LORD ARATSU DOESN'T HAVE TO GIVE ME ANYTHING.
BUT WHAT IF YOU KILL HIM AND THEN FIND OUT HE'S TELLING THE TRUTH?
THEN I'LL BE SORRY. BUT AT LEAST I'LL BE ME AGAIN.
THIS WAY I'LL NEVER BE SURE. I'LL ALWAYS JUST BE A KIND OF--BLANK SPACE.
AND YOU'RE HAPPY JUST TO MURDER SOMEONE TO FIND YOURSELF?
THAT SEEMS A LITTLE COLD, GIRL.
I LEFT HIM ALIVE, DIDN'T I?
I TRIED AND TRIED AND TRIED TO KILL HIM, BUT HE JUST STOOD THERE, LIKE A--LIKE SOME KIND OF DOCILE ANIMAL.
YOU'RE ALL JUST ANIMALS.
MORTALS. HUMANS.
STUPID-- STUPID--PIECES OF--OF MEAT! OF--

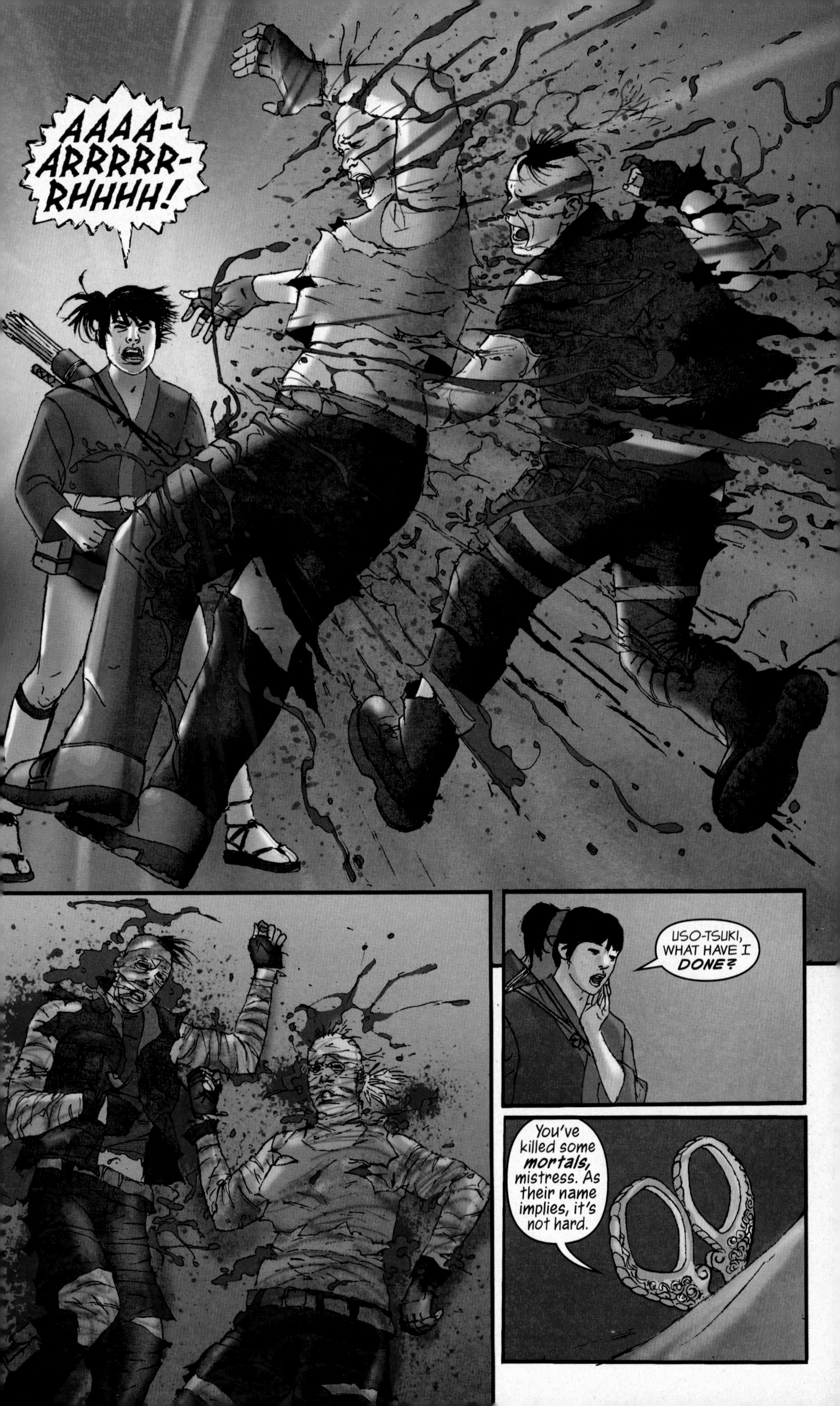
AAAA-
ARRRRR-
RHHHH!
USO-TSUKI, WHAT HAVE I DONE?
You've killed some mortals, mistress. As their name implies, it's not hard.

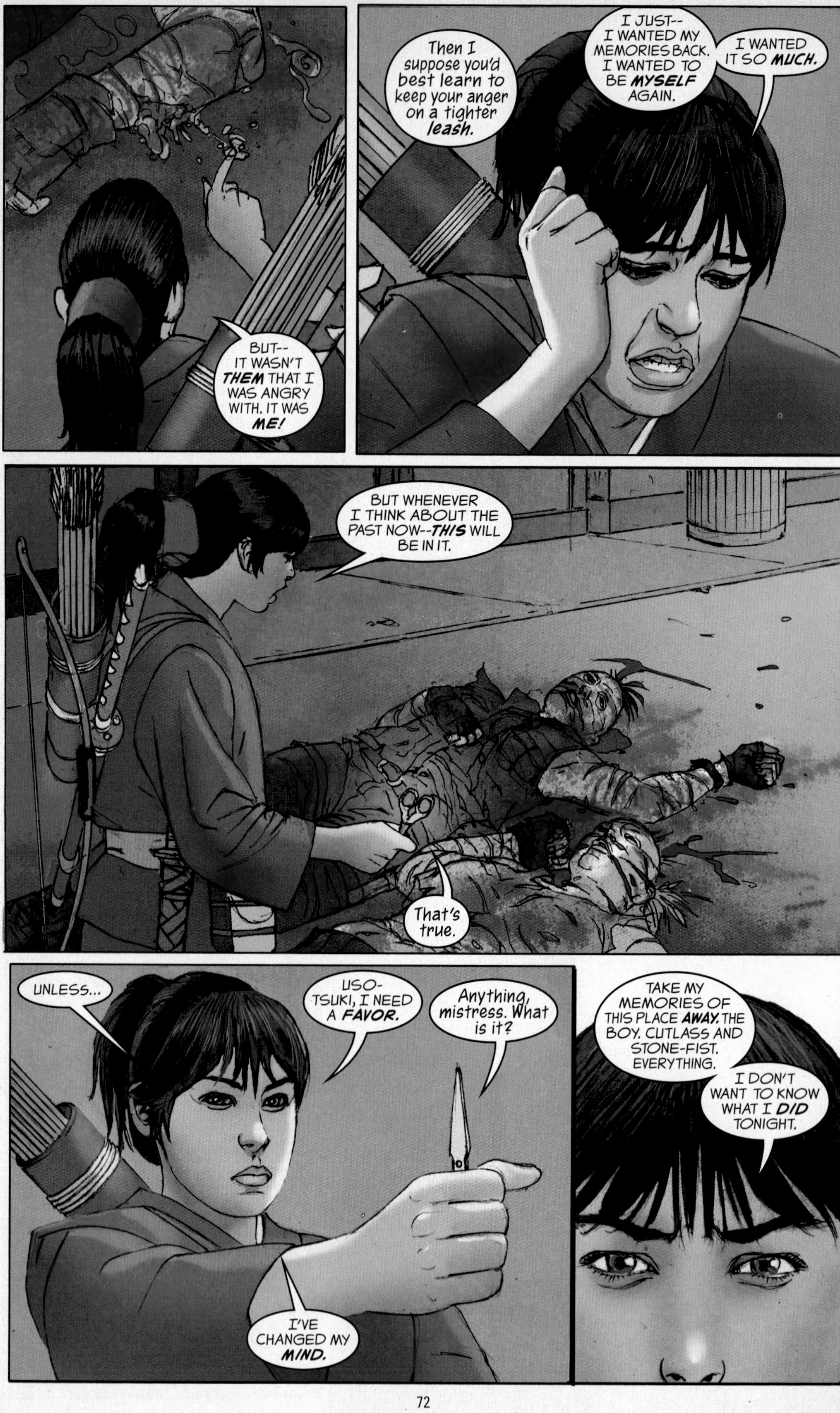
BUT-- IT WASN'T THEM THAT I WAS ANGRY WITH. IT WAS ME!
Then I suppose you'd best learn to keep your anger on a tighter leash.
I JUST-- I WANTED MY MEMORIES BACK. I WANTED TO BE MYSELF AGAIN.
I WANTED IT SO MUCH.
BUT WHENEVER I THINK ABOUT THE PAST NOW--THIS WILL BE IN IT.
That's true.
UNLESS...
USO-TSUKI, I NEED A FAVOR.
Anything, mistress. What is it?
I'VE CHANGED MY MIND.
TAKE MY MEMORIES OF THIS PLACE AWAY. THE BOY. CUTLASS AND STONE-FIST. EVERYTHING.
I DON'T WANT TO KNOW WHAT I DID TONIGHT.

But-- your memories were meant to be your *reward.* That's what you were *fighting* for.

BECAUSE I FELT THEIR *ABSENCE.* LIKE A HOLE INSIDE ME.

BUT PERHAPS IF I FORGET *ENOUGH*--

--I WON'T EVEN KNOW ANY-MORE WHAT I'M *MISSING.* AND THEN I'LL BE HAPPY.

THE BLADES DIDN'T HURT GOING IN. I WASN'T REALLY *EXPECTING* THEM TO.

BUT THE *PAST*--

--THE PAST AS IT SPILLED OUT OF ME FELT LIKE COLD *AIR* ACROSS AN ACHING TOOTH.

ALMOST A *SOUND,* AT THE LIMIT OF HEARING. MY OWN VOICE SCREAMING, HIGH ENOUGH TO SCARE THE--

--DOGS.

THE *DOGS.*

WHERE'S--?

WHERE DID SHE--?

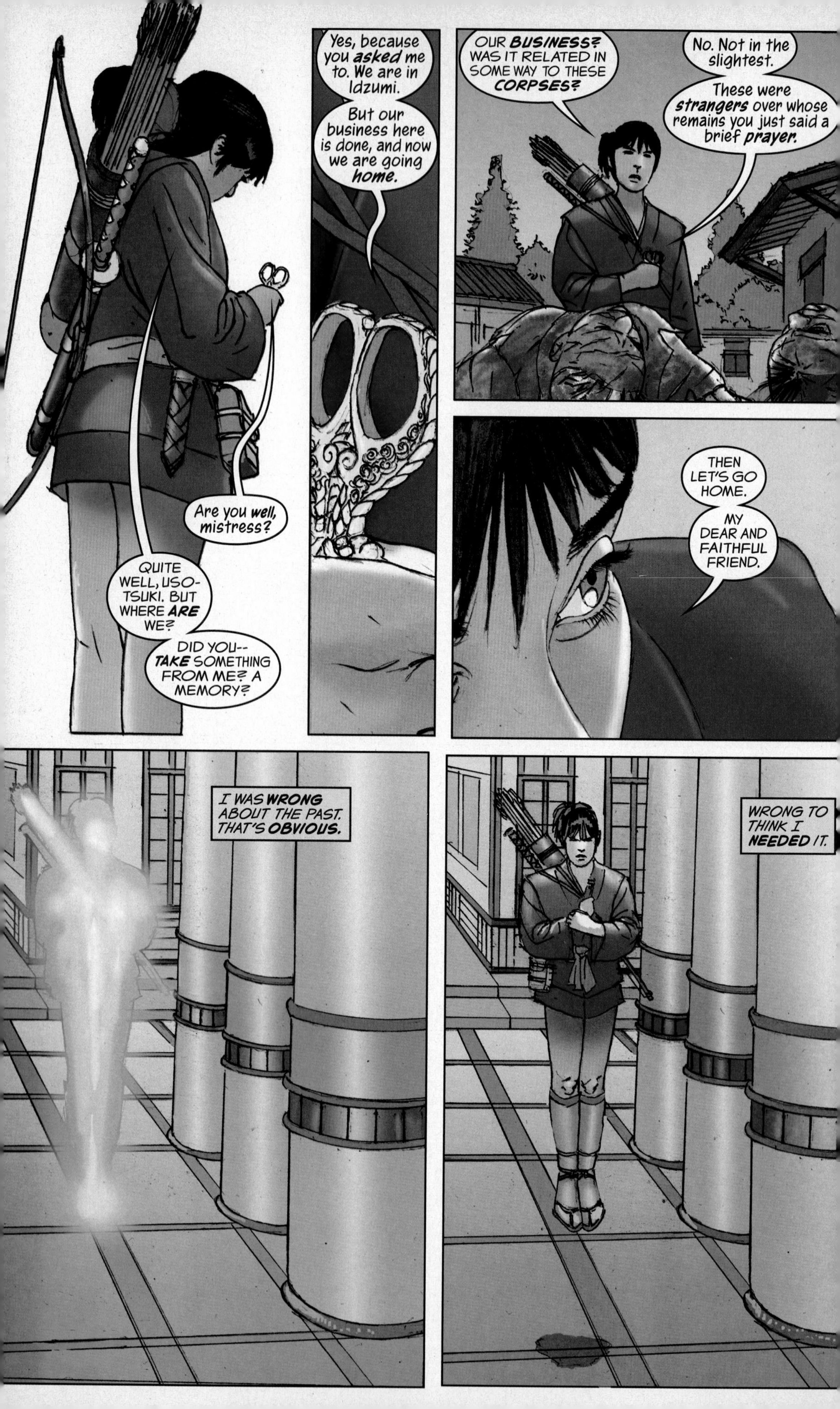
Are you well, mistress?
QUITE WELL, USO-TSUKI. BUT WHERE ARE WE?
DID YOU--TAKE SOMETHING FROM ME? A MEMORY?
Yes, because you asked me to. We are in Idzumi.
But our business here is done, and now we are going home.
OUR BUSINESS? WAS IT RELATED IN SOME WAY TO THESE CORPSES?
No. Not in the slightest.
These were strangers over whose remains you just said a brief prayer.
THEN LET'S GO HOME.
MY DEAR AND FAITHFUL FRIEND.
I WAS WRONG ABOUT THE PAST. THAT'S OBVIOUS.
WRONG TO THINK I NEEDED IT.

OR AT LEAST--THERE MUST BE A **HIGH** ROAD AND A **LOW** ROAD TO HAPPINESS.

HOW **STRANGE** NOT TO HAVE SEEN THAT BEFORE.

THAT FORGETFULNESS **ARMORS** YOU AGAINST ALMOST EVERY PAIN THERE IS.

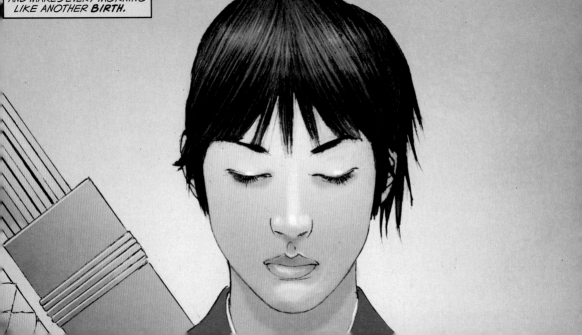

AND MAKES EVERY MORNING LIKE ANOTHER **BIRTH.**

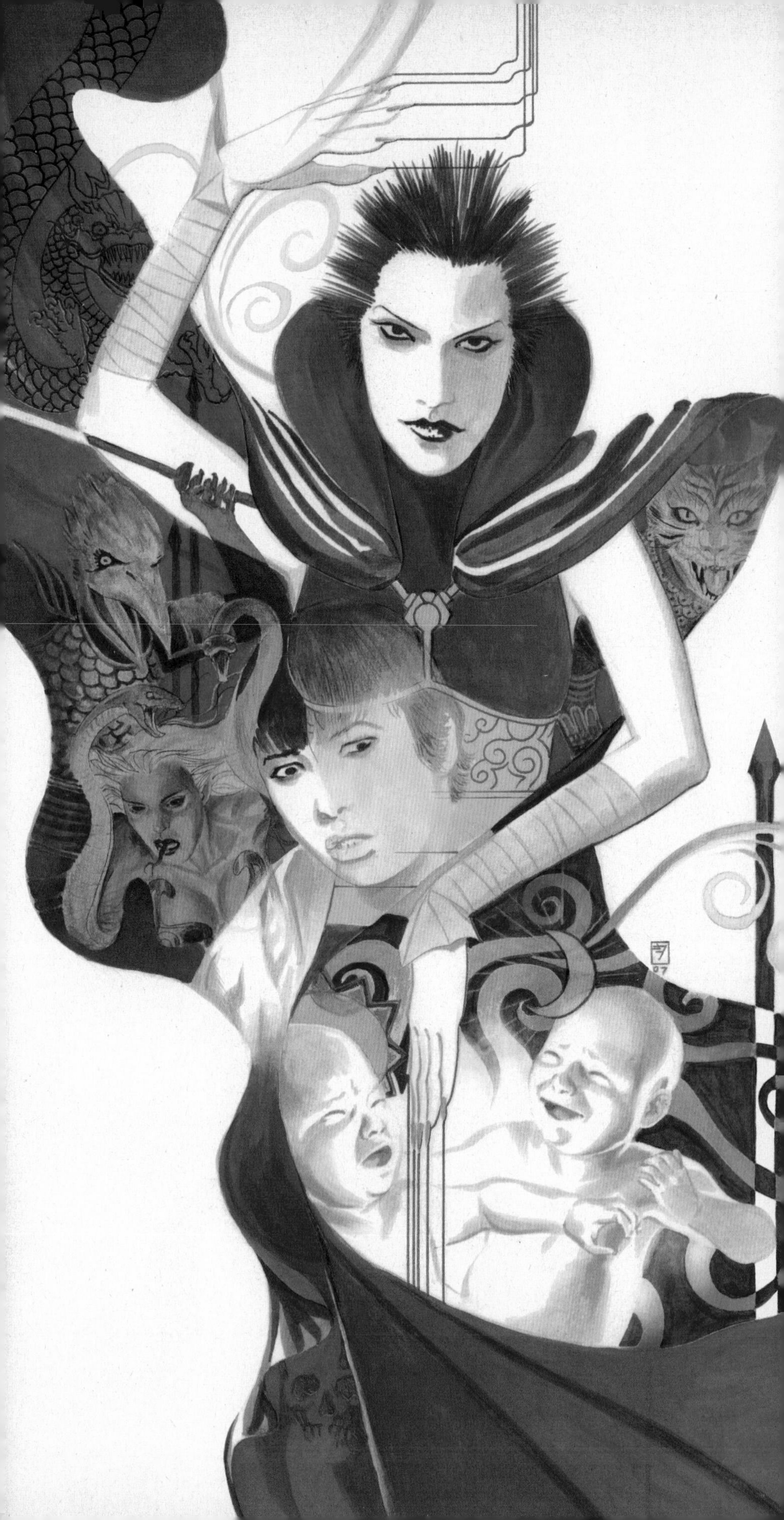

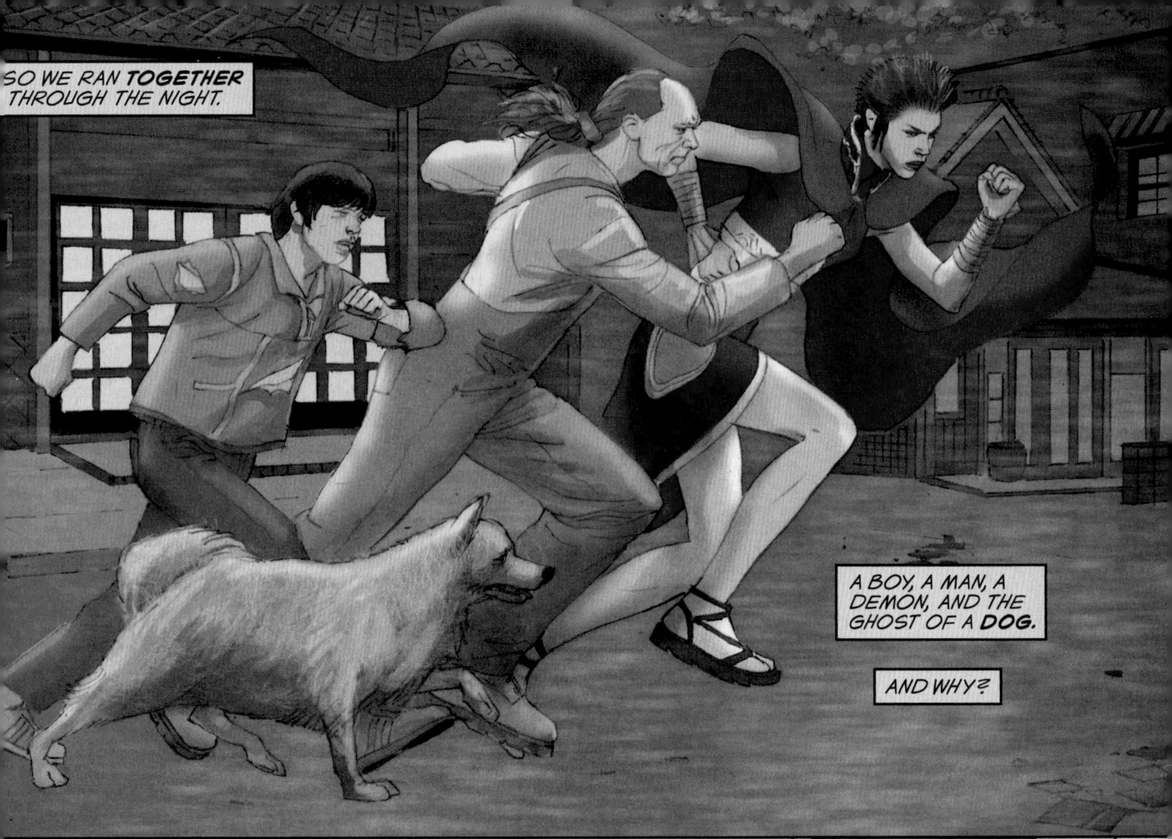
SO WE RAN TOGETHER THROUGH THE NIGHT.
A BOY, A MAN, A DEMON, AND THE GHOST OF A DOG.
AND WHY?

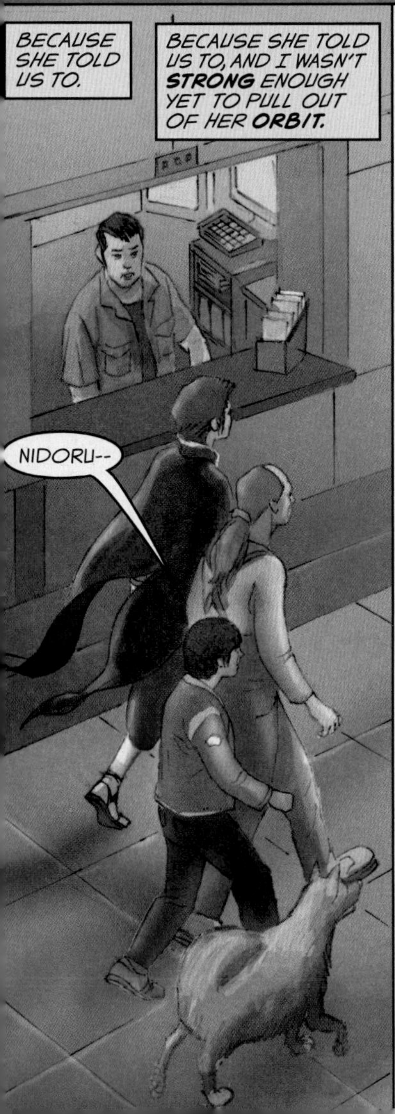
BECAUSE SHE TOLD US TO.
BECAUSE SHE TOLD US TO, AND I WASN'T STRONG ENOUGH YET TO PULL OUT OF HER ORBIT.
NIDORU--

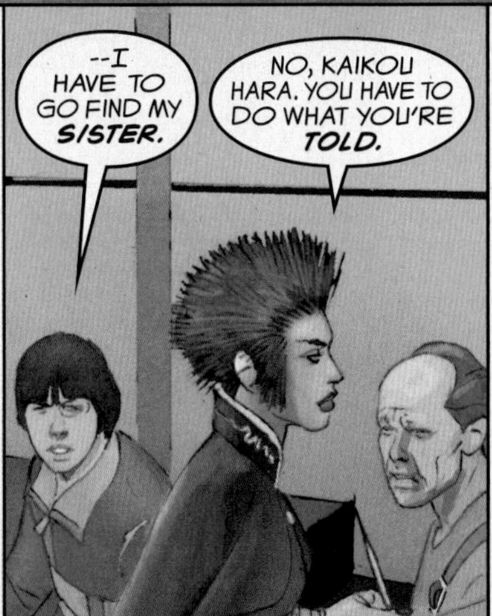
--I HAVE TO GO FIND MY SISTER.
NO, KAIKOU HARA. YOU HAVE TO DO WHAT YOU'RE TOLD.
OR ELSE YOU COULD DIE.

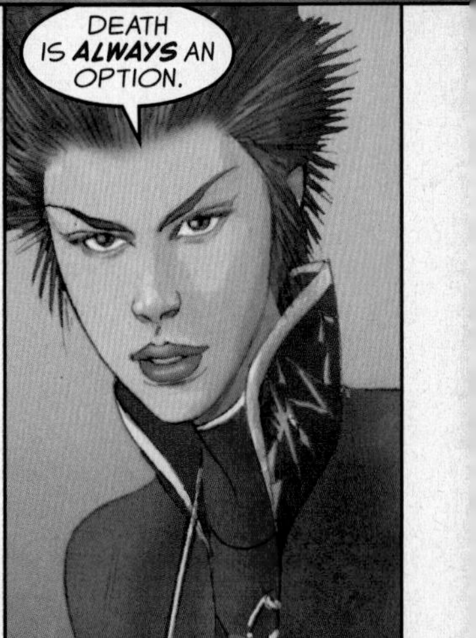
DEATH IS ALWAYS AN OPTION.

The Last Word

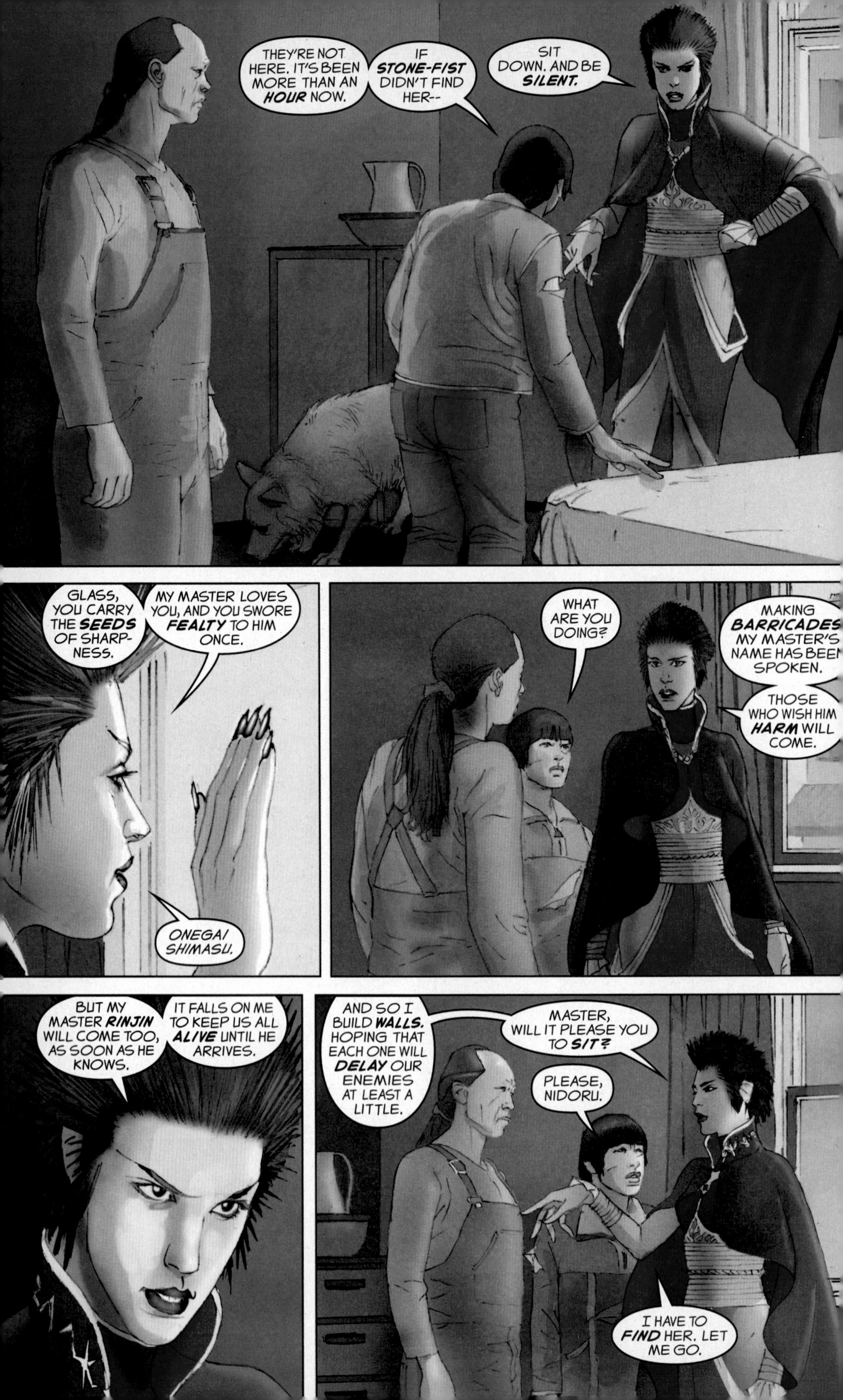

THEY'RE NOT HERE. IT'S BEEN MORE THAN AN HOUR NOW.
IF STONE-FIST DIDN'T FIND HER--
SIT DOWN. AND BE SILENT.
GLASS, YOU CARRY THE SEEDS OF SHARP-NESS.
MY MASTER LOVES YOU, AND YOU SWORE FEALTY TO HIM ONCE.
ONEGAI SHIMASU.
WHAT ARE YOU DOING?
MAKING BARRICADES. MY MASTER'S NAME HAS BEEN SPOKEN.
THOSE WHO WISH HIM HARM WILL COME.
BUT MY MASTER RINJIN WILL COME TOO, AS SOON AS HE KNOWS.
IT FALLS ON ME TO KEEP US ALL ALIVE UNTIL HE ARRIVES.
AND SO I BUILD WALLS. HOPING THAT EACH ONE WILL DELAY OUR ENEMIES AT LEAST A LITTLE.
MASTER, WILL IT PLEASE YOU TO SIT?
PLEASE, NIDORU.
I HAVE TO FIND HER. LET ME GO.

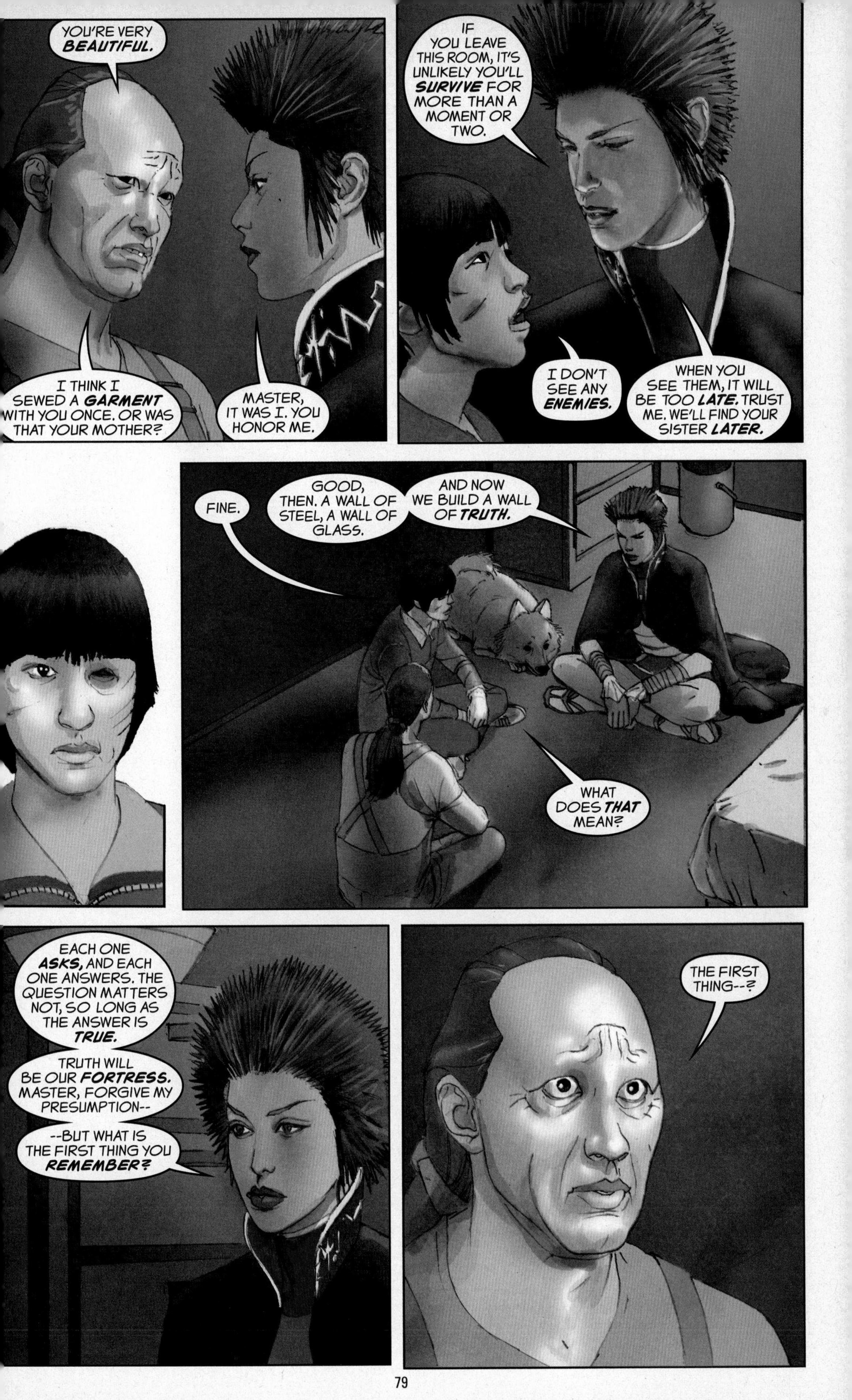
YOU'RE VERY BEAUTIFUL.
I THINK I SEWED A GARMENT WITH YOU ONCE. OR WAS THAT YOUR MOTHER?
MASTER, IT WAS I. YOU HONOR ME.
IF YOU LEAVE THIS ROOM, IT'S UNLIKELY YOU'LL SURVIVE FOR MORE THAN A MOMENT OR TWO.
I DON'T SEE ANY ENEMIES.
WHEN YOU SEE THEM, IT WILL BE TOO LATE. TRUST ME. WE'LL FIND YOUR SISTER LATER.
FINE.
GOOD, THEN. A WALL OF STEEL, A WALL OF GLASS.
AND NOW WE BUILD A WALL OF TRUTH.
WHAT DOES THAT MEAN?
EACH ONE ASKS, AND EACH ONE ANSWERS. THE QUESTION MATTERS NOT, SO LONG AS THE ANSWER IS TRUE.
TRUTH WILL BE OUR FORTRESS. MASTER, FORGIVE MY PRESUMPTION--
--BUT WHAT IS THE FIRST THING YOU REMEMBER?
THE FIRST THING--?

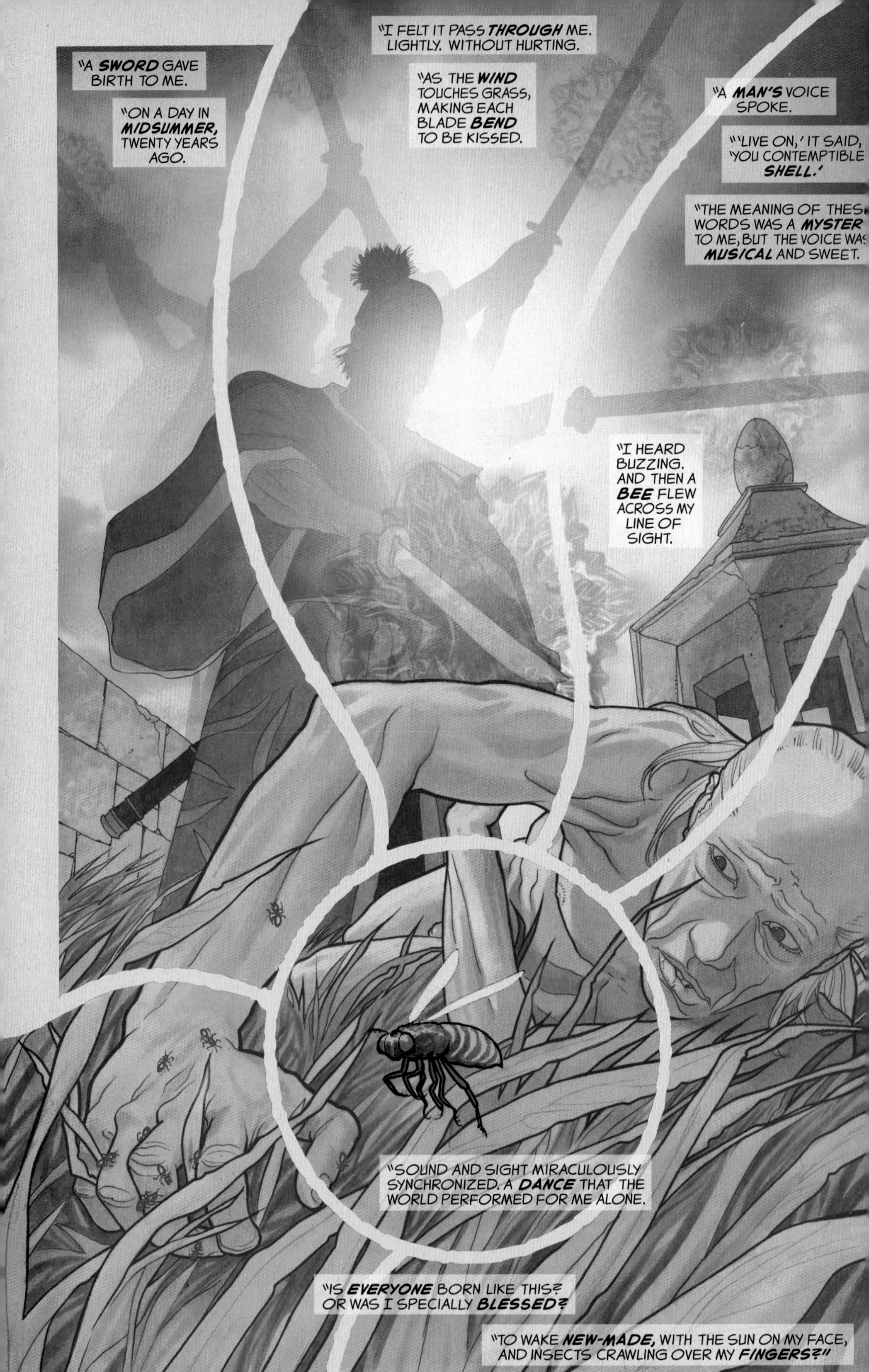
"A SWORD GAVE BIRTH TO ME.
"ON A DAY IN MIDSUMMER, TWENTY YEARS AGO.
"I FELT IT PASS THROUGH ME. LIGHTLY. WITHOUT HURTING.
"AS THE WIND TOUCHES GRASS, MAKING EACH BLADE BEND TO BE KISSED.
"A MAN'S VOICE SPOKE.
"'LIVE ON,' IT SAID, 'YOU CONTEMPTIBLE SHELL.'
"THE MEANING OF THES WORDS WAS A MYSTER TO ME, BUT THE VOICE WA MUSICAL AND SWEET.
"I HEARD BUZZING. AND THEN A BEE FLEW ACROSS MY LINE OF SIGHT.
"SOUND AND SIGHT MIRACULOUSLY SYNCHRONIZED. A DANCE THAT THE WORLD PERFORMED FOR ME ALONE.
"IS EVERYONE BORN LIKE THIS? OR WAS I SPECIALLY BLESSED?
"TO WAKE NEW-MADE, WITH THE SUN ON MY FACE, AND INSECTS CRAWLING OVER MY FINGERS?"

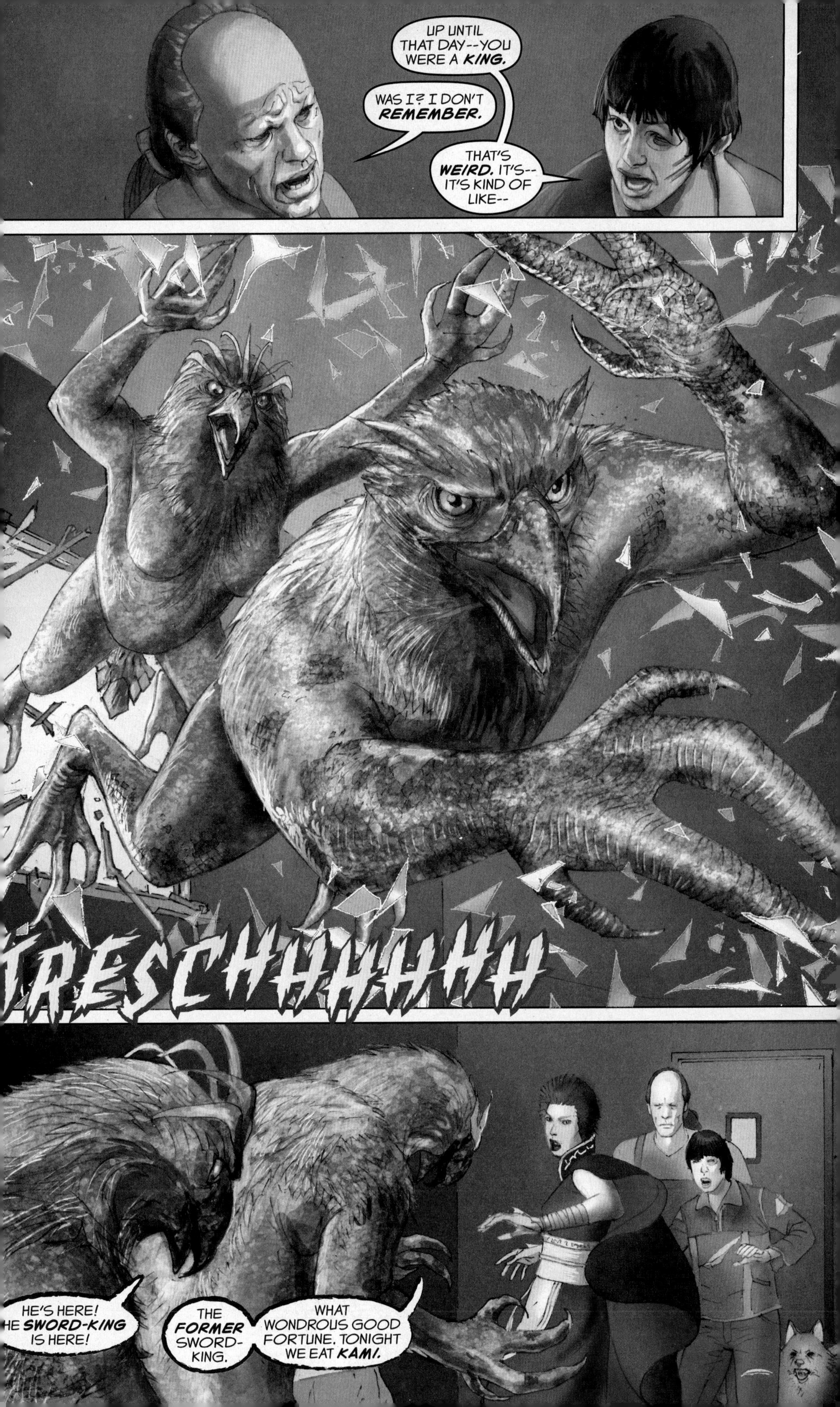
UP UNTIL THAT DAY--YOU WERE A KING.
WAS I? I DON'T REMEMBER.
THAT'S WEIRD. IT'S-- IT'S KIND OF LIKE--
RESCHHHHHH
HE'S HERE! HE SWORD-KING IS HERE!
THE FORMER SWORD-KING.
WHAT WONDROUS GOOD FORTUNE. TONIGHT WE EAT KAMI.

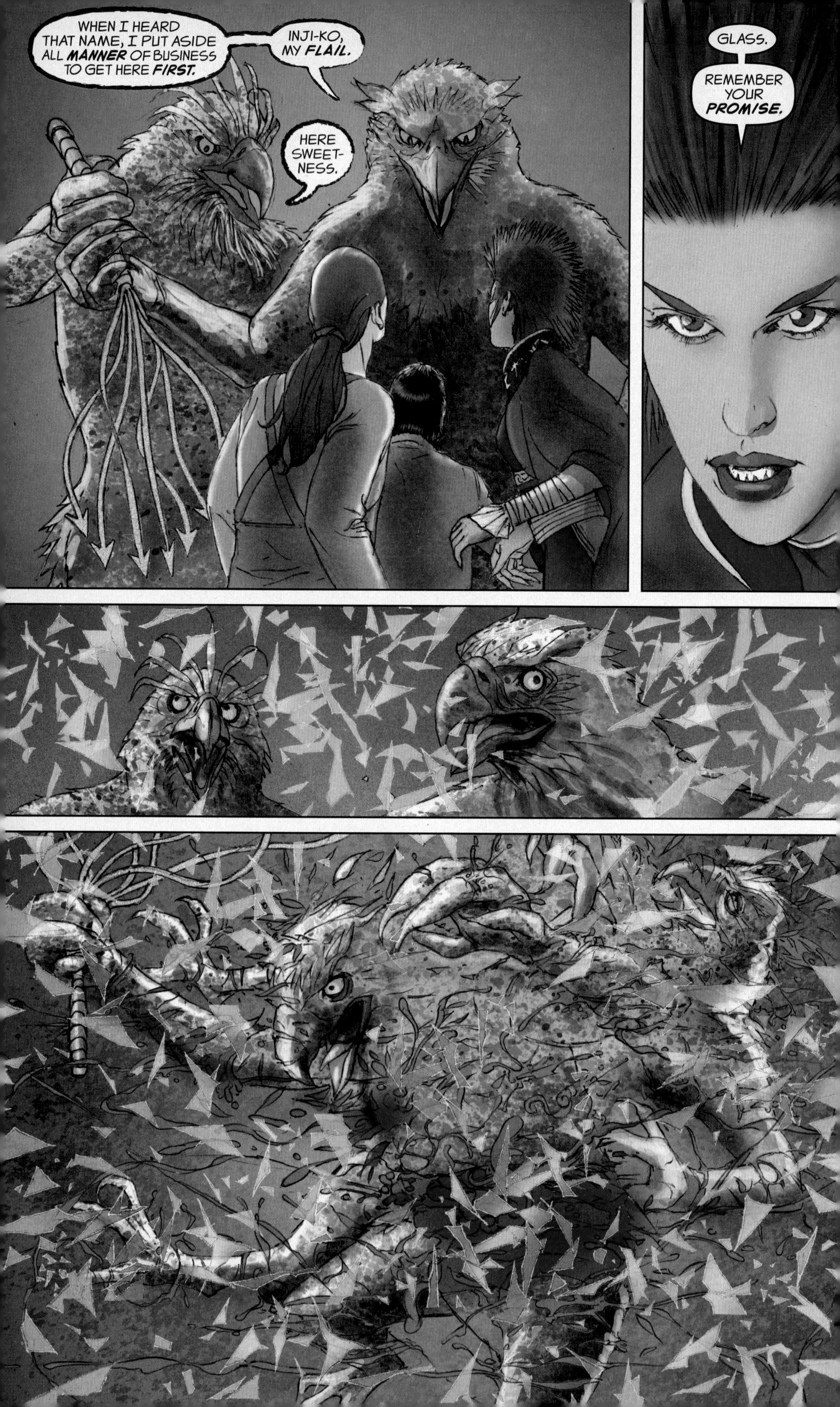
WHEN I HEARD THAT NAME, I PUT ASIDE ALL MANNER OF BUSINESS TO GET HERE FIRST.
INJI-KO, MY FLAIL.
HERE SWEET-NESS.
GLASS.
REMEMBER YOUR PROMISE.

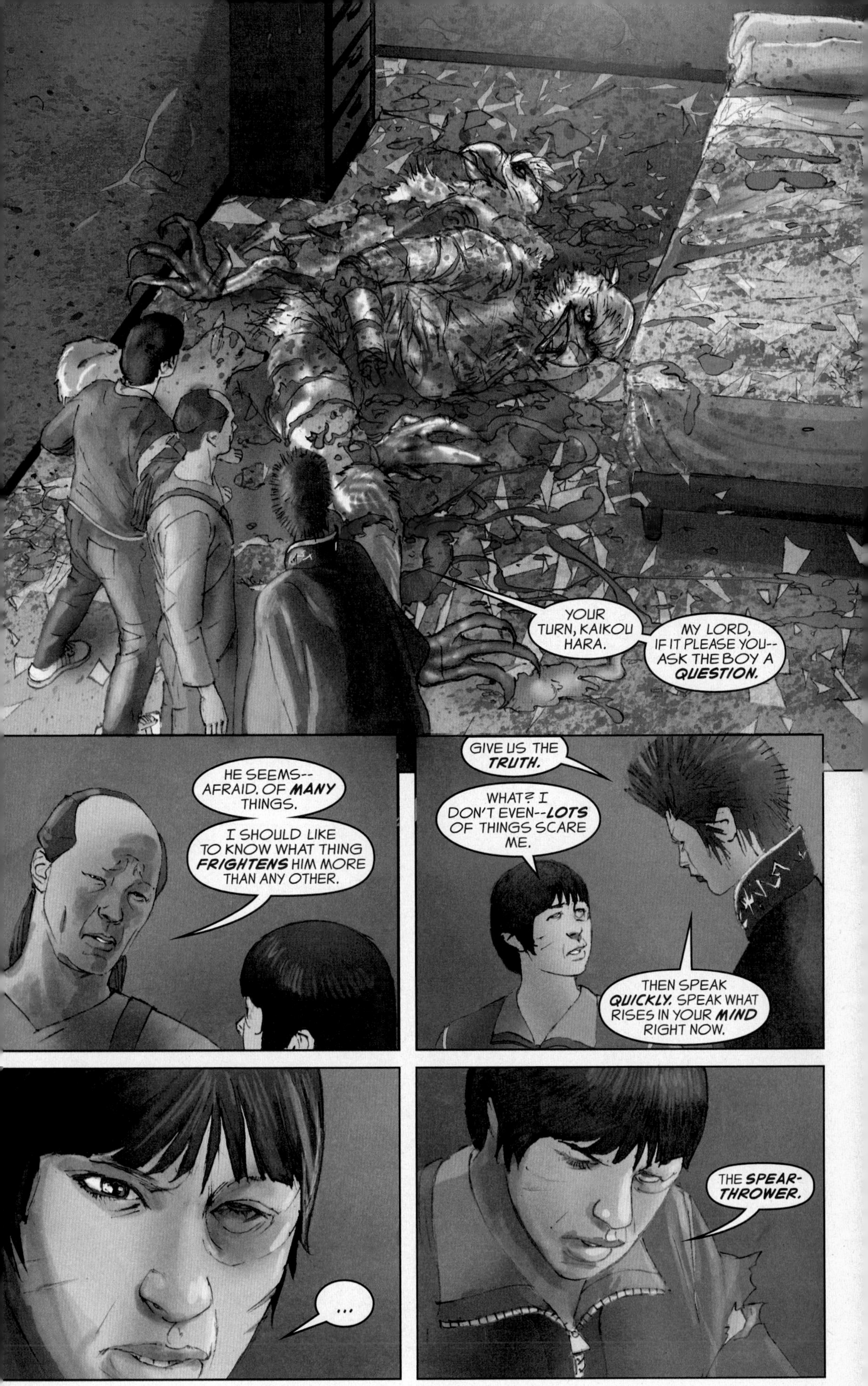
YOUR TURN, KAIKOU HARA.
MY LORD, IF IT PLEASE YOU-- ASK THE BOY A QUESTION.
HE SEEMS-- AFRAID. OF MANY THINGS.
I SHOULD LIKE TO KNOW WHAT THING FRIGHTENS HIM MORE THAN ANY OTHER.
GIVE US THE TRUTH.
WHAT? I DON'T EVEN--LOTS OF THINGS SCARE ME.
THEN SPEAK QUICKLY. SPEAK WHAT RISES IN YOUR MIND RIGHT NOW.
...
THE SPEAR-THROWER.

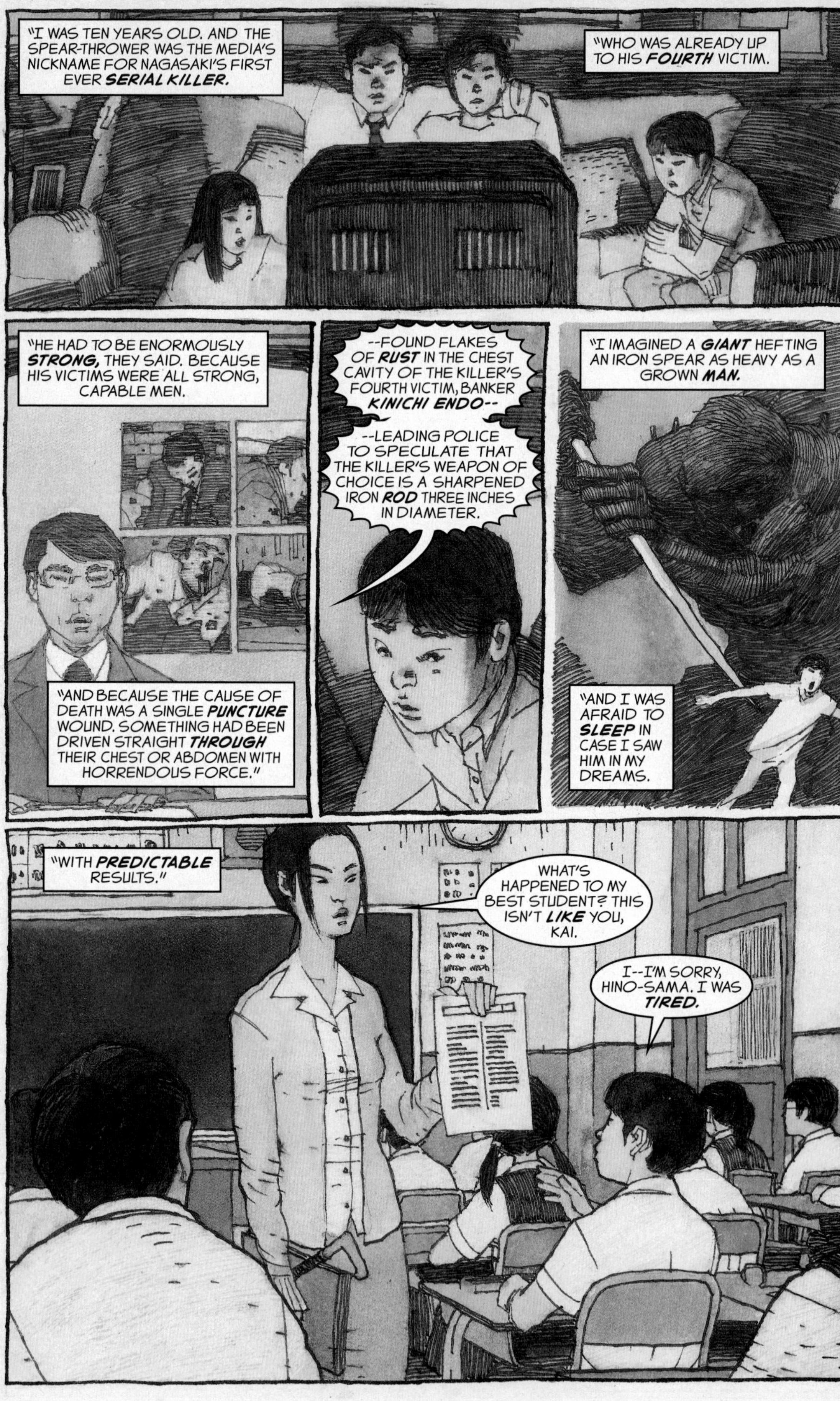
"I WAS TEN YEARS OLD. AND THE SPEAR-THROWER WAS THE MEDIA'S NICKNAME FOR NAGASAKI'S FIRST EVER SERIAL KILLER.
"WHO WAS ALREADY UP TO HIS FOURTH VICTIM.
"HE HAD TO BE ENORMOUSLY STRONG, THEY SAID. BECAUSE HIS VICTIMS WERE ALL STRONG, CAPABLE MEN.
"AND BECAUSE THE CAUSE OF DEATH WAS A SINGLE PUNCTURE WOUND. SOMETHING HAD BEEN DRIVEN STRAIGHT THROUGH THEIR CHEST OR ABDOMEN WITH HORRENDOUS FORCE."
--FOUND FLAKES OF RUST IN THE CHEST CAVITY OF THE KILLER'S FOURTH VICTIM, BANKER KINICHI ENDO--
--LEADING POLICE TO SPECULATE THAT THE KILLER'S WEAPON OF CHOICE IS A SHARPENED IRON ROD THREE INCHES IN DIAMETER.
"I IMAGINED A GIANT HEFTING AN IRON SPEAR AS HEAVY AS A GROWN MAN.
"AND I WAS AFRAID TO SLEEP IN CASE I SAW HIM IN MY DREAMS.
"WITH PREDICTABLE RESULTS."
WHAT'S HAPPENED TO MY BEST STUDENT? THIS ISN'T LIKE YOU, KAI.
I--I'M SORRY, HINO-SAMA. I WAS TIRED.

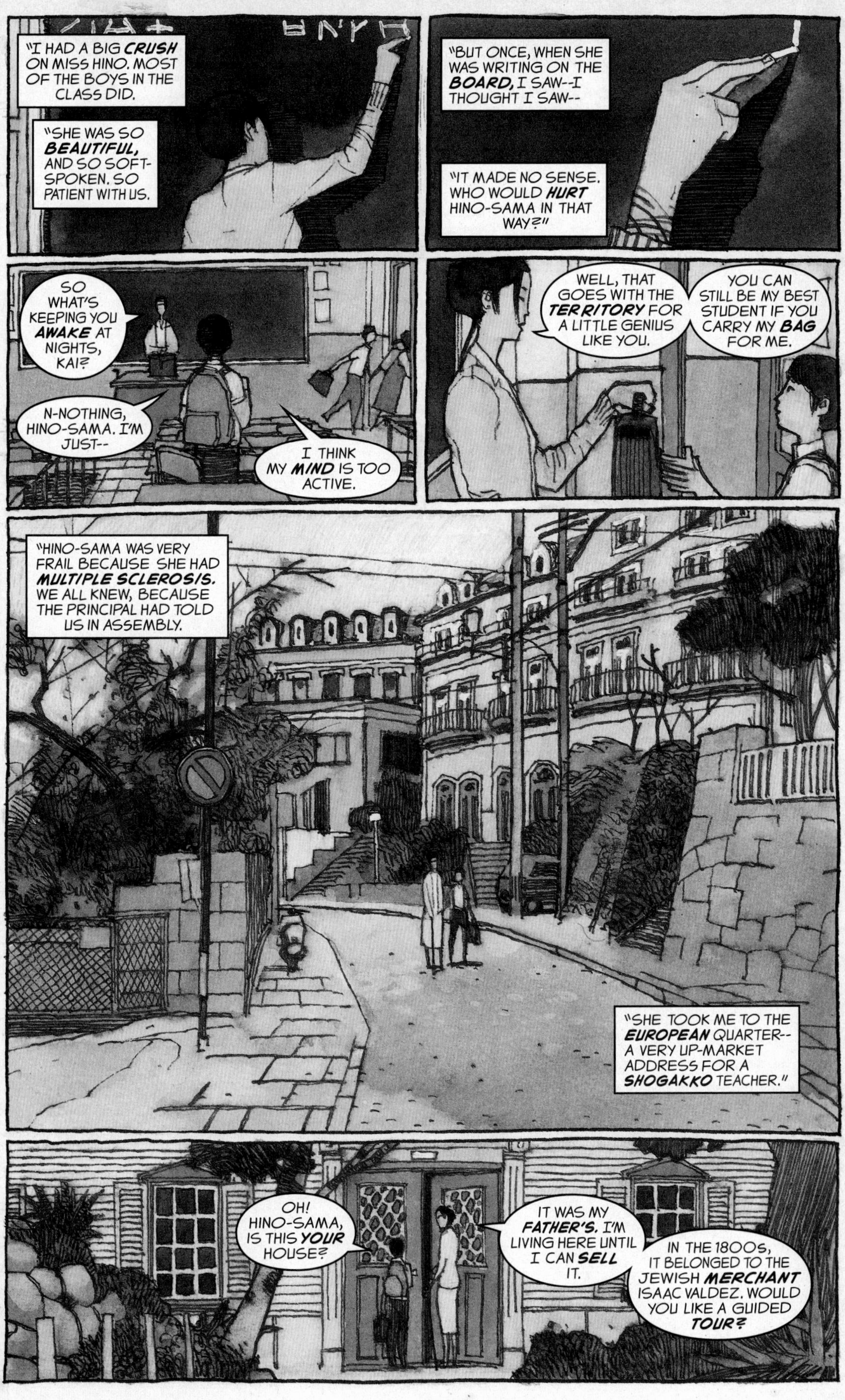
"I HAD A BIG CRUSH ON MISS HINO. MOST OF THE BOYS IN THE CLASS DID.
"SHE WAS SO BEAUTIFUL, AND SO SOFT-SPOKEN. SO PATIENT WITH US.
"BUT ONCE, WHEN SHE WAS WRITING ON THE BOARD, I SAW--I THOUGHT I SAW--
"IT MADE NO SENSE. WHO WOULD HURT HINO-SAMA IN THAT WAY?"
SO WHAT'S KEEPING YOU AWAKE AT NIGHTS, KAI?
N-NOTHING, HINO-SAMA. I'M JUST--
I THINK MY MIND IS TOO ACTIVE.
WELL, THAT GOES WITH THE TERRITORY FOR A LITTLE GENIUS LIKE YOU.
YOU CAN STILL BE MY BEST STUDENT IF YOU CARRY MY BAG FOR ME.
"HINO-SAMA WAS VERY FRAIL BECAUSE SHE HAD MULTIPLE SCLEROSIS. WE ALL KNEW, BECAUSE THE PRINCIPAL HAD TOLD US IN ASSEMBLY.
"SHE TOOK ME TO THE EUROPEAN QUARTER--A VERY UP-MARKET ADDRESS FOR A SHOGAKKO TEACHER."
OH! HINO-SAMA, IS THIS YOUR HOUSE?
IT WAS MY FATHER'S. I'M LIVING HERE UNTIL I CAN SELL IT.
IN THE 1800s, IT BELONGED TO THE JEWISH MERCHANT ISAAC VALDEZ. WOULD YOU LIKE A GUIDED TOUR?

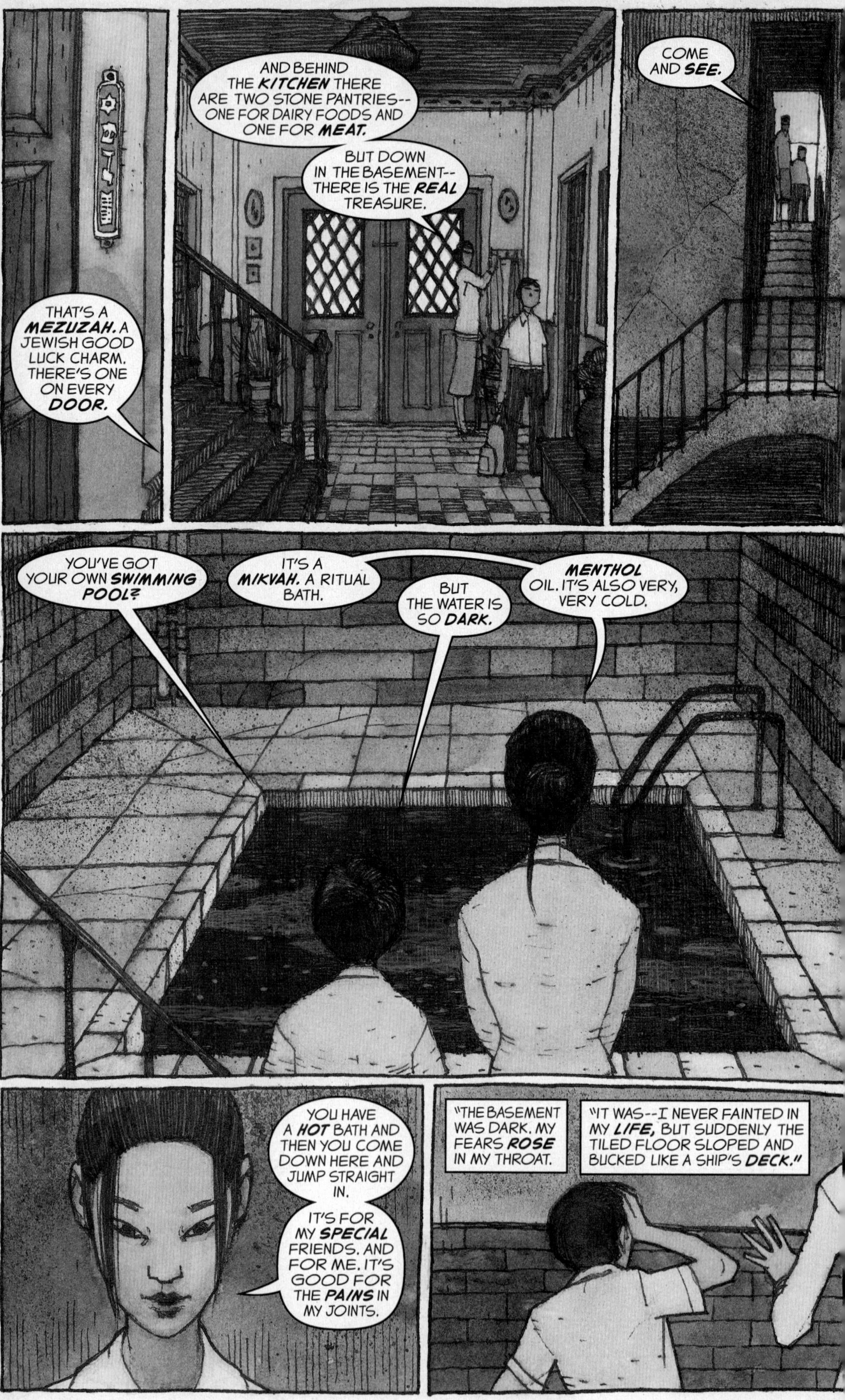
THAT'S A MEZUZAH. A JEWISH GOOD LUCK CHARM. THERE'S ONE ON EVERY DOOR.
AND BEHIND THE KITCHEN THERE ARE TWO STONE PANTRIES-- ONE FOR DAIRY FOODS AND ONE FOR MEAT.
BUT DOWN IN THE BASEMENT-- THERE IS THE REAL TREASURE.
COME AND SEE.
YOU'VE GOT YOUR OWN SWIMMING POOL?
IT'S A MIKVAH. A RITUAL BATH.
BUT THE WATER IS SO DARK.
MENTHOL OIL. IT'S ALSO VERY, VERY COLD.
YOU HAVE A HOT BATH AND THEN YOU COME DOWN HERE AND JUMP STRAIGHT IN.
IT'S FOR MY SPECIAL FRIENDS. AND FOR ME. IT'S GOOD FOR THE PAINS IN MY JOINTS.
"THE BASEMENT WAS DARK. MY FEARS ROSE IN MY THROAT.
"IT WAS--I NEVER FAINTED IN MY LIFE, BUT SUDDENLY THE TILED FLOOR SLOPED AND BUCKED LIKE A SHIP'S DECK."

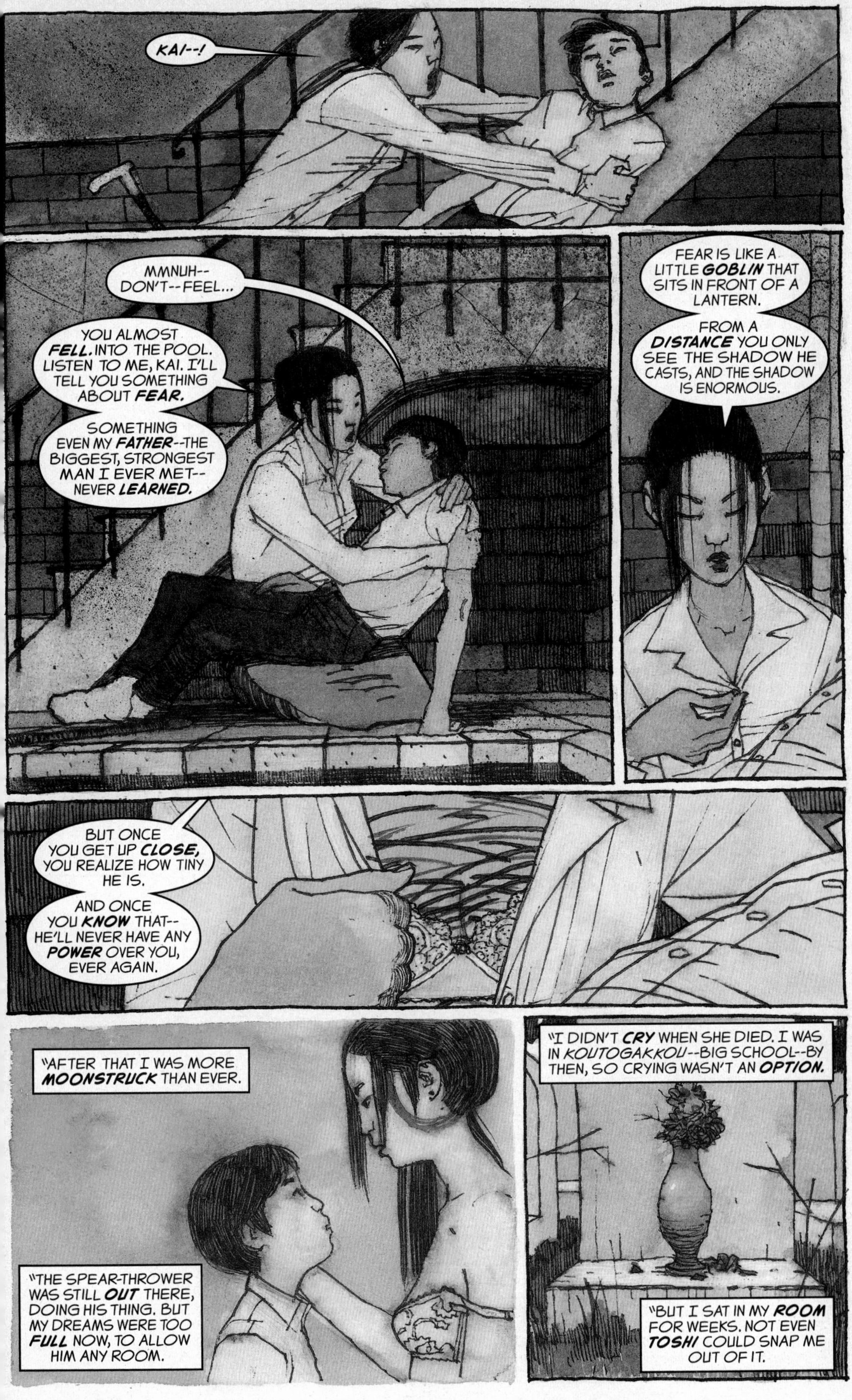
KAI--!
MMNUH-- DON'T--FEEL...
YOU ALMOST FELL. INTO THE POOL. LISTEN TO ME, KAI. I'LL TELL YOU SOMETHING ABOUT FEAR.
SOMETHING EVEN MY FATHER--THE BIGGEST, STRONGEST MAN I EVER MET-- NEVER LEARNED.
FEAR IS LIKE A LITTLE GOBLIN THAT SITS IN FRONT OF A LANTERN.
FROM A DISTANCE YOU ONLY SEE THE SHADOW HE CASTS, AND THE SHADOW IS ENORMOUS.
BUT ONCE YOU GET UP CLOSE, YOU REALIZE HOW TINY HE IS.
AND ONCE YOU KNOW THAT-- HE'LL NEVER HAVE ANY POWER OVER YOU, EVER AGAIN.
"AFTER THAT I WAS MORE MOONSTRUCK THAN EVER.
"THE SPEAR-THROWER WAS STILL OUT THERE, DOING HIS THING. BUT MY DREAMS WERE TOO FULL NOW, TO ALLOW HIM ANY ROOM.
"I DIDN'T CRY WHEN SHE DIED. I WAS IN KOUTOGAKKOU--BIG SCHOOL--BY THEN, SO CRYING WASN'T AN OPTION.
"BUT I SAT IN MY ROOM FOR WEEKS. NOT EVEN TOSHI COULD SNAP ME OUT OF IT.

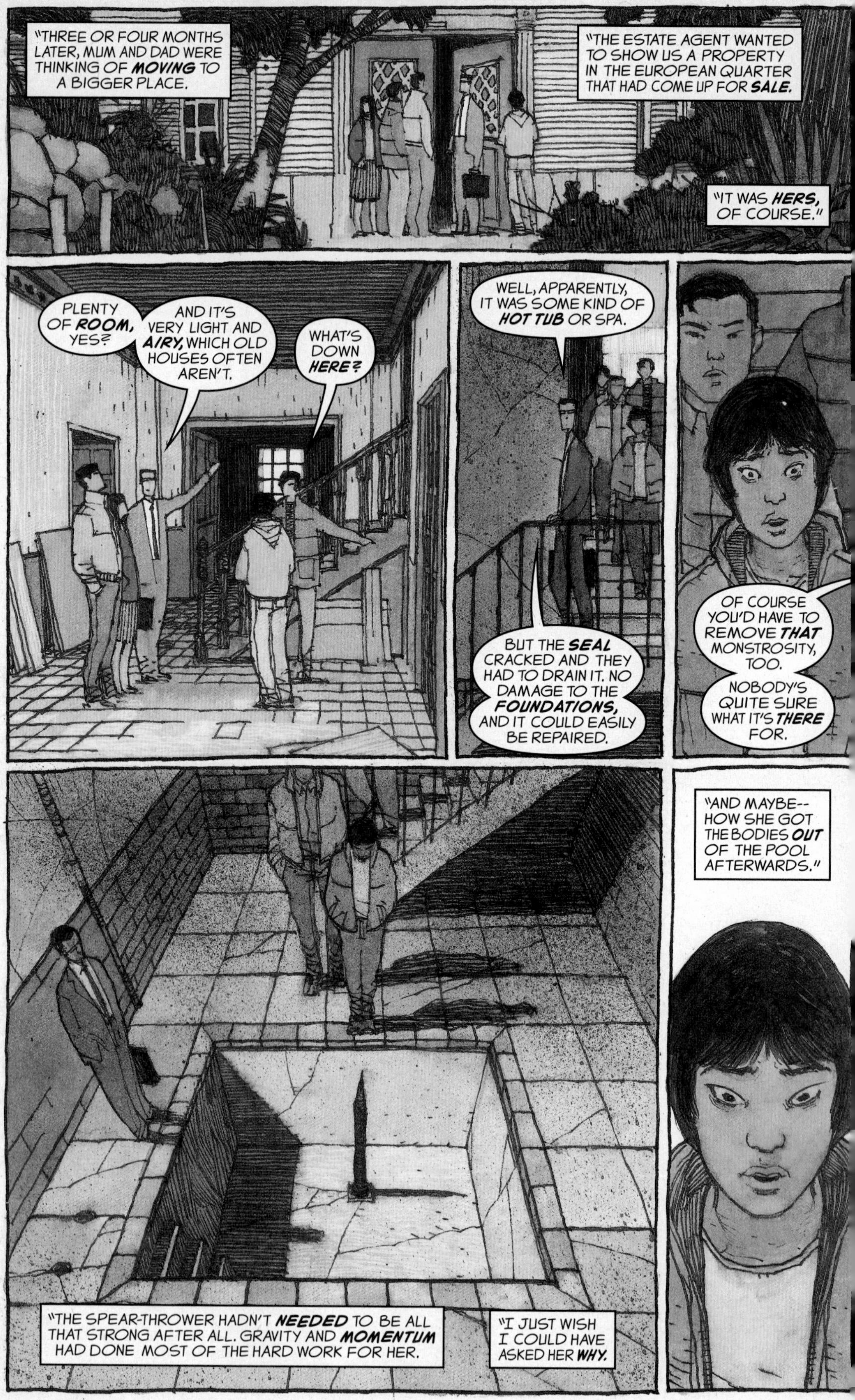
"THREE OR FOUR MONTHS LATER, MUM AND DAD WERE THINKING OF MOVING TO A BIGGER PLACE.
"THE ESTATE AGENT WANTED TO SHOW US A PROPERTY IN THE EUROPEAN QUARTER THAT HAD COME UP FOR SALE.
"IT WAS HERS, OF COURSE."
PLENTY OF ROOM, YES?
AND IT'S VERY LIGHT AND AIRY, WHICH OLD HOUSES OFTEN AREN'T.
WHAT'S DOWN HERE?
WELL, APPARENTLY, IT WAS SOME KIND OF HOT TUB OR SPA.
BUT THE SEAL CRACKED AND THEY HAD TO DRAIN IT. NO DAMAGE TO THE FOUNDATIONS, AND IT COULD EASILY BE REPAIRED.
OF COURSE YOU'D HAVE TO REMOVE THAT MONSTROSITY, TOO.
NOBODY'S QUITE SURE WHAT IT'S THERE FOR.
"THE SPEAR-THROWER HADN'T NEEDED TO BE ALL THAT STRONG AFTER ALL. GRAVITY AND MOMENTUM HAD DONE MOST OF THE HARD WORK FOR HER.
"I JUST WISH I COULD HAVE ASKED HER WHY.
"AND MAYBE-- HOW SHE GOT THE BODIES OUT OF THE POOL AFTERWARDS."

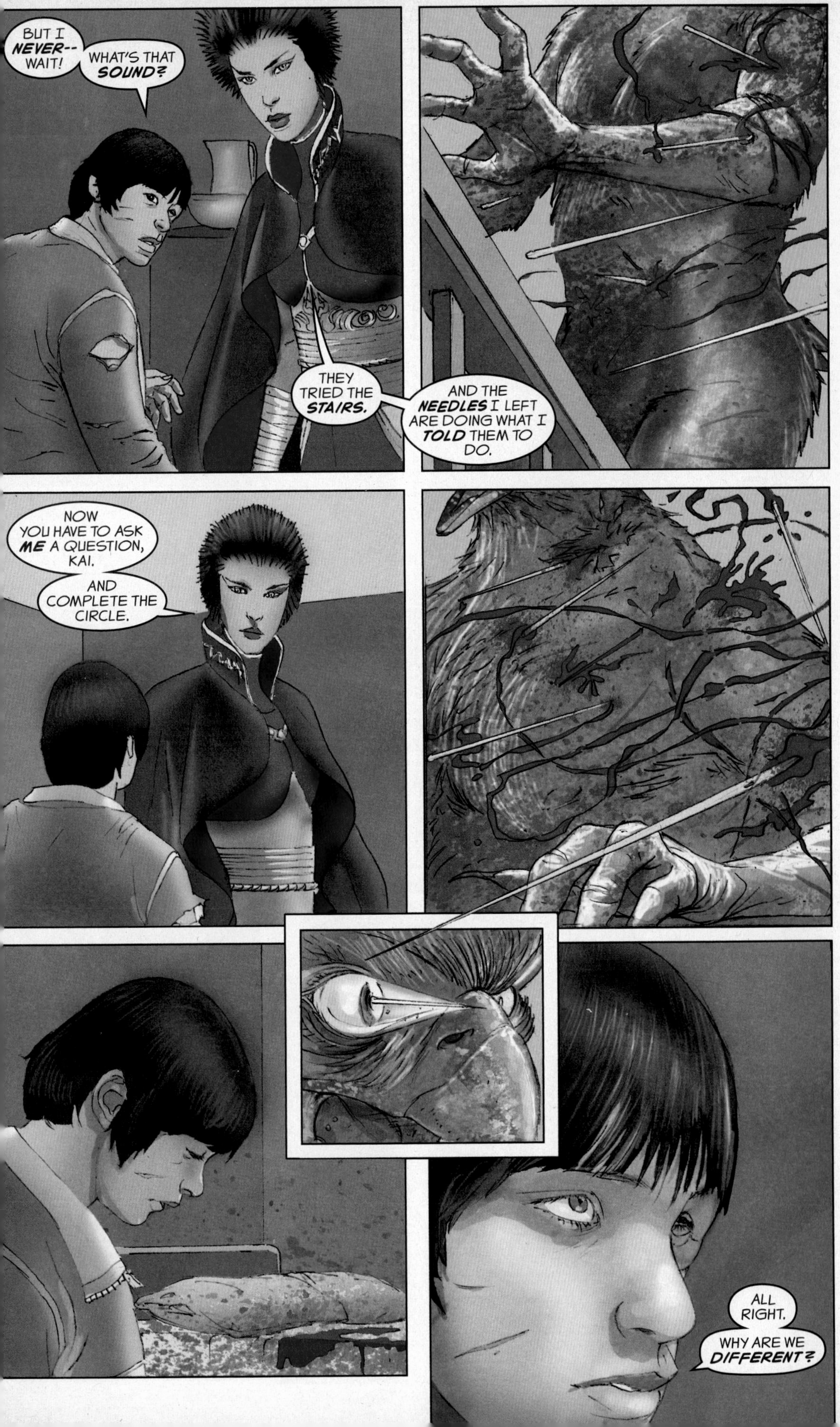
BUT I NEVER-- WAIT!
WHAT'S THAT SOUND?
THEY TRIED THE STAIRS.
AND THE NEEDLES I LEFT ARE DOING WHAT I TOLD THEM TO DO.
NOW YOU HAVE TO ASK ME A QUESTION, KAI.
AND COMPLETE THE CIRCLE.
ALL RIGHT.
WHY ARE WE DIFFERENT?

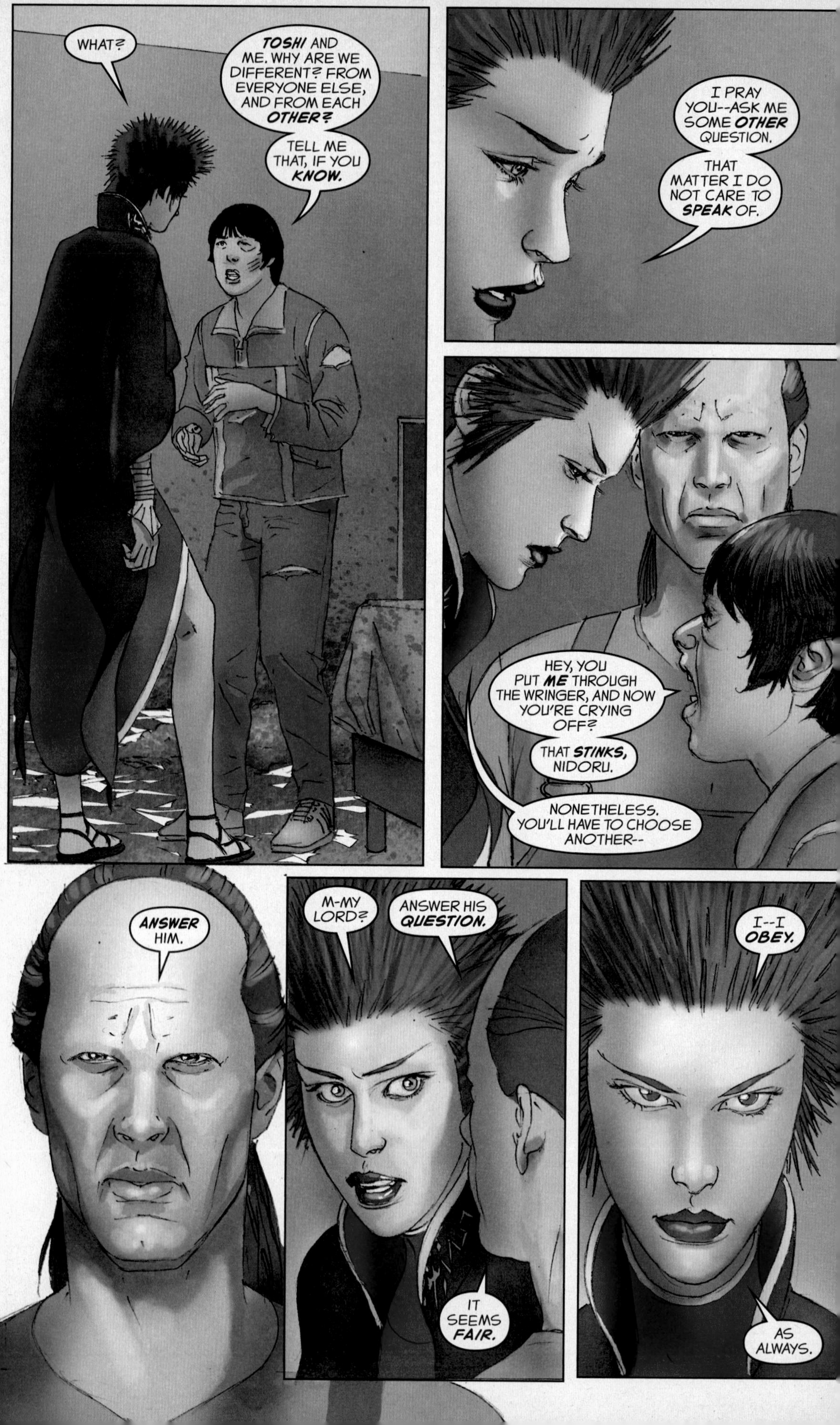
WHAT?
TOSHI AND ME. WHY ARE WE DIFFERENT? FROM EVERYONE ELSE, AND FROM EACH OTHER?
TELL ME THAT, IF YOU KNOW.
I PRAY YOU--ASK ME SOME OTHER QUESTION.
THAT MATTER I DO NOT CARE TO SPEAK OF.
HEY, YOU PUT ME THROUGH THE WRINGER, AND NOW YOU'RE CRYING OFF?
THAT STINKS, NIDORU.
NONETHELESS. YOU'LL HAVE TO CHOOSE ANOTHER--
ANSWER HIM.
M-MY LORD?
ANSWER HIS QUESTION.
IT SEEMS FAIR.
I--I OBEY.
AS ALWAYS.

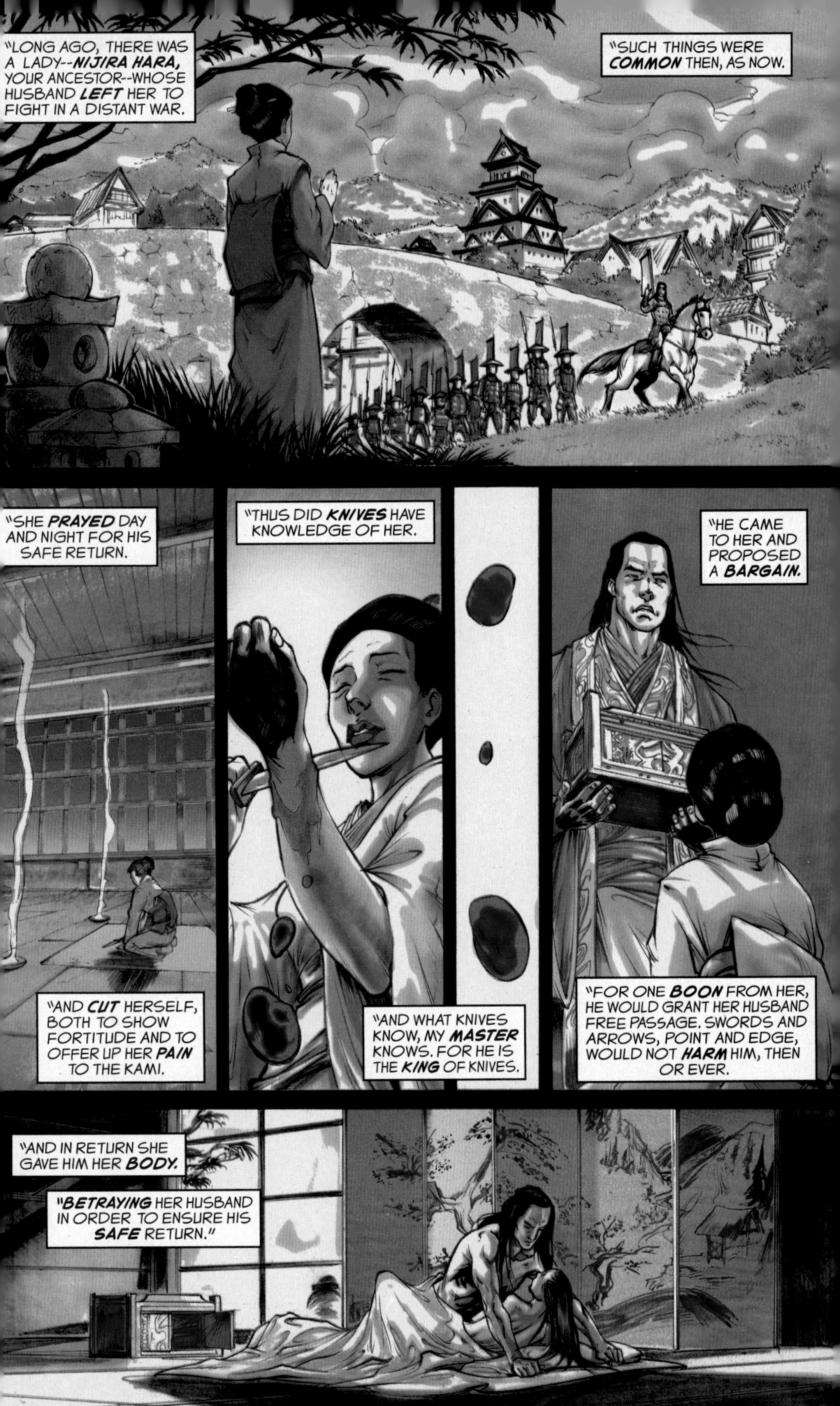
"LONG AGO, THERE WAS A LADY--NIJIRA HARA, YOUR ANCESTOR--WHOSE HUSBAND LEFT HER TO FIGHT IN A DISTANT WAR.
"SUCH THINGS WERE COMMON THEN, AS NOW.
"SHE PRAYED DAY AND NIGHT FOR HIS SAFE RETURN.
"AND CUT HERSELF, BOTH TO SHOW FORTITUDE AND TO OFFER UP HER PAIN TO THE KAMI.
"THUS DID KNIVES HAVE KNOWLEDGE OF HER.
"AND WHAT KNIVES KNOW, MY MASTER KNOWS. FOR HE IS THE KING OF KNIVES.
"HE CAME TO HER AND PROPOSED A BARGAIN.
"FOR ONE BOON FROM HER, HE WOULD GRANT HER HUSBAND FREE PASSAGE. SWORDS AND ARROWS, POINT AND EDGE, WOULD NOT HARM HIM, THEN OR EVER.
"AND IN RETURN SHE GAVE HIM HER BODY.
"BETRAYING HER HUSBAND IN ORDER TO ENSURE HIS SAFE RETURN."

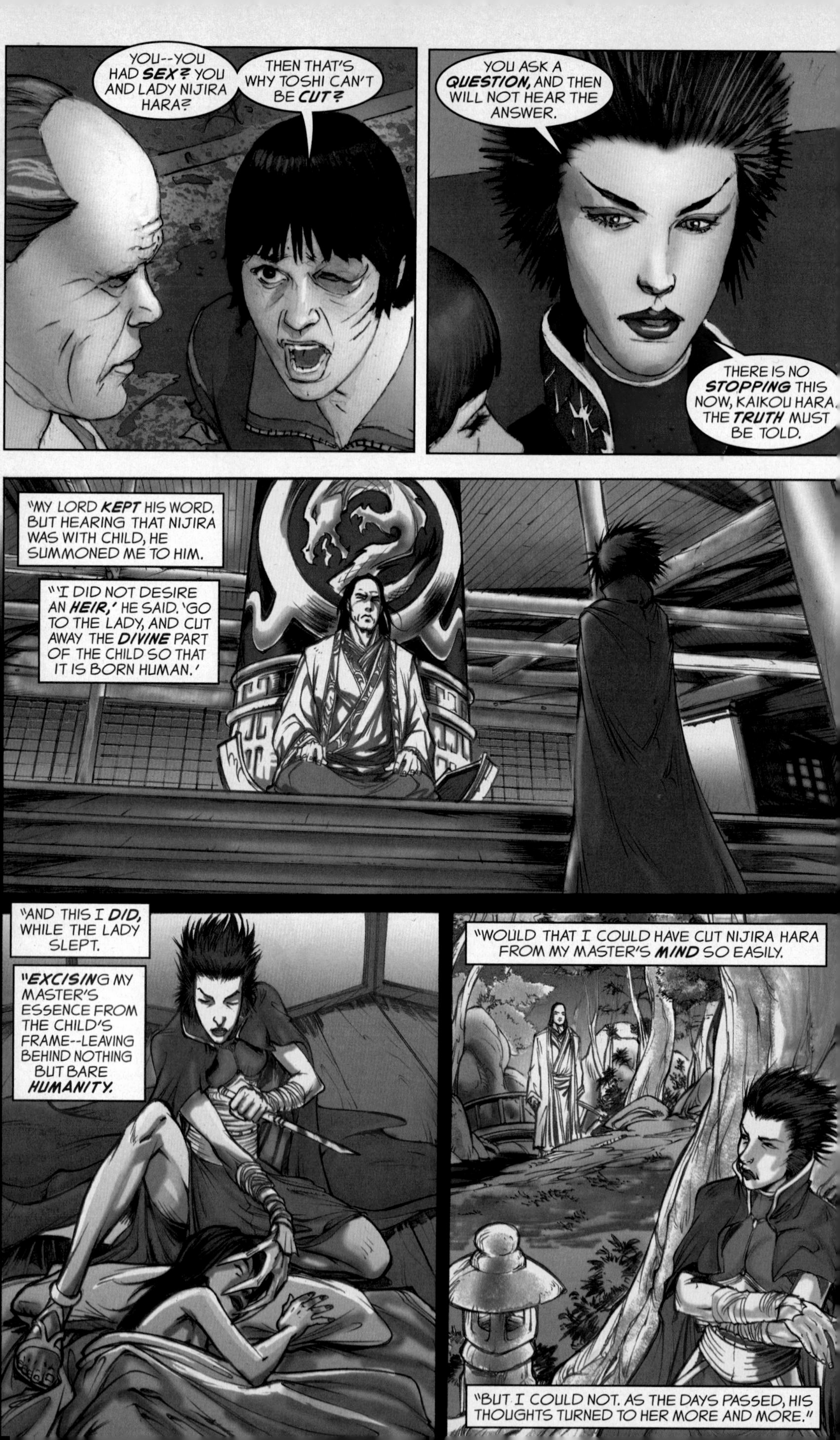
YOU--YOU HAD SEX? YOU AND LADY NIJIRA HARA?
THEN THAT'S WHY TOSHI CAN'T BE CUT?
YOU ASK A QUESTION, AND THEN WILL NOT HEAR THE ANSWER.
THERE IS NO STOPPING THIS NOW, KAIKOU HARA. THE TRUTH MUST BE TOLD.
"MY LORD KEPT HIS WORD. BUT HEARING THAT NIJIRA WAS WITH CHILD, HE SUMMONED ME TO HIM.
"'I DID NOT DESIRE AN HEIR,' HE SAID. 'GO TO THE LADY, AND CUT AWAY THE DIVINE PART OF THE CHILD SO THAT IT IS BORN HUMAN.'
"AND THIS I DID, WHILE THE LADY SLEPT.
"EXCISING MY MASTER'S ESSENCE FROM THE CHILD'S FRAME--LEAVING BEHIND NOTHING BUT BARE HUMANITY.
"WOULD THAT I COULD HAVE CUT NIJIRA HARA FROM MY MASTER'S MIND SO EASILY.
"BUT I COULD NOT. AS THE DAYS PASSED, HIS THOUGHTS TURNED TO HER MORE AND MORE."

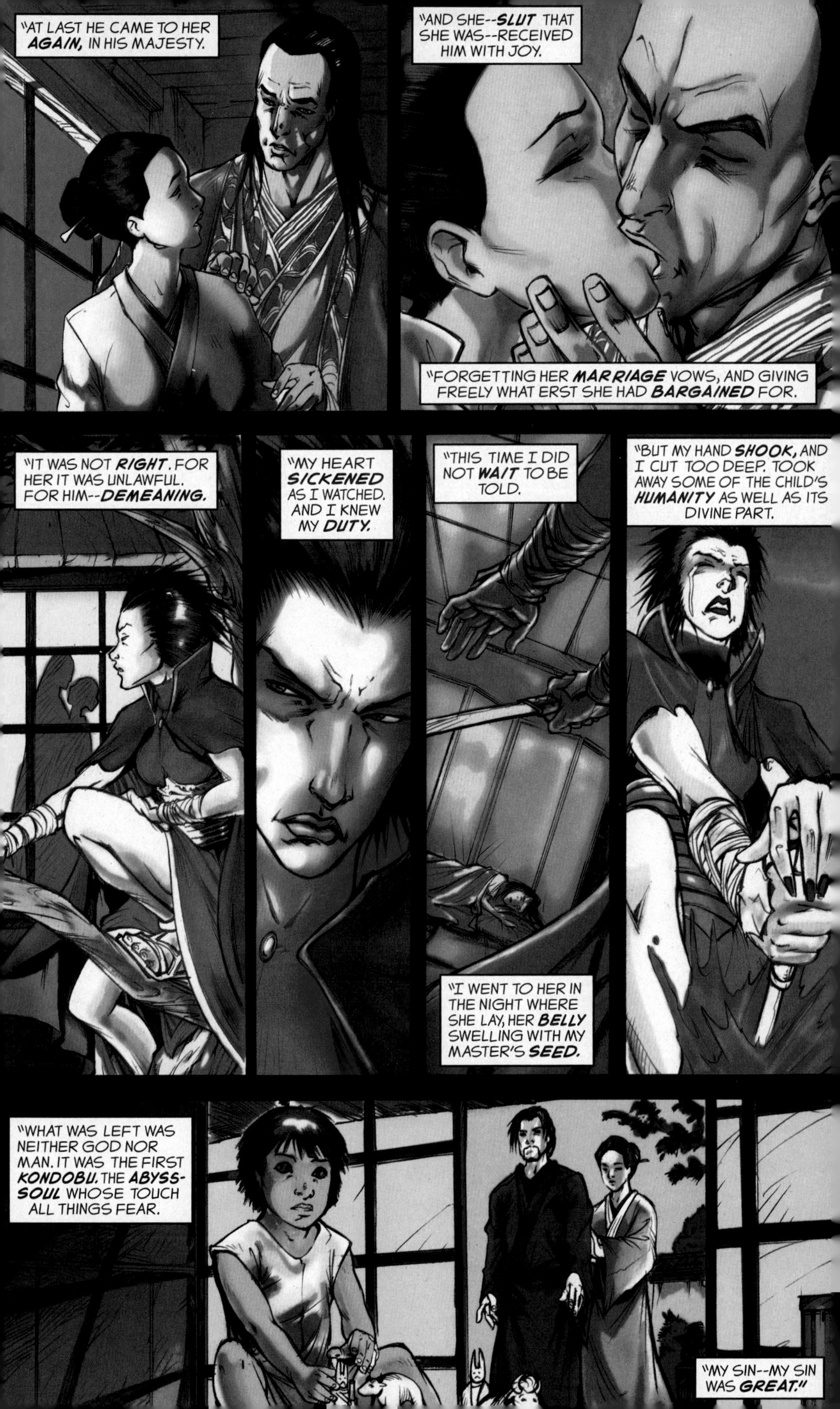
"AT LAST HE CAME TO HER AGAIN, IN HIS MAJESTY.
"AND SHE--SLUT THAT SHE WAS--RECEIVED HIM WITH JOY.
"FORGETTING HER MARRIAGE VOWS, AND GIVING FREELY WHAT ERST SHE HAD BARGAINED FOR.
"IT WAS NOT RIGHT. FOR HER IT WAS UNLAWFUL. FOR HIM--DEMEANING.
"MY HEART SICKENED AS I WATCHED. AND I KNEW MY DUTY.
"THIS TIME I DID NOT WAIT TO BE TOLD.
"I WENT TO HER IN THE NIGHT WHERE SHE LAY, HER BELLY SWELLING WITH MY MASTER'S SEED.
"BUT MY HAND SHOOK, AND I CUT TOO DEEP. TOOK AWAY SOME OF THE CHILD'S HUMANITY AS WELL AS ITS DIVINE PART.
"WHAT WAS LEFT WAS NEITHER GOD NOR MAN. IT WAS THE FIRST KONDOBU. THE ABYSS-SOUL WHOSE TOUCH ALL THINGS FEAR.
"MY SIN--MY SIN WAS GREAT."

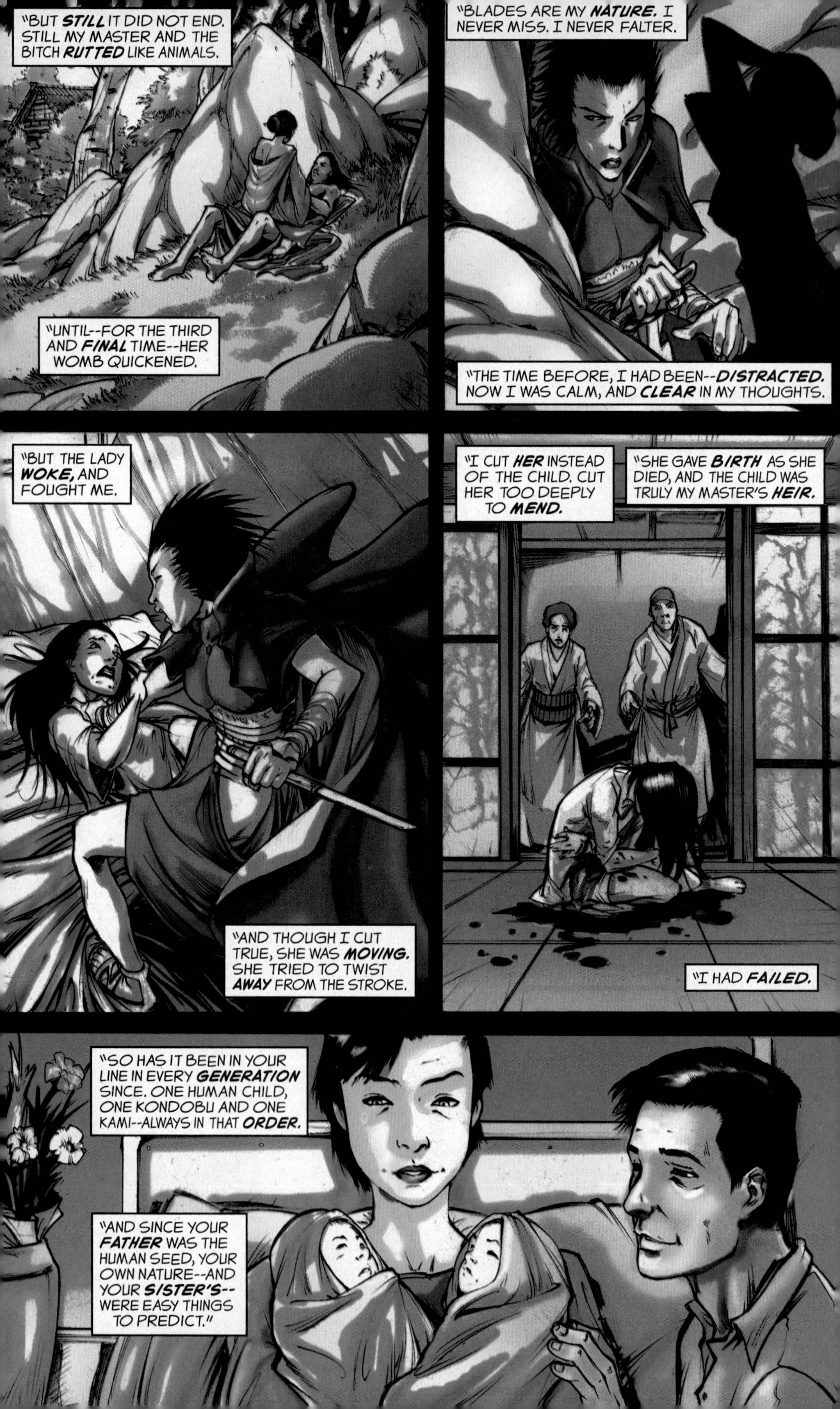
"BUT STILL IT DID NOT END. STILL MY MASTER AND THE BITCH RUTTED LIKE ANIMALS.
"UNTIL--FOR THE THIRD AND FINAL TIME--HER WOMB QUICKENED.
"BLADES ARE MY NATURE. I NEVER MISS. I NEVER FALTER.
"THE TIME BEFORE, I HAD BEEN--DISTRACTED. NOW I WAS CALM, AND CLEAR IN MY THOUGHTS.
"BUT THE LADY WOKE, AND FOUGHT ME.
"AND THOUGH I CUT TRUE, SHE WAS MOVING. SHE TRIED TO TWIST AWAY FROM THE STROKE.
"I CUT HER INSTEAD OF THE CHILD. CUT HER TOO DEEPLY TO MEND.
"SHE GAVE BIRTH AS SHE DIED, AND THE CHILD WAS TRULY MY MASTER'S HEIR.
"I HAD FAILED.
"SO HAS IT BEEN IN YOUR LINE IN EVERY GENERATION SINCE. ONE HUMAN CHILD, ONE KONDOBU AND ONE KAMI--ALWAYS IN THAT ORDER.
"AND SINCE YOUR FATHER WAS THE HUMAN SEED, YOUR OWN NATURE--AND YOUR SISTER'S--WERE EASY THINGS TO PREDICT."

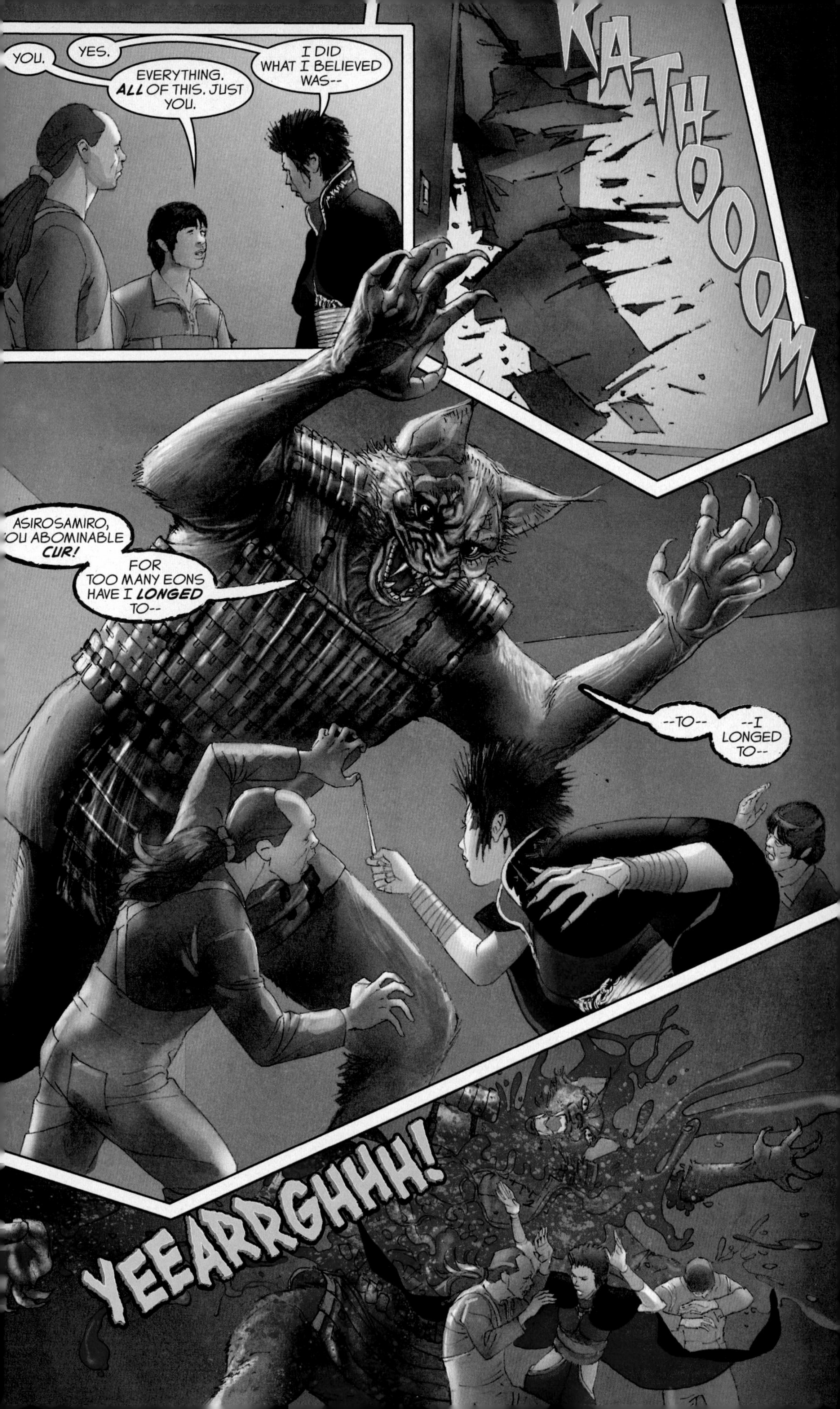
YOU.
YES.
EVERYTHING. ALL OF THIS. JUST YOU.
I DID WHAT I BELIEVED WAS--
KATHOOOOM
ASIROSAMIRO, YOU ABOMINABLE CUR!
FOR TOO MANY EONS HAVE I LONGED TO--
--TO--
--I LONGED TO--
YEEARRGHHH!

M-MY GOD!

THE WALL OF WORDS HELD.

YOU SPOKE *TRULY* ABOUT YOUR FEARS.

AND SO DID *YOU*, ABOUT YOUR SIN.

YES. THOUGH I WISH WITH ALL MY *HEART* THAT I COULD HAVE LIED.

I SEE YOUR PAIN IN YOUR FACE, AND IT *SHAME* ME. I CAN ONLY OFFER--

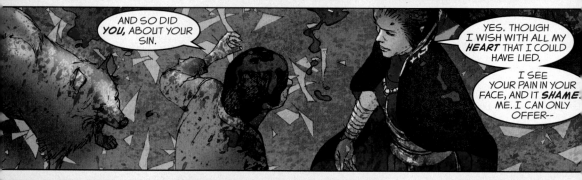

NO, NO, NIDORU. PLEASE!

LET'S HAVE NO TALK OF *SHAME*.

THIS IS A *JOYOUS* OCCASION. MINSTRELS SHOULD SING, AND MUSICIANS *PLAY* FOR US.

FIREWORKS SHOULD PAINT THE SKIES.

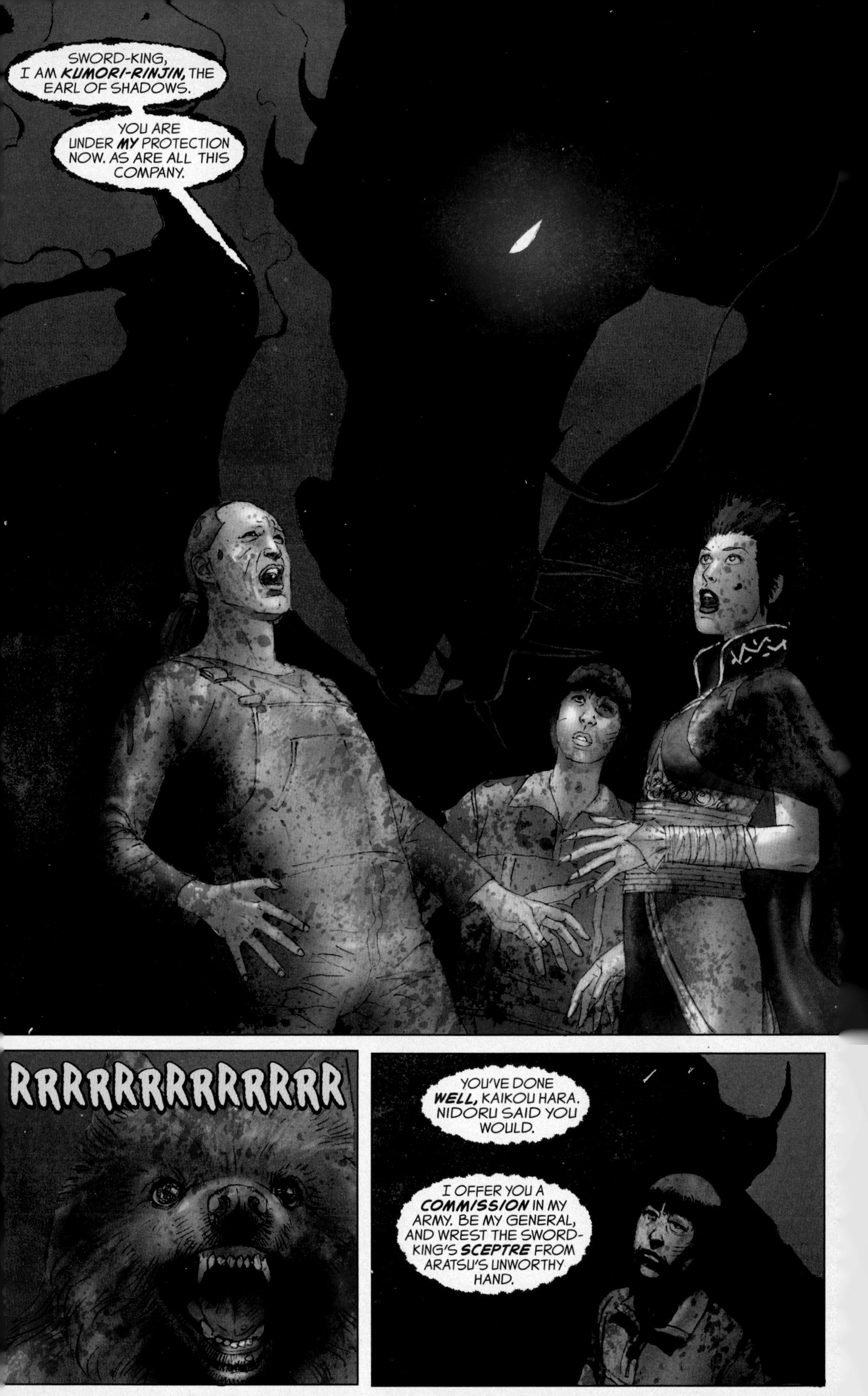
SWORD-KING, I AM KUMORI-RINJIN, THE EARL OF SHADOWS.
YOU ARE UNDER MY PROTECTION NOW. AS ARE ALL THIS COMPANY.
RRRRRRRRRRRRRR
YOU'VE DONE WELL, KAIKOU HARA. NIDORU SAID YOU WOULD.
I OFFER YOU A COMMISSION IN MY ARMY. BE MY GENERAL, AND WREST THE SWORD-KING'S SCEPTRE FROM ARATSU'S UNWORTHY HAND.

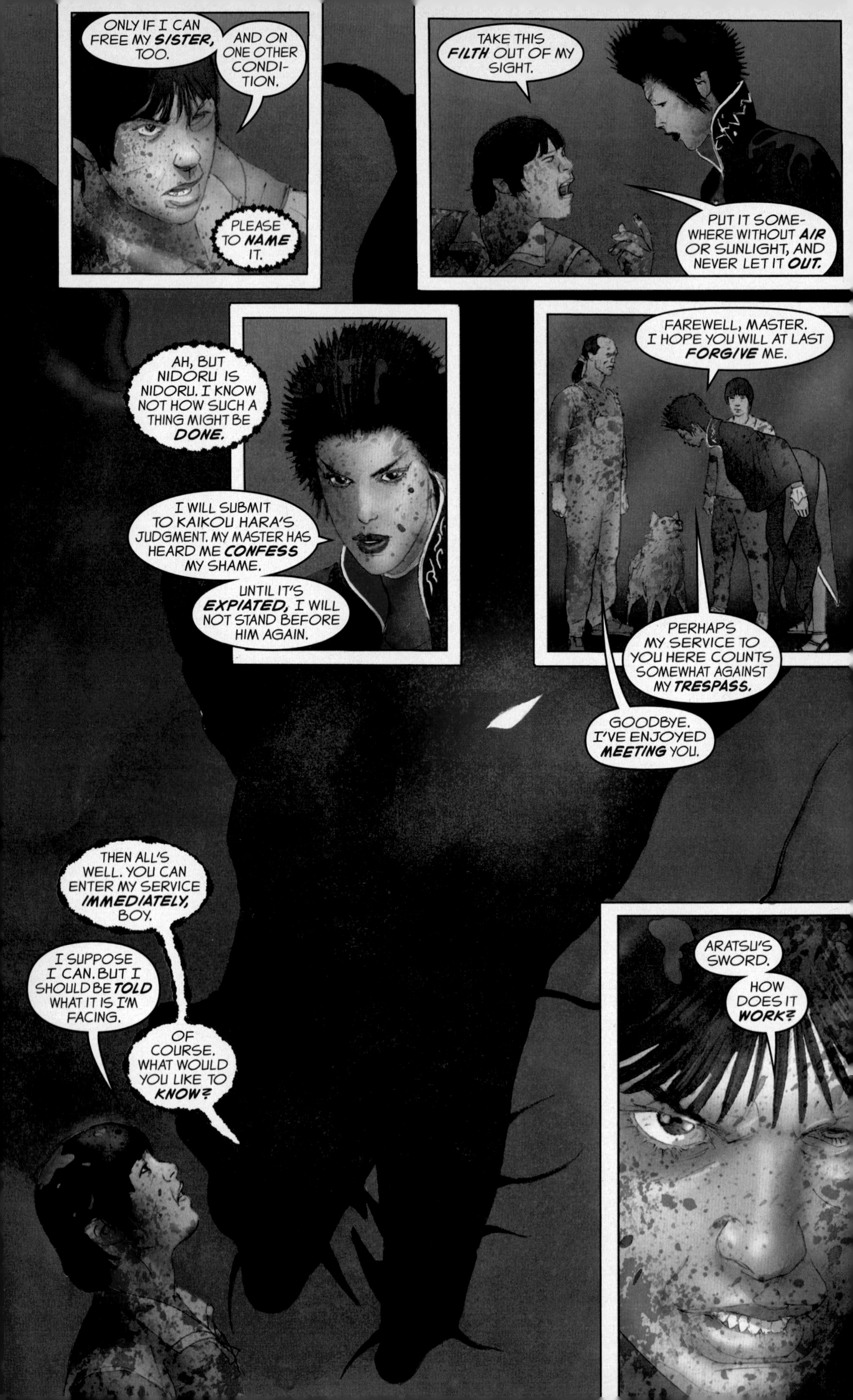
ONLY IF I CAN FREE MY SISTER, TOO.
AND ON ONE OTHER CONDITION.
PLEASE TO NAME IT.
TAKE THIS FILTH OUT OF MY SIGHT.
PUT IT SOMEWHERE WITHOUT AIR OR SUNLIGHT, AND NEVER LET IT OUT.
AH, BUT NIDORU IS NIDORU. I KNOW NOT HOW SUCH A THING MIGHT BE DONE.
I WILL SUBMIT TO KAIKOU HARA'S JUDGMENT. MY MASTER HAS HEARD ME CONFESS MY SHAME.
UNTIL IT'S EXPIATED, I WILL NOT STAND BEFORE HIM AGAIN.
FAREWELL, MASTER. I HOPE YOU WILL AT LAST FORGIVE ME.
PERHAPS MY SERVICE TO YOU HERE COUNTS SOMEWHAT AGAINST MY TRESPASS.
GOODBYE. I'VE ENJOYED MEETING YOU.
THEN ALL'S WELL. YOU CAN ENTER MY SERVICE IMMEDIATELY, BOY.
I SUPPOSE I CAN. BUT I SHOULD BE TOLD WHAT IT IS I'M FACING.
OF COURSE. WHAT WOULD YOU LIKE TO KNOW?
ARATSU'S SWORD.
HOW DOES IT WORK?

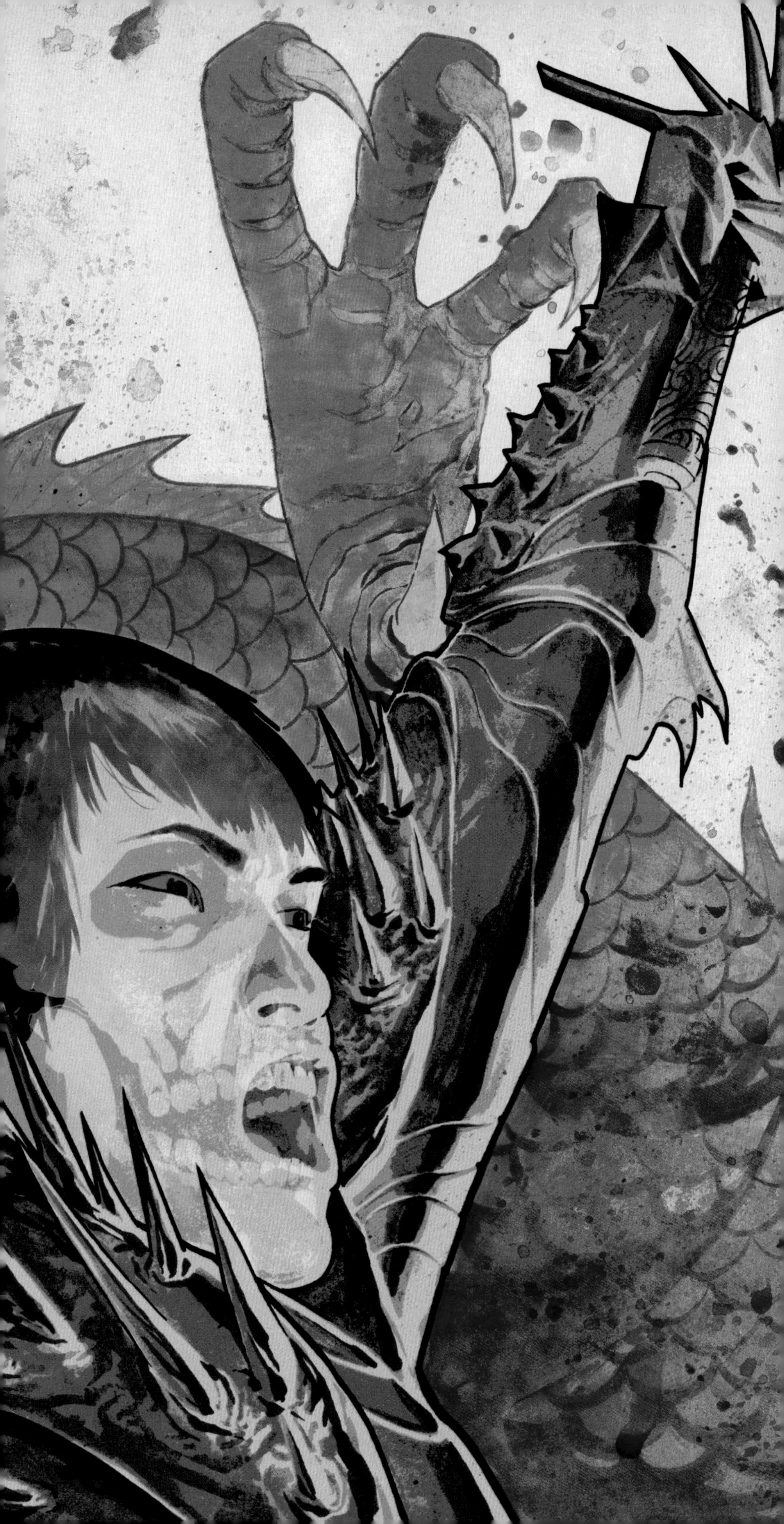

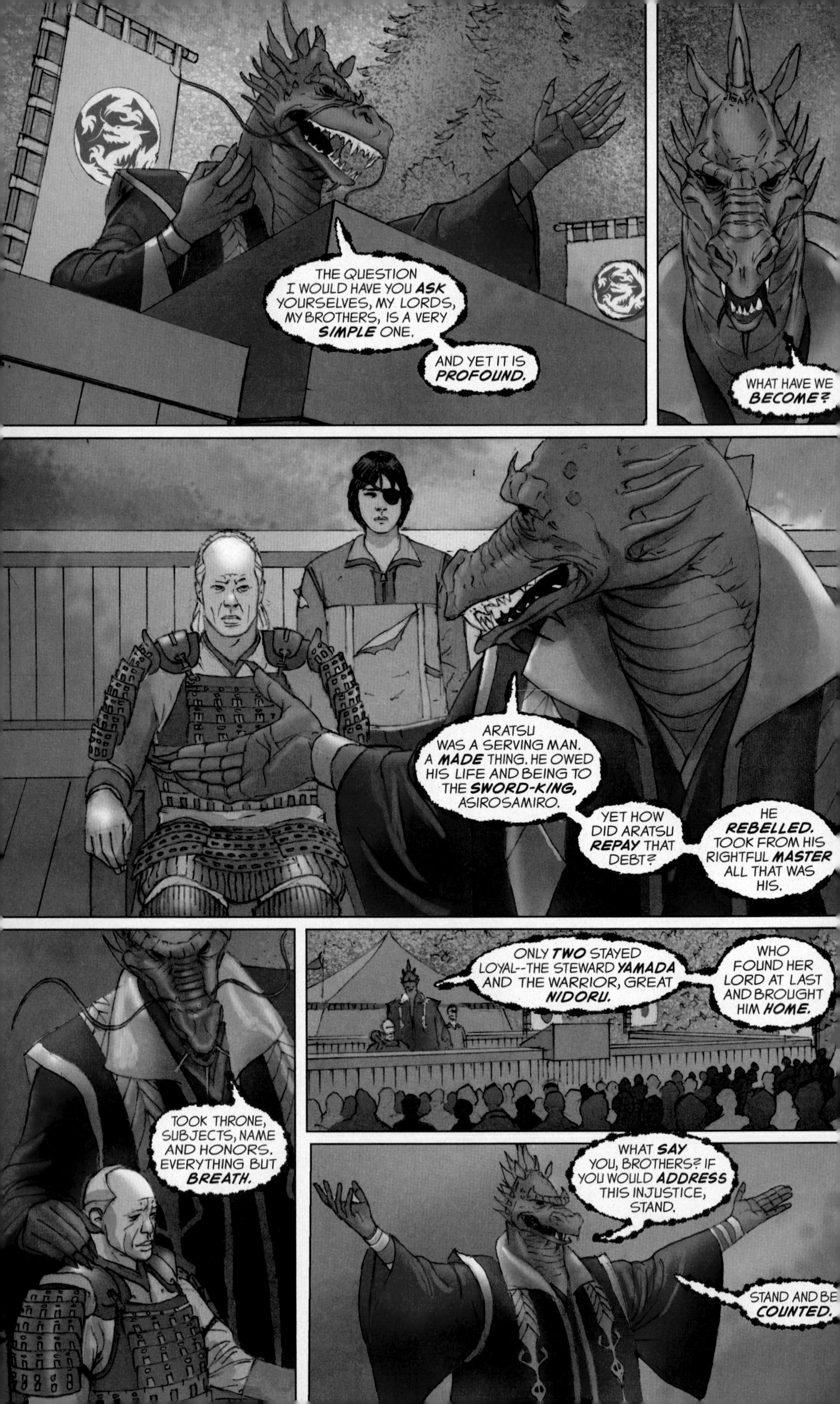
THE QUESTION I WOULD HAVE YOU ASK YOURSELVES, MY LORDS, MY BROTHERS, IS A VERY SIMPLE ONE.
AND YET IT IS PROFOUND.
WHAT HAVE WE BECOME?
ARATSU WAS A SERVING MAN. A MADE THING. HE OWED HIS LIFE AND BEING TO THE SWORD-KING, ASIROSAMIRO.
YET HOW DID ARATSU REPAY THAT DEBT?
HE REBELLED. TOOK FROM HIS RIGHTFUL MASTER ALL THAT WAS HIS.
TOOK THRONE, SUBJECTS, NAME AND HONORS. EVERYTHING BUT BREATH.
ONLY TWO STAYED LOYAL--THE STEWARD YAMADA AND THE WARRIOR, GREAT NIDORU.
WHO FOUND HER LORD AT LAST AND BROUGHT HIM HOME.
WHAT SAY YOU, BROTHERS? IF YOU WOULD ADDRESS THIS INJUSTICE, STAND.
STAND AND BE COUNTED.

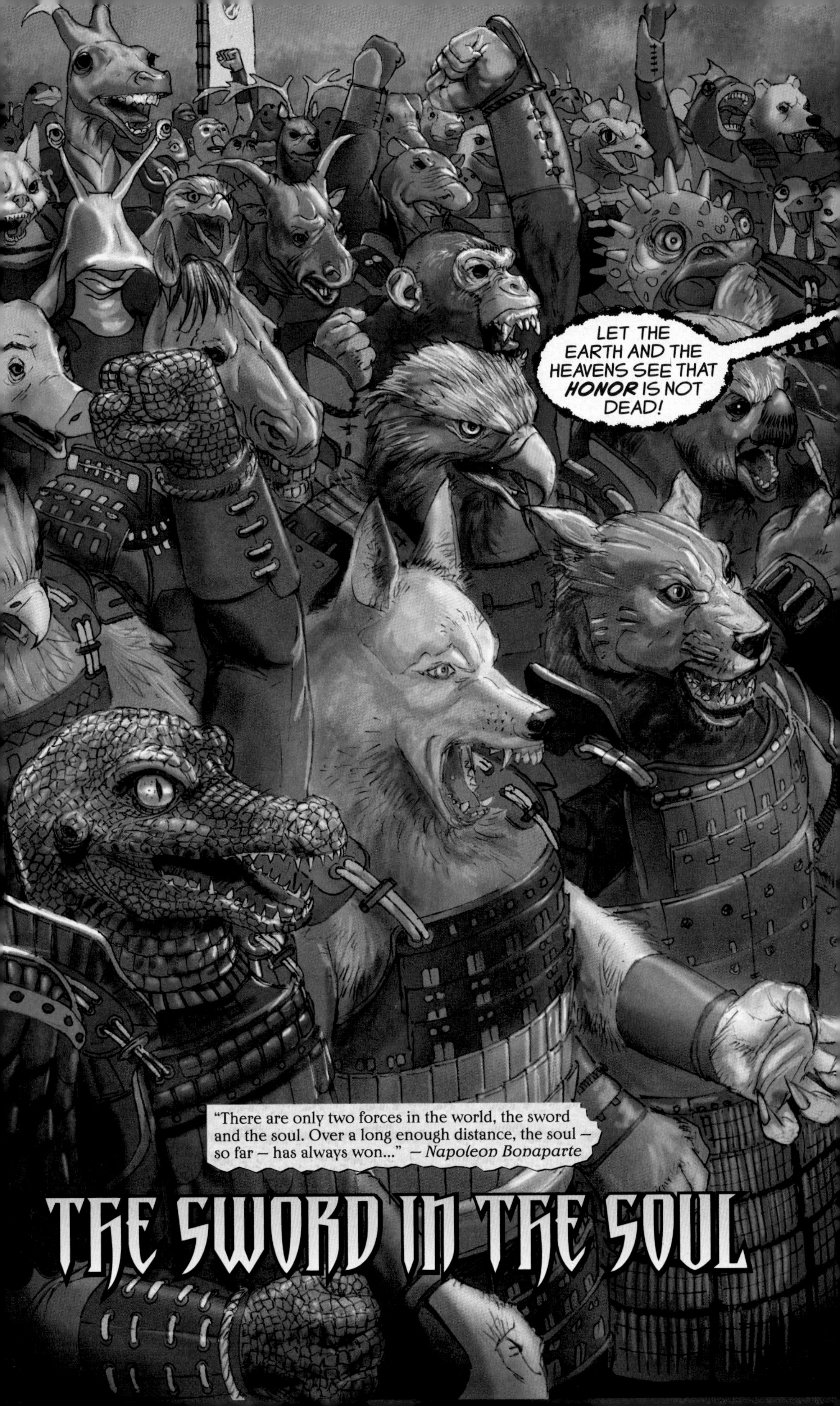
LET THE EARTH AND THE HEAVENS SEE THAT HONOR IS NOT DEAD!
"There are only two forces in the world, the sword and the soul. Over a long enough distance, the soul — so far — has always won..." — Napoleon Bonaparte
THE SWORD IN THE SOUL

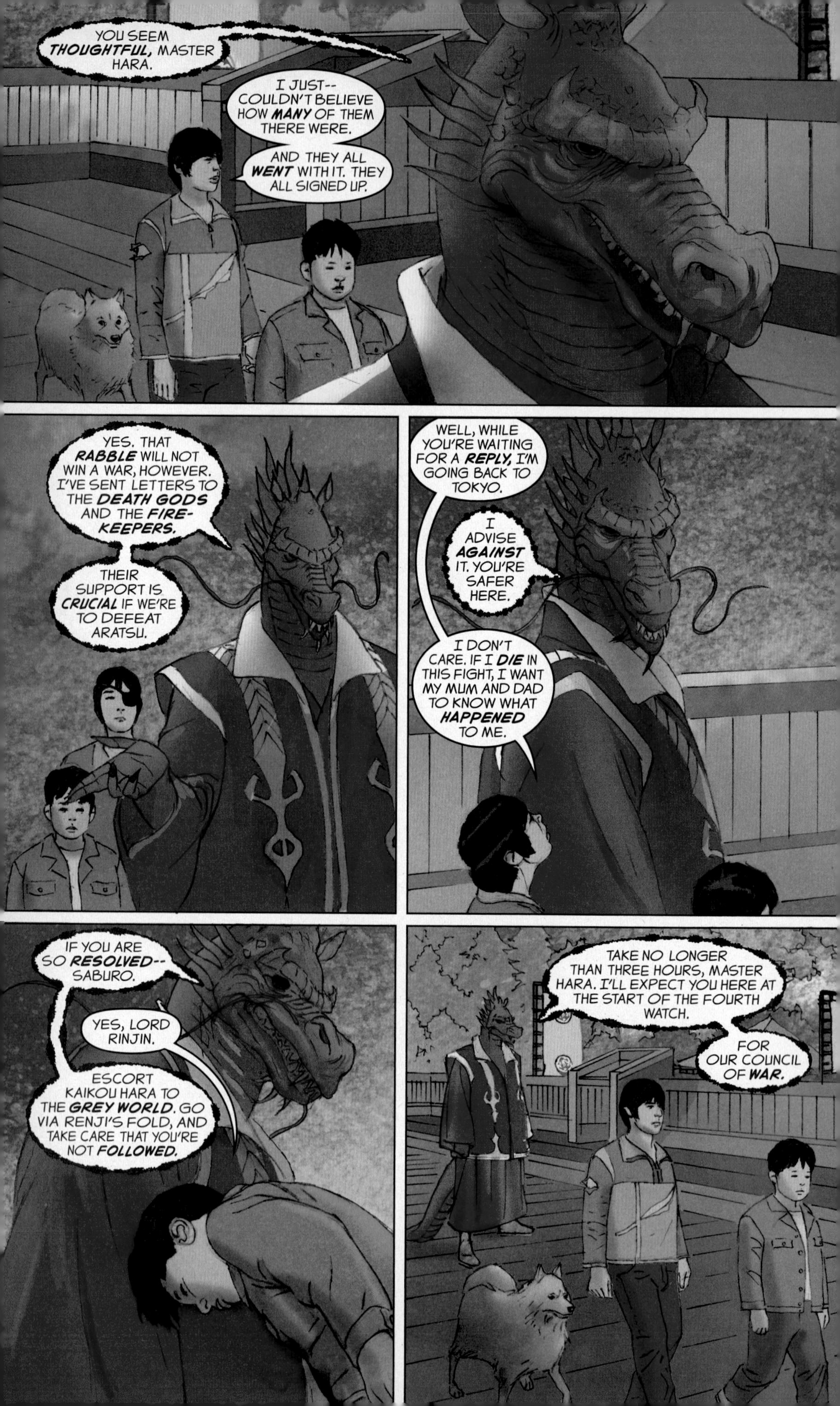
YOU SEEM THOUGHTFUL, MASTER HARA.
I JUST-- COULDN'T BELIEVE HOW MANY OF THEM THERE WERE.
AND THEY ALL WENT WITH IT. THEY ALL SIGNED UP.
YES. THAT RABBLE WILL NOT WIN A WAR, HOWEVER. I'VE SENT LETTERS TO THE DEATH GODS AND THE FIRE-KEEPERS.
THEIR SUPPORT IS CRUCIAL IF WE'RE TO DEFEAT ARATSU.
WELL, WHILE YOU'RE WAITING FOR A REPLY, I'M GOING BACK TO TOKYO.
I ADVISE AGAINST IT. YOU'RE SAFER HERE.
I DON'T CARE. IF I DIE IN THIS FIGHT, I WANT MY MUM AND DAD TO KNOW WHAT HAPPENED TO ME.
IF YOU ARE SO RESOLVED-- SABURO.
YES, LORD RINJIN.
ESCORT KAIKOU HARA TO THE GREY WORLD. GO VIA RENJI'S FOLD, AND TAKE CARE THAT YOU'RE NOT FOLLOWED.
TAKE NO LONGER THAN THREE HOURS, MASTER HARA. I'LL EXPECT YOU HERE AT THE START OF THE FOURTH WATCH.
FOR OUR COUNCIL OF WAR.

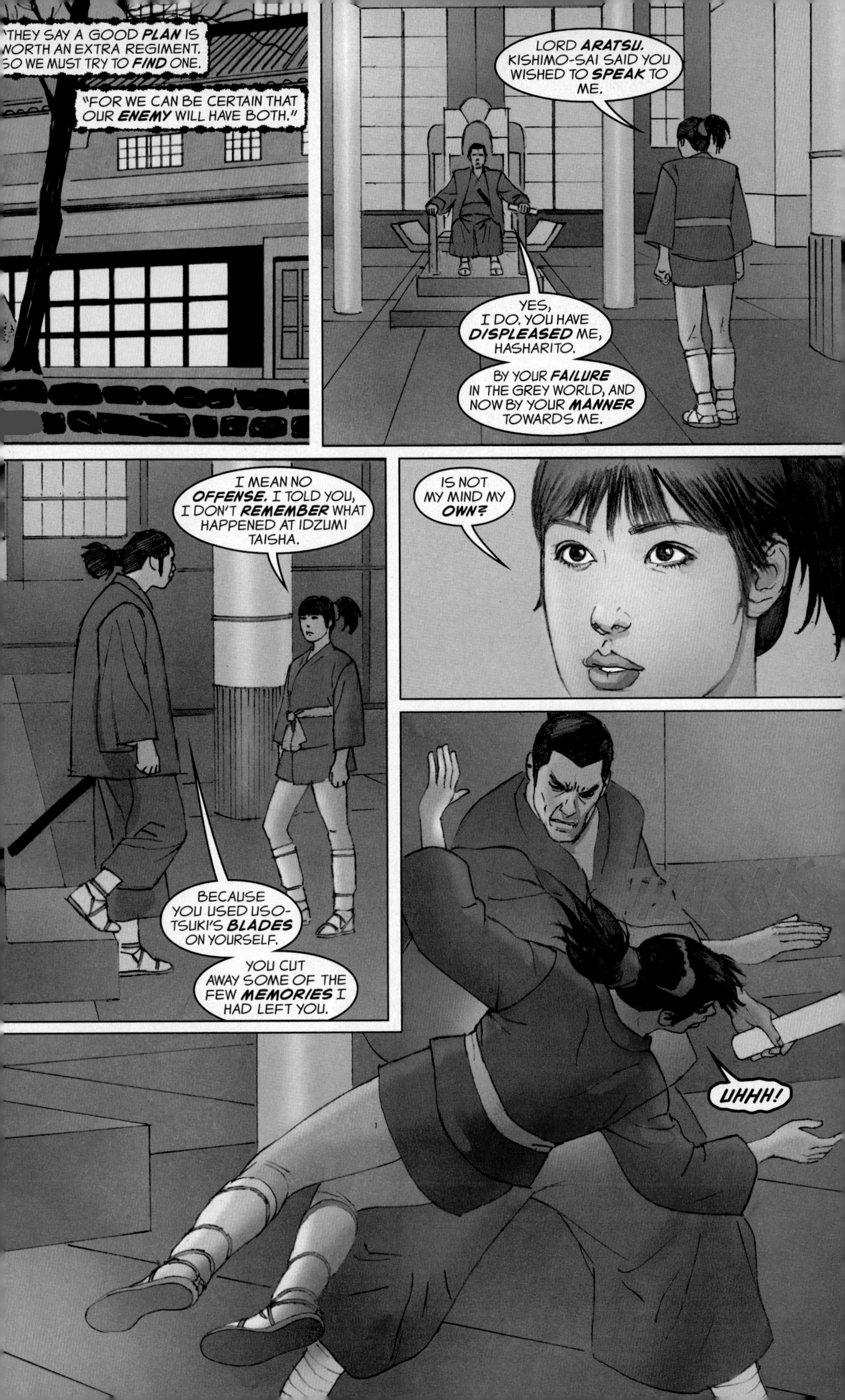
"THEY SAY A GOOD PLAN IS WORTH AN EXTRA REGIMENT. SO WE MUST TRY TO FIND ONE.
"FOR WE CAN BE CERTAIN THAT OUR ENEMY WILL HAVE BOTH."
LORD ARATSU. KISHIMO-SAI SAID YOU WISHED TO SPEAK TO ME.
YES, I DO. YOU HAVE DISPLEASED ME, HASHARITO.
BY YOUR FAILURE IN THE GREY WORLD, AND NOW BY YOUR MANNER TOWARDS ME.
I MEAN NO OFFENSE. I TOLD YOU, I DON'T REMEMBER WHAT HAPPENED AT IDZUMI TAISHA.
BECAUSE YOU USED USO-TSUKI'S BLADES ON YOURSELF.
YOU CUT AWAY SOME OF THE FEW MEMORIES I HAD LEFT YOU.
IS NOT MY MIND MY OWN?
UHHH!

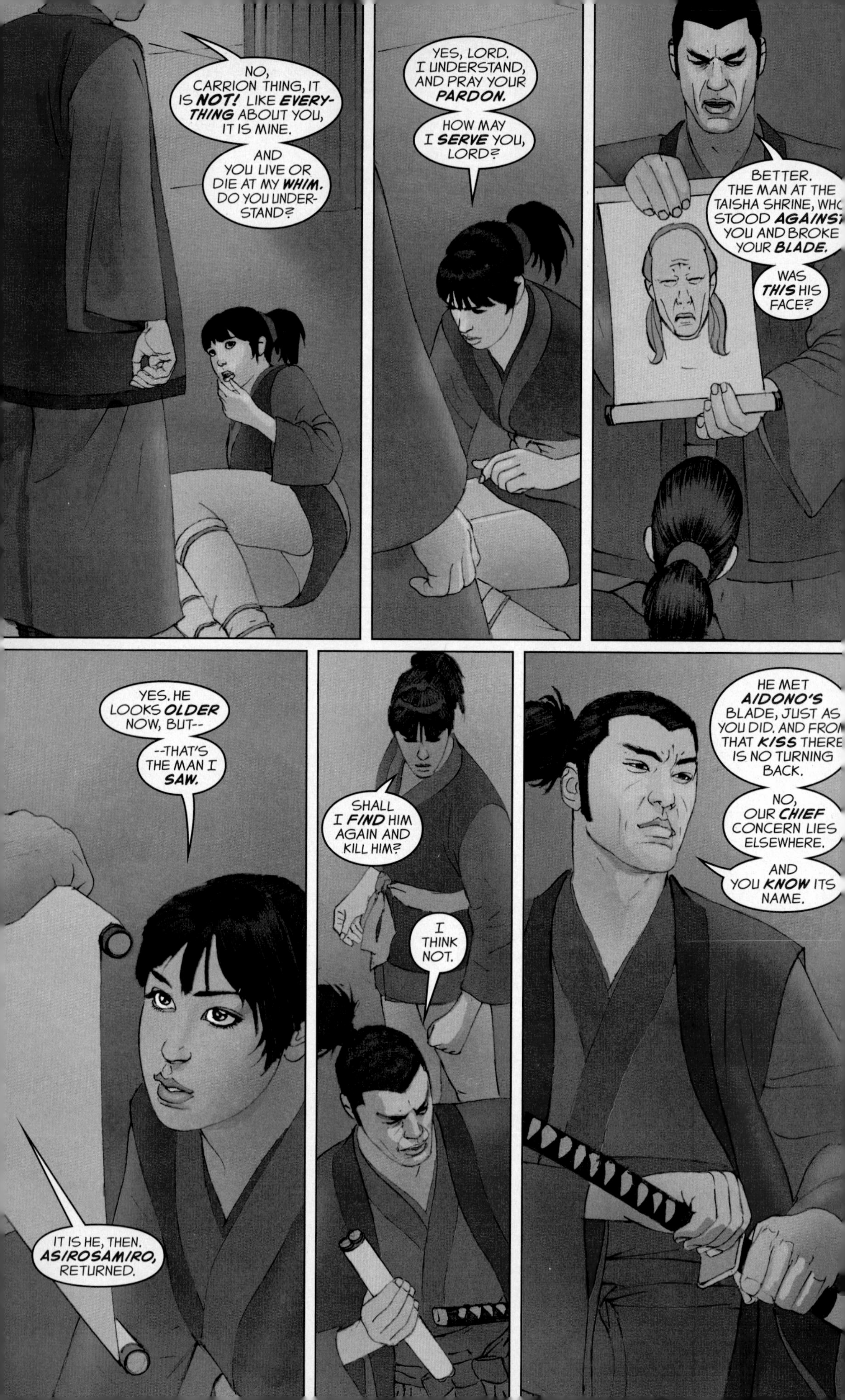
NO, CARRION THING, IT IS NOT! LIKE EVERYTHING ABOUT YOU, IT IS MINE.
AND YOU LIVE OR DIE AT MY WHIM. DO YOU UNDERSTAND?
YES, LORD. I UNDERSTAND, AND PRAY YOUR PARDON.
HOW MAY I SERVE YOU, LORD?
BETTER. THE MAN AT THE TAISHA SHRINE, WHO STOOD AGAINST YOU AND BROKE YOUR BLADE.
WAS THIS HIS FACE?
YES. HE LOOKS OLDER NOW, BUT--
--THAT'S THE MAN I SAW.
IT IS HE, THEN. ASIROSAMIRO, RETURNED.
SHALL I FIND HIM AGAIN AND KILL HIM?
I THINK NOT.
HE MET AIDONO'S BLADE, JUST AS YOU DID. AND FROM THAT KISS THERE IS NO TURNING BACK.
NO, OUR CHIEF CONCERN LIES ELSEWHERE.
AND YOU KNOW ITS NAME.

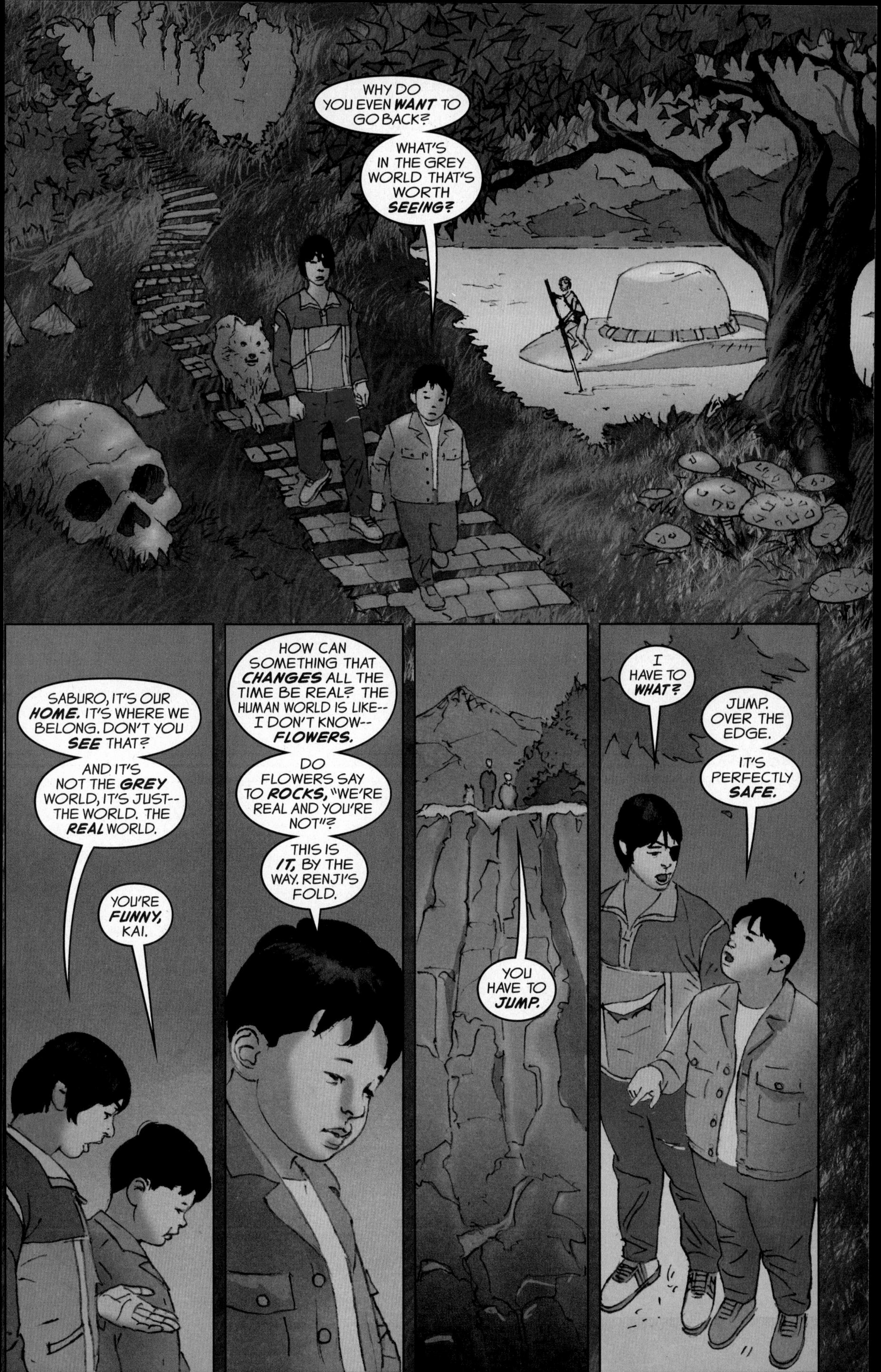
WHY DO YOU EVEN WANT TO GO BACK?
WHAT'S IN THE GREY WORLD THAT'S WORTH SEEING?
SABURO, IT'S OUR HOME. IT'S WHERE WE BELONG. DON'T YOU SEE THAT?
AND IT'S NOT THE GREY WORLD, IT'S JUST-- THE WORLD. THE REAL WORLD.
YOU'RE FUNNY, KAI.
HOW CAN SOMETHING THAT CHANGES ALL THE TIME BE REAL? THE HUMAN WORLD IS LIKE-- I DON'T KNOW-- FLOWERS.
DO FLOWERS SAY TO ROCKS, "WE'RE REAL AND YOU'RE NOT"?
THIS IS IT, BY THE WAY. RENJI'S FOLD.
YOU HAVE TO JUMP.
I HAVE TO WHAT?
JUMP. OVER THE EDGE.
IT'S PERFECTLY SAFE.

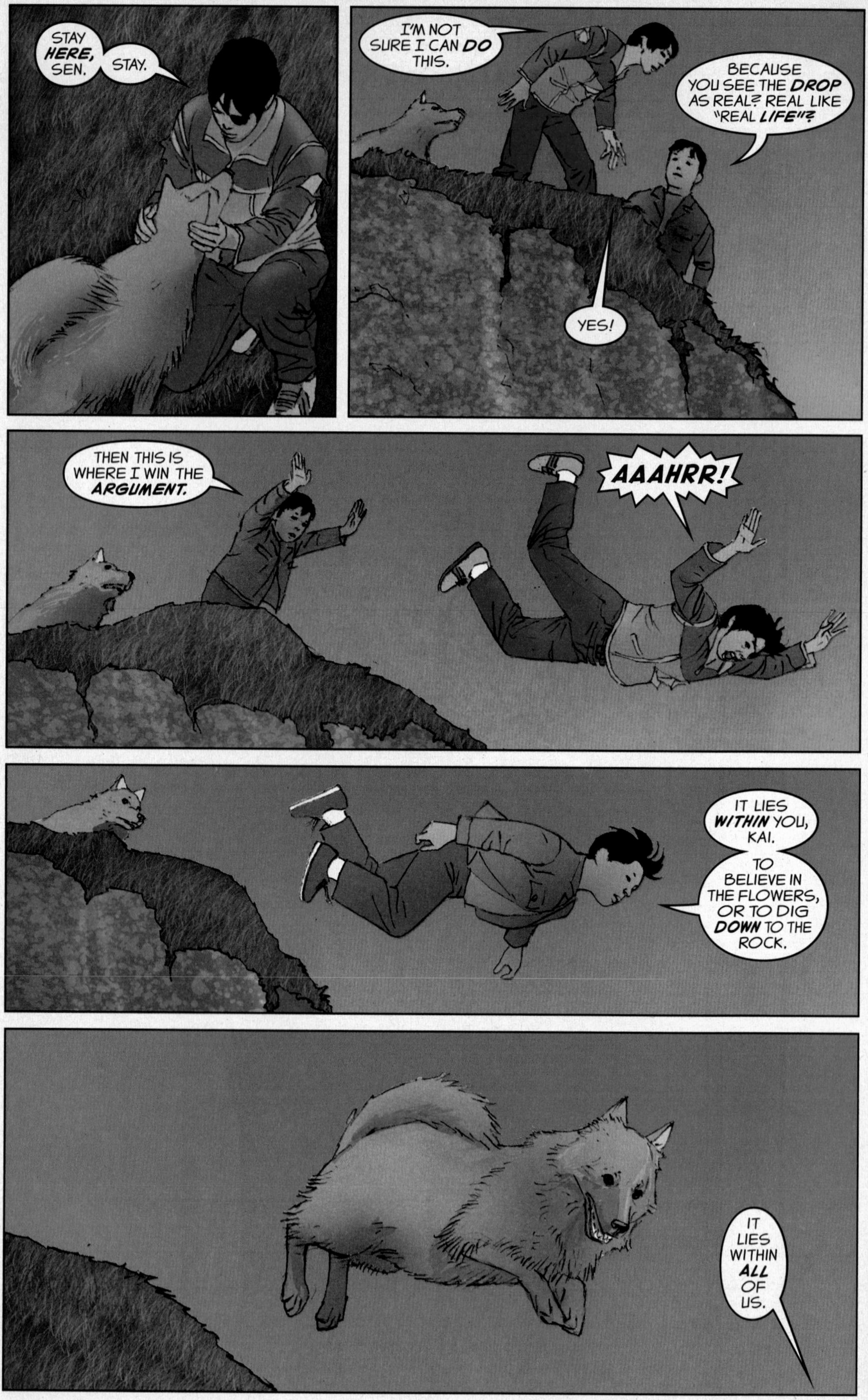
STAY **HERE,** SEN.
STAY.
I'M NOT SURE I CAN **DO** THIS.
BECAUSE YOU SEE THE **DROP** AS REAL? REAL LIKE "REAL **LIFE**"?
YES!
THEN THIS IS WHERE I WIN THE **ARGUMENT.**
AAAHRR!
IT LIES **WITHIN** YOU, KAI.
TO BELIEVE IN THE FLOWERS, OR TO DIG **DOWN** TO THE ROCK.
IT LIES WITHIN **ALL** OF US.

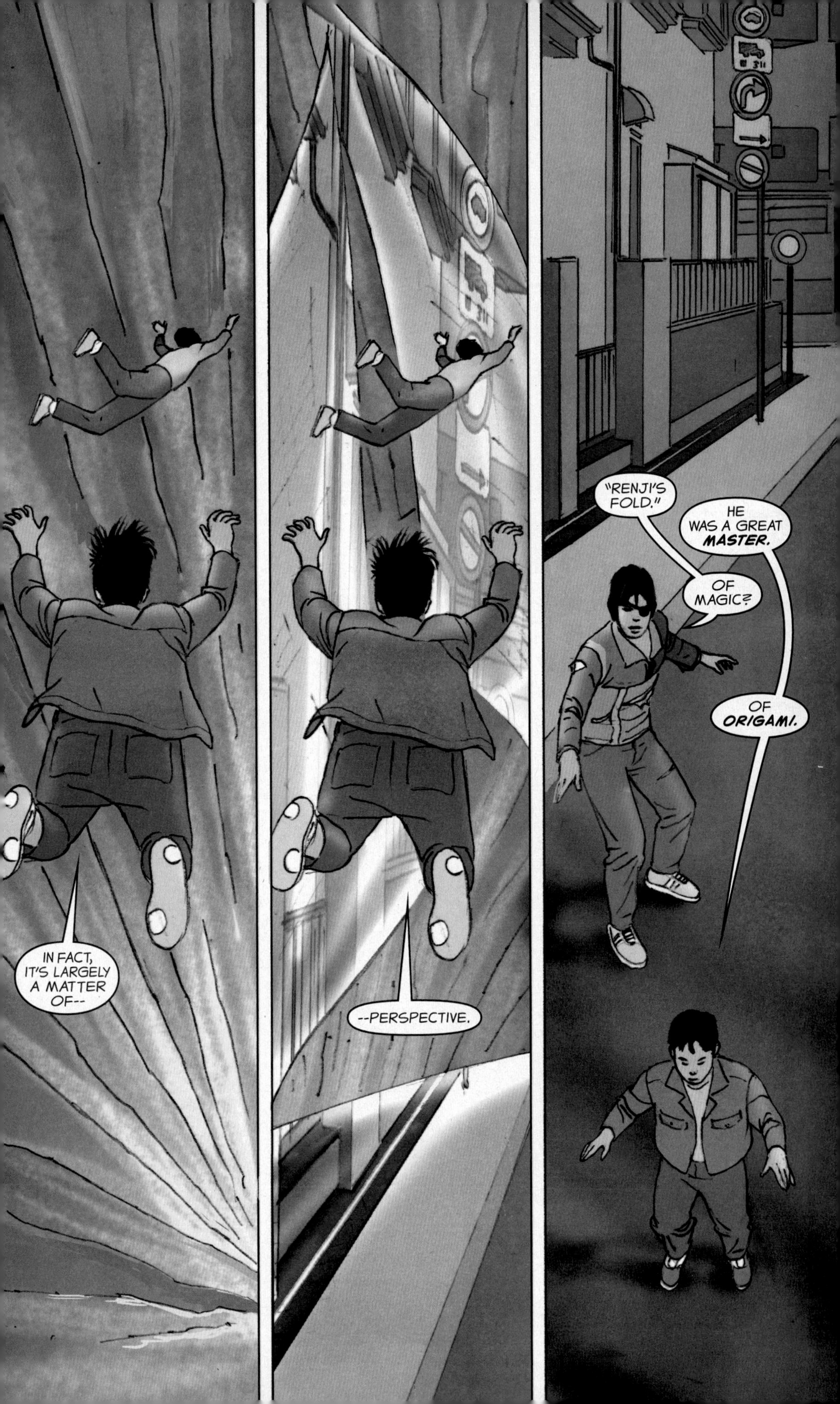
IN FACT, IT'S LARGELY A MATTER OF--
--PERSPECTIVE.
"RENJI'S FOLD."
HE WAS A GREAT **MASTER.**
OF MAGIC?
OF **ORIGAMI.**

SO YOU SERVE THE LORD OF CLOSED DOORS?

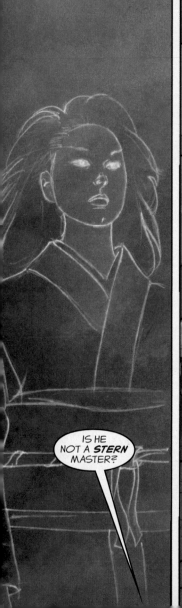

IS HE NOT A **STERN** MASTER?

HARSH, BUT FAIR, I'D SAY. HE **FLOGGED** ME ONCE FOR STARING AT HIS DAUGHTER. FORTY STROKES.

BUT HE BADE THE TORTURER STOP THE WOUNDS WITH **MERCURY**, AFTER.

THE **SHADOW-DRAGON**, THOUGH, HE'S A DEEP ONE, ISN'T HE?

KEEPS THAT HUMAN **BOY** AT HIS SIDE, THAT NEVER HAS A WORD TO SAY FOR ITSELF. SOME KIND OF **PET**, I'M THINKING.

THAT'S NO HUMAN.

THAT'S A **KONDOBU**.

AAAA!

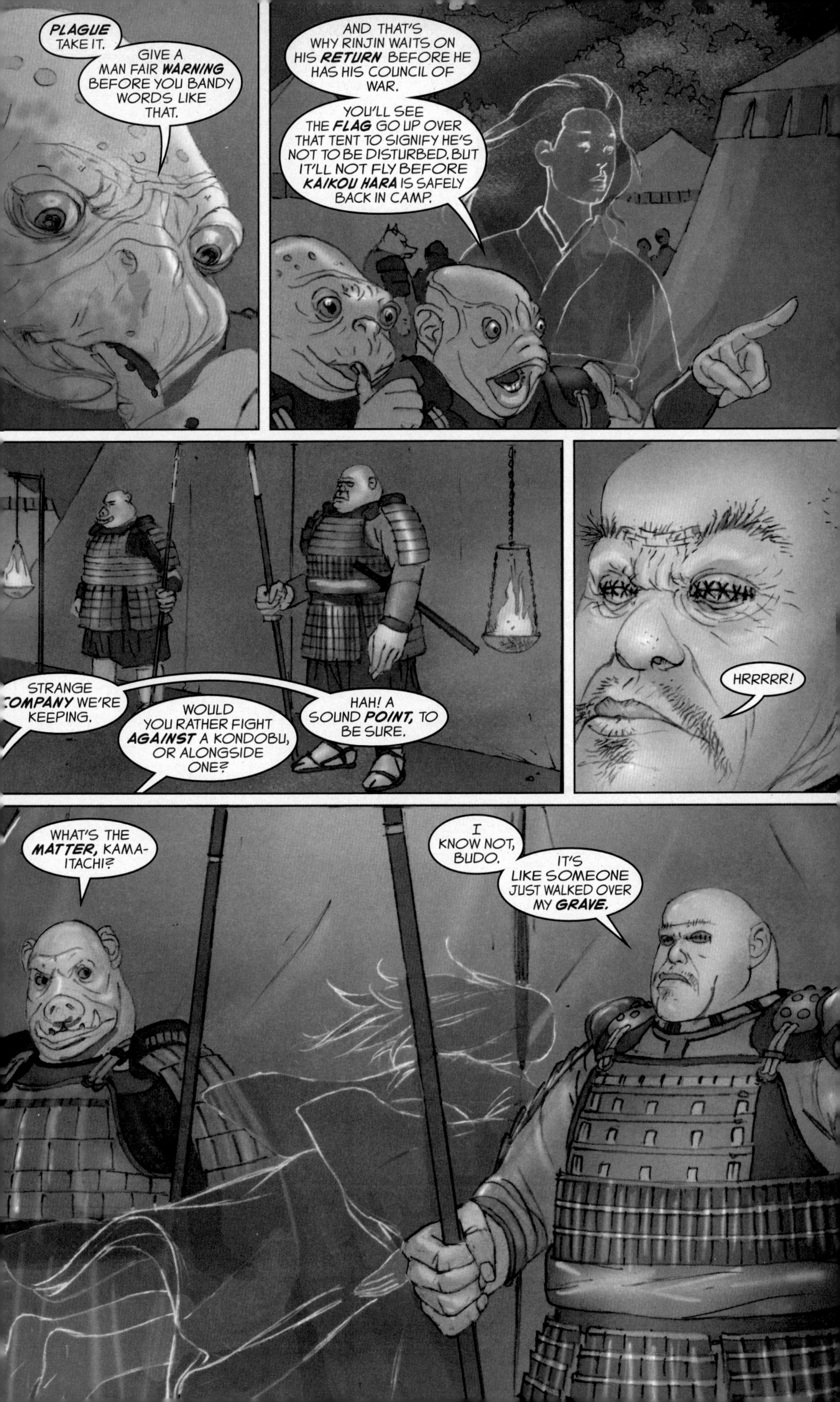
PLAGUE TAKE IT.
GIVE A MAN FAIR WARNING BEFORE YOU BANDY WORDS LIKE THAT.
AND THAT'S WHY RINJIN WAITS ON HIS RETURN BEFORE HE HAS HIS COUNCIL OF WAR.
YOU'LL SEE THE FLAG GO UP OVER THAT TENT TO SIGNIFY HE'S NOT TO BE DISTURBED. BUT IT'LL NOT FLY BEFORE KAIKOU HARA IS SAFELY BACK IN CAMP.
STRANGE COMPANY WE'RE KEEPING.
WOULD YOU RATHER FIGHT AGAINST A KONDOBU, OR ALONGSIDE ONE?
HAH! A SOUND POINT, TO BE SURE.
HRRRRR!
WHAT'S THE MATTER, KAMA-ITACHI?
I KNOW NOT, BUDO.
IT'S LIKE SOMEONE JUST WALKED OVER MY GRAVE.

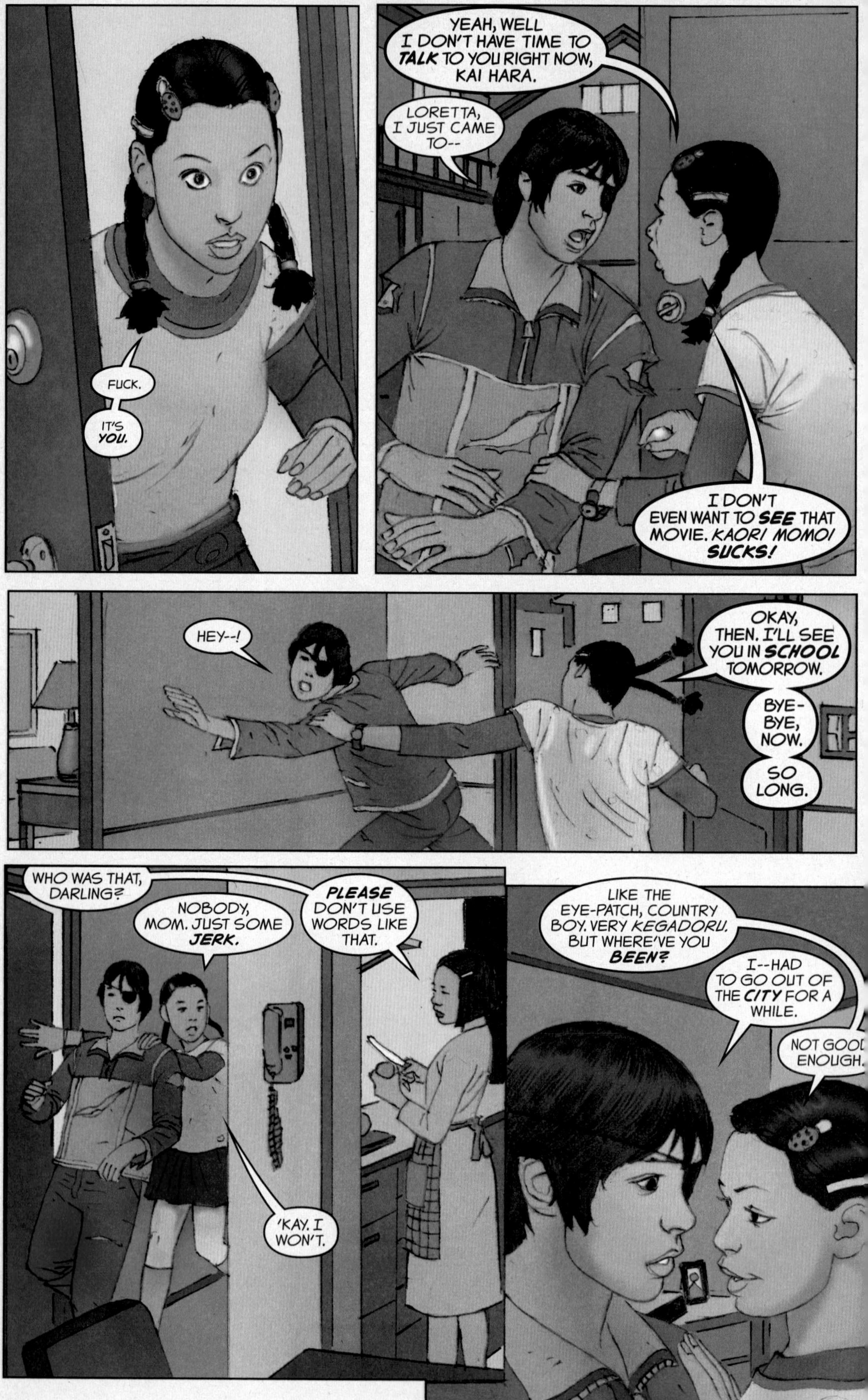
FUCK.
IT'S YOU.
YEAH, WELL I DON'T HAVE TIME TO TALK TO YOU RIGHT NOW, KAI HARA.
LORETTA, I JUST CAME TO--
I DON'T EVEN WANT TO SEE THAT MOVIE. KAORI MOMOI SUCKS!
HEY--!
OKAY, THEN. I'LL SEE YOU IN SCHOOL TOMORROW.
BYE-BYE, NOW.
SO LONG.
WHO WAS THAT, DARLING?
NOBODY, MOM. JUST SOME JERK.
PLEASE DON'T USE WORDS LIKE THAT.
'KAY. I WON'T.
LIKE THE EYE-PATCH, COUNTRY BOY. VERY KEGADORU. BUT WHERE'VE YOU BEEN?
I--HAD TO GO OUT OF THE CITY FOR A WHILE.
NOT GOOD ENOUGH.

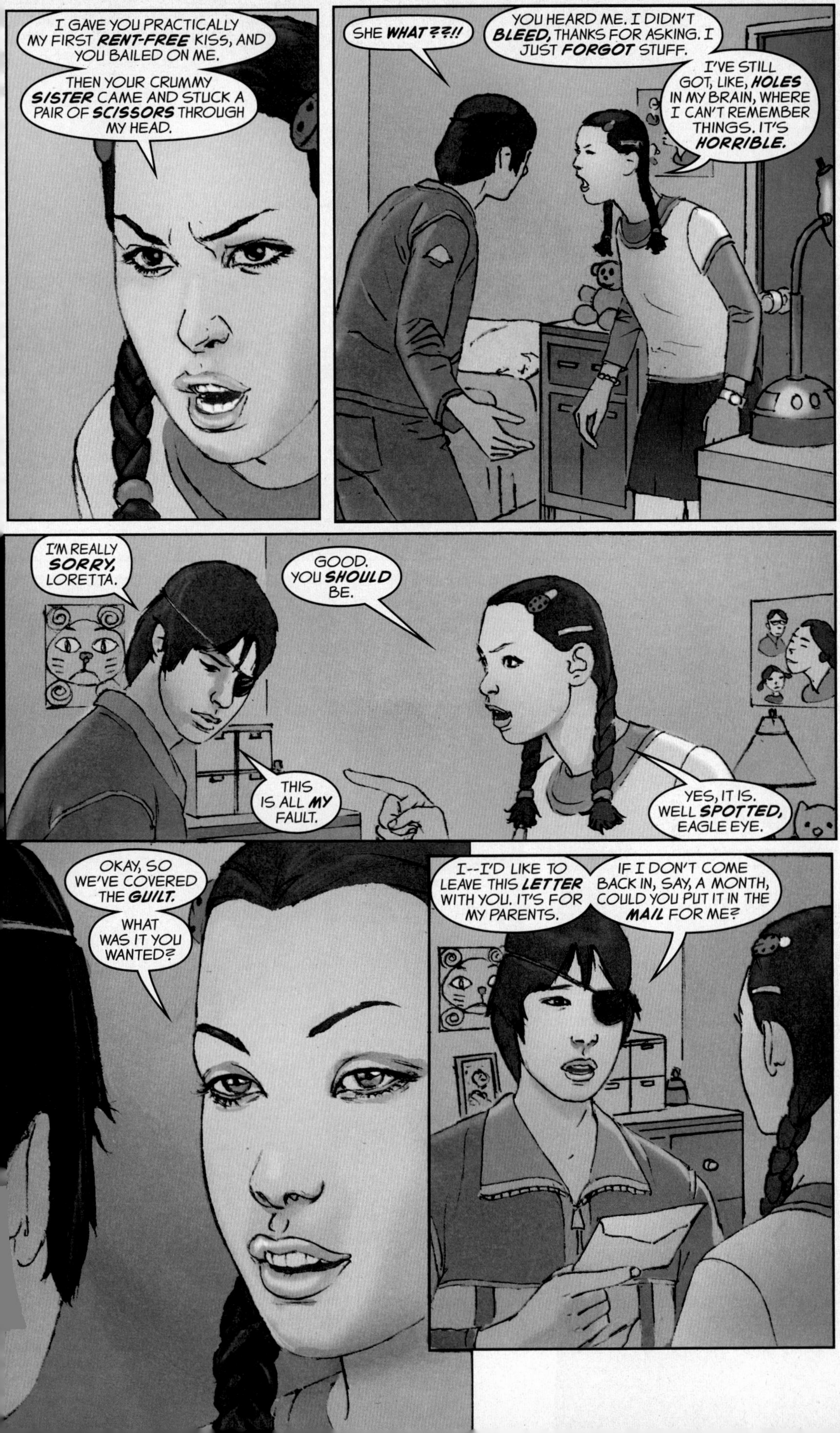

I GAVE YOU PRACTICALLY MY FIRST RENT-FREE KISS, AND YOU BAILED ON ME.
THEN YOUR CRUMMY SISTER CAME AND STUCK A PAIR OF SCISSORS THROUGH MY HEAD.
SHE WHAT??!!
YOU HEARD ME. I DIDN'T BLEED, THANKS FOR ASKING. I JUST FORGOT STUFF.
I'VE STILL GOT, LIKE, HOLES IN MY BRAIN, WHERE I CAN'T REMEMBER THINGS. IT'S HORRIBLE.
I'M REALLY SORRY, LORETTA.
GOOD. YOU SHOULD BE.
THIS IS ALL MY FAULT.
YES, IT IS. WELL SPOTTED, EAGLE EYE.
OKAY, SO WE'VE COVERED THE GUILT.
WHAT WAS IT YOU WANTED?
I--I'D LIKE TO LEAVE THIS LETTER WITH YOU. IT'S FOR MY PARENTS.
IF I DON'T COME BACK IN, SAY, A MONTH, COULD YOU PUT IT IN THE MAIL FOR ME?

OKAY, YOU **GOT** IT.

BUT IS THAT WHAT YOU **REALLY** CAME HERE FOR, COUNTRY BOY?

UMM-- YES. WHY ELSE?

I THOUGHT MAYBE YOU CAME TO PAY YOUR **DEBTS**.

"SEX SLAVE FOR A **DAY.**" REMEMBER?

I--THAT WAS--I THOUGHT YOU WERE JUST-- YOU KNOW, JOKING.

ABOUT **SEX?** UH-UH.

LORETTA, I DON'T **HAVE** A DAY.

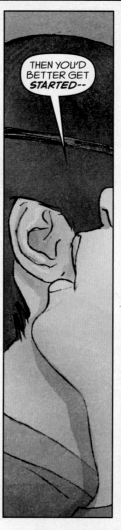

THEN YOU'D BETTER GET **STARTED**--

--HADN'T YOU?

112

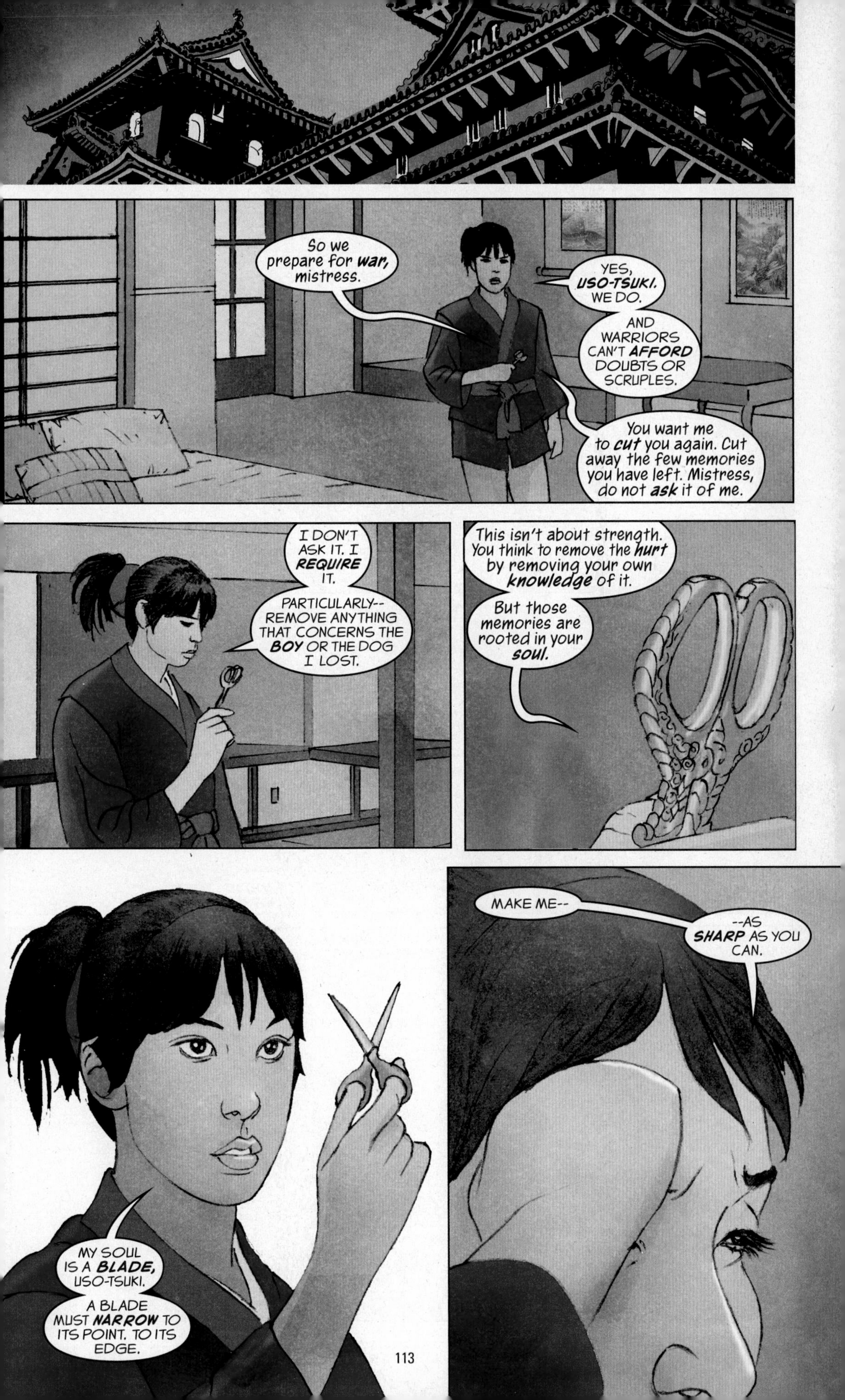
So we prepare for war, mistress.
YES, USO-TSUKI. WE DO.
AND WARRIORS CAN'T AFFORD DOUBTS OR SCRUPLES.
You want me to cut you again. Cut away the few memories you have left. Mistress, do not ask it of me.
I DON'T ASK IT. I REQUIRE IT.
PARTICULARLY-- REMOVE ANYTHING THAT CONCERNS THE BOY OR THE DOG I LOST.
This isn't about strength. You think to remove the hurt by removing your own knowledge of it.
But those memories are rooted in your soul.
MY SOUL IS A BLADE, USO-TSUKI.
A BLADE MUST NARROW TO ITS POINT. TO ITS EDGE.
MAKE ME--
--AS SHARP AS YOU CAN.

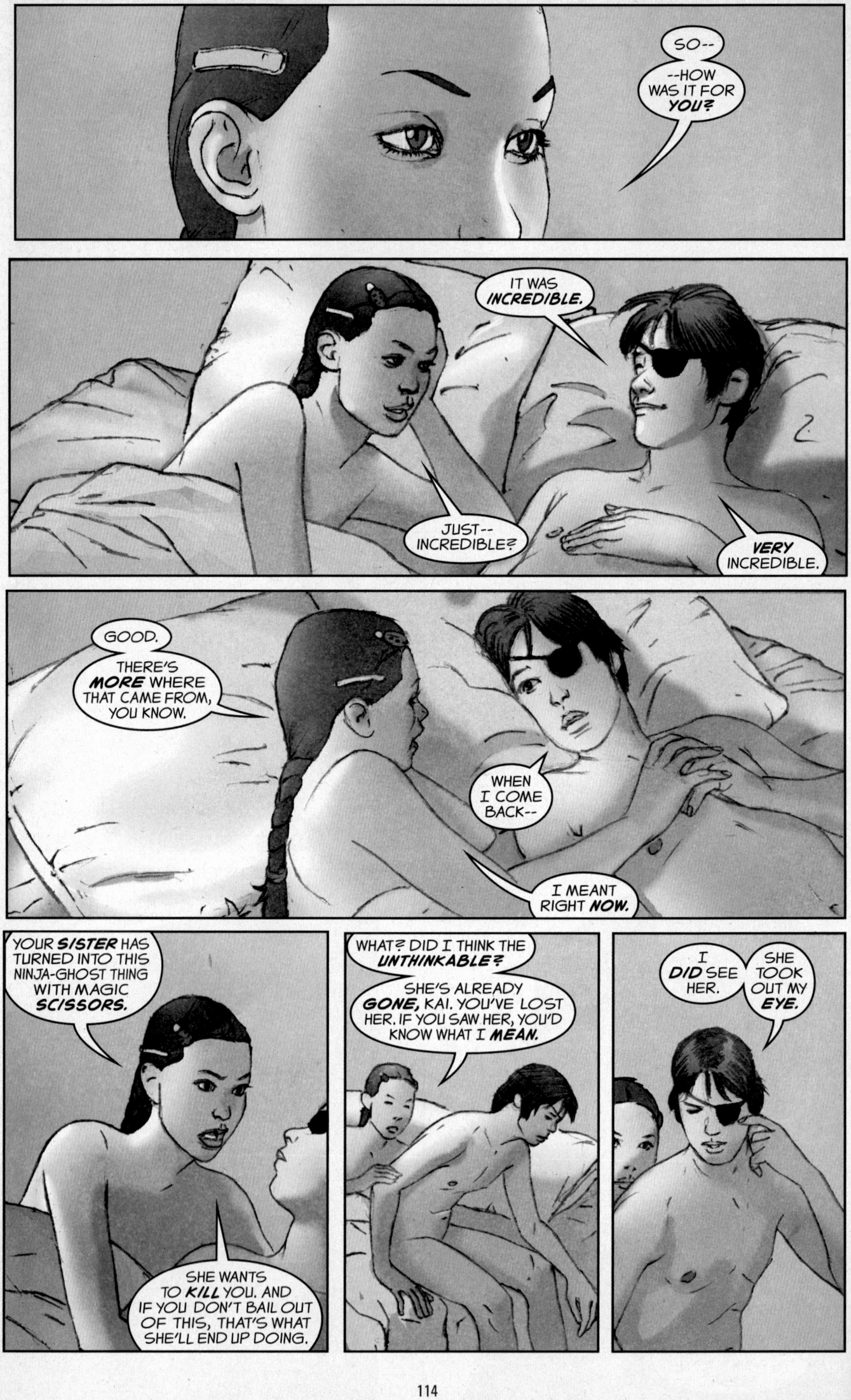
SO--
--HOW WAS IT FOR YOU?
IT WAS INCREDIBLE.
JUST-- INCREDIBLE?
VERY INCREDIBLE.
GOOD.
THERE'S MORE WHERE THAT CAME FROM, YOU KNOW.
WHEN I COME BACK--
I MEANT RIGHT NOW.
YOUR SISTER HAS TURNED INTO THIS NINJA-GHOST THING WITH MAGIC SCISSORS.
SHE WANTS TO KILL YOU. AND IF YOU DON'T BAIL OUT OF THIS, THAT'S WHAT SHE'LL END UP DOING.
WHAT? DID I THINK THE UNTHINKABLE?
SHE'S ALREADY GONE, KAI. YOU'VE LOST HER. IF YOU SAW HER, YOU'D KNOW WHAT I MEAN.
I DID SEE HER.
SHE TOOK OUT MY EYE.

IS THAT A WEIRD *METAPHOR*, OR--NO, YOU REALLY *MEAN* IT, DON'T YOU?

SHIT, KAI, WHAT ARE YOU TRYING TO DO? OFFER HER A *TWO-FOR-ONE* DEAL?

I JUST--I HAVE TO FIND HER. I'M REALLY *CLOSE* NOW. I'VE GOT HELP.

PSYCHIATRIC HELP, YOU MEAN? SHE'S A *KILLER,* KAI. YOU'RE--A NICE GUY WITH A *LITTLE-BOY-LOST* VIBE I FIND KIND OF SEXY.

SHE WILL FUCKING *EAT* YOU ALIVE.

MAYBE SHE *WILL.* BUT I CAN'T JUST GIVE UP ON HER, LORETTA.

YES, YOU *CAN.* RIGHT NOW, YOU *CAN.*

BEFORE IT GETS EVEN SICKER AND BLOODIER AND *STUPIDER* THAN IT ALREADY IS.

YOU CAN SAY *GOODBYE.*

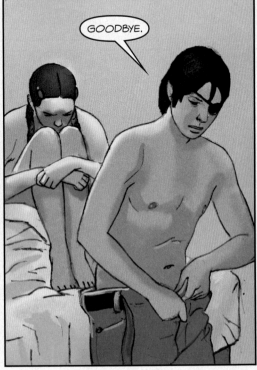

GOODBYE.

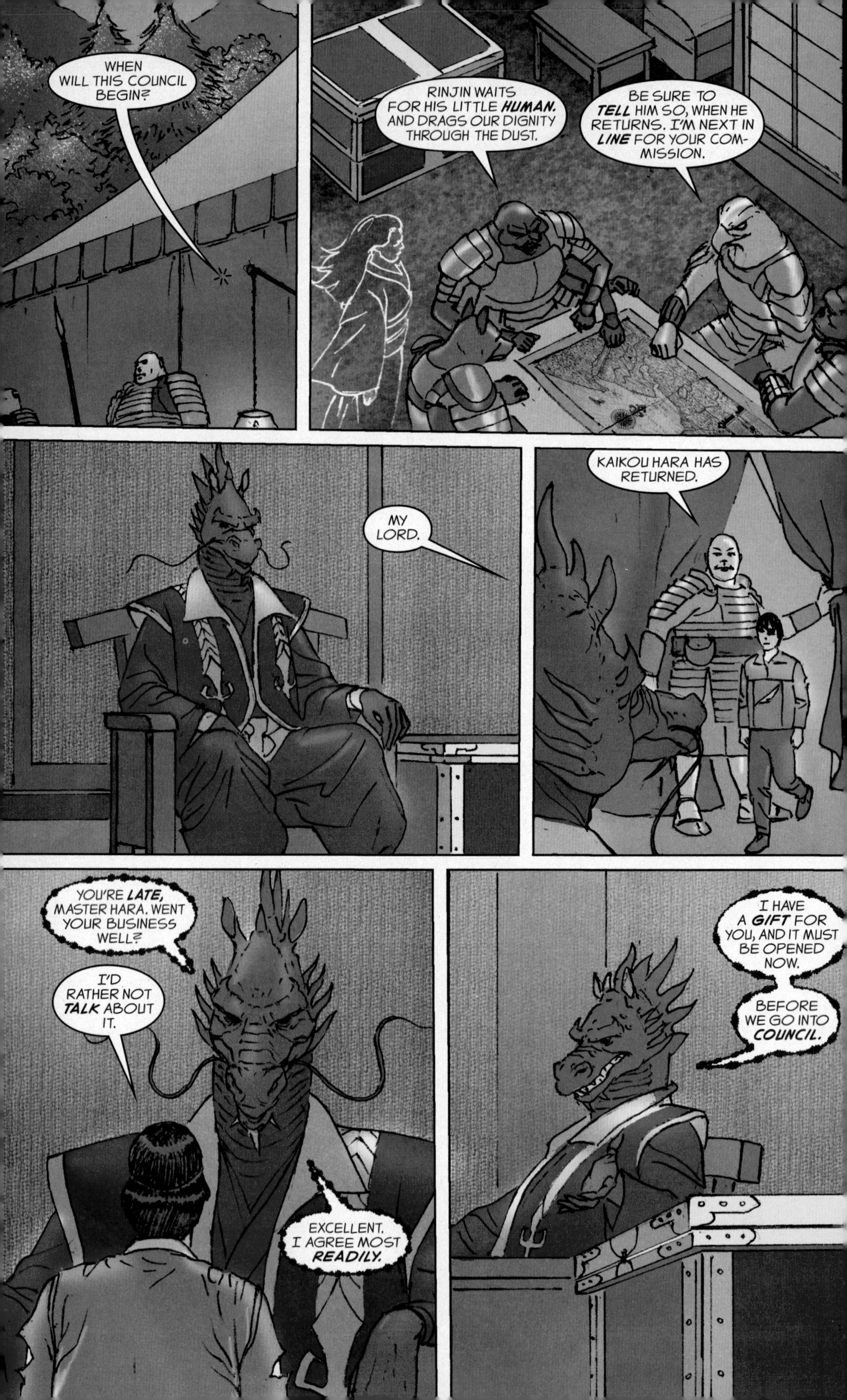
WHEN WILL THIS COUNCIL BEGIN?
RINJIN WAITS FOR HIS LITTLE HUMAN. AND DRAGS OUR DIGNITY THROUGH THE DUST.
BE SURE TO TELL HIM SO, WHEN HE RETURNS. I'M NEXT IN LINE FOR YOUR COMMISSION.
MY LORD.
KAIKOU HARA HAS RETURNED.
YOU'RE LATE, MASTER HARA. WENT YOUR BUSINESS WELL?
I'D RATHER NOT TALK ABOUT IT.
EXCELLENT. I AGREE MOST READILY.
I HAVE A GIFT FOR YOU, AND IT MUST BE OPENED NOW.
BEFORE WE GO INTO COUNCIL.

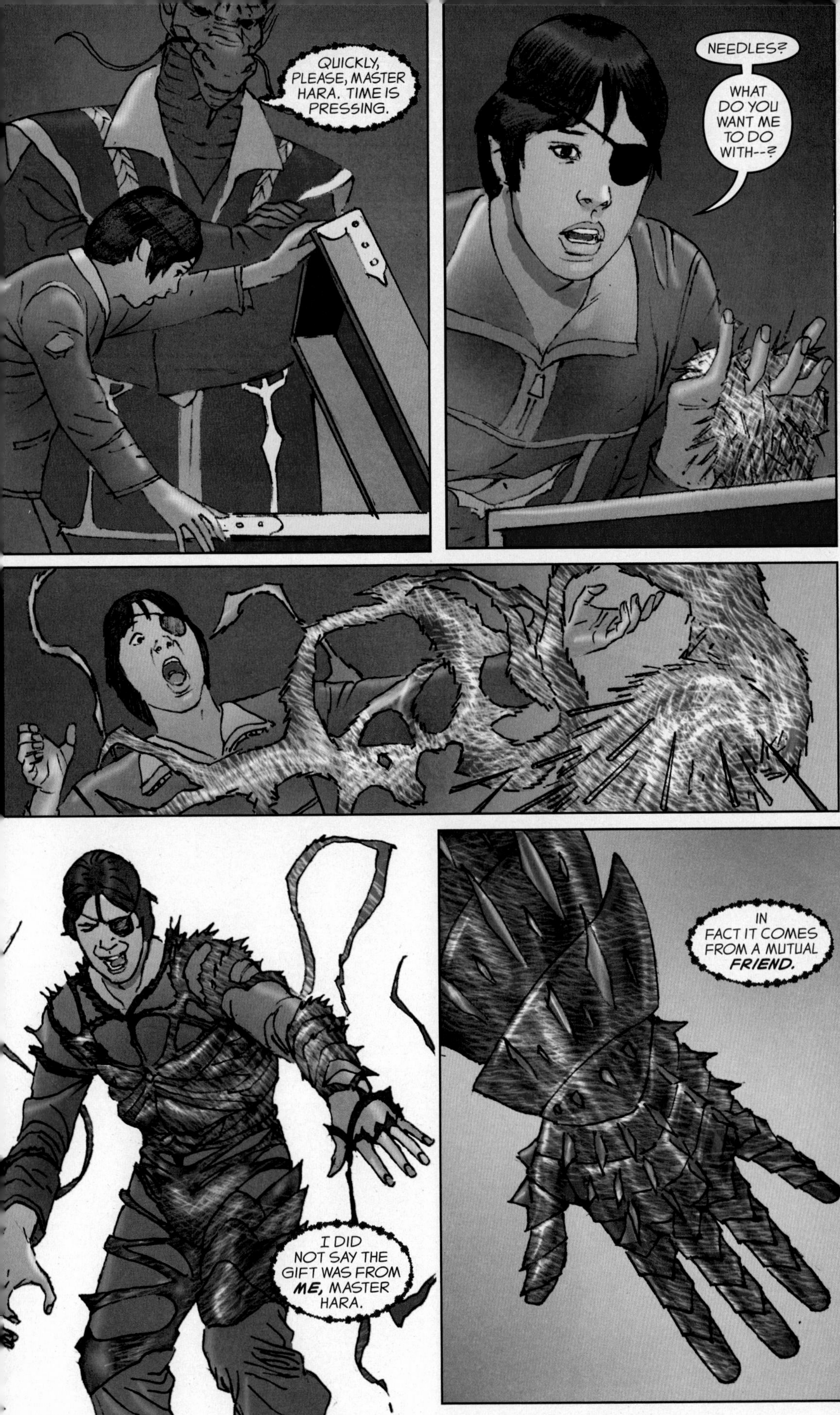
QUICKLY, PLEASE, MASTER HARA. TIME IS PRESSING.
NEEDLES?
WHAT DO YOU WANT ME TO DO WITH--?
I DID NOT SAY THE GIFT WAS FROM ME, MASTER HARA.
IN FACT IT COMES FROM A MUTUAL FRIEND.

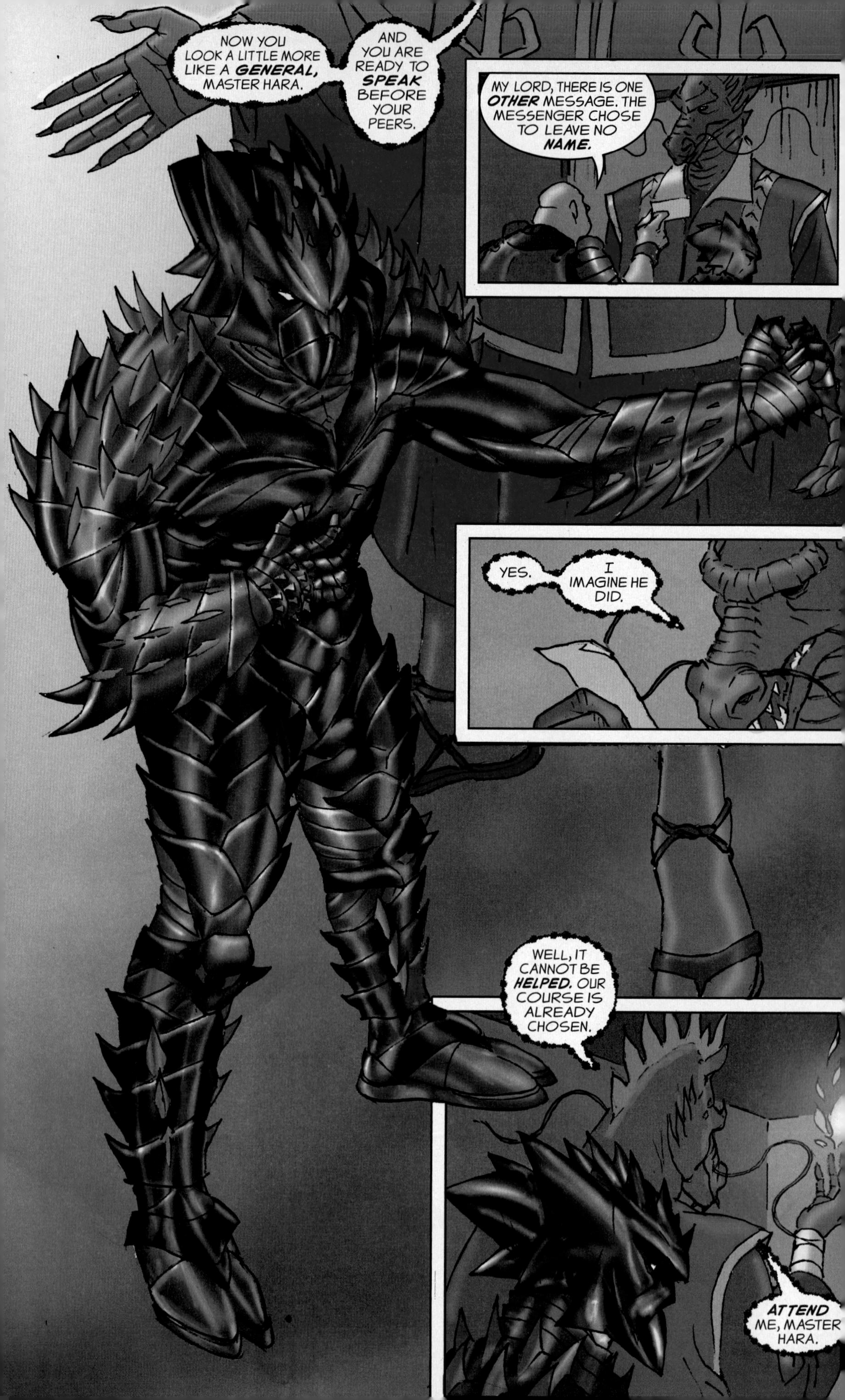
NOW YOU LOOK A LITTLE MORE LIKE A **GENERAL,** MASTER HARA.
AND YOU ARE READY TO **SPEAK** BEFORE YOUR PEERS.
MY LORD, THERE IS ONE **OTHER** MESSAGE. THE MESSENGER CHOSE TO LEAVE NO **NAME.**
YES.
I IMAGINE HE DID.
WELL, IT CANNOT BE **HELPED.** OUR COURSE IS ALREADY CHOSEN.
ATTEND ME, MASTER HARA.

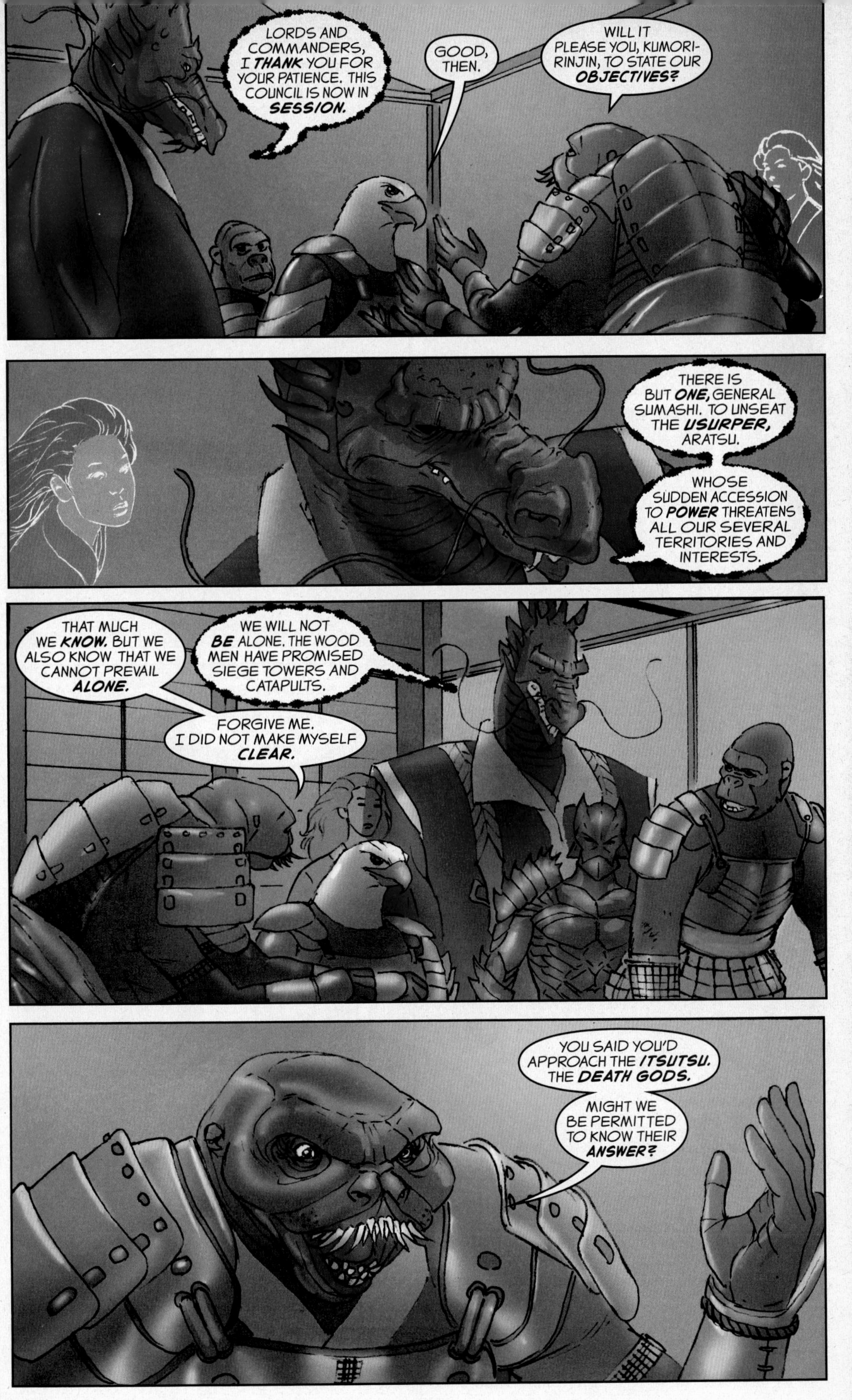
LORDS AND COMMANDERS, I THANK YOU FOR YOUR PATIENCE. THIS COUNCIL IS NOW IN SESSION.
GOOD, THEN.
WILL IT PLEASE YOU, KUMORI-RINJIN, TO STATE OUR OBJECTIVES?
THERE IS BUT ONE, GENERAL SUMASHI. TO UNSEAT THE USURPER, ARATSU.
WHOSE SUDDEN ACCESSION TO POWER THREATENS ALL OUR SEVERAL TERRITORIES AND INTERESTS.
THAT MUCH WE KNOW. BUT WE ALSO KNOW THAT WE CANNOT PREVAIL ALONE.
WE WILL NOT BE ALONE. THE WOOD MEN HAVE PROMISED SIEGE TOWERS AND CATAPULTS.
FORGIVE ME. I DID NOT MAKE MYSELF CLEAR.
YOU SAID YOU'D APPROACH THE ITSUTSU. THE DEATH GODS.
MIGHT WE BE PERMITTED TO KNOW THEIR ANSWER?

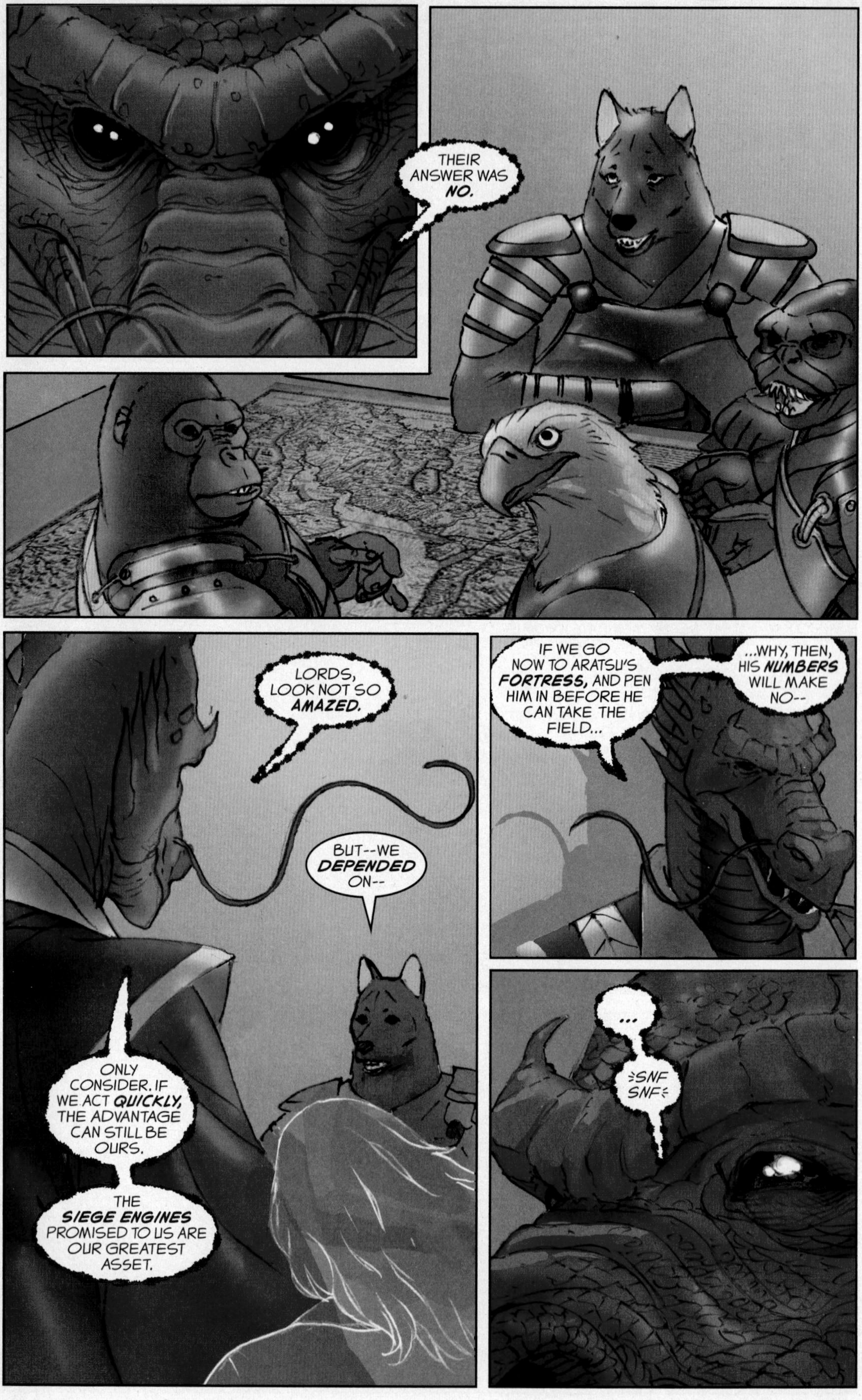
THEIR ANSWER WAS NO.
LORDS, LOOK NOT SO AMAZED.
BUT--WE DEPENDED ON--
ONLY CONSIDER. IF WE ACT QUICKLY, THE ADVANTAGE CAN STILL BE OURS.
THE SIEGE ENGINES PROMISED TO US ARE OUR GREATEST ASSET.
IF WE GO NOW TO ARATSU'S FORTRESS, AND PEN HIM IN BEFORE HE CAN TAKE THE FIELD...
...WHY, THEN, HIS NUMBERS WILL MAKE NO--
...
SNF SNF

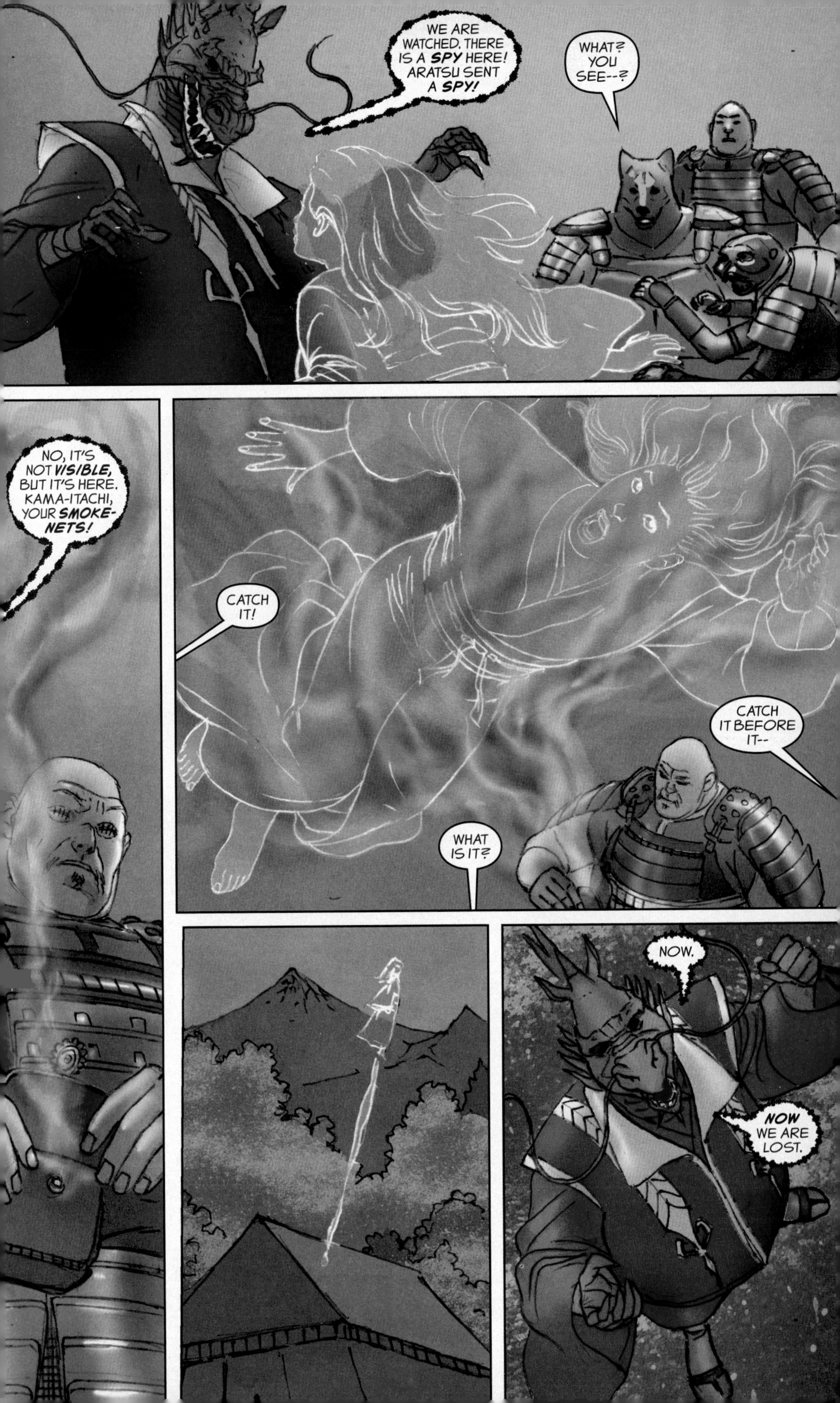

WE ARE WATCHED. THERE IS A SPY HERE! ARATSU SENT A SPY!
WHAT? YOU SEE--?
NO, IT'S NOT VISIBLE, BUT IT'S HERE. KAMA-ITACHI, YOUR SMOKE-NETS!
CATCH IT!
CATCH IT BEFORE IT--
WHAT IS IT?
NOW.
NOW WE ARE LOST.

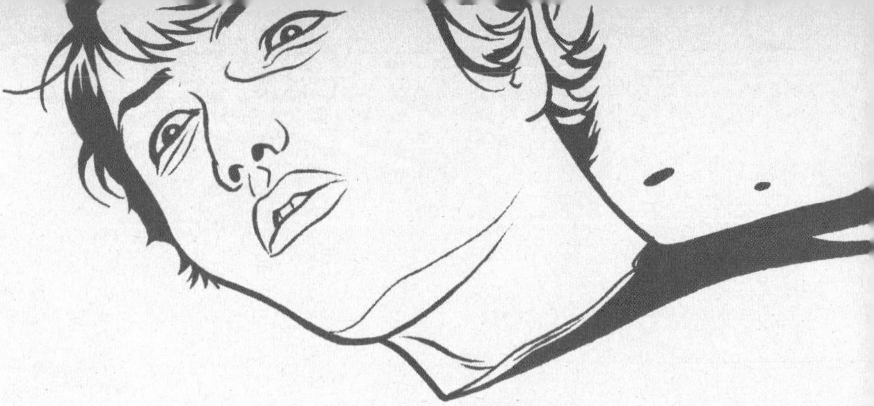

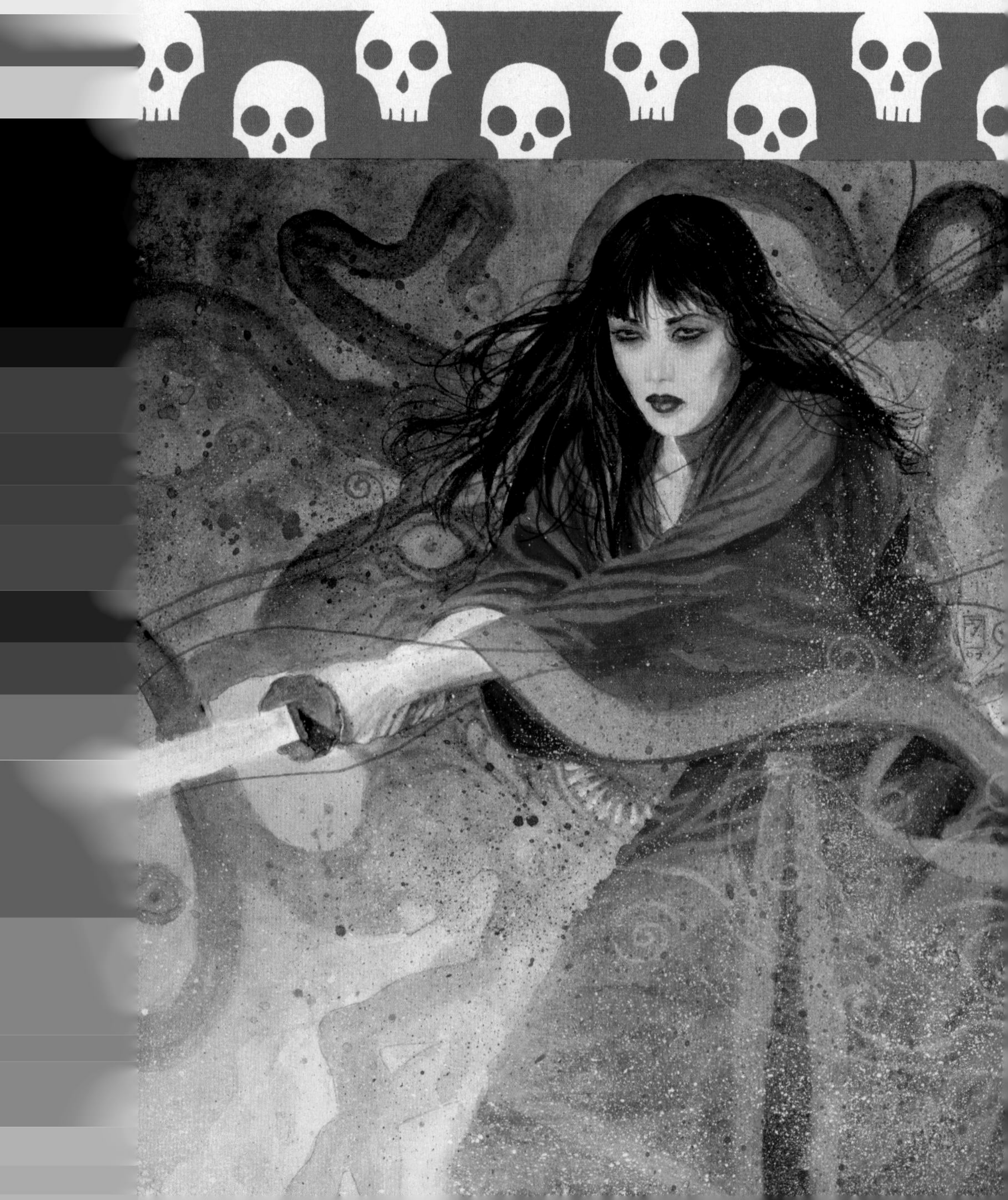

KILL HER, WARRIORS. KILL THIS **CHILD** YOU SEE BEFORE YOU.

ALL ATTACKS, ALL **WEAPONS**, ARE PERMISSIBLE. AND LORD ARATSU'S BOUNTY GOES TO **ALL** OF YOU IF ANY **ONE** SUCCEEDS.

YOU MUST **DIE**, LITTLE ONE, SO THAT WE MAY **PROSPER**.

BUT GIVE US YOUR **PARDON**, AND YOU'LL HAVE SUCH MERCY AS WE CAN GRANT.

A **QUICK** DEATH, AND NO DISHONOR.

MY PARDON? YOU **HAVE** IT, SOLDIER.

BUT YOUR MERCY WON'T BE **REQUIRED**.

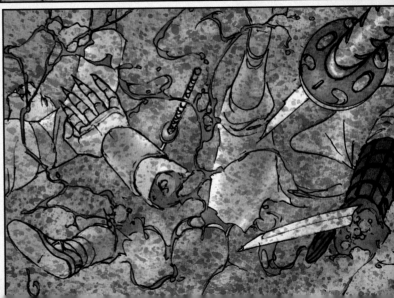

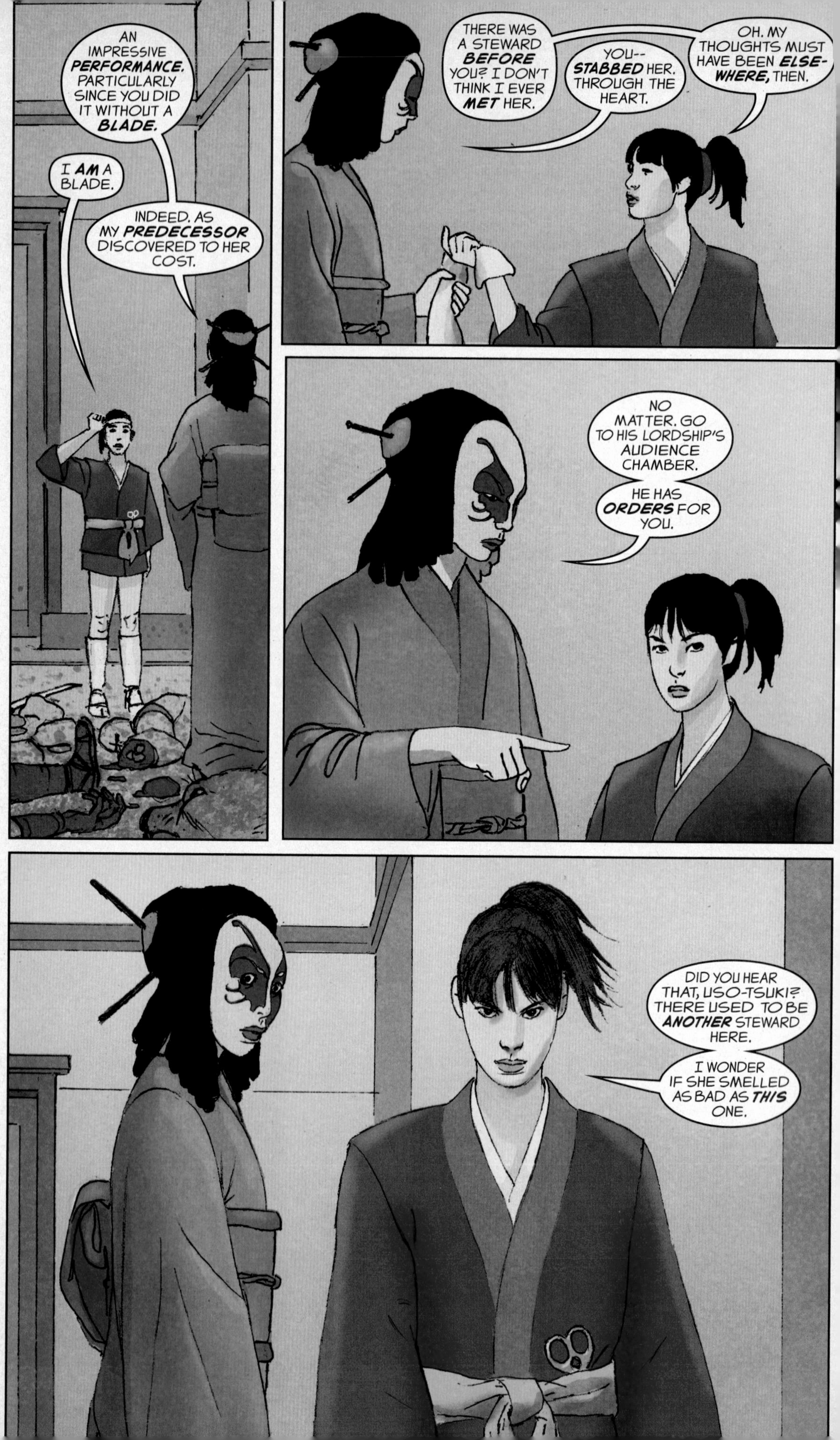
AN IMPRESSIVE PERFORMANCE. PARTICULARLY SINCE YOU DID IT WITHOUT A BLADE.
I AM A BLADE.
INDEED. AS MY PREDECESSOR DISCOVERED TO HER COST.
THERE WAS A STEWARD BEFORE YOU? I DON'T THINK I EVER MET HER.
YOU-- STABBED HER. THROUGH THE HEART.
OH. MY THOUGHTS MUST HAVE BEEN ELSEWHERE, THEN.
NO MATTER. GO TO HIS LORDSHIP'S AUDIENCE CHAMBER.
HE HAS ORDERS FOR YOU.
DID YOU HEAR THAT, USO-TSUKI? THERE USED TO BE ANOTHER STEWARD HERE.
I WONDER IF SHE SMELLED AS BAD AS THIS ONE.

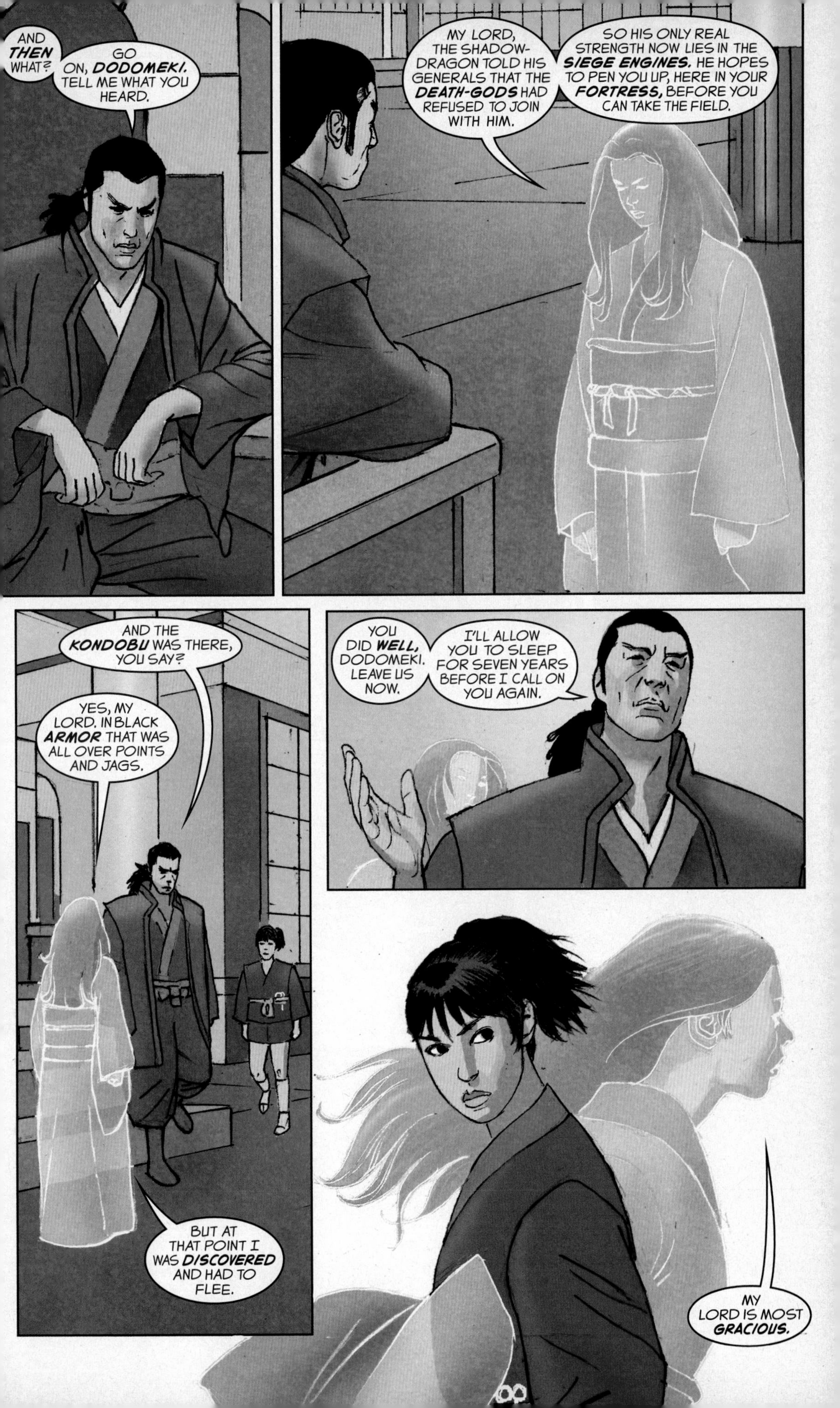
AND THEN WHAT?
GO ON, DODOMEKI. TELL ME WHAT YOU HEARD.
MY LORD, THE SHADOW-DRAGON TOLD HIS GENERALS THAT THE DEATH-GODS HAD REFUSED TO JOIN WITH HIM.
SO HIS ONLY REAL STRENGTH NOW LIES IN THE SIEGE ENGINES. HE HOPES TO PEN YOU UP, HERE IN YOUR FORTRESS, BEFORE YOU CAN TAKE THE FIELD.
AND THE KONDOBU WAS THERE, YOU SAY?
YES, MY LORD. IN BLACK ARMOR THAT WAS ALL OVER POINTS AND JAGS.
BUT AT THAT POINT I WAS DISCOVERED AND HAD TO FLEE.
YOU DID WELL, DODOMEKI. LEAVE US NOW.
I'LL ALLOW YOU TO SLEEP FOR SEVEN YEARS BEFORE I CALL ON YOU AGAIN.
MY LORD IS MOST GRACIOUS.

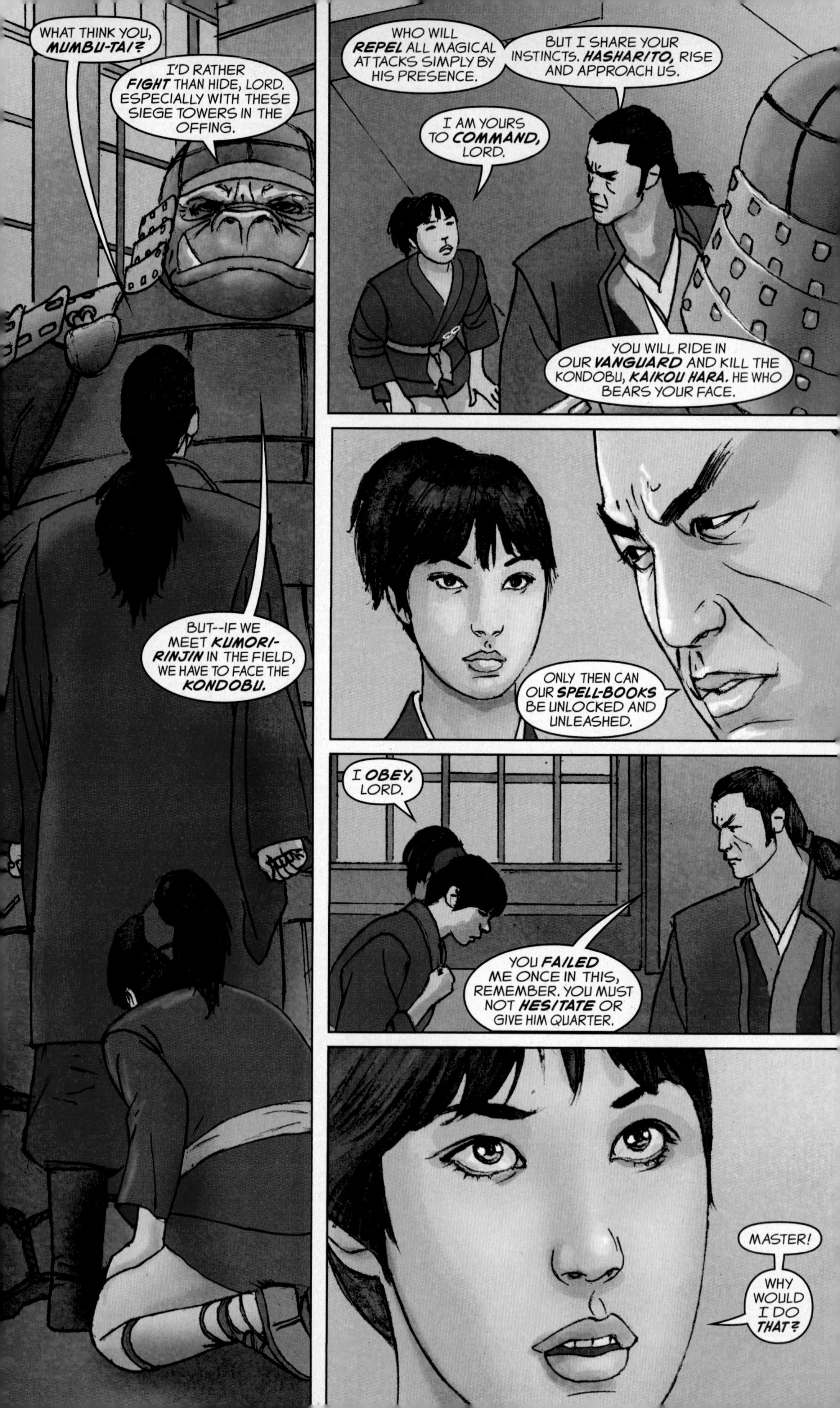
WHAT THINK YOU, MUMBU-TAI?
I'D RATHER FIGHT THAN HIDE, LORD. ESPECIALLY WITH THESE SIEGE TOWERS IN THE OFFING.
BUT--IF WE MEET KUMORI-RINJIN IN THE FIELD, WE HAVE TO FACE THE KONDOBU.
WHO WILL REPEL ALL MAGICAL ATTACKS SIMPLY BY HIS PRESENCE.
BUT I SHARE YOUR INSTINCTS. HASHARITO, RISE AND APPROACH US.
I AM YOURS TO COMMAND, LORD.
YOU WILL RIDE IN OUR VANGUARD AND KILL THE KONDOBU, KAIKOU HARA. HE WHO BEARS YOUR FACE.
ONLY THEN CAN OUR SPELL-BOOKS BE UNLOCKED AND UNLEASHED.
I OBEY, LORD.
YOU FAILED ME ONCE IN THIS, REMEMBER. YOU MUST NOT HESITATE OR GIVE HIM QUARTER.
MASTER!
WHY WOULD I DO THAT?

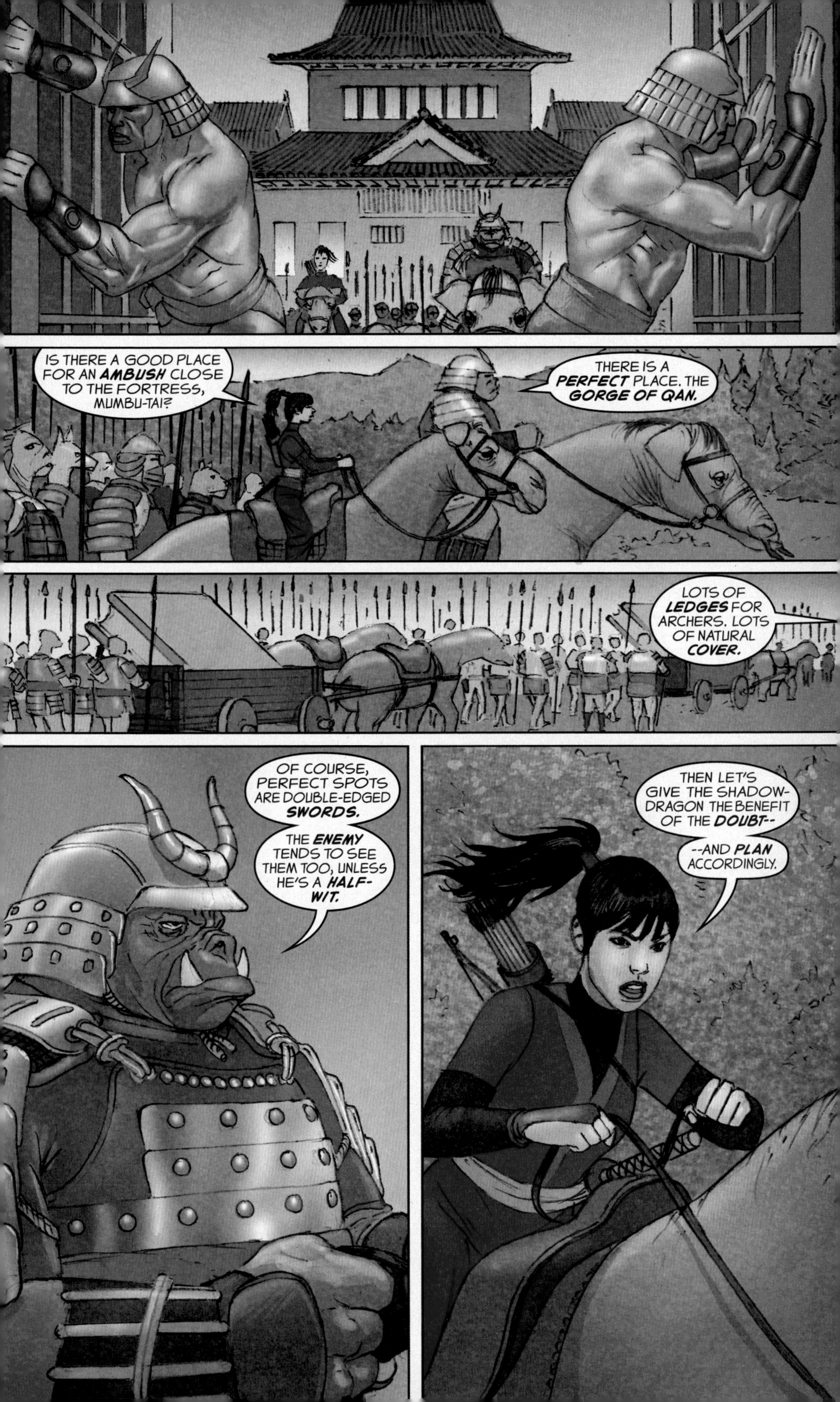
IS THERE A GOOD PLACE FOR AN AMBUSH CLOSE TO THE FORTRESS, MUMBU-TAI?
THERE IS A PERFECT PLACE. THE GORGE OF QAN.
LOTS OF LEDGES FOR ARCHERS. LOTS OF NATURAL COVER.
OF COURSE, PERFECT SPOTS ARE DOUBLE-EDGED SWORDS.
THE ENEMY TENDS TO SEE THEM TOO, UNLESS HE'S A HALF-WIT.
THEN LET'S GIVE THE SHADOW-DRAGON THE BENEFIT OF THE DOUBT--
--AND PLAN ACCORDINGLY.

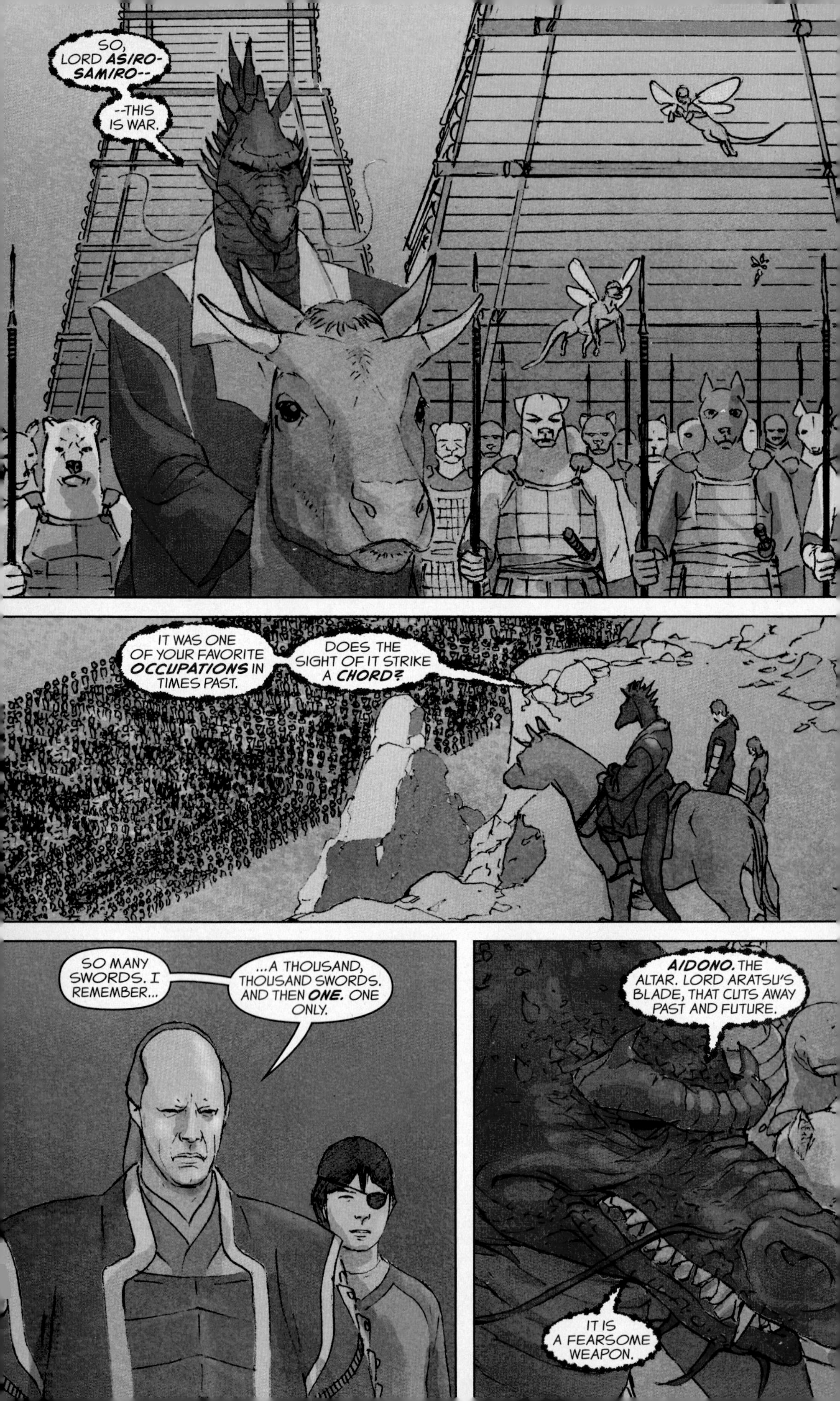
SO, LORD ASIRO-SAMIRO--
--THIS IS WAR.
IT WAS ONE OF YOUR FAVORITE OCCUPATIONS IN TIMES PAST.
DOES THE SIGHT OF IT STRIKE A CHORD?
SO MANY SWORDS. I REMEMBER...
...A THOUSAND, THOUSAND SWORDS. AND THEN ONE. ONE ONLY.
AIDONO. THE ALTAR. LORD ARATSU'S BLADE, THAT CUTS AWAY PAST AND FUTURE.
IT IS A FEARSOME WEAPON.

YOU SEEM **TROUBLED,** MASTER ARA. ARE YOU HAVING SECOND **THOUGHTS** ABOUT OUR STRATEGY?

NO. BUT I'M NO **FIGHTER,** LORD RINJIN.

I DON'T KNOW IF I CAN DO **ANY** OF THIS.

DO YOU KNOW THE **ORIGAMI** SCULPTURE CALLED THE DRAGON?

NO.

IT IS EXTREMELY **INTRICATE.**

AND IN MAKING IT YOU MUST PASS THROUGH MANY **INTERMEDIATE** FORMS.

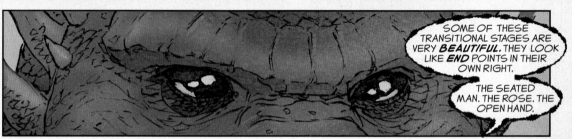

SOME OF THESE TRANSITIONAL STAGES ARE VERY **BEAUTIFUL.** THEY LOOK LIKE **END** POINTS IN THEIR OWN RIGHT.

THE SEATED MAN. THE ROSE. THE OPEN HAND.

I **APOLOGIZE** FOR THE LABORED ANALOGY.

BUT LIFE FOLDS EACH OF US INTO **MANY** CURIOUS SHAPES BEFORE WE FINALLY BECOME WHAT WE ARE **MEANT** TO BE.

EXALTED ONE, YOU ASKED FOR THE **KONDOBU'S ARMOR** TO BE BROUGHT TO YOU.

INDEED I **DID.**

TIME TO SILENCE YOUR **DOUBTS,** KAIKOU--

--AND BECOME THE **DRAGON.**

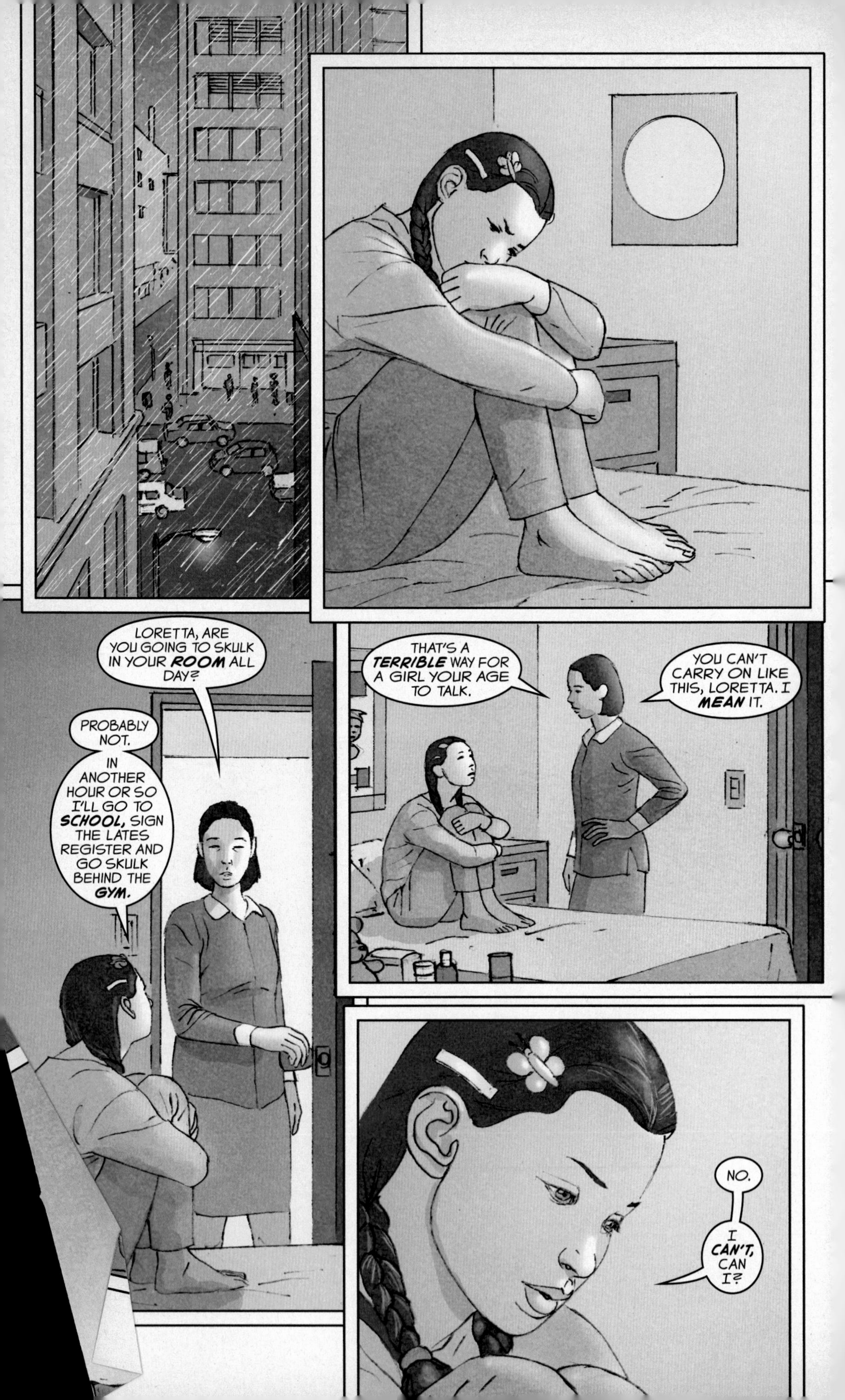
LORETTA, ARE YOU GOING TO SKULK IN YOUR ROOM ALL DAY?
PROBABLY NOT.
IN ANOTHER HOUR OR SO I'LL GO TO SCHOOL, SIGN THE LATES REGISTER AND GO SKULK BEHIND THE GYM.
THAT'S A TERRIBLE WAY FOR A GIRL YOUR AGE TO TALK.
YOU CAN'T CARRY ON LIKE THIS, LORETTA. I MEAN IT.
NO.
I CAN'T, CAN I?

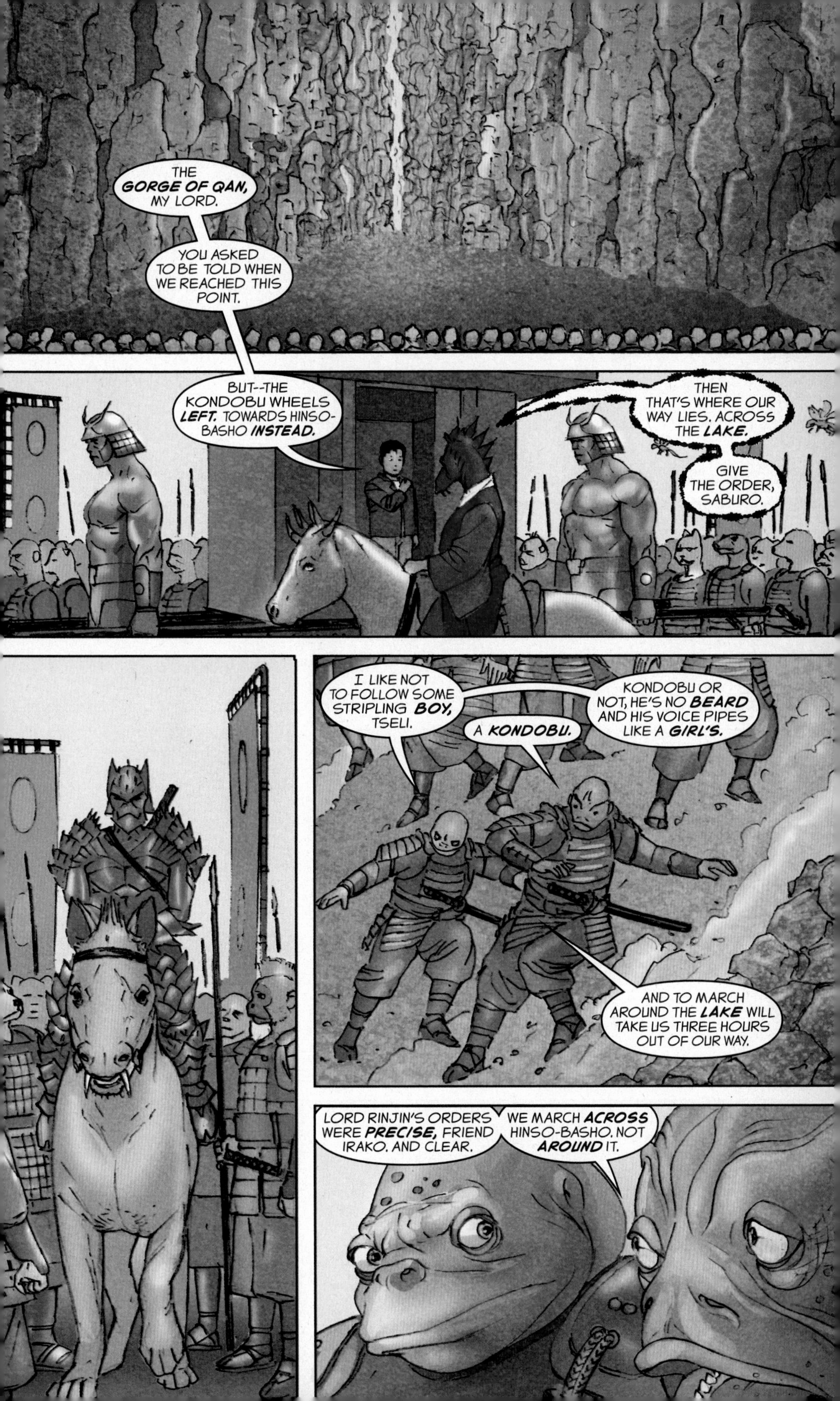
THE GORGE OF QAN, MY LORD.
YOU ASKED TO BE TOLD WHEN WE REACHED THIS POINT.
BUT--THE KONDOBU WHEELS LEFT. TOWARDS HINSO-BASHO INSTEAD.
THEN THAT'S WHERE OUR WAY LIES. ACROSS THE LAKE.
GIVE THE ORDER, SABURO.
I LIKE NOT TO FOLLOW SOME STRIPLING BOY, TSELI.
A KONDOBU.
KONDOBU OR NOT, HE'S NO BEARD AND HIS VOICE PIPES LIKE A GIRL'S.
AND TO MARCH AROUND THE LAKE WILL TAKE US THREE HOURS OUT OF OUR WAY.
LORD RINJIN'S ORDERS WERE PRECISE, FRIEND IRAKO. AND CLEAR.
WE MARCH ACROSS HINSO-BASHO. NOT AROUND IT.

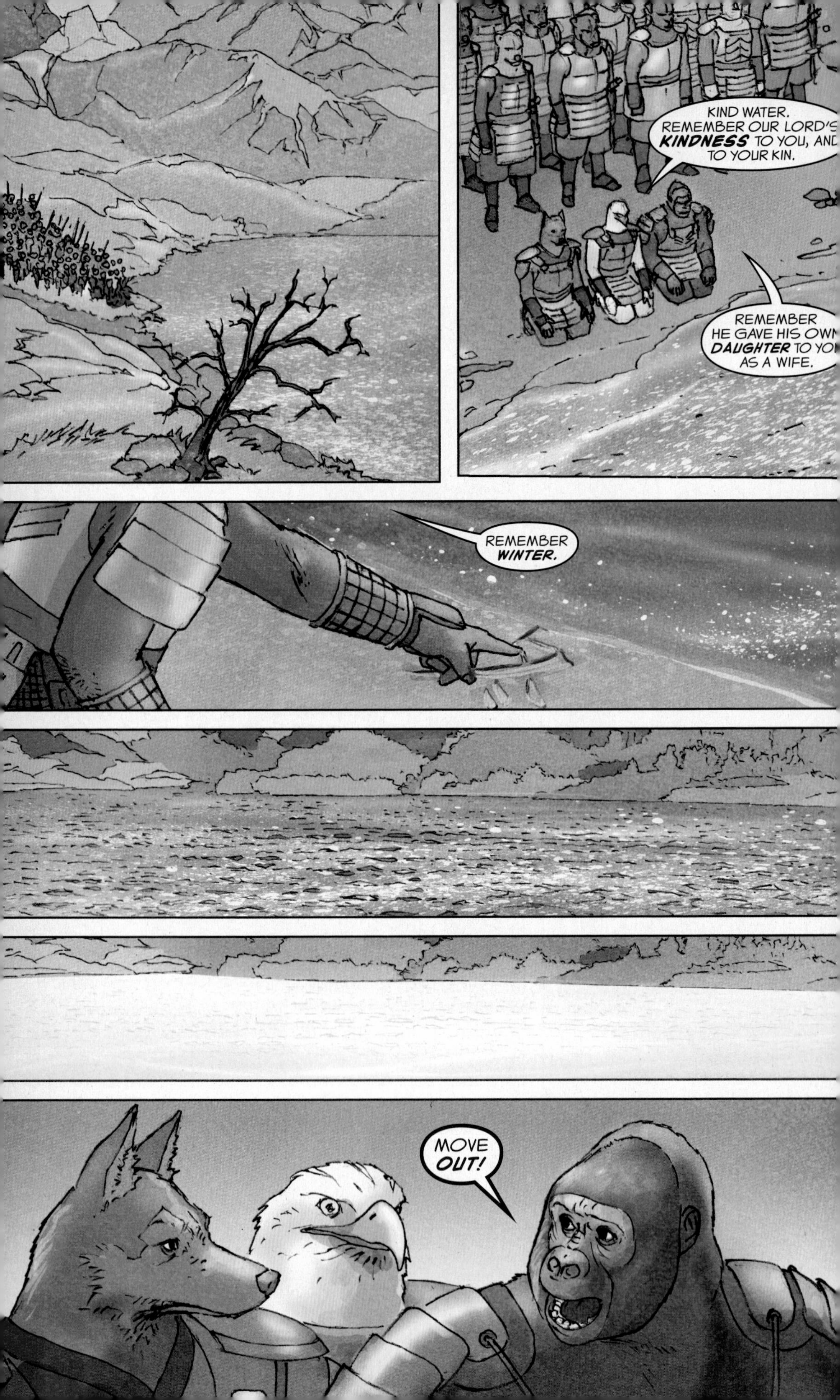

KIND WATER. REMEMBER OUR LORD'S **KINDNESS** TO YOU, AND TO YOUR KIN.
REMEMBER HE GAVE HIS OWN **DAUGHTER** TO YOU AS A WIFE.
REMEMBER **WINTER.**
MOVE **OUT!**

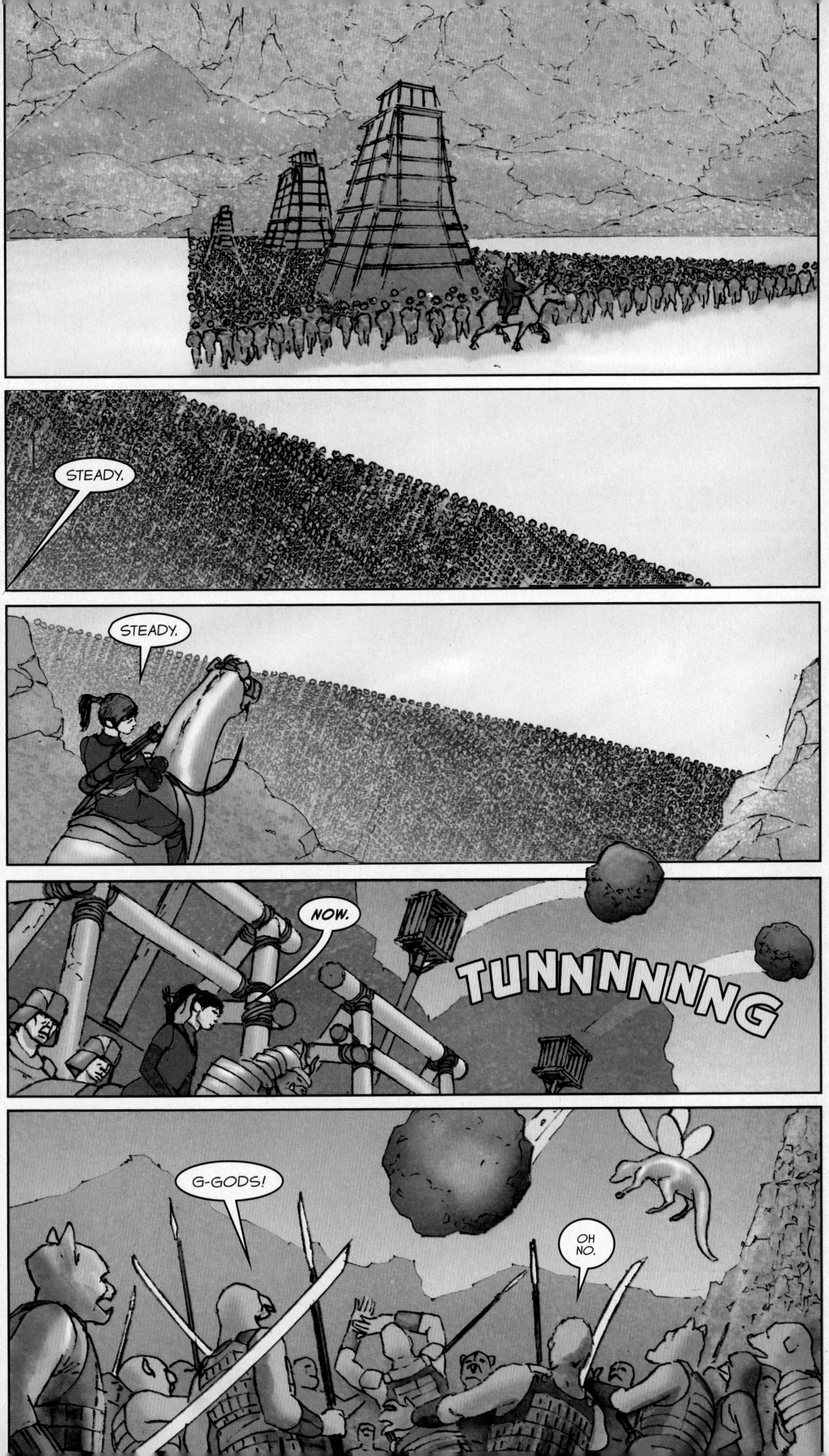
STEADY.
STEADY.
NOW.
TUNNNNNNG
G-GODS!
OH NO.

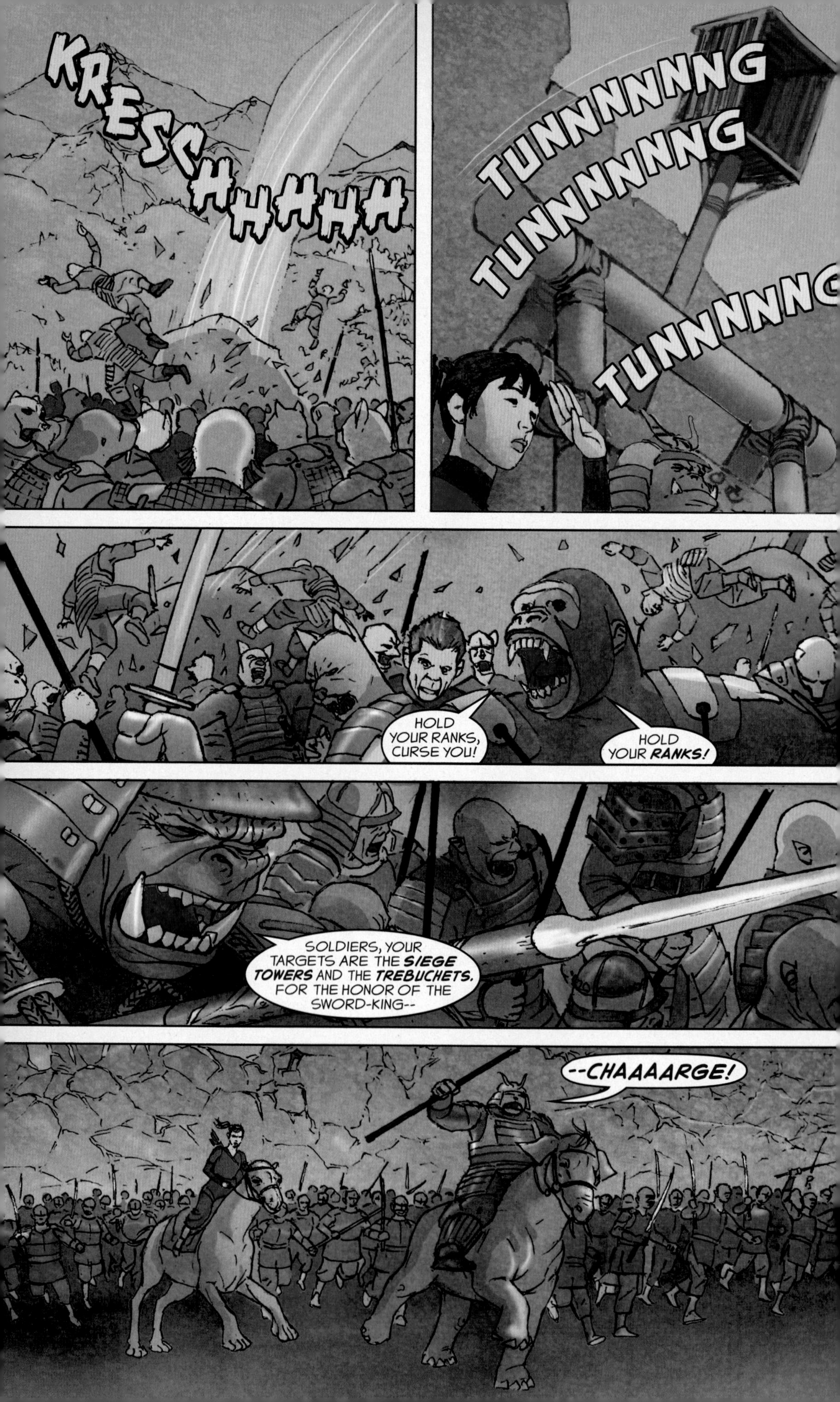
KRESCHHHHH
TUNNNNNNG
TUNNNNNNG
TUNNNNNNG
HOLD YOUR RANKS, CURSE YOU!
HOLD YOUR RANKS!
SOLDIERS, YOUR TARGETS ARE THE SIEGE TOWERS AND THE TREBUCHETS. FOR THE HONOR OF THE SWORD-KING--
--CHAAAARGE!

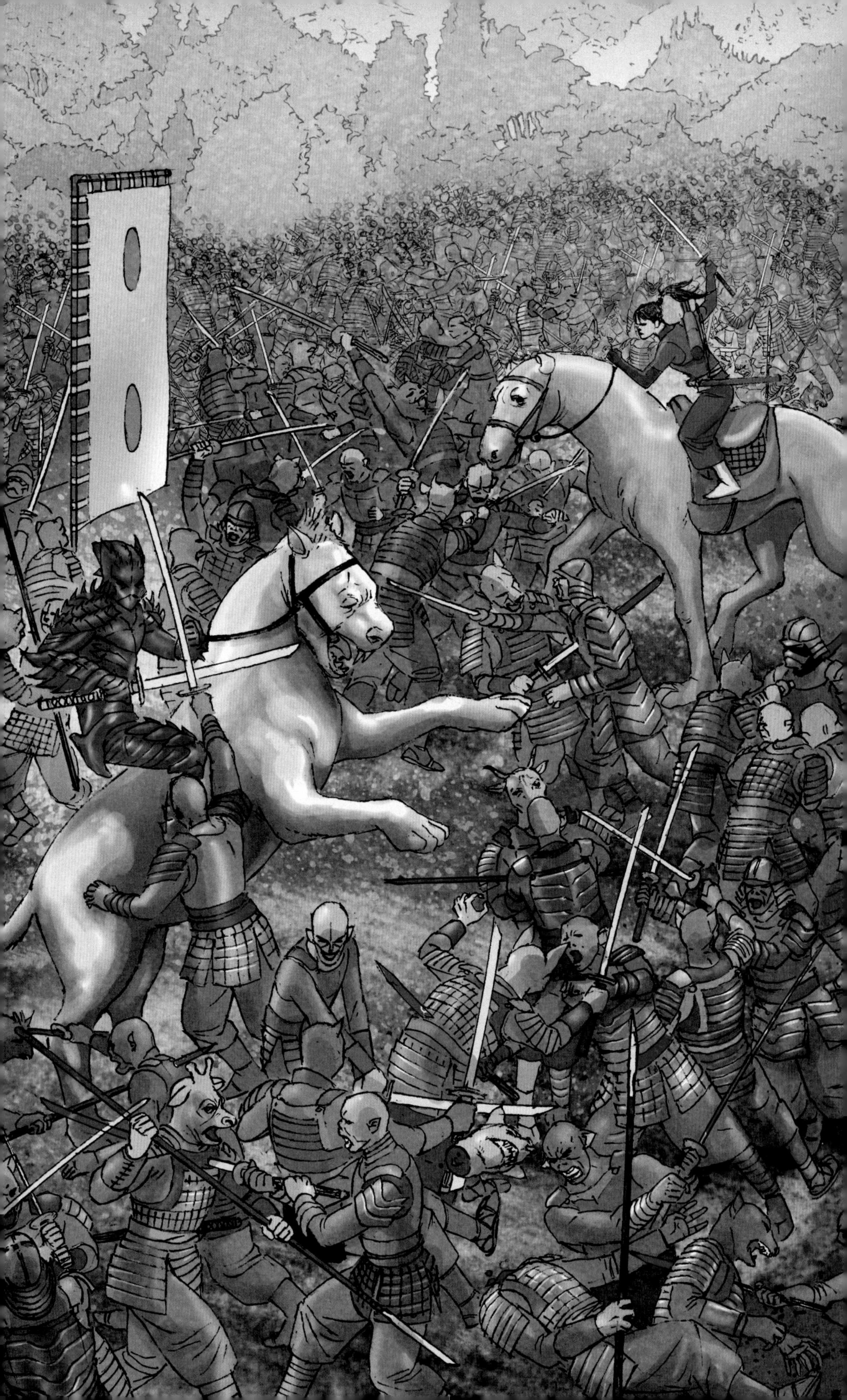

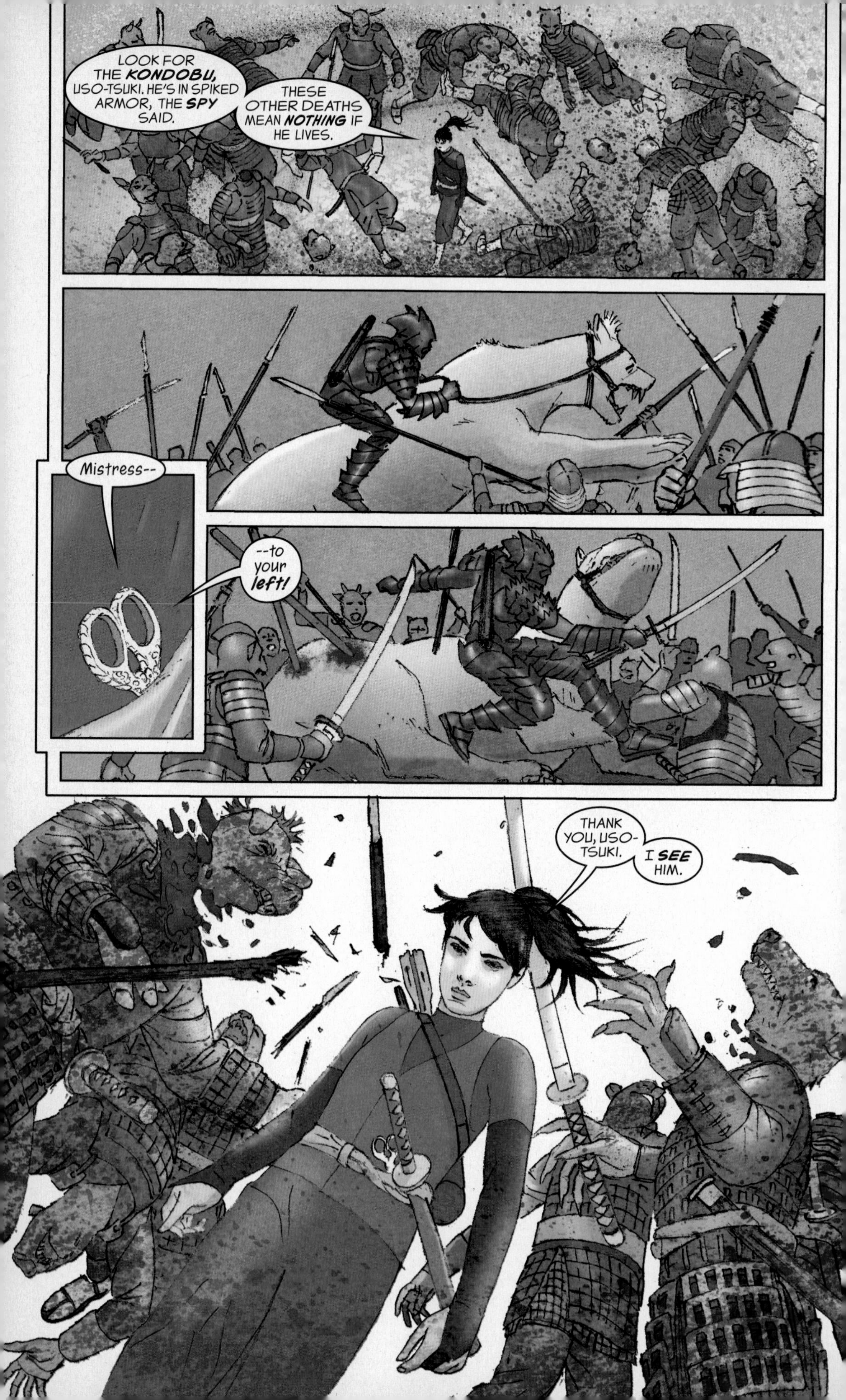
LOOK FOR THE KONDOBU, USO-TSUKI. HE'S IN SPIKED ARMOR, THE SPY SAID.
THESE OTHER DEATHS MEAN NOTHING IF HE LIVES.
Mistress--
--to your left!
THANK YOU, USO-TSUKI.
I SEE HIM.

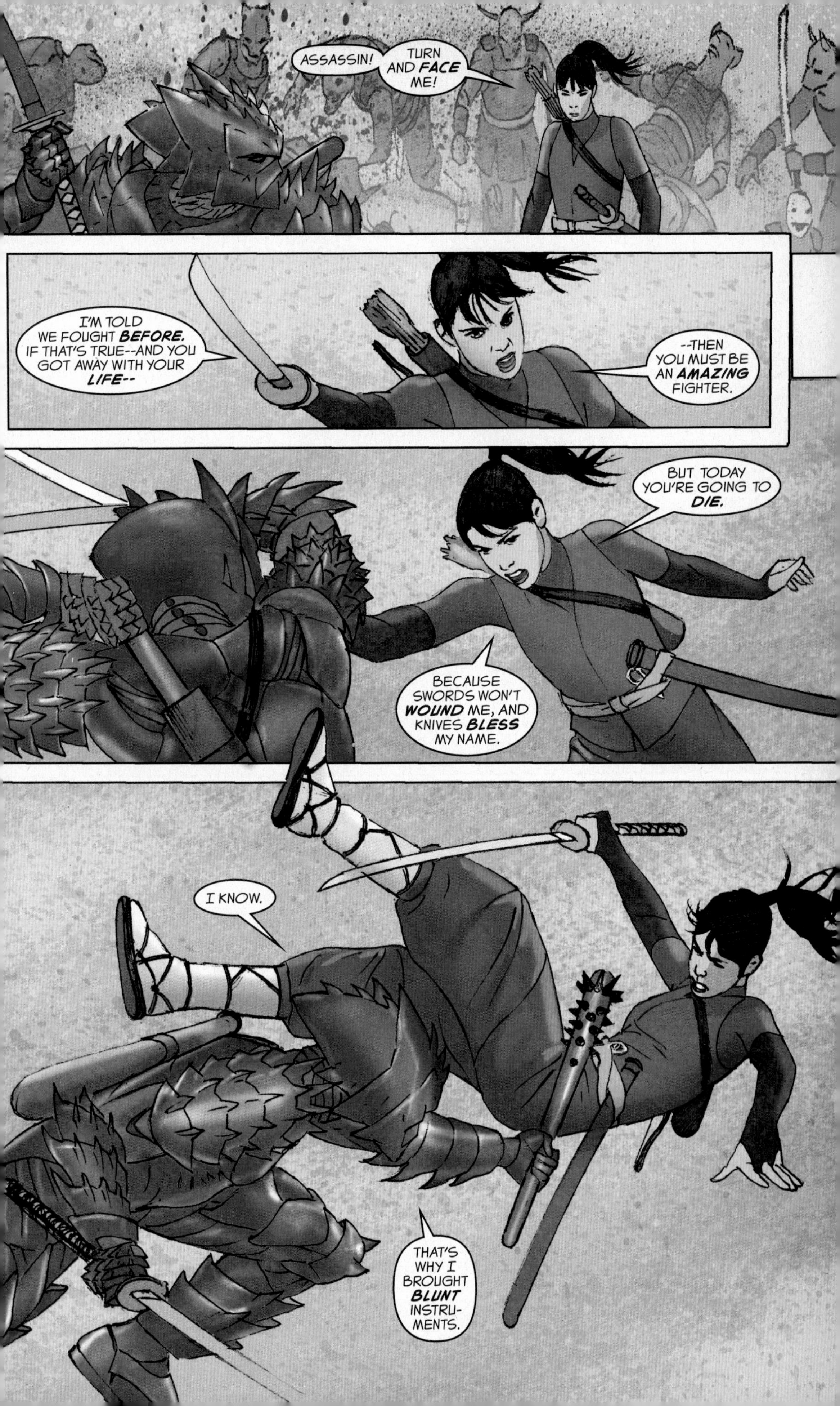

ASSASSIN!
TURN AND FACE ME!
I'M TOLD WE FOUGHT BEFORE. IF THAT'S TRUE--AND YOU GOT AWAY WITH YOUR LIFE--
--THEN YOU MUST BE AN AMAZING FIGHTER.
BUT TODAY YOU'RE GOING TO DIE.
BECAUSE SWORDS WON'T WOUND ME, AND KNIVES BLESS MY NAME.
I KNOW.
THAT'S WHY I BROUGHT BLUNT INSTRU-MENTS.

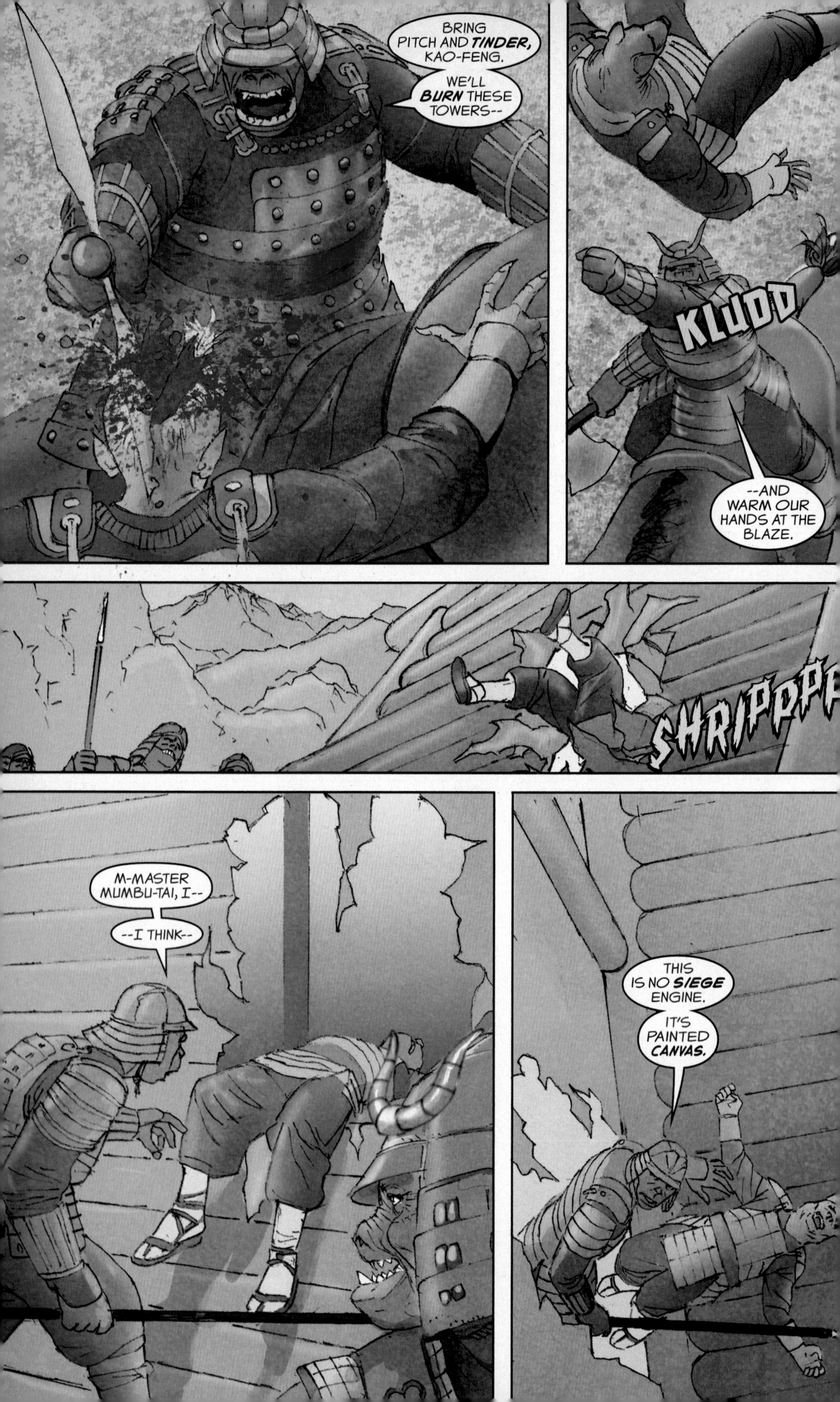

BRING PITCH AND *TINDER,* KAO-FENG.
WE'LL *BURN* THESE TOWERS--
KLUDD
--AND WARM OUR HANDS AT THE BLAZE.
SHRIPPP
M-MASTER MUMBU-TAI, I--
--I THINK--
THIS IS NO *SIEGE* ENGINE.
IT'S PAINTED *CANVAS.*

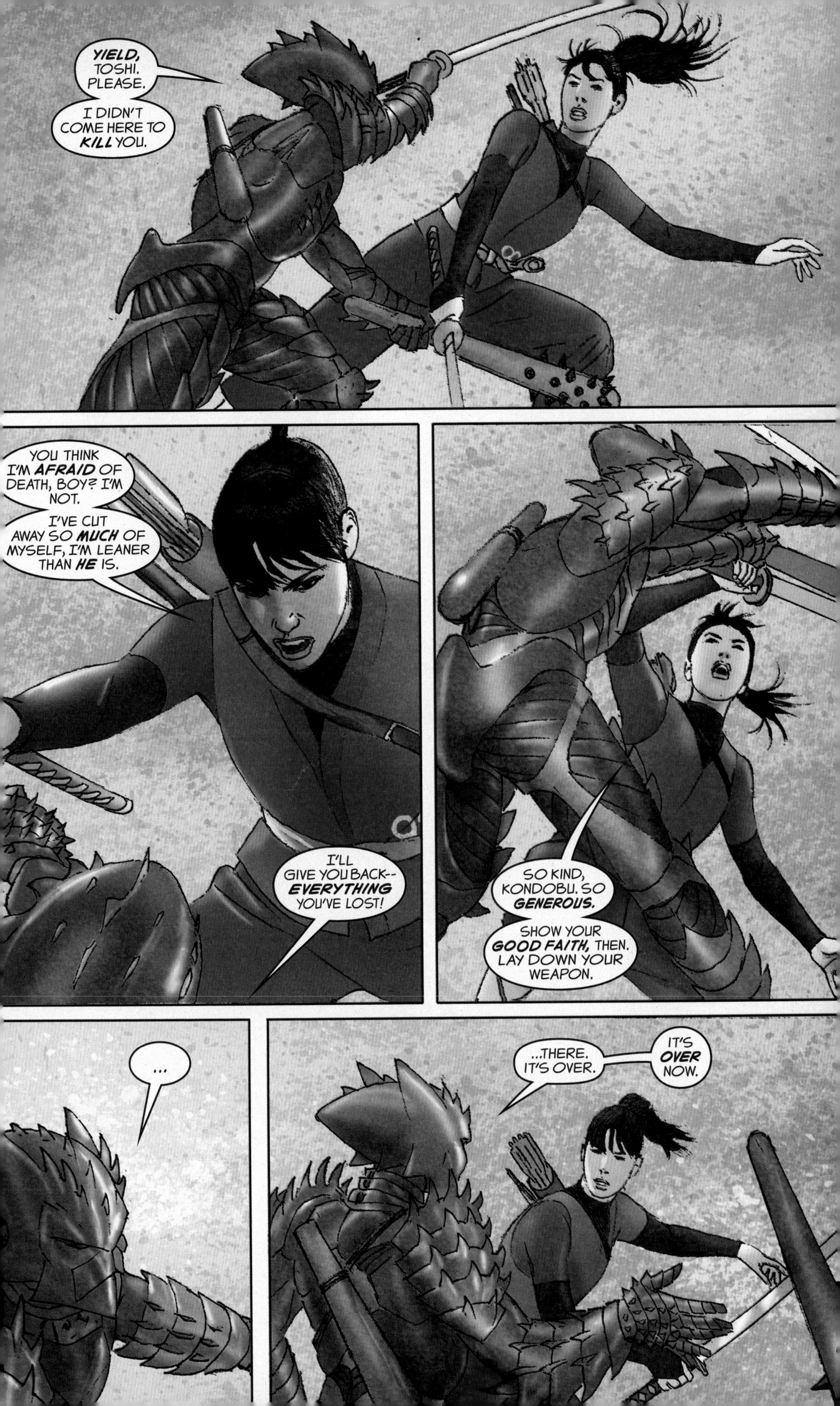
YIELD, TOSHI. PLEASE.
I DIDN'T COME HERE TO KILL YOU.
YOU THINK I'M AFRAID OF DEATH, BOY? I'M NOT.
I'VE CUT AWAY SO MUCH OF MYSELF, I'M LEANER THAN HE IS.
I'LL GIVE YOU BACK-- EVERYTHING YOU'VE LOST!
SO KIND, KONDOBU. SO GENEROUS.
SHOW YOUR GOOD FAITH, THEN. LAY DOWN YOUR WEAPON.
...
...THERE. IT'S OVER.
IT'S OVER NOW.

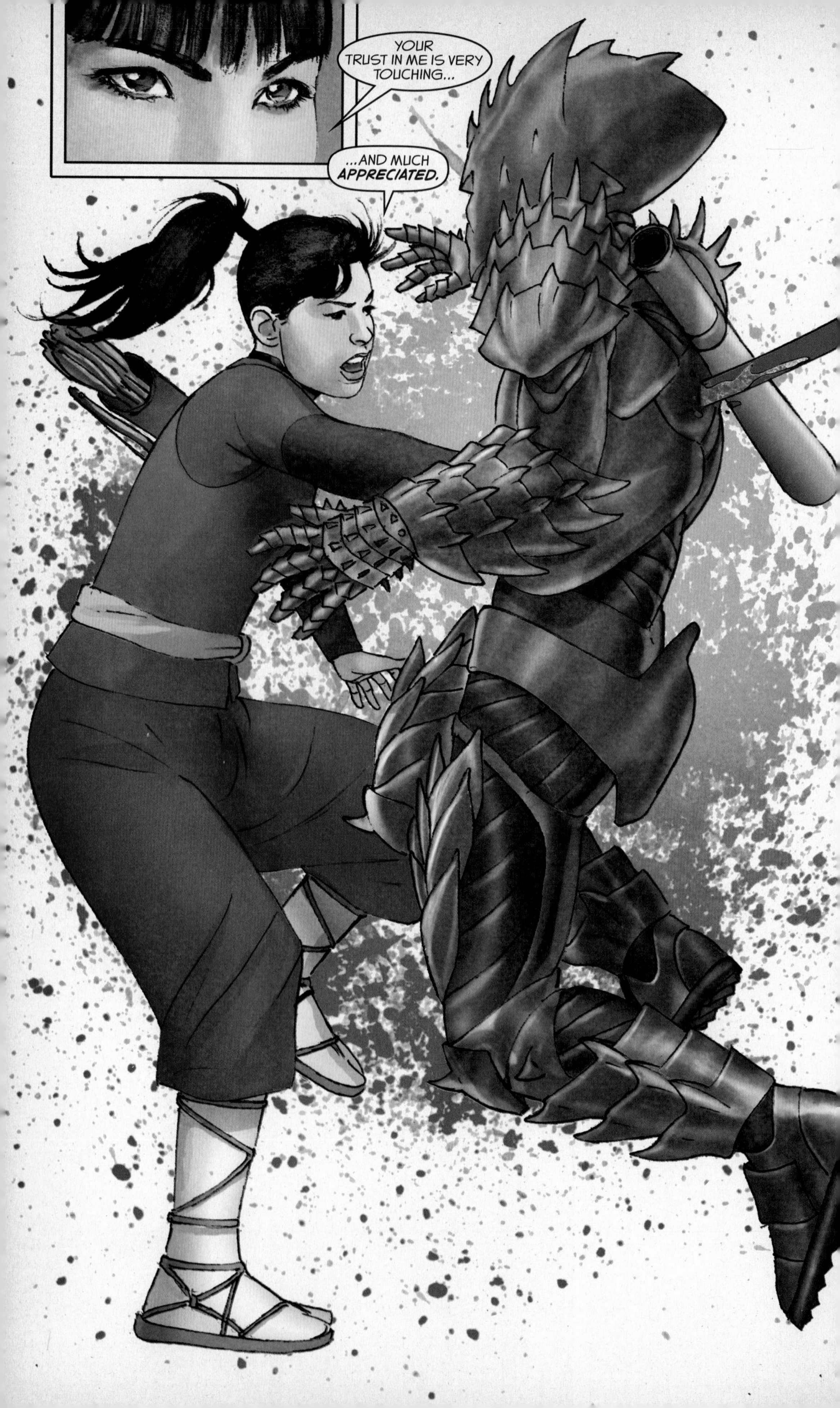

YOUR TRUST IN ME IS VERY TOUCHING...
...AND MUCH APPRECIATED.

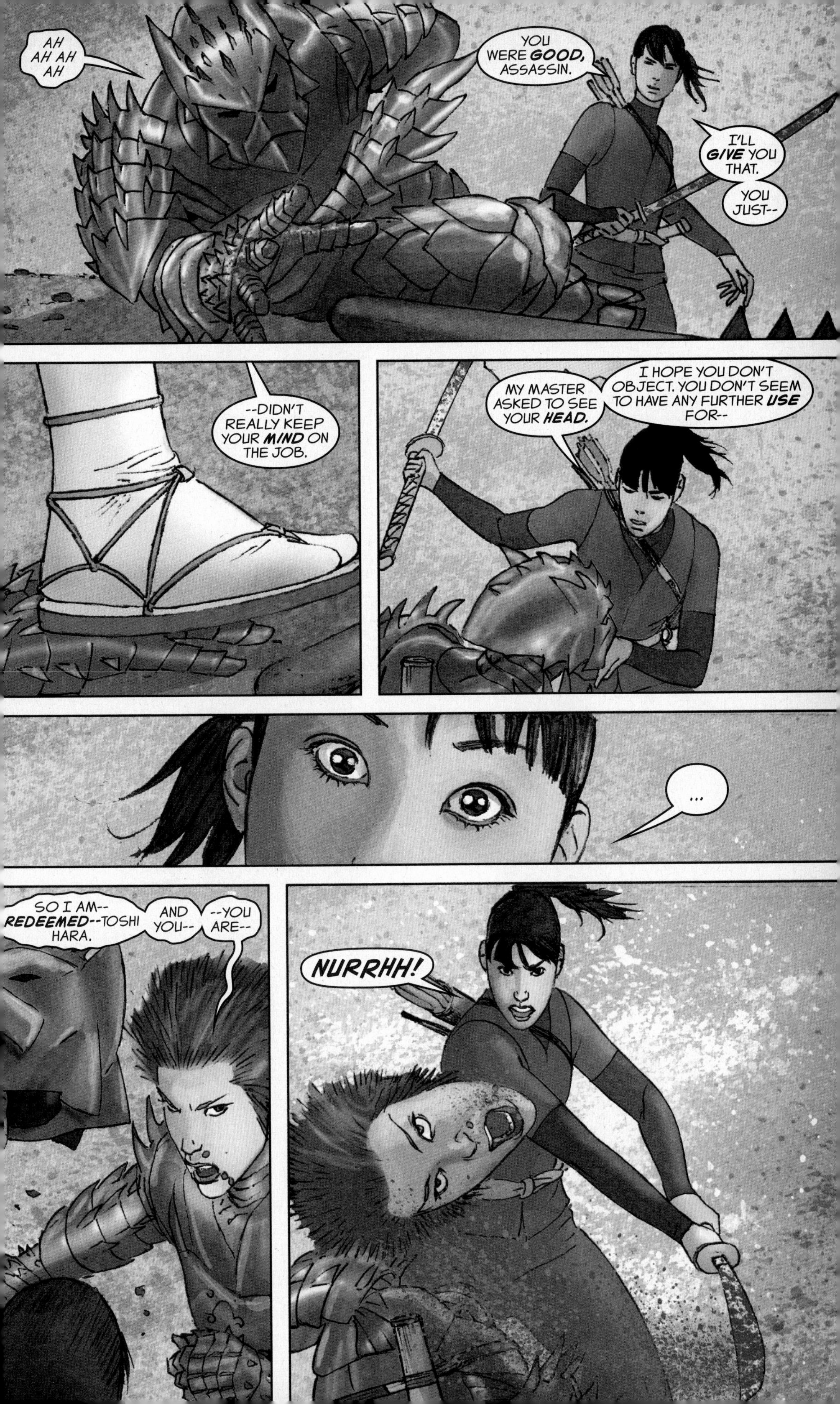
AH AH AH AH
YOU WERE GOOD, ASSASSIN.
I'LL GIVE YOU THAT.
YOU JUST--
--DIDN'T REALLY KEEP YOUR MIND ON THE JOB.
MY MASTER ASKED TO SEE YOUR HEAD.
I HOPE YOU DON'T OBJECT. YOU DON'T SEEM TO HAVE ANY FURTHER USE FOR--
...
SO I AM-- REDEEMED--TOSHI HARA.
AND YOU--
--YOU ARE--
NURRHH!

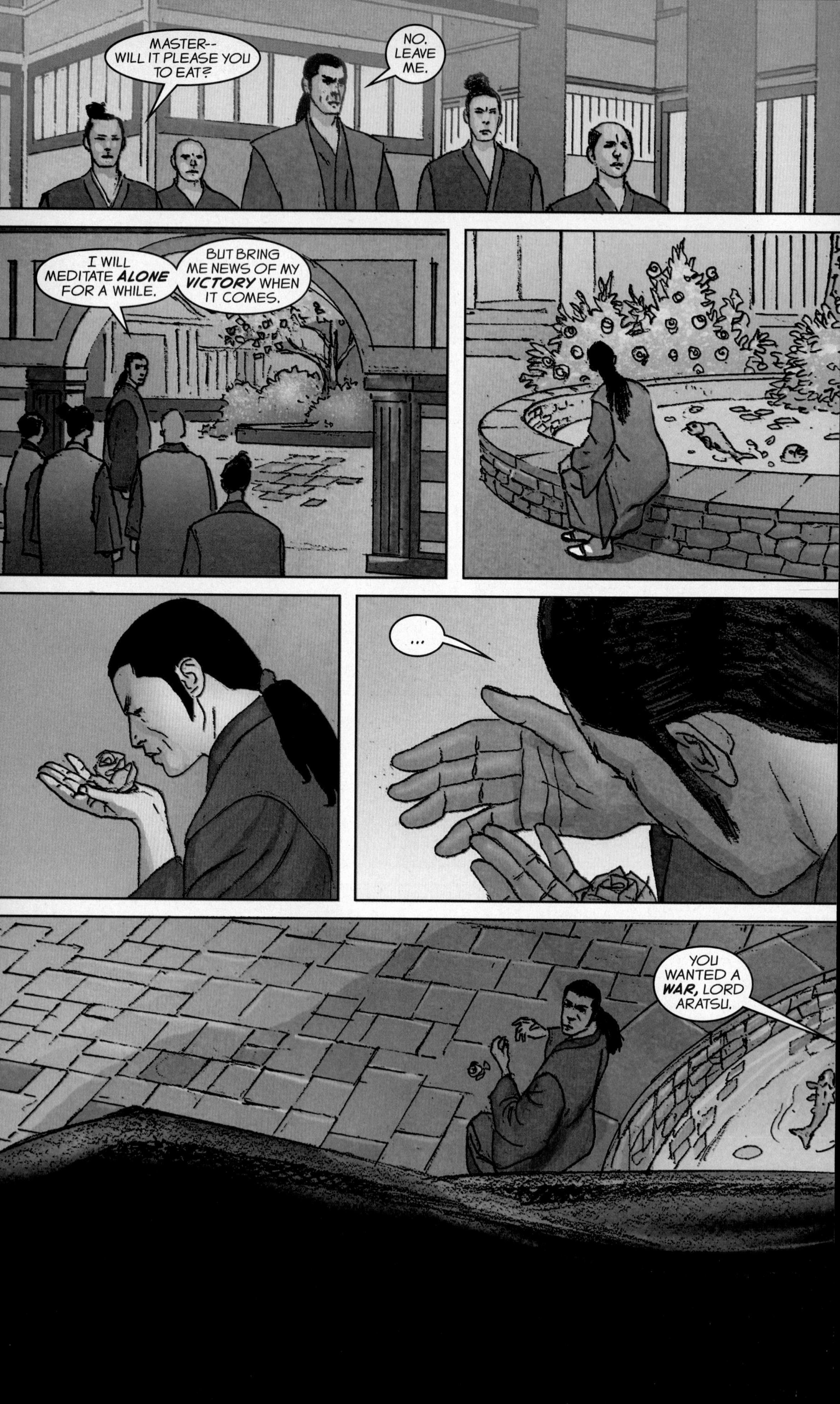

MASTER-- WILL IT PLEASE YOU TO EAT?
NO. LEAVE ME.
I WILL MEDITATE ALONE FOR A WHILE.
BUT BRING ME NEWS OF MY VICTORY WHEN IT COMES.
...
YOU WANTED A WAR, LORD ARATSU.

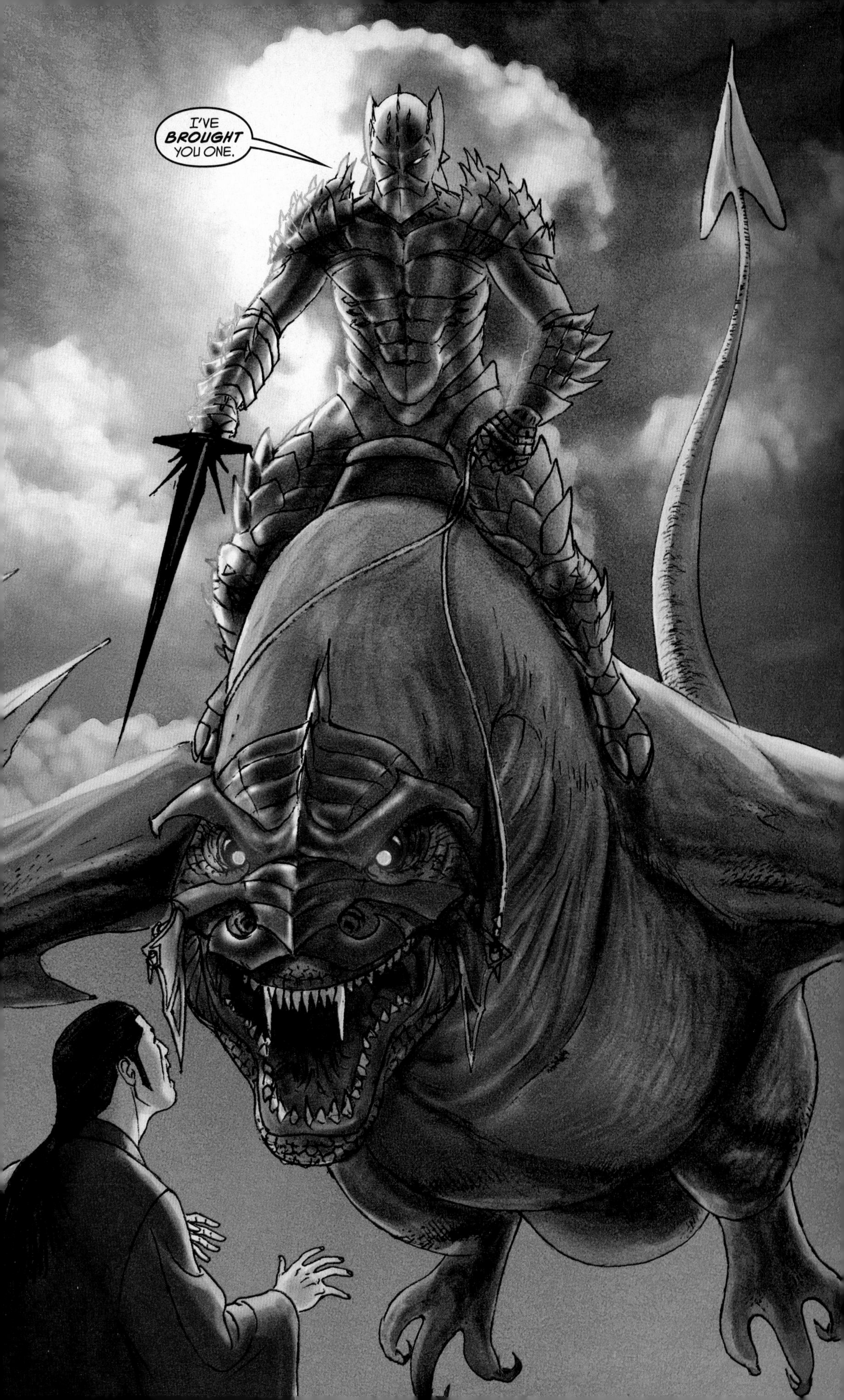
I'VE BROUGHT YOU ONE.

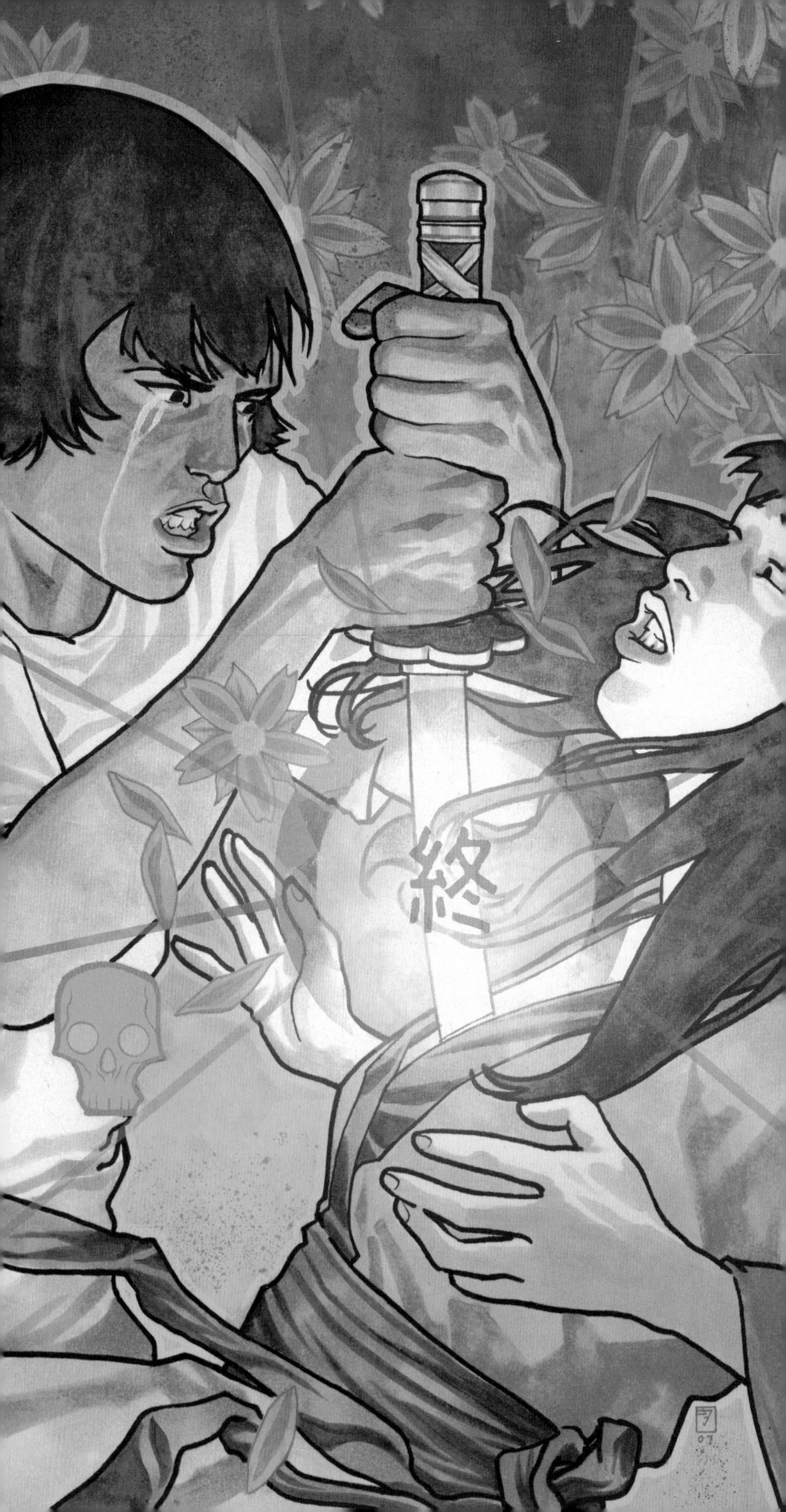
終

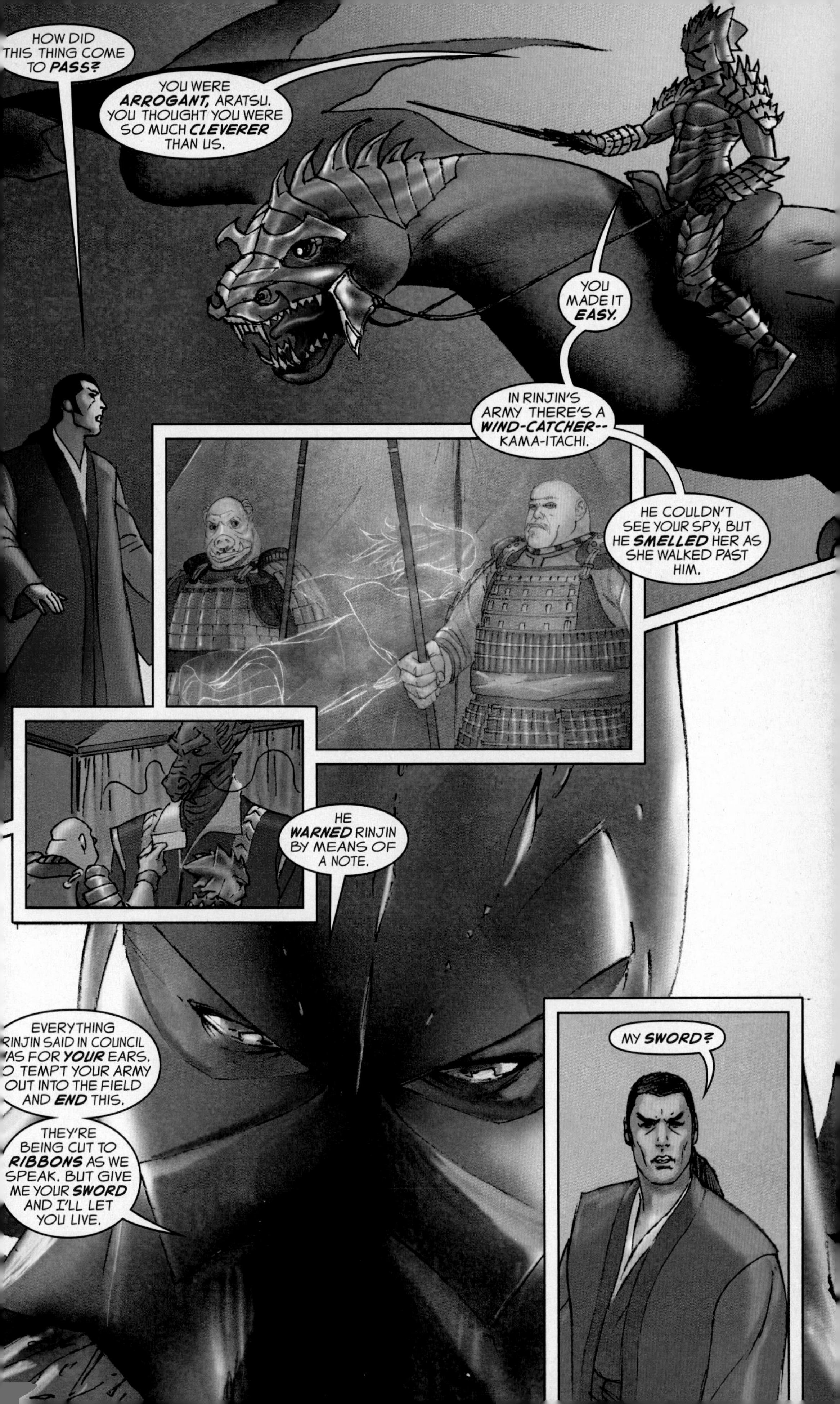
HOW DID THIS THING COME TO PASS?
YOU WERE ARROGANT, ARATSU. YOU THOUGHT YOU WERE SO MUCH CLEVERER THAN US.
YOU MADE IT EASY.
IN RINJIN'S ARMY THERE'S A WIND-CATCHER-- KAMA-ITACHI.
HE COULDN'T SEE YOUR SPY, BUT HE SMELLED HER AS SHE WALKED PAST HIM.
HE WARNED RINJIN BY MEANS OF A NOTE.
EVERYTHING RINJIN SAID IN COUNCIL AS FOR YOUR EARS. O TEMPT YOUR ARMY OUT INTO THE FIELD AND END THIS.
THEY'RE BEING CUT TO RIBBONS AS WE SPEAK. BUT GIVE ME YOUR SWORD AND I'LL LET YOU LIVE.
MY SWORD?

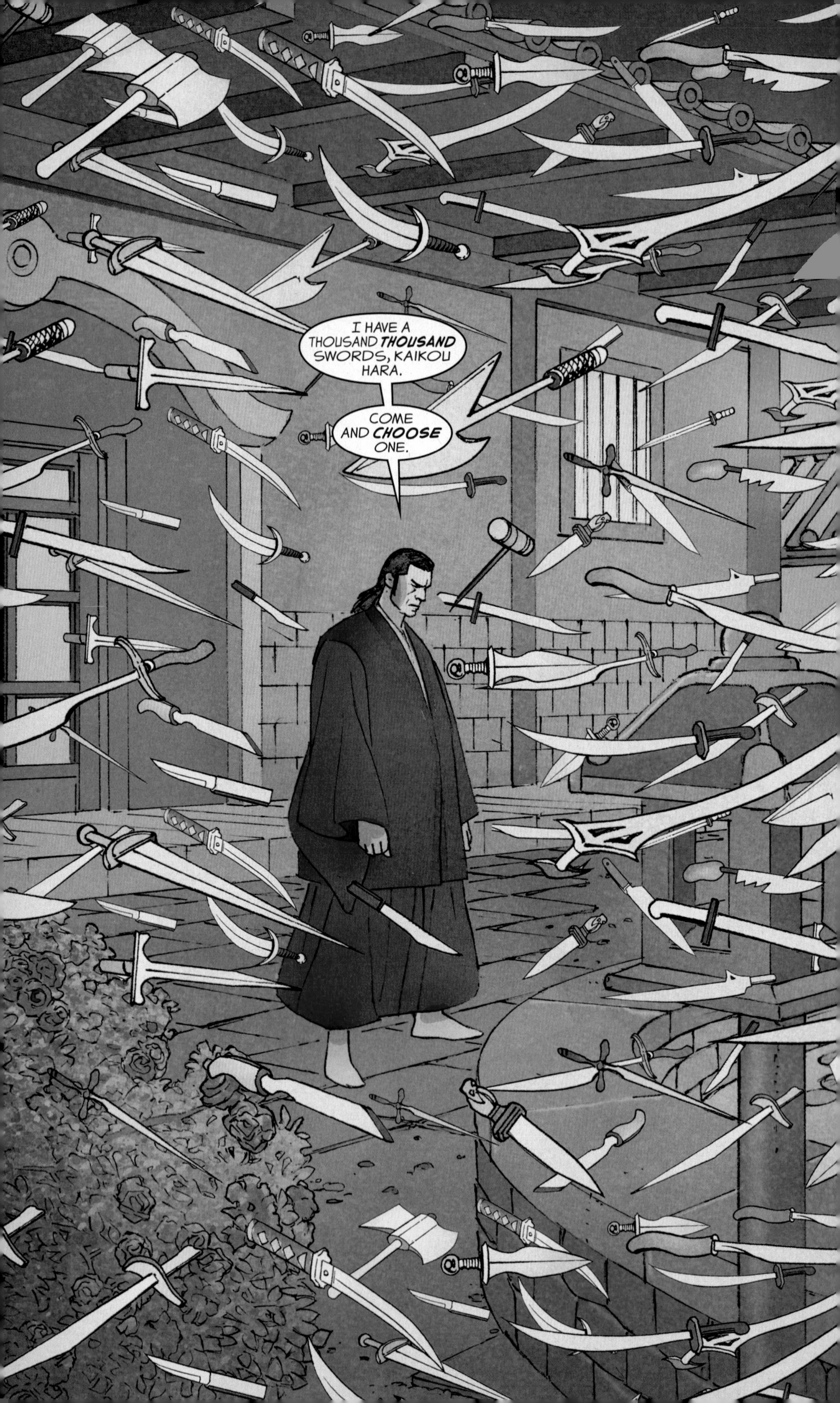
I HAVE A THOUSAND **THOUSAND** SWORDS, KAIKOU HARA.
COME AND **CHOOSE** ONE.

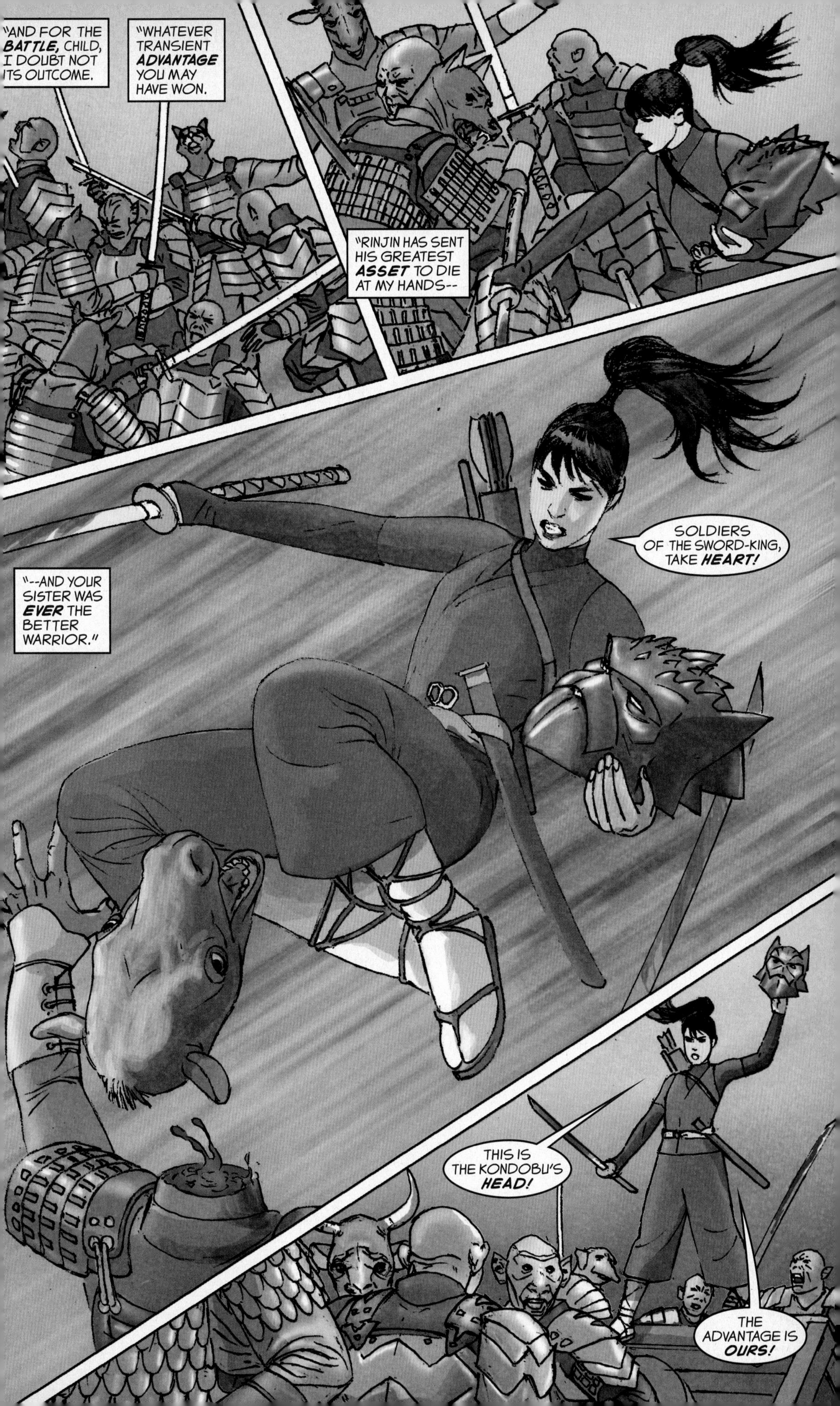

"AND FOR THE BATTLE, CHILD, I DOUBT NOT ITS OUTCOME.
"WHATEVER TRANSIENT ADVANTAGE YOU MAY HAVE WON.
"RINJIN HAS SENT HIS GREATEST ASSET TO DIE AT MY HANDS--
SOLDIERS OF THE SWORD-KING, TAKE HEART!
"--AND YOUR SISTER WAS EVER THE BETTER WARRIOR."
THIS IS THE KONDOBU'S HEAD!
THE ADVANTAGE IS OURS!

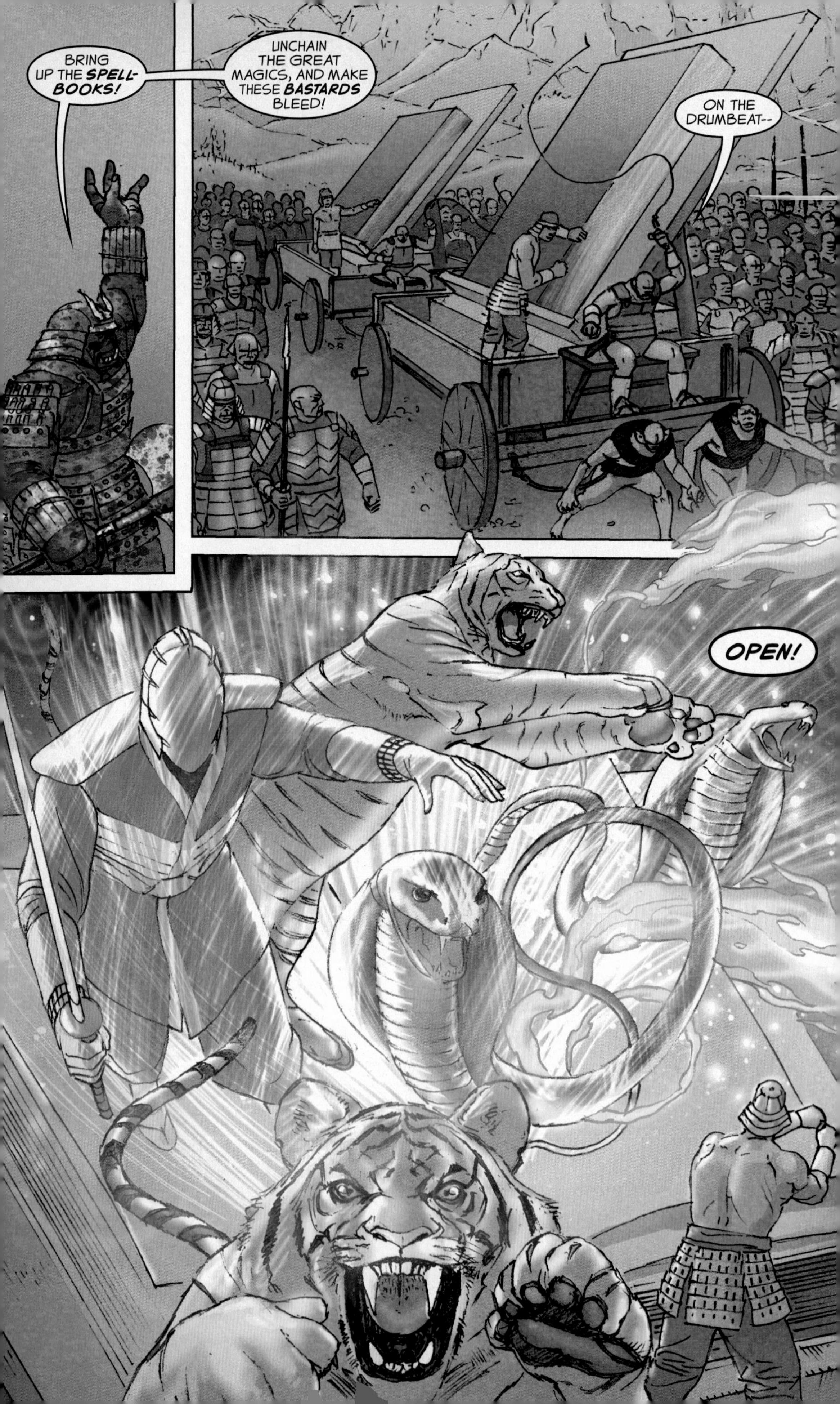
BRING UP THE SPELL-BOOKS!
UNCHAIN THE GREAT MAGICS, AND MAKE THESE BASTARDS BLEED!
ON THE DRUMBEAT--
OPEN!

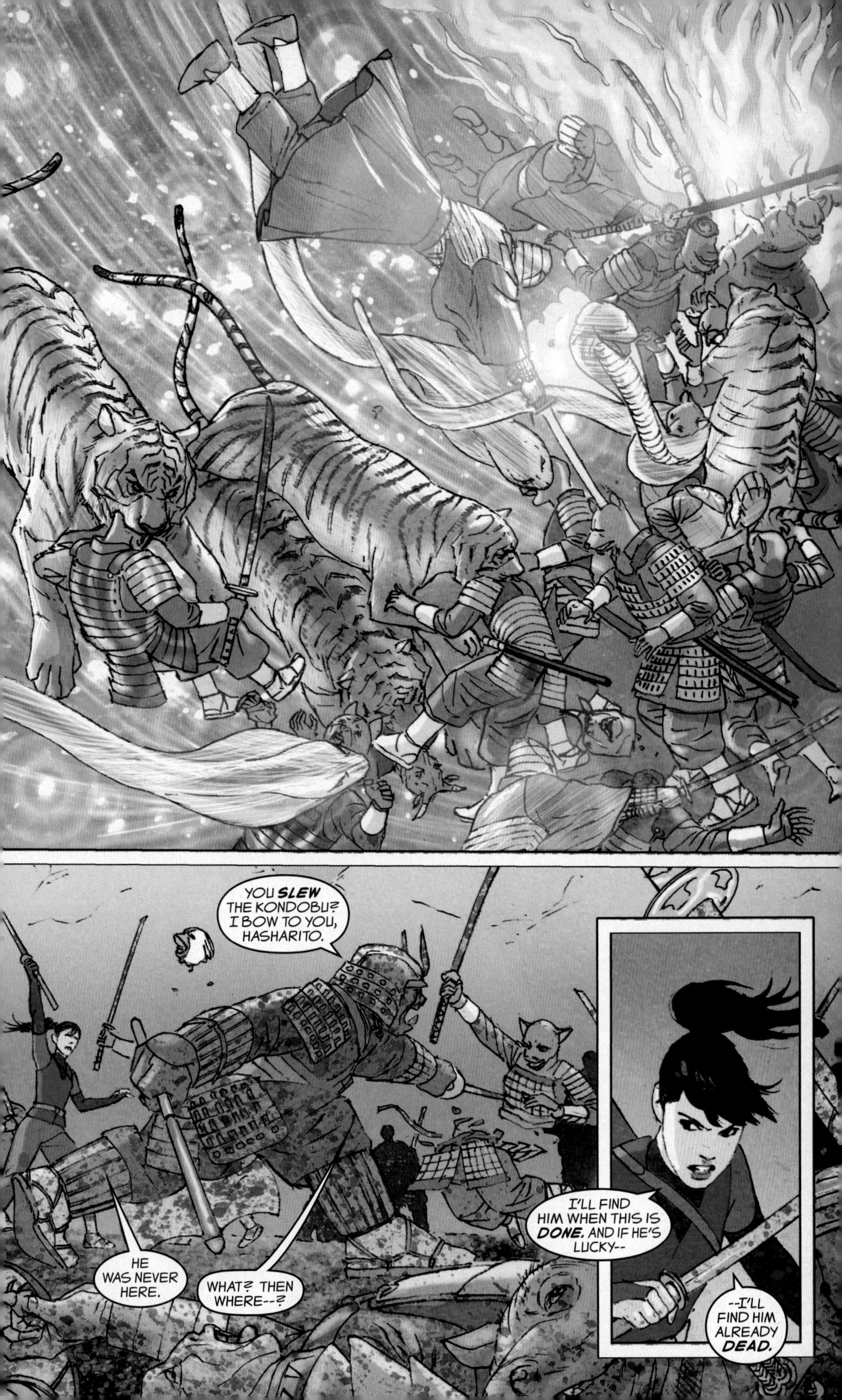
YOU **SLEW** THE KONDOBU? I BOW TO YOU, HASHARITO.
HE WAS NEVER HERE.
WHAT? THEN WHERE--?
I'LL FIND HIM WHEN THIS IS **DONE.** AND IF HE'S LUCKY--
--I'LL FIND HIM ALREADY **DEAD.**

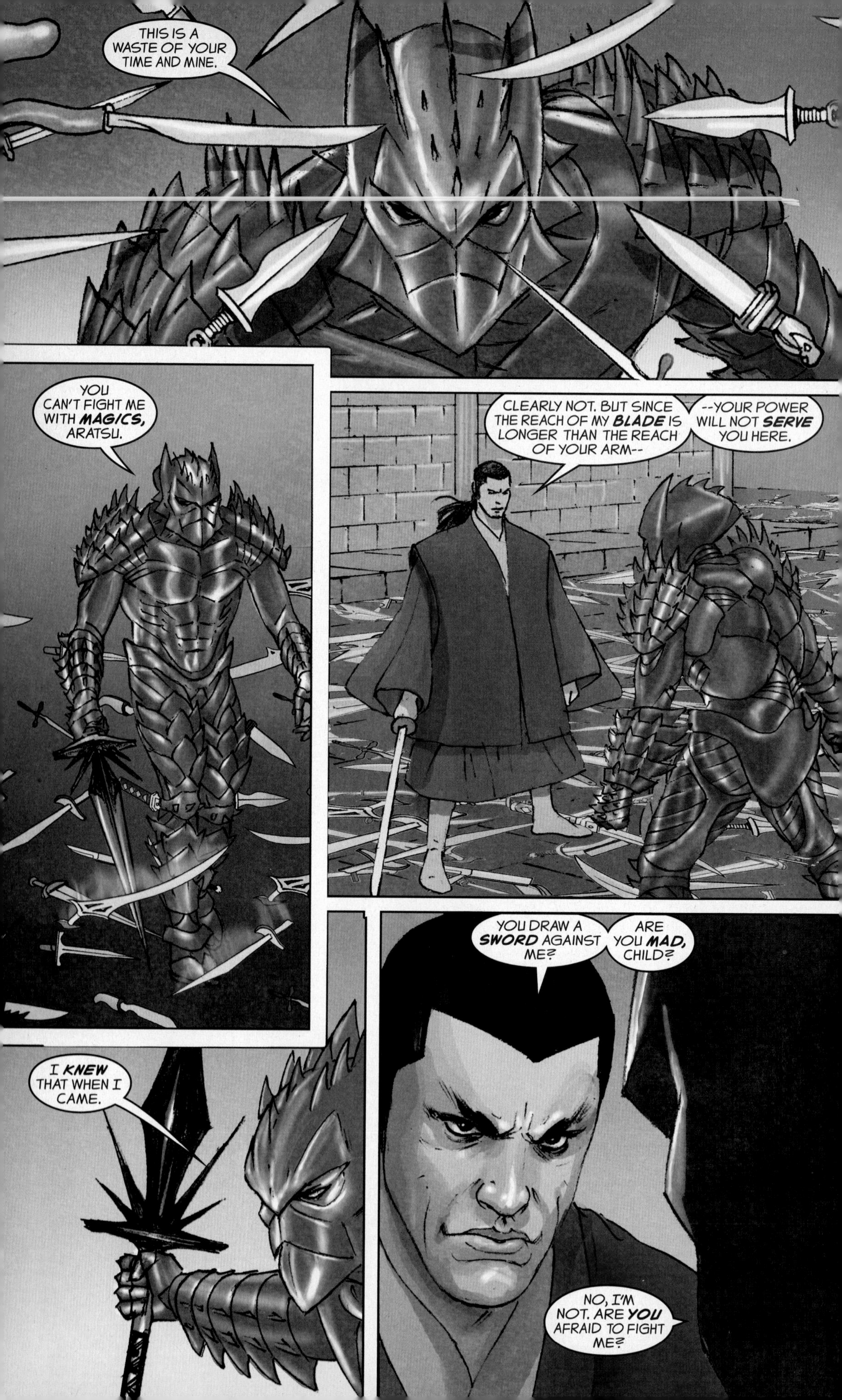
THIS IS A WASTE OF YOUR TIME AND MINE.
YOU CAN'T FIGHT ME WITH MAGICS, ARATSU.
CLEARLY NOT. BUT SINCE THE REACH OF MY BLADE IS LONGER THAN THE REACH OF YOUR ARM--
--YOUR POWER WILL NOT SERVE YOU HERE.
YOU DRAW A SWORD AGAINST ME?
ARE YOU MAD, CHILD?
I KNEW THAT WHEN I CAME.
NO, I'M NOT. ARE YOU AFRAID TO FIGHT ME?

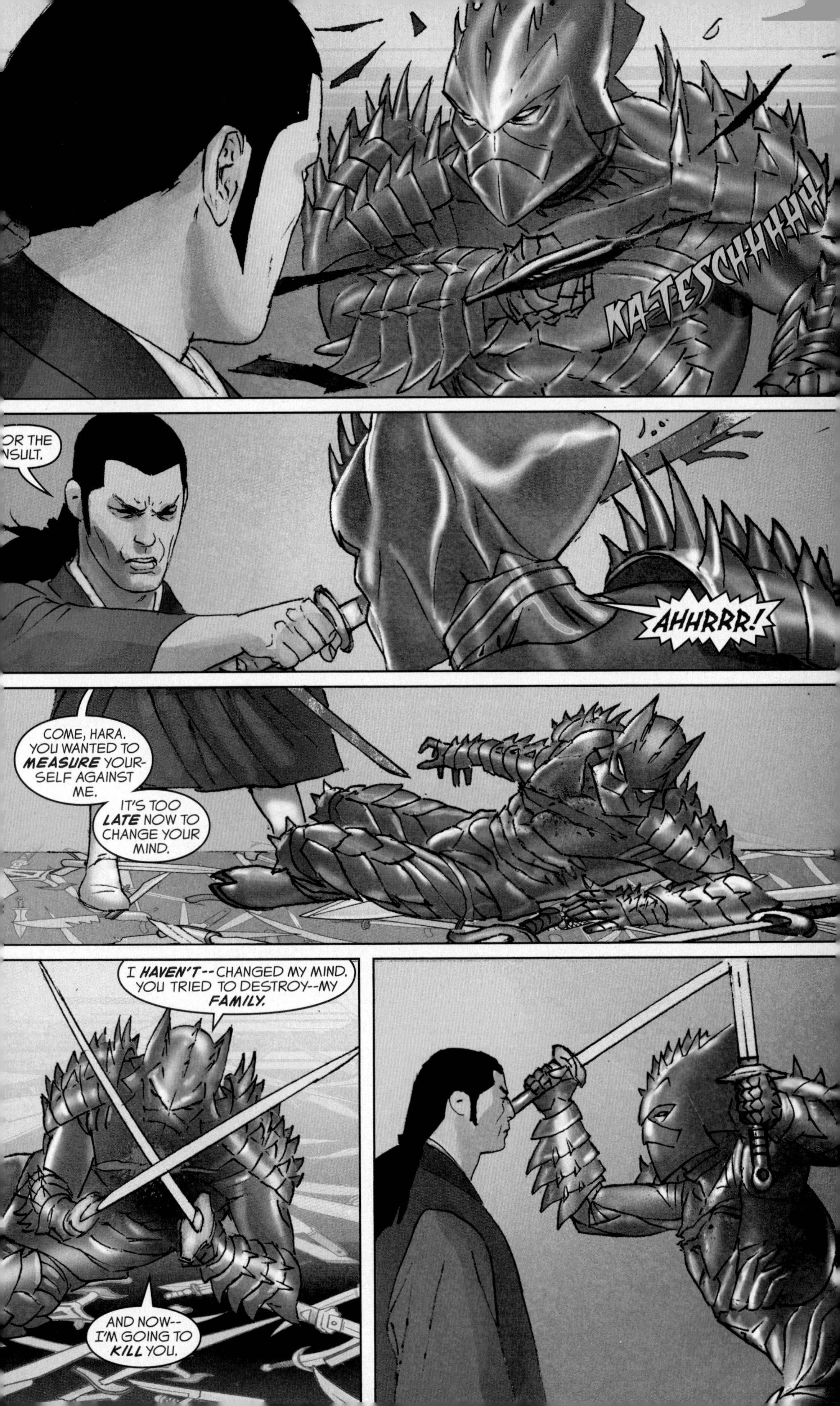
KA-TESCHHHAH
OR THE NSULT.
AHHRRR!
COME, HARA. YOU WANTED TO MEASURE YOURSELF AGAINST ME.
IT'S TOO LATE NOW TO CHANGE YOUR MIND.
I HAVEN'T--CHANGED MY MIND. YOU TRIED TO DESTROY--MY FAMILY.
AND NOW-- I'M GOING TO KILL YOU.

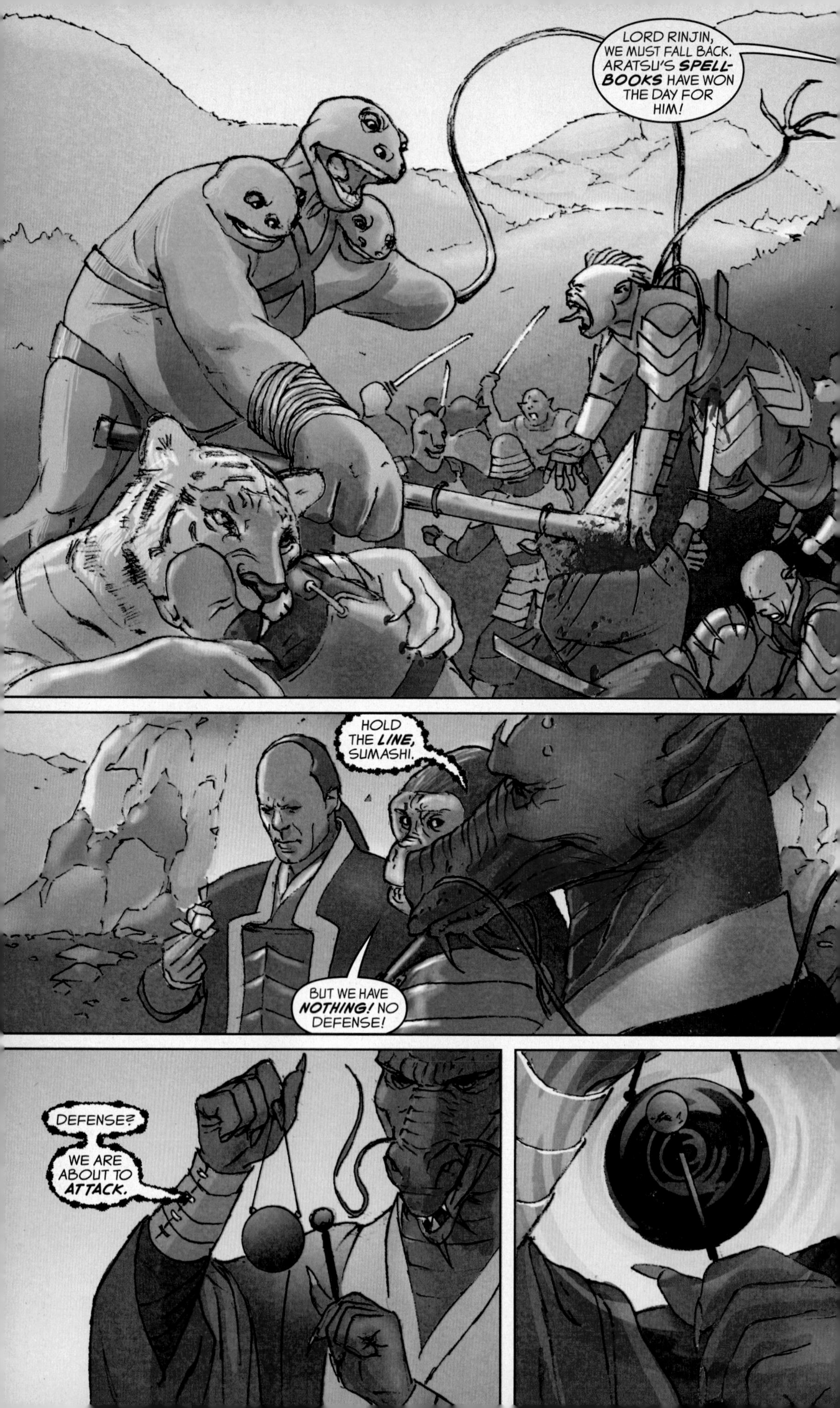
LORD RINJIN, WE MUST FALL BACK. ARATSU'S SPELL-BOOKS HAVE WON THE DAY FOR HIM!
HOLD THE LINE, SUMASHI.
BUT WE HAVE NOTHING! NO DEFENSE!
DEFENSE?
WE ARE ABOUT TO ATTACK.

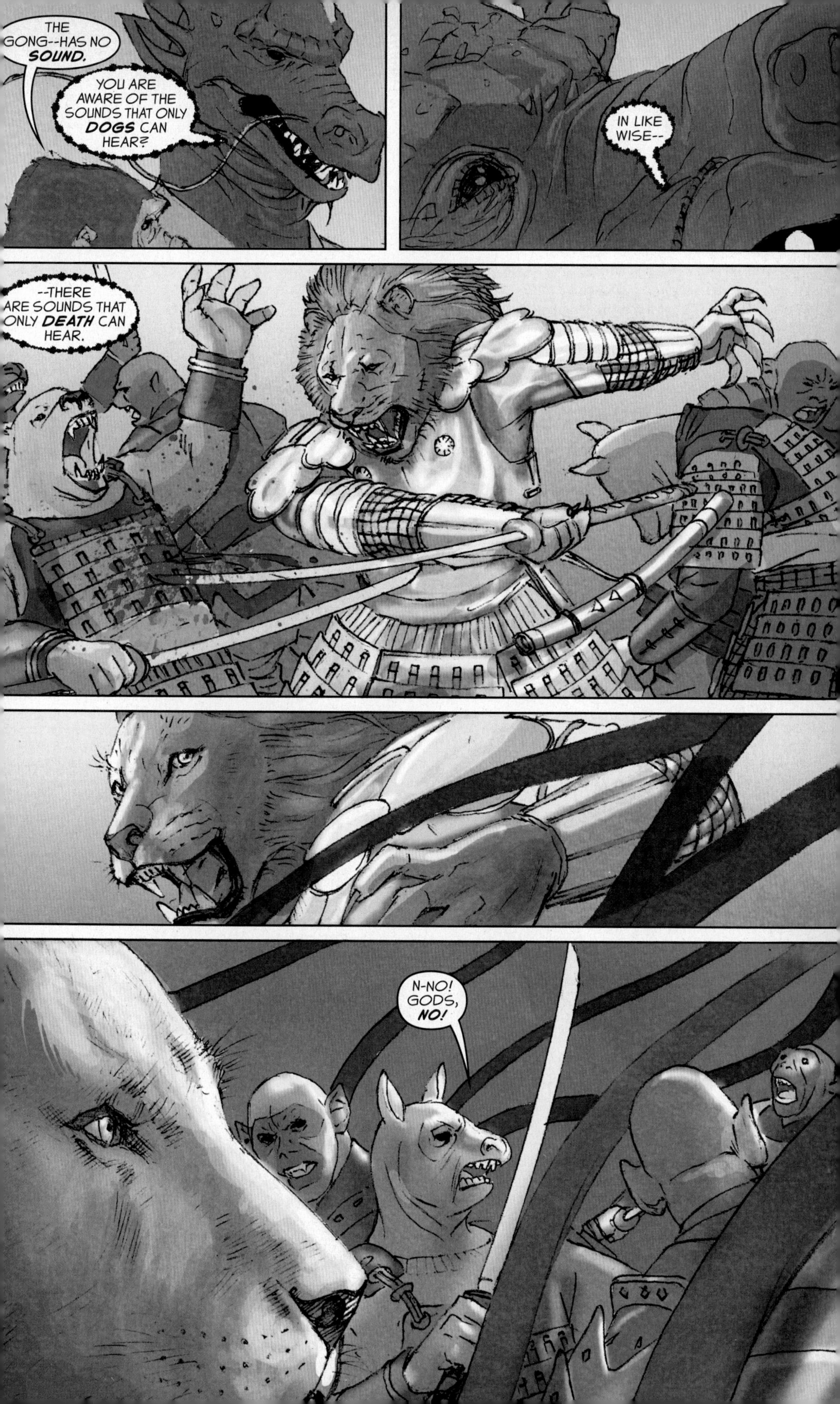
THE GONG--HAS NO **SOUND.**
YOU ARE AWARE OF THE SOUNDS THAT ONLY **DOGS** CAN HEAR?
IN LIKE WISE--
--THERE ARE SOUNDS THAT ONLY **DEATH** CAN HEAR.
N-NO! GODS, **NO!**

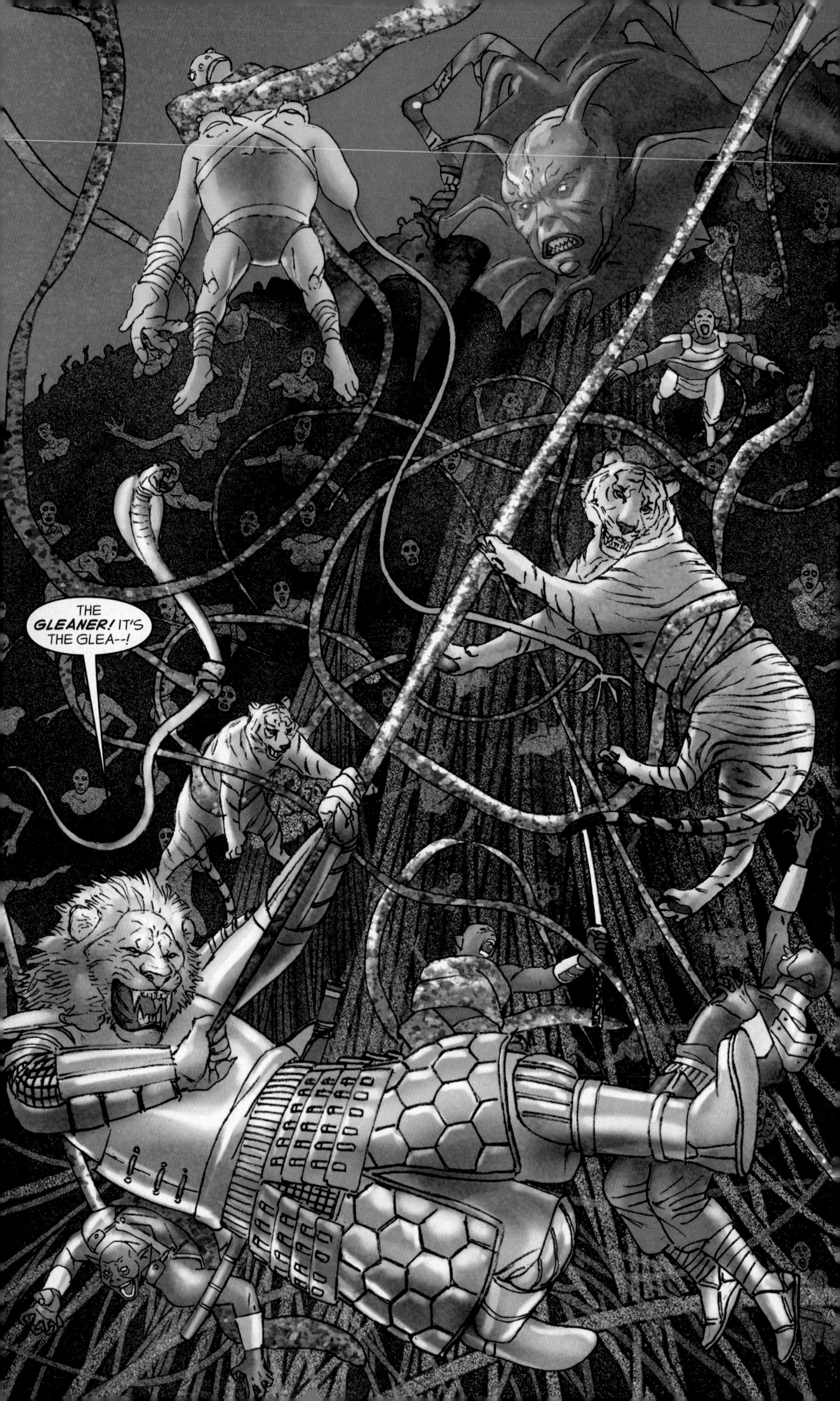
THE GLEANER! IT'S THE GLEA--!

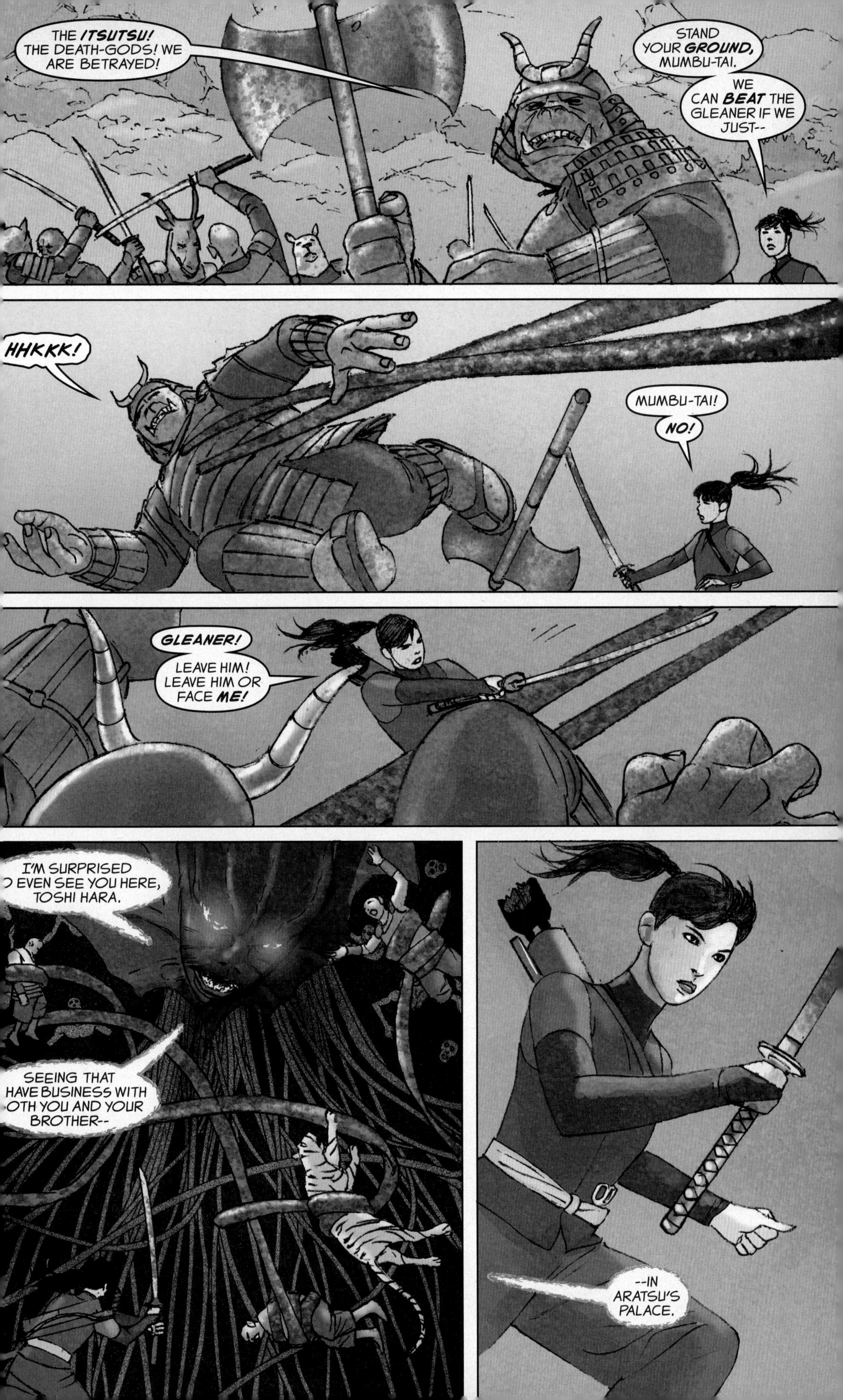

THE ITSUTSU! THE DEATH-GODS! WE ARE BETRAYED!
STAND YOUR GROUND, MUMBU-TAI.
WE CAN BEAT THE GLEANER IF WE JUST--
HHKKK!
MUMBU-TAI! NO!
GLEANER!
LEAVE HIM! LEAVE HIM OR FACE ME!
I'M SURPRISED
EVEN SEE YOU HERE, TOSHI HARA.
SEEING THAT
HAVE BUSINESS WITH
OTH YOU AND YOUR BROTHER--
--IN ARATSU'S PALACE.

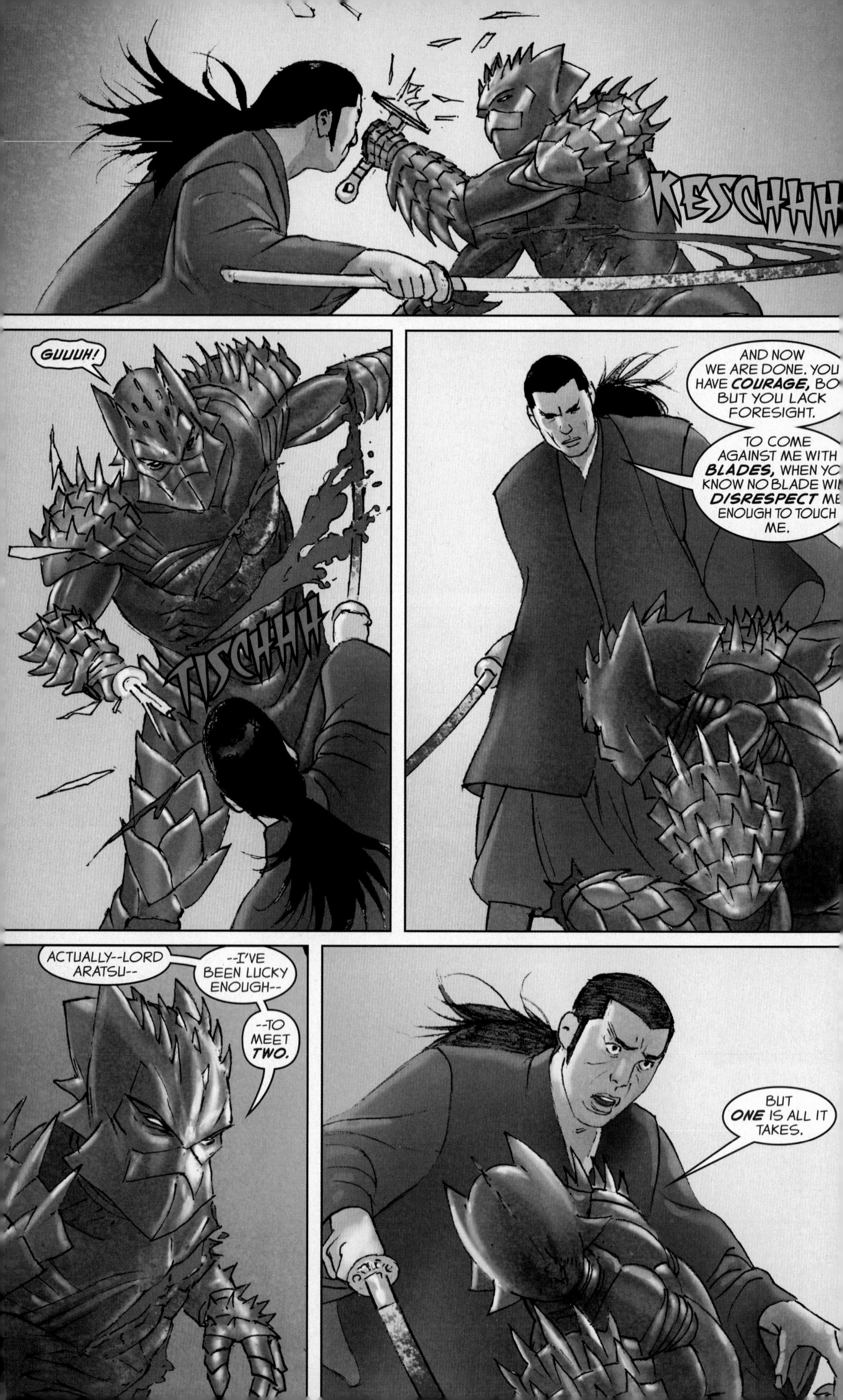
KESCHHH
GUUUH!
TISCHHH
AND NOW WE ARE DONE. YOU HAVE COURAGE, BO BUT YOU LACK FORESIGHT.
TO COME AGAINST ME WITH BLADES, WHEN YO KNOW NO BLADE WI DISRESPECT ME ENOUGH TO TOUCH ME.
ACTUALLY--LORD ARATSU--
--I'VE BEEN LUCKY ENOUGH--
--TO MEET TWO.
BUT ONE IS ALL IT TAKES.

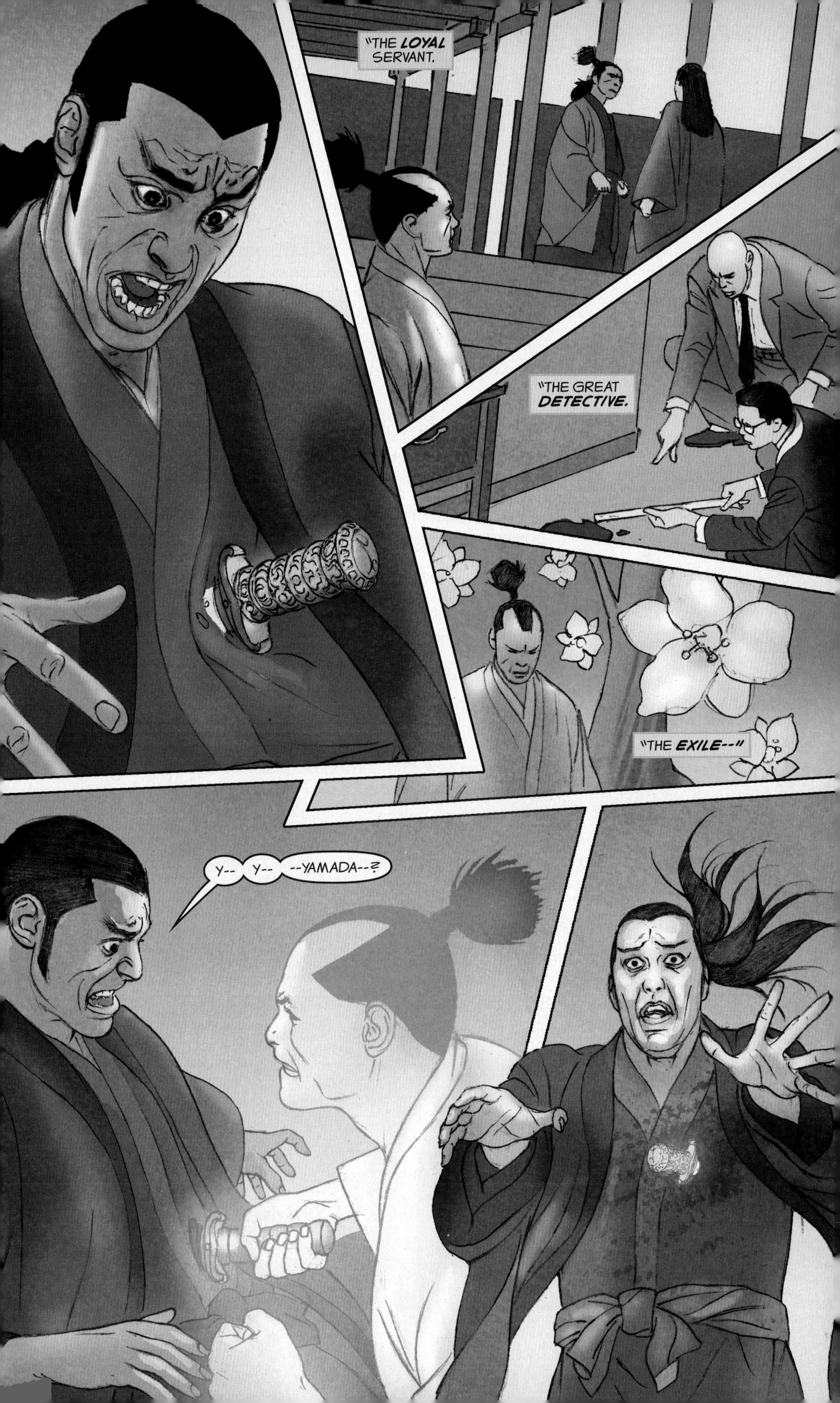

"THE LOYAL SERVANT.
"THE GREAT DETECTIVE.
"THE EXILE--"
Y--
Y--
--YAMADA--?

YOU MUST KEEP MOVING, KAIKOU. YOU MUST FIND THE SWORD.

THE SWORD THAT STEALS THE PAST.

HUH HUH HUH

YAMADA, IS THIS THE ONE? IS THIS *AIDONO*?

I DO NOT THINK SO, KAIKOU. HE KEEPS *THAT* BLADE IN HIS AUDIENCE CHAMBER.

BESIDE THE *CHAIR* IN WHICH HE SITS.

TELL ME-- THE WAY.

HUH.

AND KEEP ME *MOVING*--IF I STOP.

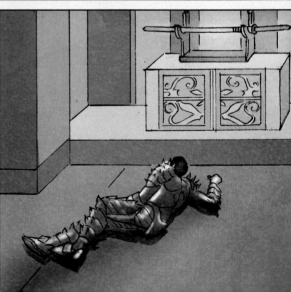

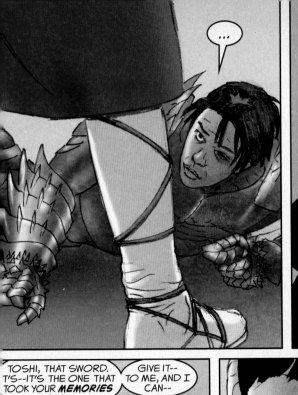

...

VERY *CLEVER.*

T-TOSHI!

ALL OF IT. I'M REALLY IMPRESSED.

TOSHI, THAT SWORD. T'S--IT'S THE ONE THAT TOOK YOUR *MEMORIES* AWAY.

GIVE IT-- TO ME, AND I CAN--

GIVE YOU A *WEAPON?* WHAT AN INTERESTING SUGGESTION.

I C--CAN TAKE AWAY ITS *POWER,* WITH MY TOUCH. *CURE* YOU.

OF COURSE.

JUST LET ME--*TOUCH* IT.

WELL--

--PERHAPS I *WILL.*

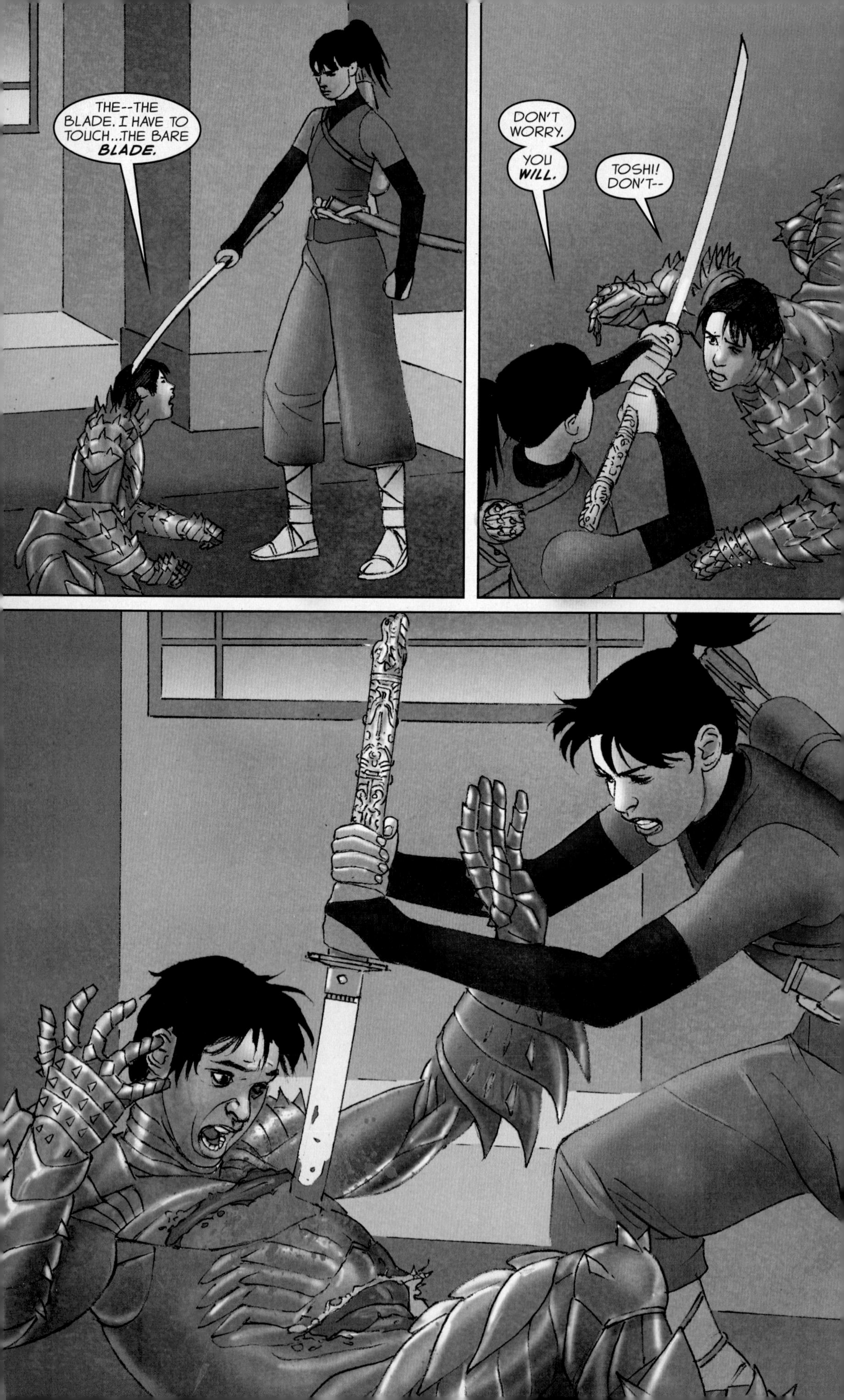
THE--THE BLADE. I HAVE TO TOUCH...THE BARE **BLADE.**
DON'T WORRY.
YOU **WILL.**
TOSHI! DON'T--

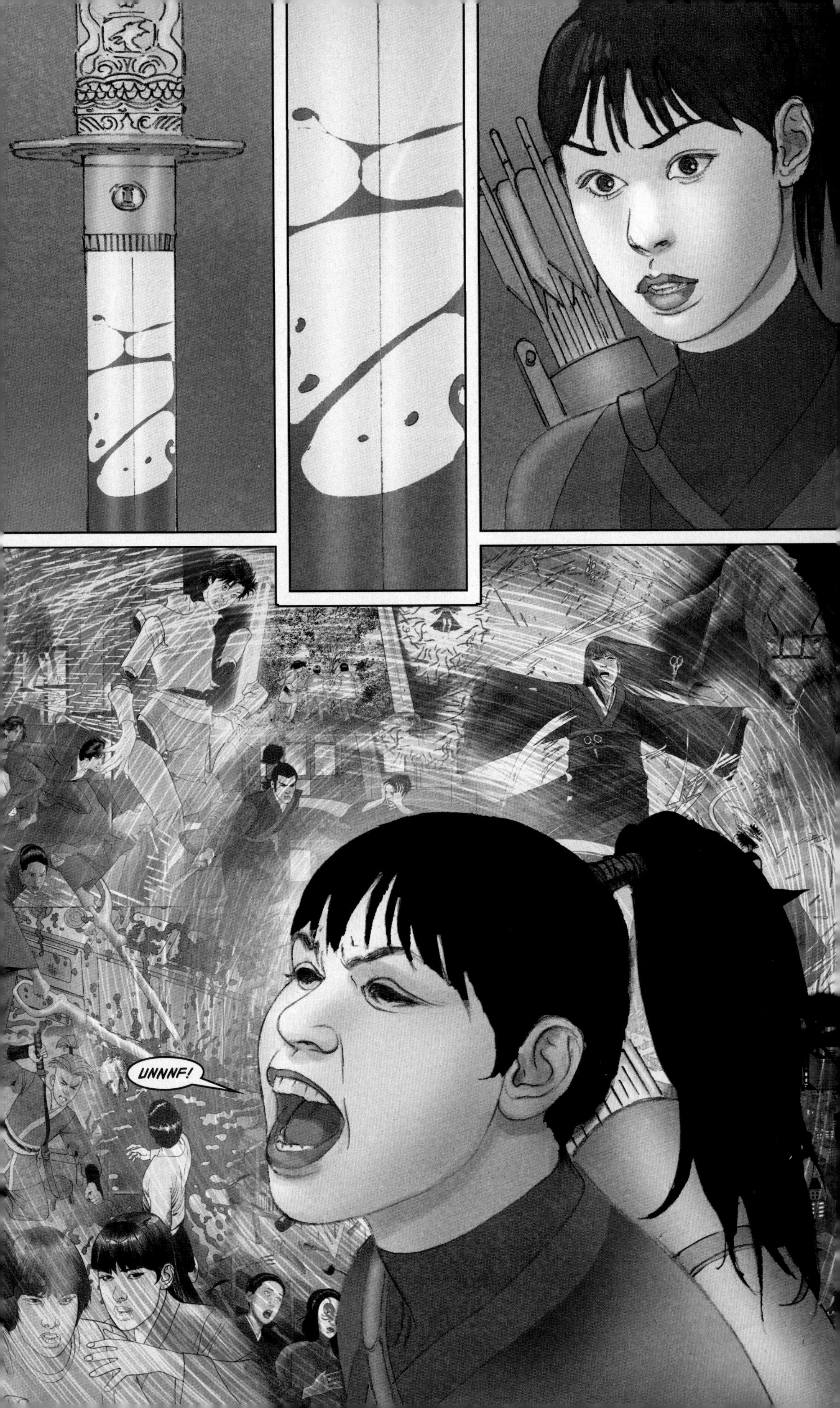
UNNNF!

AAH. YES.

MY LORD RINJIN.

MY LORD ASIROSAMIRO.

IT *APPEARS* I AM AT WAR.

INDEED. AND HAPPILY, I BELIEVE YOU ARE THE *VICTOR*.

IF YOU KNOW ME, AND *YOURSELF*, IT FOLLOWS THAT THE USURPER IS *DEAD* AND HIS POWER BROKEN.

YOU DID ALL THIS ON *MY* BEHALF?

WELL, WITH A VIEW TO SUITABLE *RECOMPENSE*.

OF COURSE.

AND WITH SOME *ASSISTANCE* FROM OTHER INTERESTED PARTIES.

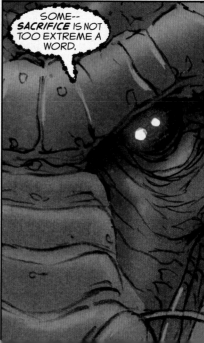

SOME-- *SACRIFICE* IS NOT TOO EXTREME A WORD.

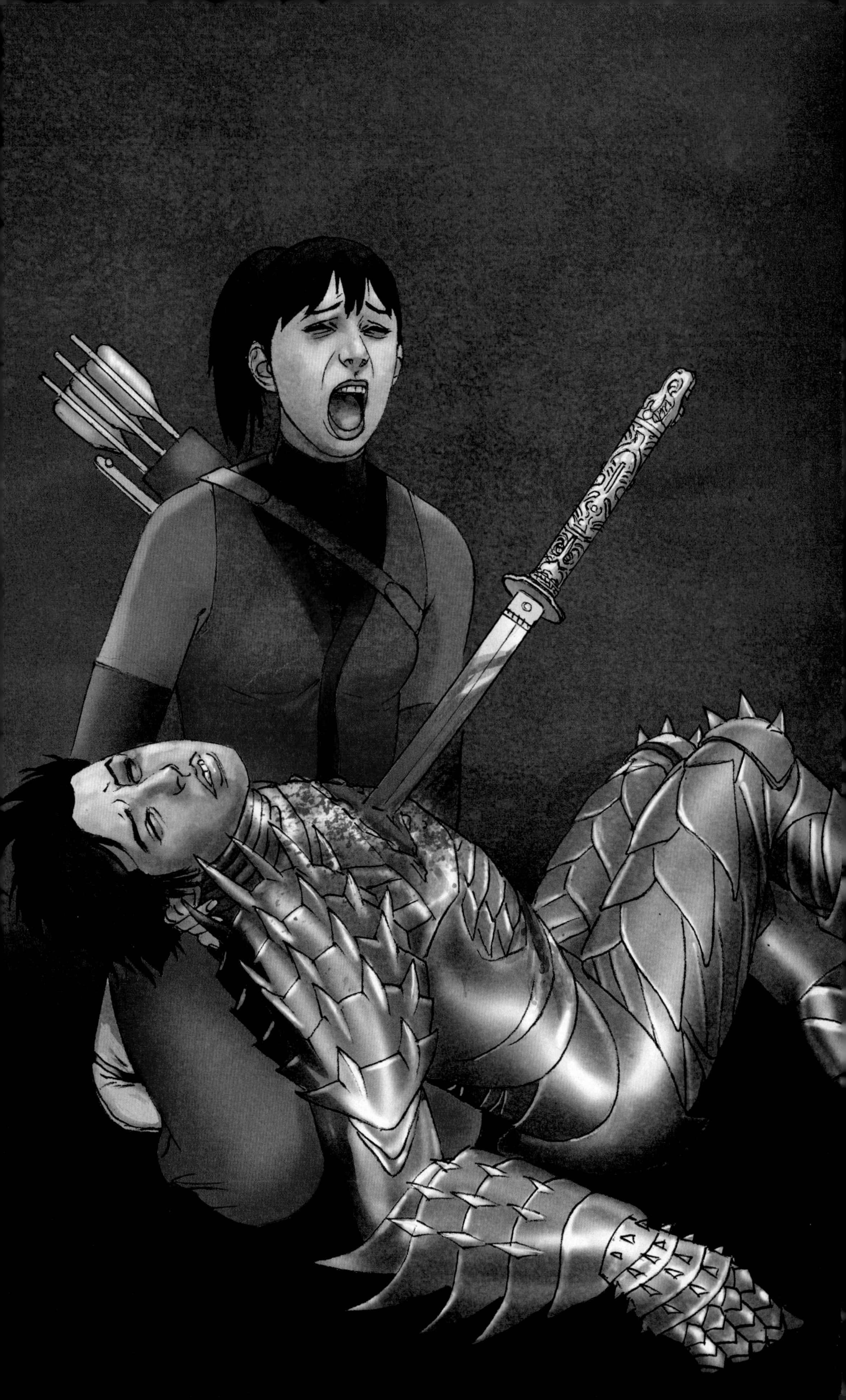

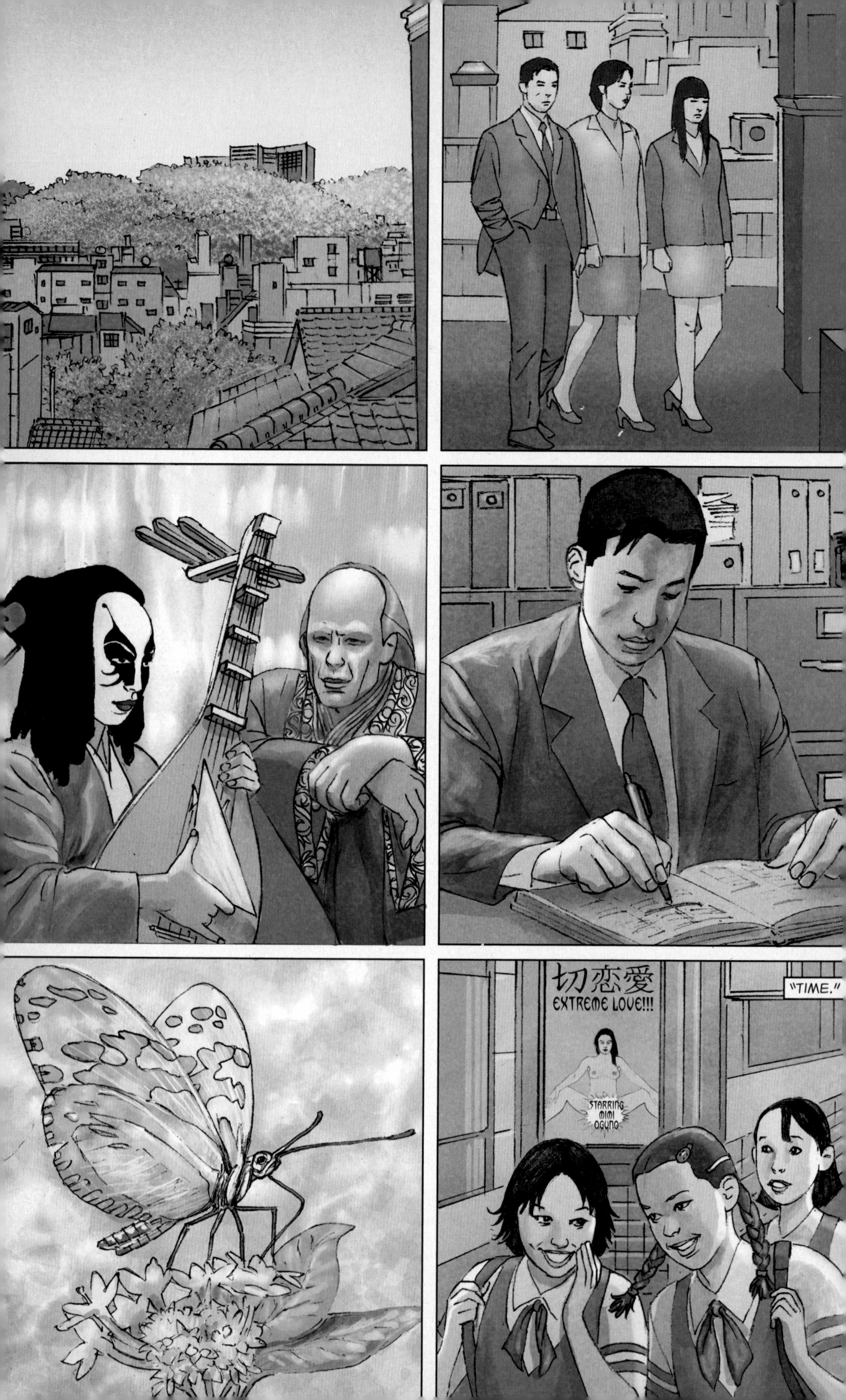

切恋愛
EXTREME LOVE!!!
STARRING
MIMI
OGUNO
"TIME."

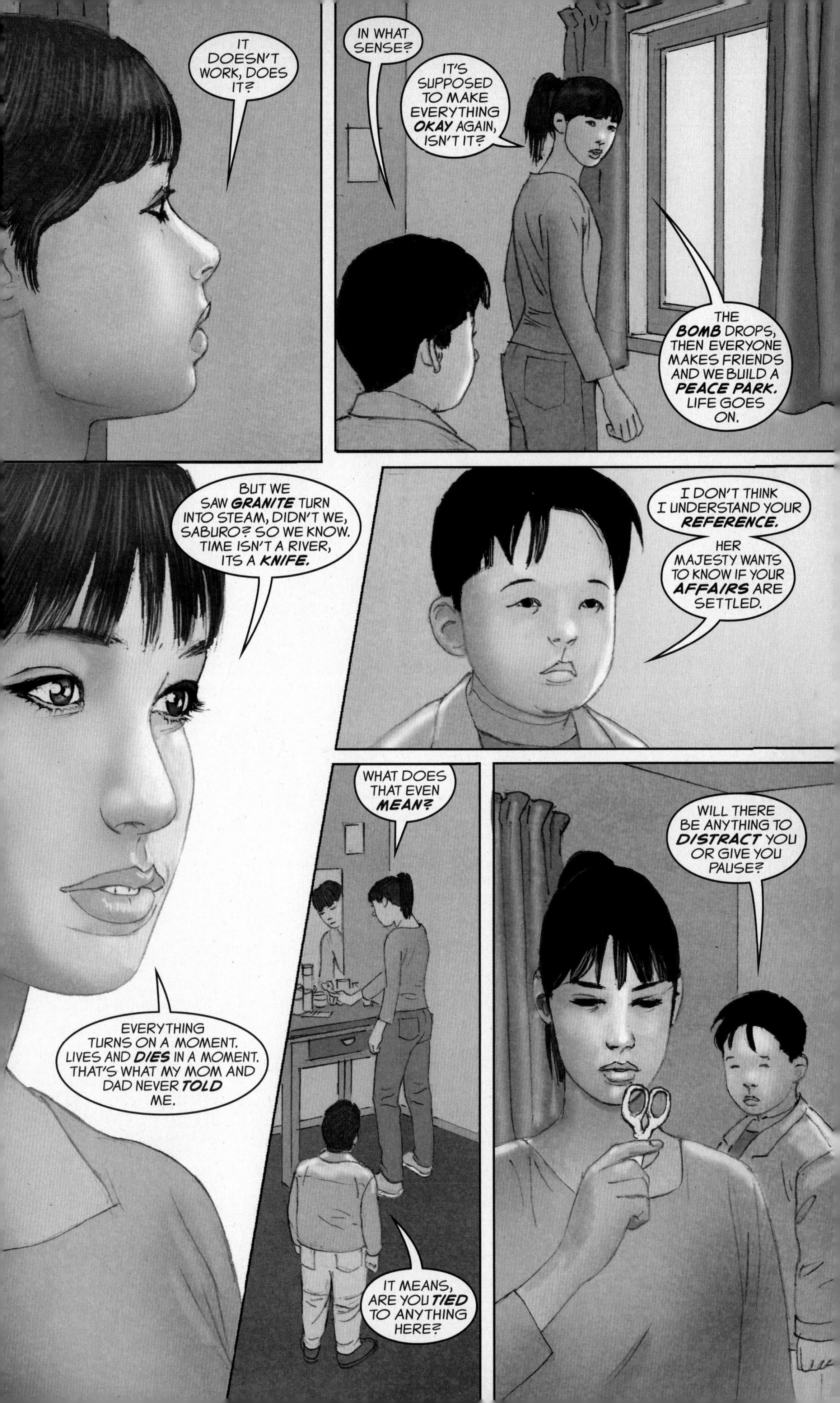

IT DOESN'T WORK, DOES IT?
IN WHAT SENSE?
IT'S SUPPOSED TO MAKE EVERYTHING OKAY AGAIN, ISN'T IT?
THE BOMB DROPS, THEN EVERYONE MAKES FRIENDS AND WE BUILD A PEACE PARK. LIFE GOES ON.
BUT WE SAW GRANITE TURN INTO STEAM, DIDN'T WE, SABURO? SO WE KNOW. TIME ISN'T A RIVER, ITS A KNIFE.
I DON'T THINK I UNDERSTAND YOUR REFERENCE.
HER MAJESTY WANTS TO KNOW IF YOUR AFFAIRS ARE SETTLED.
EVERYTHING TURNS ON A MOMENT. LIVES AND DIES IN A MOMENT. THAT'S WHAT MY MOM AND DAD NEVER TOLD ME.
WHAT DOES THAT EVEN MEAN?
IT MEANS, ARE YOU TIED TO ANYTHING HERE?
WILL THERE BE ANYTHING TO DISTRACT YOU OR GIVE YOU PAUSE?

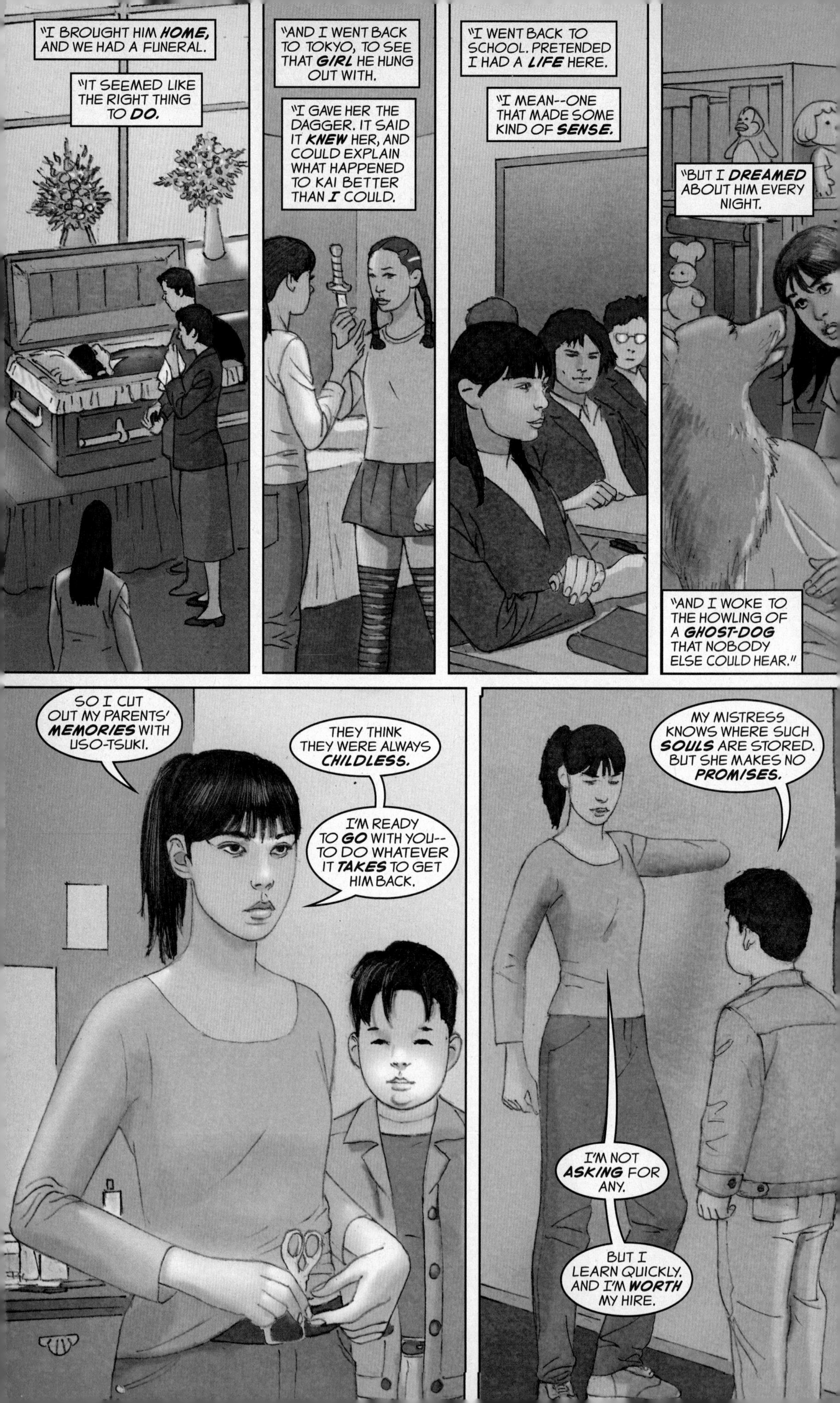

"I BROUGHT HIM **HOME,** AND WE HAD A FUNERAL.
"IT SEEMED LIKE THE RIGHT THING TO **DO.**
"AND I WENT BACK TO TOKYO, TO SEE THAT **GIRL** HE HUNG OUT WITH.
"I GAVE HER THE DAGGER. IT SAID IT **KNEW** HER, AND COULD EXPLAIN WHAT HAPPENED TO KAI BETTER THAN **I** COULD.
"I WENT BACK TO SCHOOL. PRETENDED I HAD A **LIFE** HERE.
"I MEAN--ONE THAT MADE SOME KIND OF **SENSE.**
"BUT I **DREAMED** ABOUT HIM EVERY NIGHT.
"AND I WOKE TO THE HOWLING OF A **GHOST-DOG** THAT NOBODY ELSE COULD HEAR."
SO I CUT OUT MY PARENTS' **MEMORIES** WITH USO-TSUKI.
THEY THINK THEY WERE ALWAYS **CHILDLESS.**
I'M READY TO **GO** WITH YOU-- TO DO WHATEVER IT **TAKES** TO GET HIM BACK.
MY MISTRESS KNOWS WHERE SUCH **SOULS** ARE STORED. BUT SHE MAKES NO **PROMISES.**
I'M NOT **ASKING** FOR ANY.
BUT I LEARN QUICKLY. AND I'M **WORTH** MY HIRE.

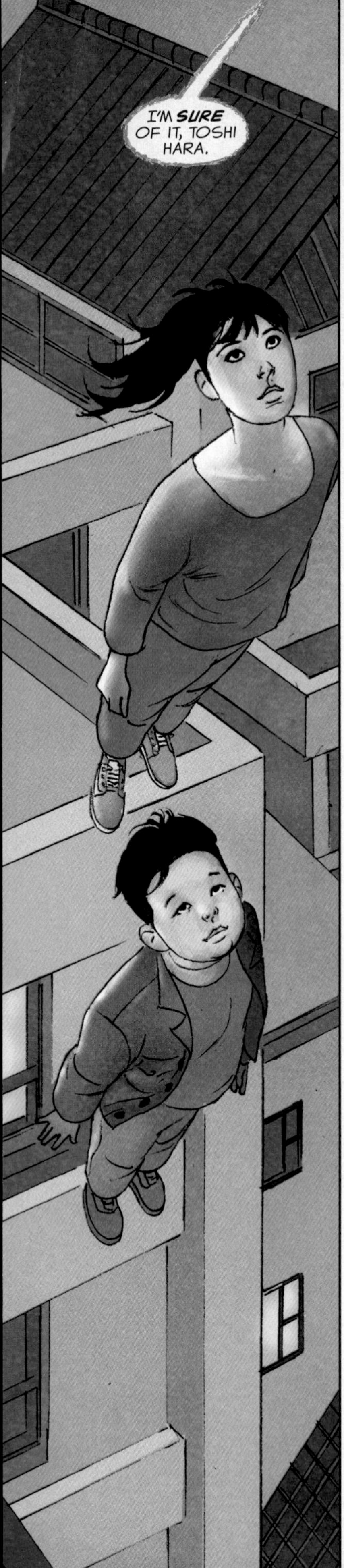
I'M SURE OF IT, TOSHI HARA.

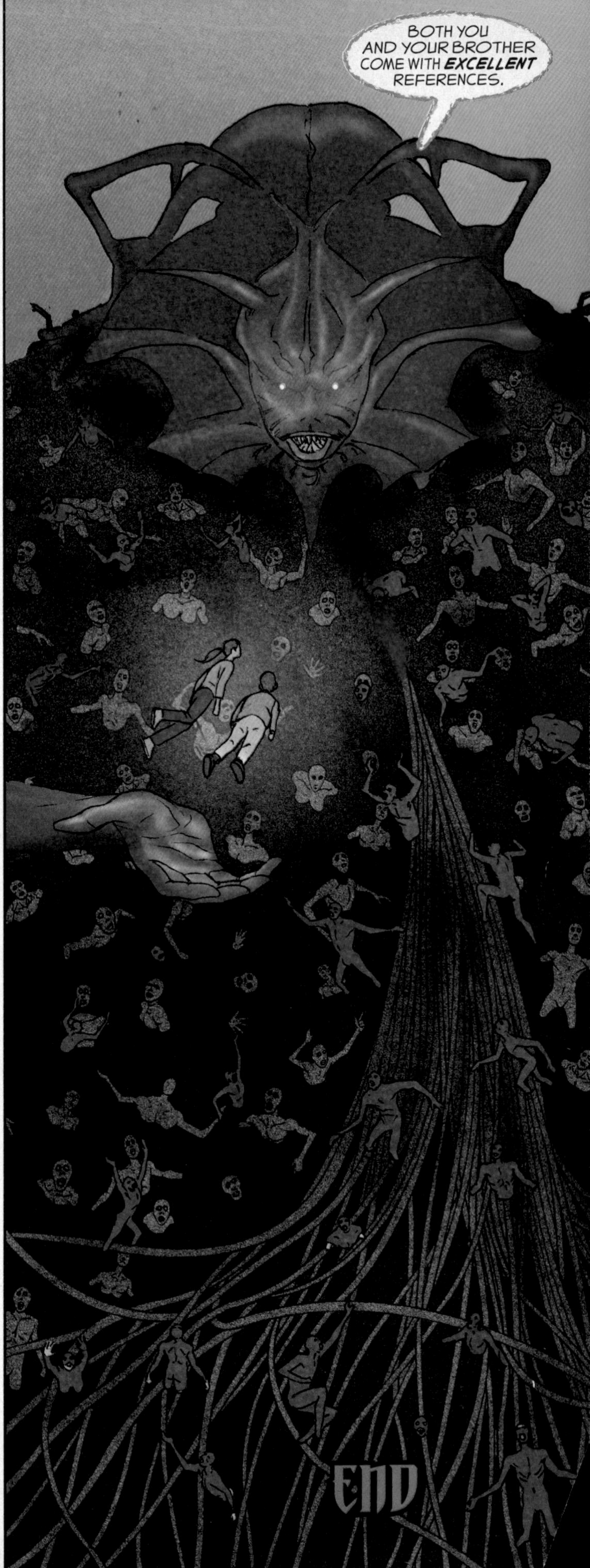
BOTH YOU AND YOUR BROTHER COME WITH EXCELLENT REFERENCES.
END

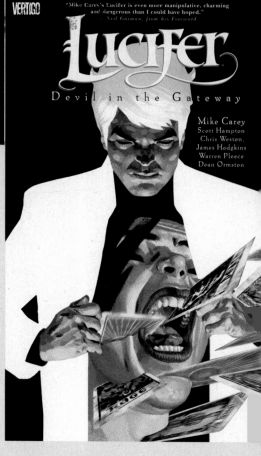

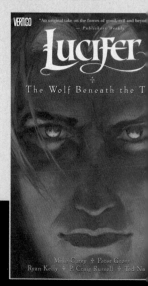